I am on a quest to find a mechanical pencil that best suits me. It can't be too heavy or too light, and it has to feel like part of my own hand. So far the one I paid 100 yen for seems to be the best.

—**Katsura Hoshino**

Shiga Prefecture native Katsura Hoshino's hit manga series *D.Gray-man* has been serialized in *Weekly Shonen Jump* since 2004. Katsura's debut manga, "Continue," appeared for the first time in *Weekly Shonen Jump* in 2003.

Katsura adores cats.

D.GRAY-MAN
VOL. 7
SHONEN JUMP ADVANCED
Manga Edition

STORY AND ART BY
KATSURA HOSHINO

English Adaptation/Lance Caselman
Translation/Toshifumi Yoshida
Touch-up Art & Lettering/Kelle Han
Design/Yukiko Whitley
Editor/Gary Leach

VP, Production/Alvin Lu
VP, Sales & Product Marketing/Gonzalo Ferreyra
VP, Creative/Linda Espinosa
Publisher/Hyoe Narita

D.GRAY-MAN © 2004 by Katsura Hoshino. All rights reserved.
First published in Japan in 2004 by SHUEISHA Inc., Tokyo.
English translation rights arranged by SHUEISHA Inc.

The rights of the author(s) of the work(s) in this publication to be so identified have been asserted in accordance with the Copyright, Designs and Patents Act 1988. A CIP catalogue record for this book is available from the British Library.

Printed in the U.S.A.

Published by VIZ Media, LLC
P.O. Box 77010
San Francisco, CA 94107

10 9 8 7 6 5 4
First printing, November 2007
Fourth printing, February 2010

www.viz.com

www.shonenjump.com

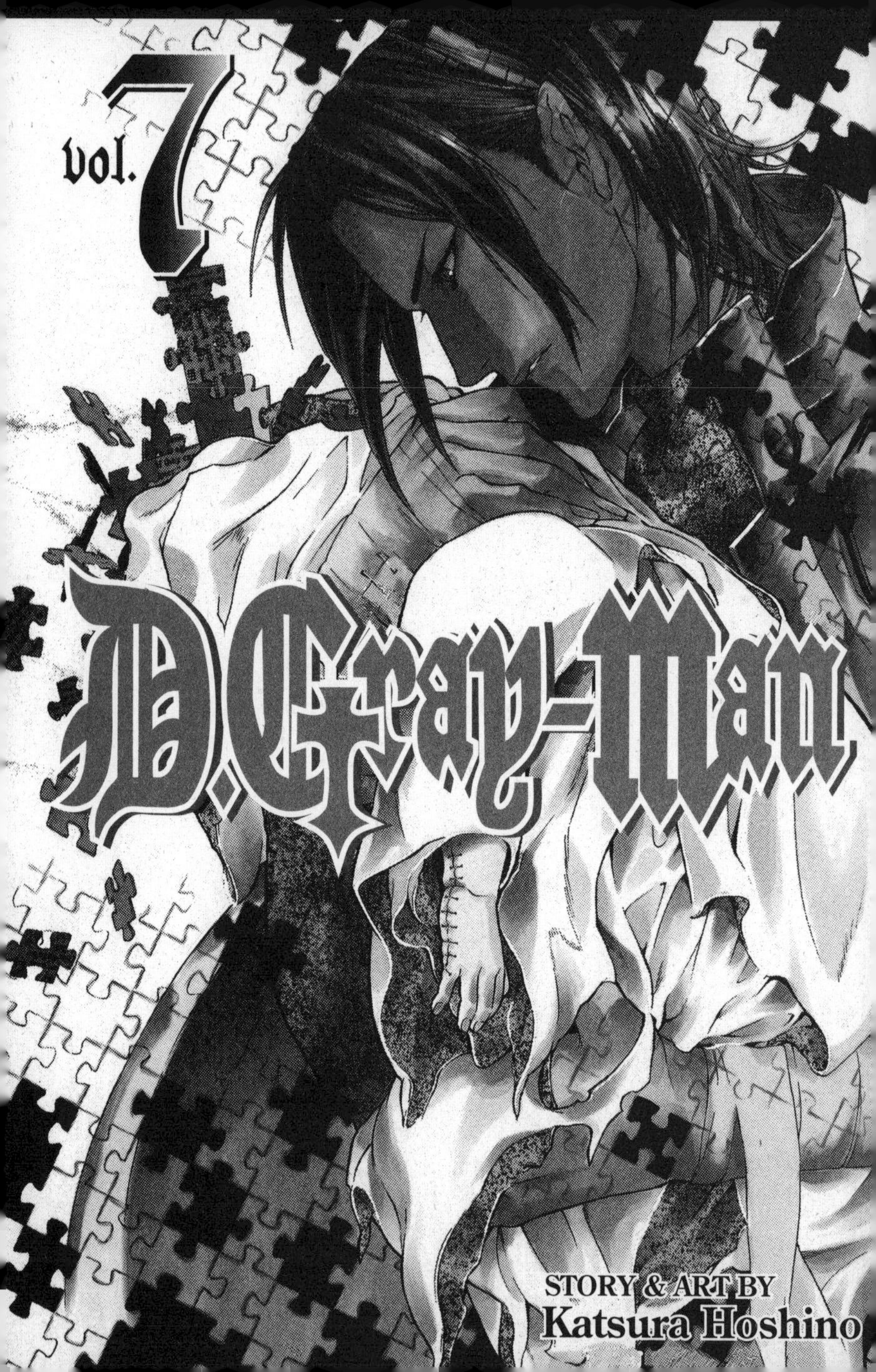
vol. 7
D.Gray-man
STORY & ART BY
Katsura Hoshino

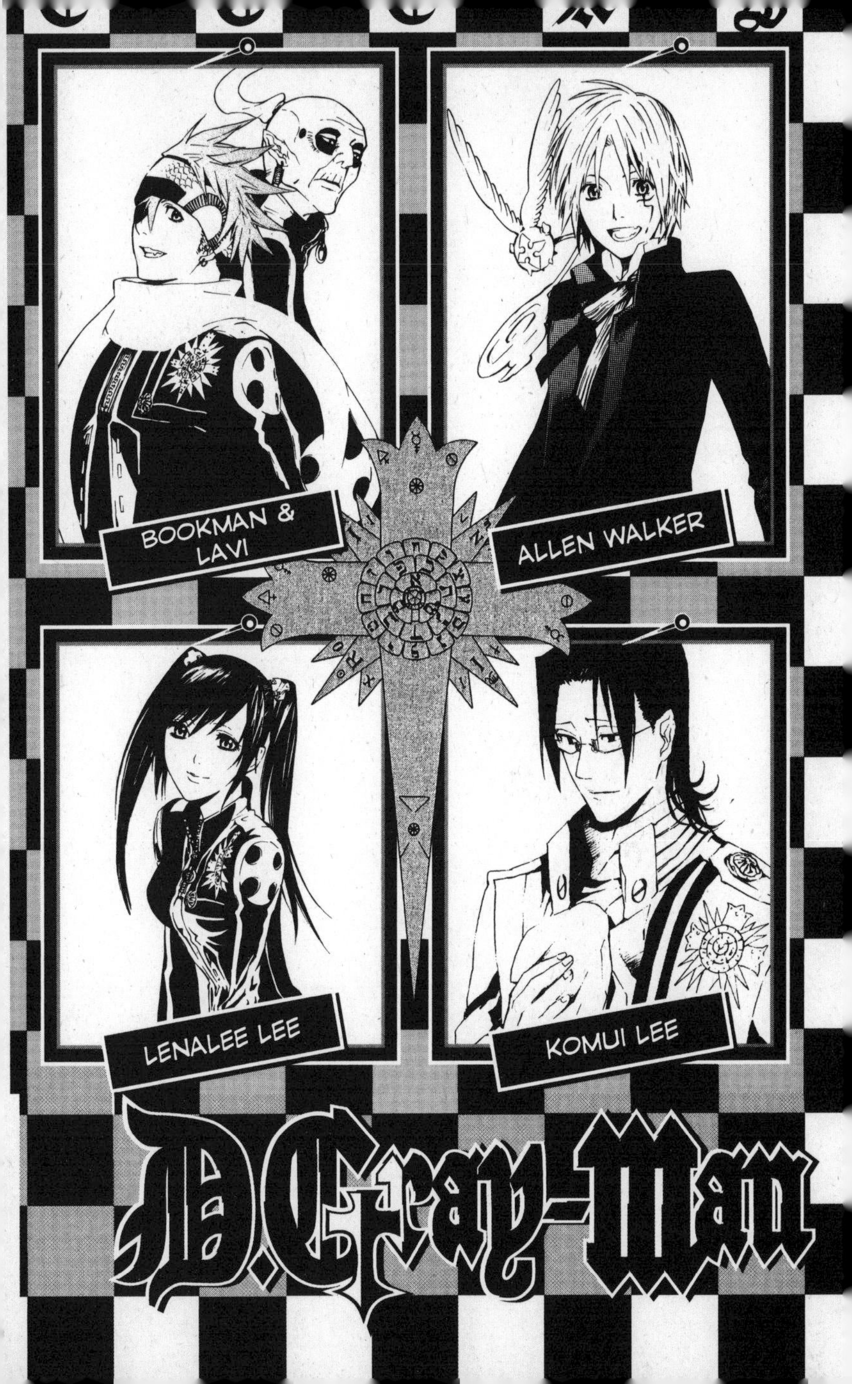
ALLEN WALKER
BOOKMAN & LAVI
KOMUI LEE
LENALEE LEE
D.Gray-man

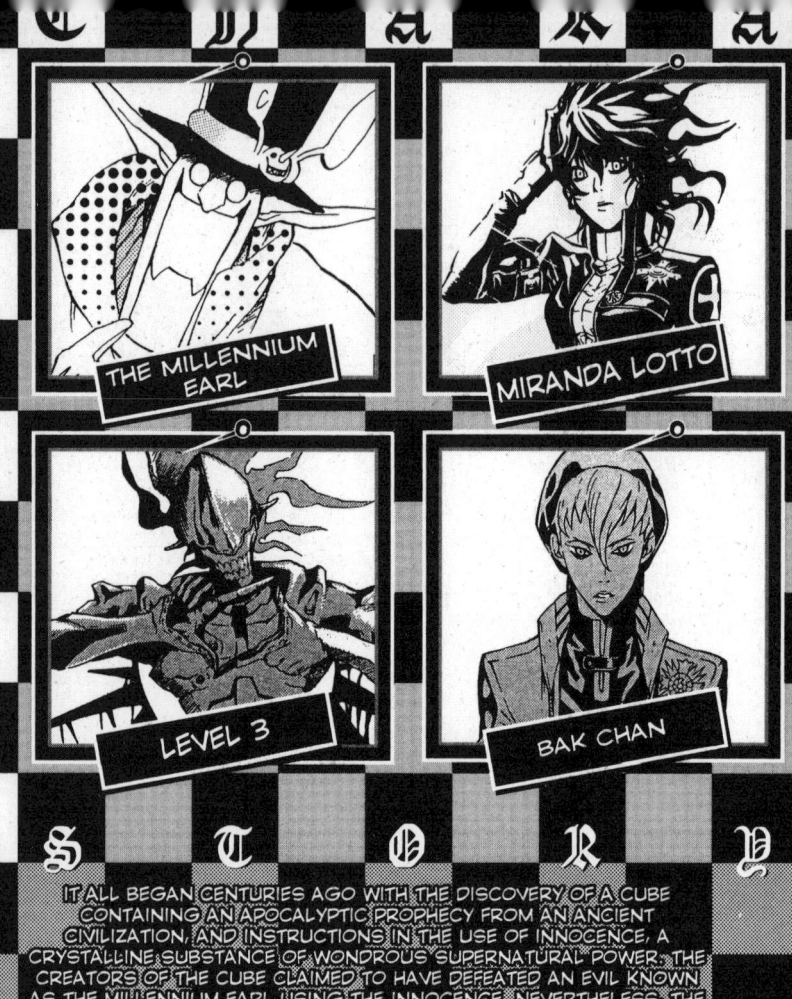

CHARA

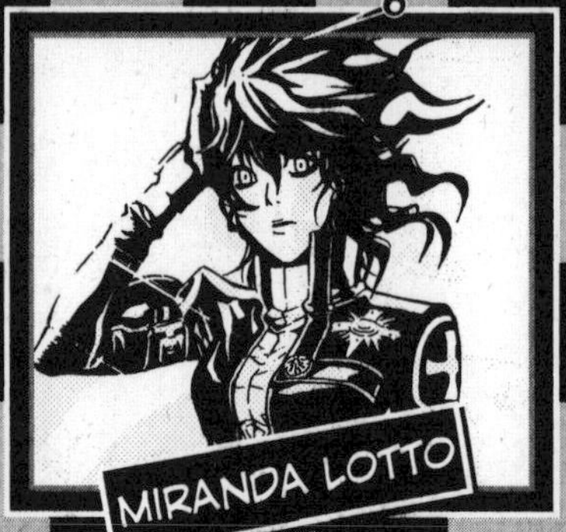
MIRANDA LOTTO

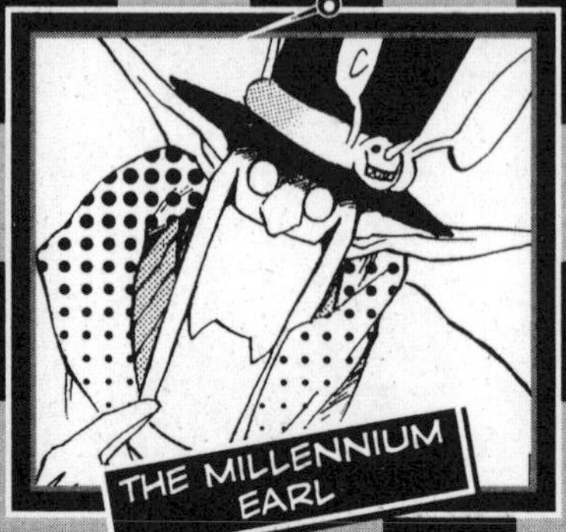
THE MILLENNIUM EARL

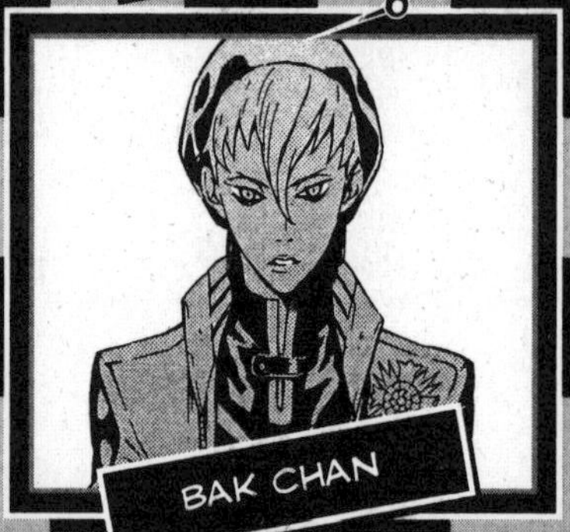
BAK CHAN

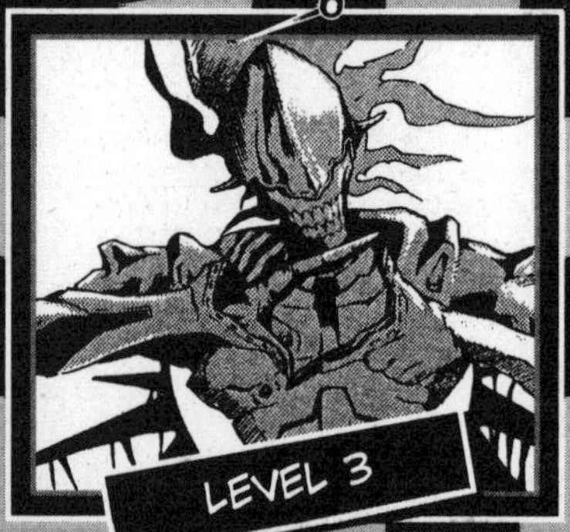
LEVEL 3

STORY

IT ALL BEGAN CENTURIES AGO WITH THE DISCOVERY OF A CUBE CONTAINING AN APOCALYPTIC PROPHECY FROM AN ANCIENT CIVILIZATION, AND INSTRUCTIONS IN THE USE OF INNOCENCE, A CRYSTALLINE SUBSTANCE OF WONDROUS SUPERNATURAL POWER. THE CREATORS OF THE CUBE CLAIMED TO HAVE DEFEATED AN EVIL KNOWN AS THE MILLENNIUM EARL USING THE INNOCENCE. NEVERTHELESS, THE WORLD WAS DESTROYED BY THE GREAT FLOOD OF THE OLD TESTAMENT. NOW TO AVERT A SECOND END OF THE WORLD, A GROUP OF EXORCISTS WIELDING WEAPONS MADE OF INNOCENCE MUST BATTLE THE MILLENNIUM EARL AND HIS TERRIBLE MINIONS, THE AKUMA.

EN ROUTE TO JAPAN, ALLEN FINDS HIMSELF IN THE PATH OF A VAST SWARM OF AKUMA! HOWEVER THEIR TARGET IS NOT THE SHIP, BUT A FALLEN ONE NAMED SUMAN DARK. ALLEN MANAGES TO SAVE SUMAN FROM HIS FALLEN STATE ONLY TO SEE HIM TORN APART BY MAN-EATING GOLEMS. BUT ALLEN SOON DISCOVERS THAT GOLEMS ARE THE LEAST OF HIS WORRIES AS HE FACES TYKI MIKK, WHO HAS THE POWER TO PASS THROUGH SOLID MATTER--EVEN LIVING FLESH. BEFORE HE CAN DEFEND HIMSELF, ALLEN FINDS HIS INNOCENCE PULVERIZED, AND HIS LIFE SWIFTLY DRAINING FROM HIS PUNCTURED HEART...

D.GRAY-MAN
Vol. 7

CONTENTS

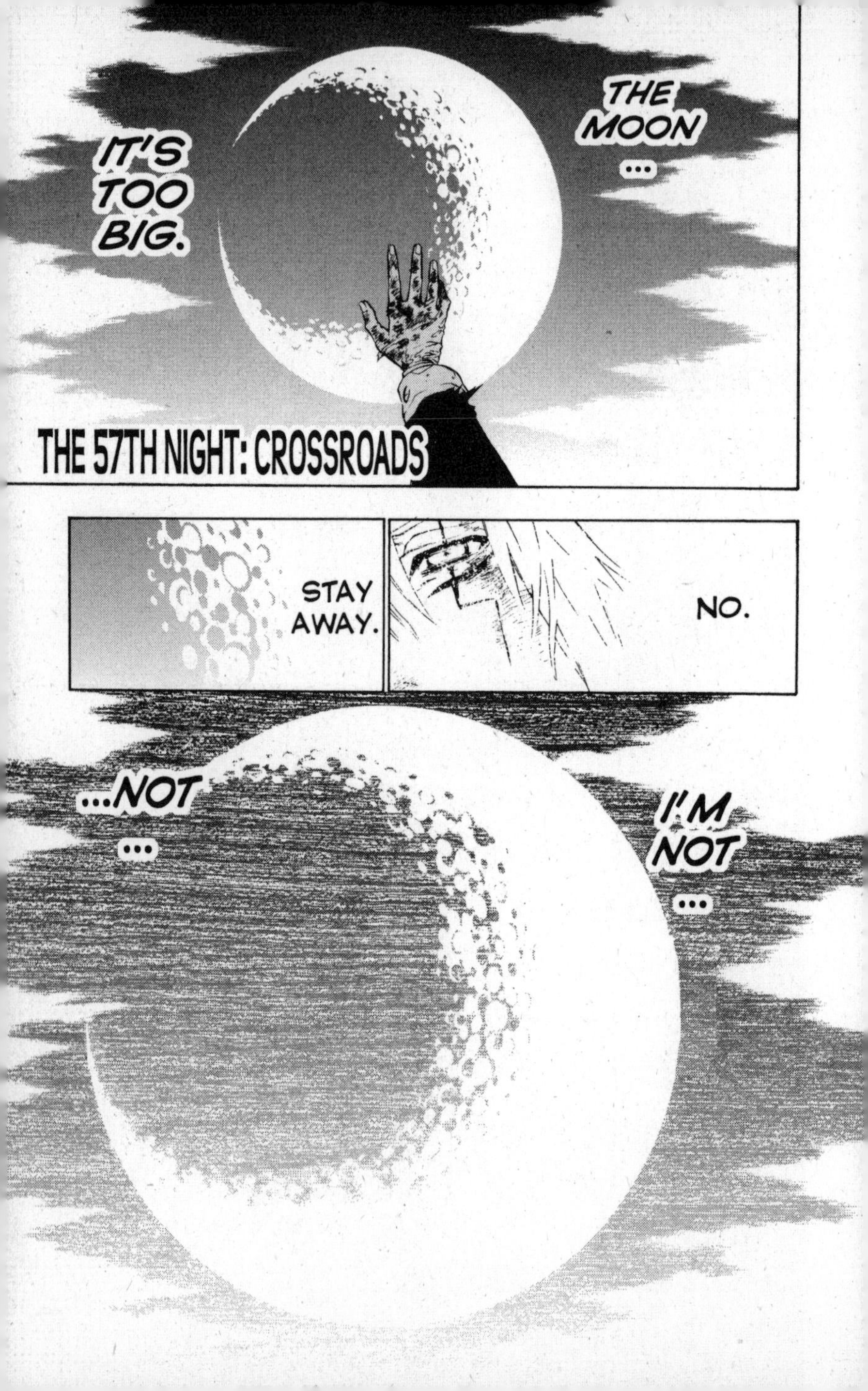
THE MOON...
IT'S TOO BIG.
THE 57TH NIGHT: CROSSROADS
NO.
STAY AWAY.
I'M NOT...
...NOT...

THE 57TH NIGHT: CROSSROADS

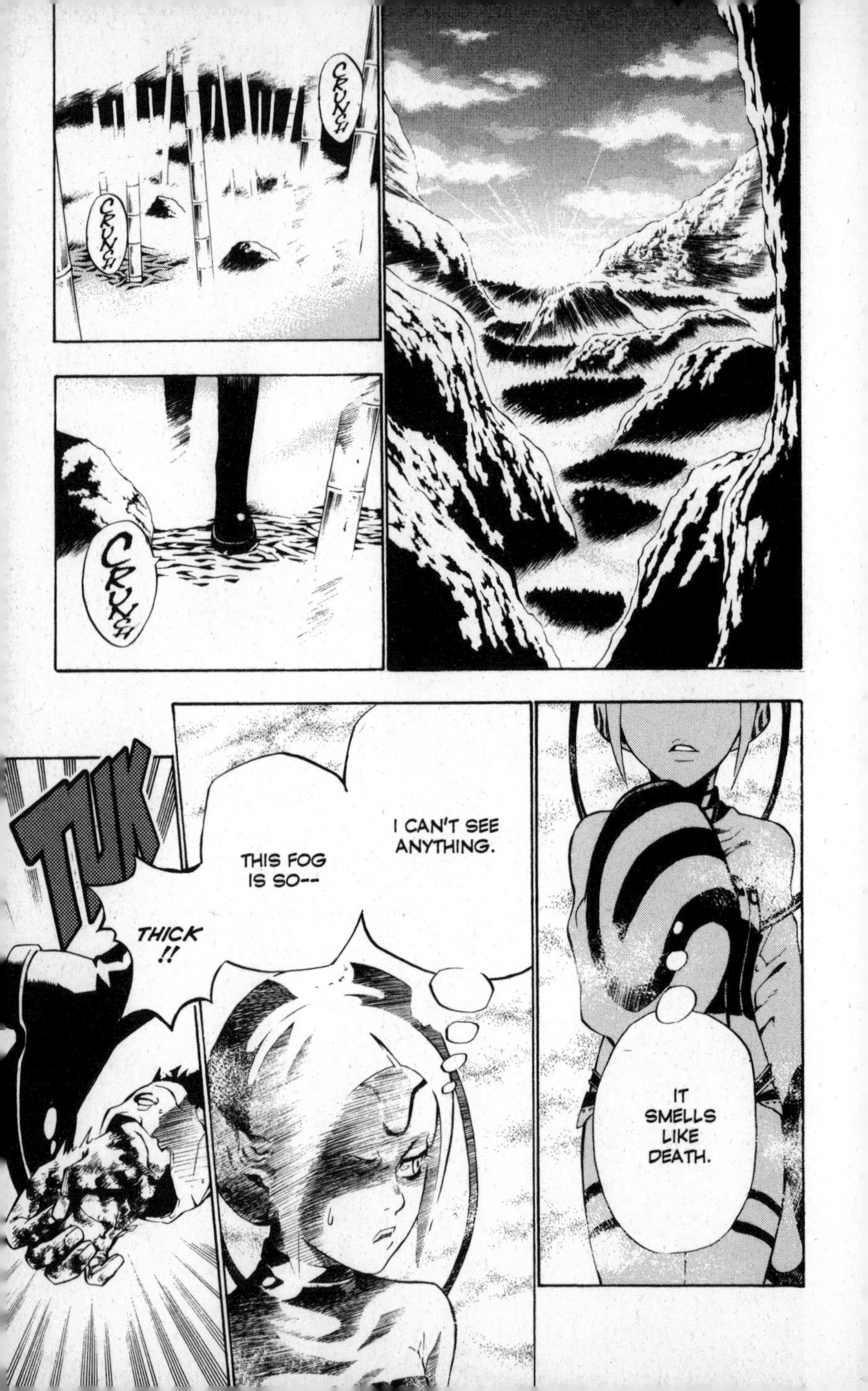
CRUNCH
CRUNCH
CRUNCH
IT SMELLS LIKE DEATH.
I CAN'T SEE ANYTHING.
THIS FOG IS SO--
TUK
THICK!!

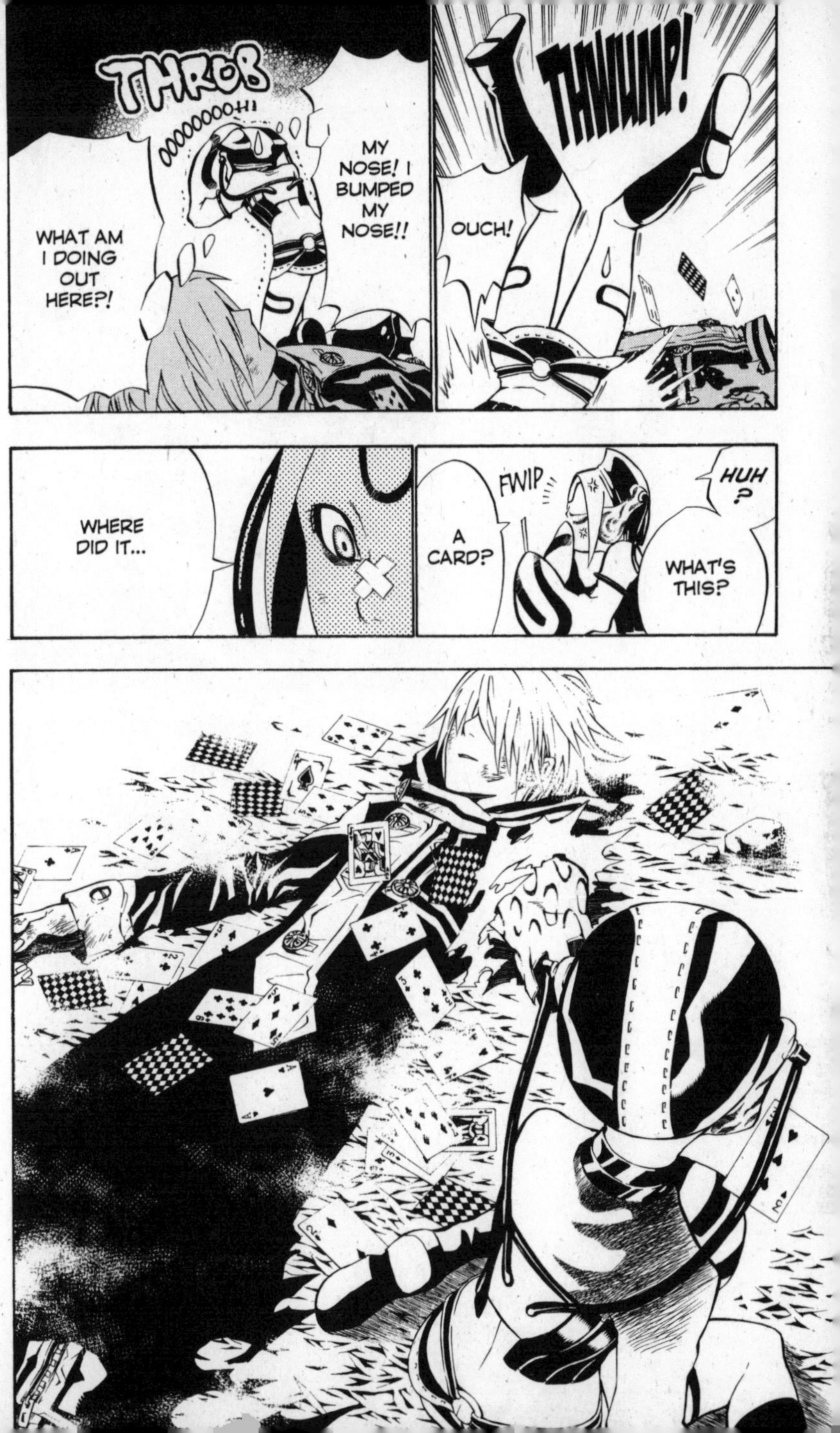
THWUMP!
OUCH!
THROB
OOOOOOOOH!!
MY NOSE! I BUMPED MY NOSE!!
WHAT AM I DOING OUT HERE?!
HUH?
WHAT'S THIS?
FWIP
A CARD?
WHERE DID IT...

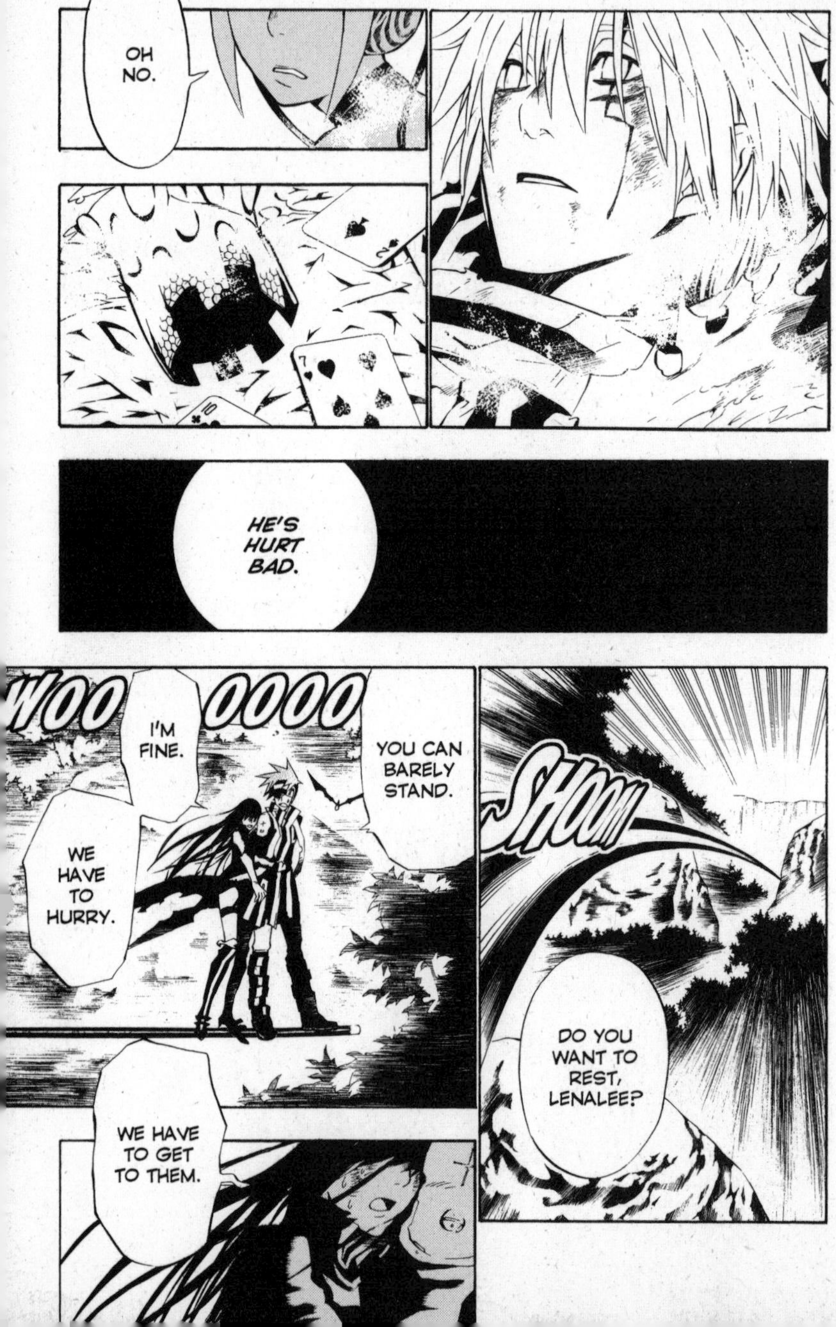
OH NO.
HE'S HURT BAD.
SHOOM
DO YOU WANT TO REST, LENALEE?
WOO OOOO
YOU CAN BARELY STAND.
I'M FINE.
WE HAVE TO HURRY.
WE HAVE TO GET TO THEM.

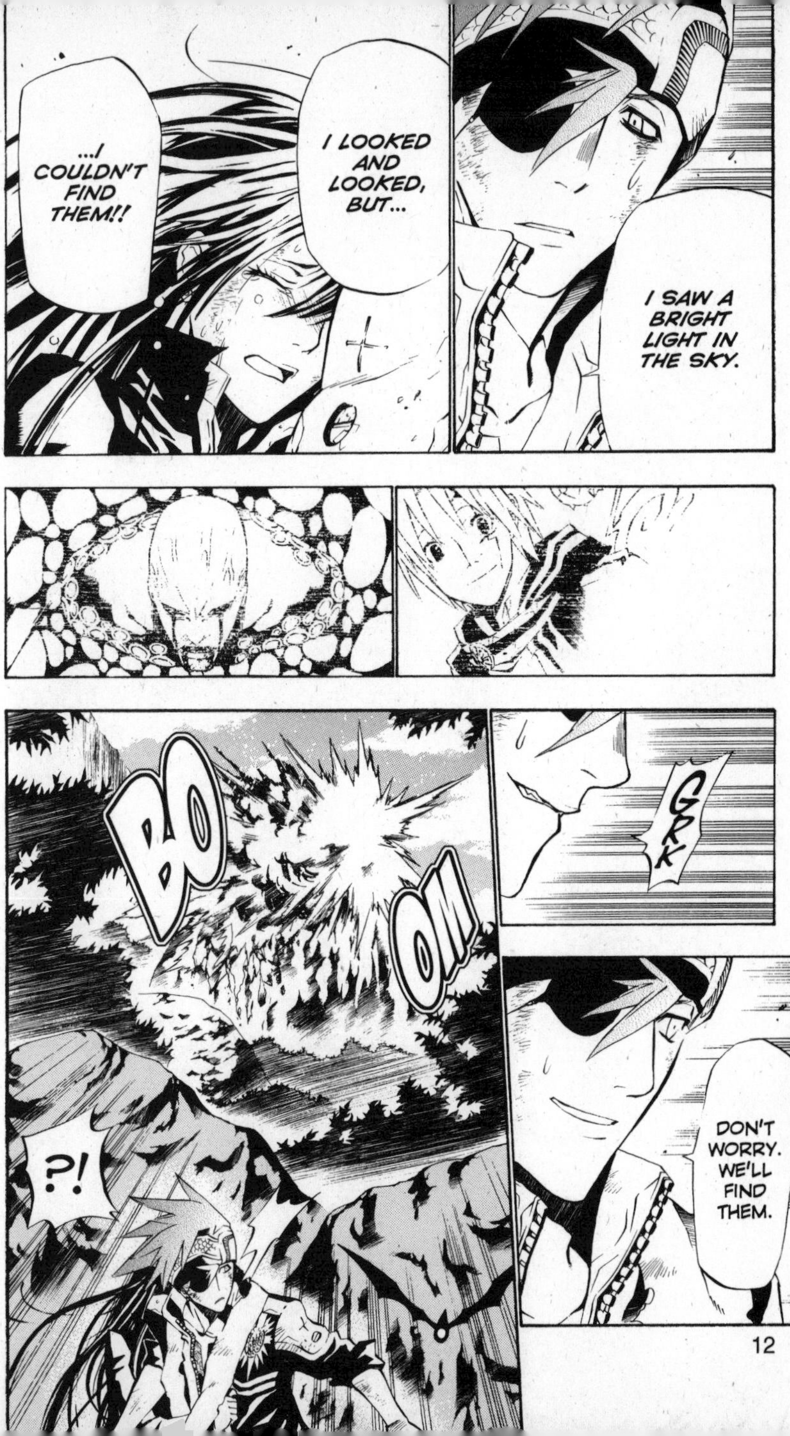
I SAW A BRIGHT LIGHT IN THE SKY.
I LOOKED AND LOOKED, BUT...
...I COULDN'T FIND THEM!!
GRK
DON'T WORRY. WE'LL FIND THEM.
BOOM
?!

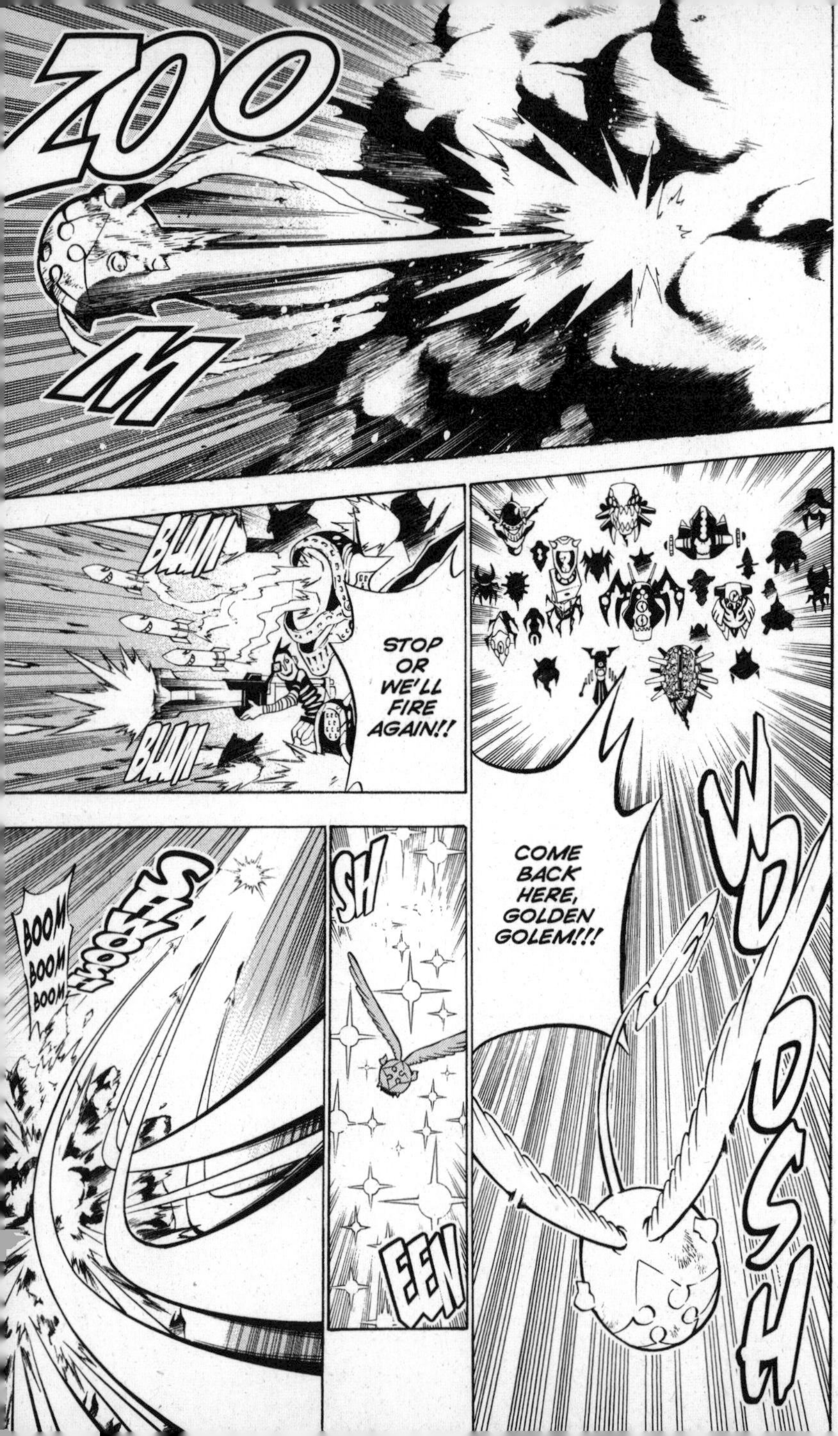
ZOOM
COME BACK HERE, GOLDEN GOLEM!!!
WOOSH
STOP OR WE'LL FIRE AGAIN!!
BLAM
BLAM
SH
EEN
SHWOOM
BOOM BOOM BOOM

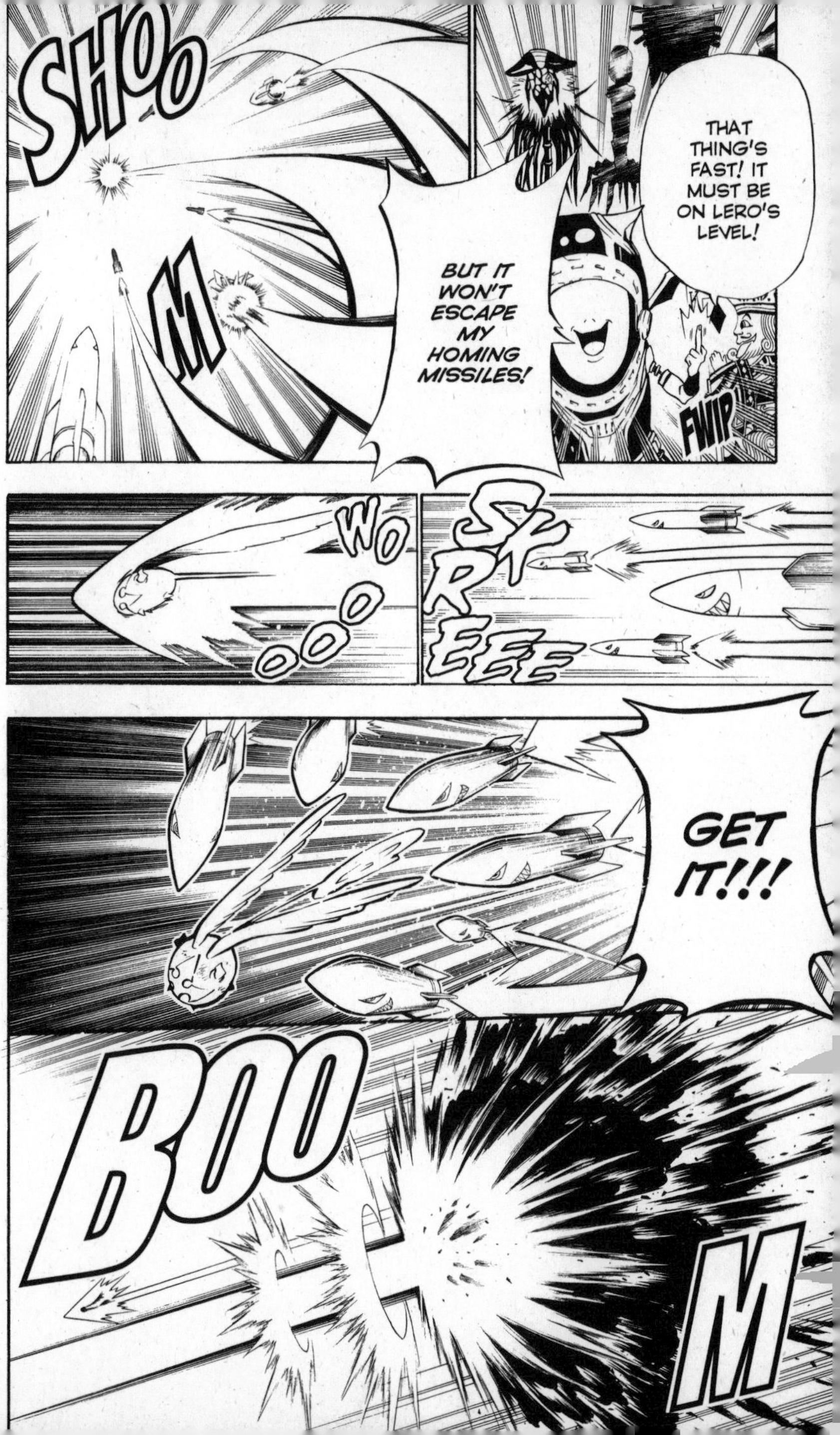
THAT THING'S FAST! IT MUST BE ON LERO'S LEVEL!
FWIP
BUT IT WON'T ESCAPE MY HOMING MISSILES!
SHOOM
SKREEE
WOOOOOO
GET IT!!!
BOOM

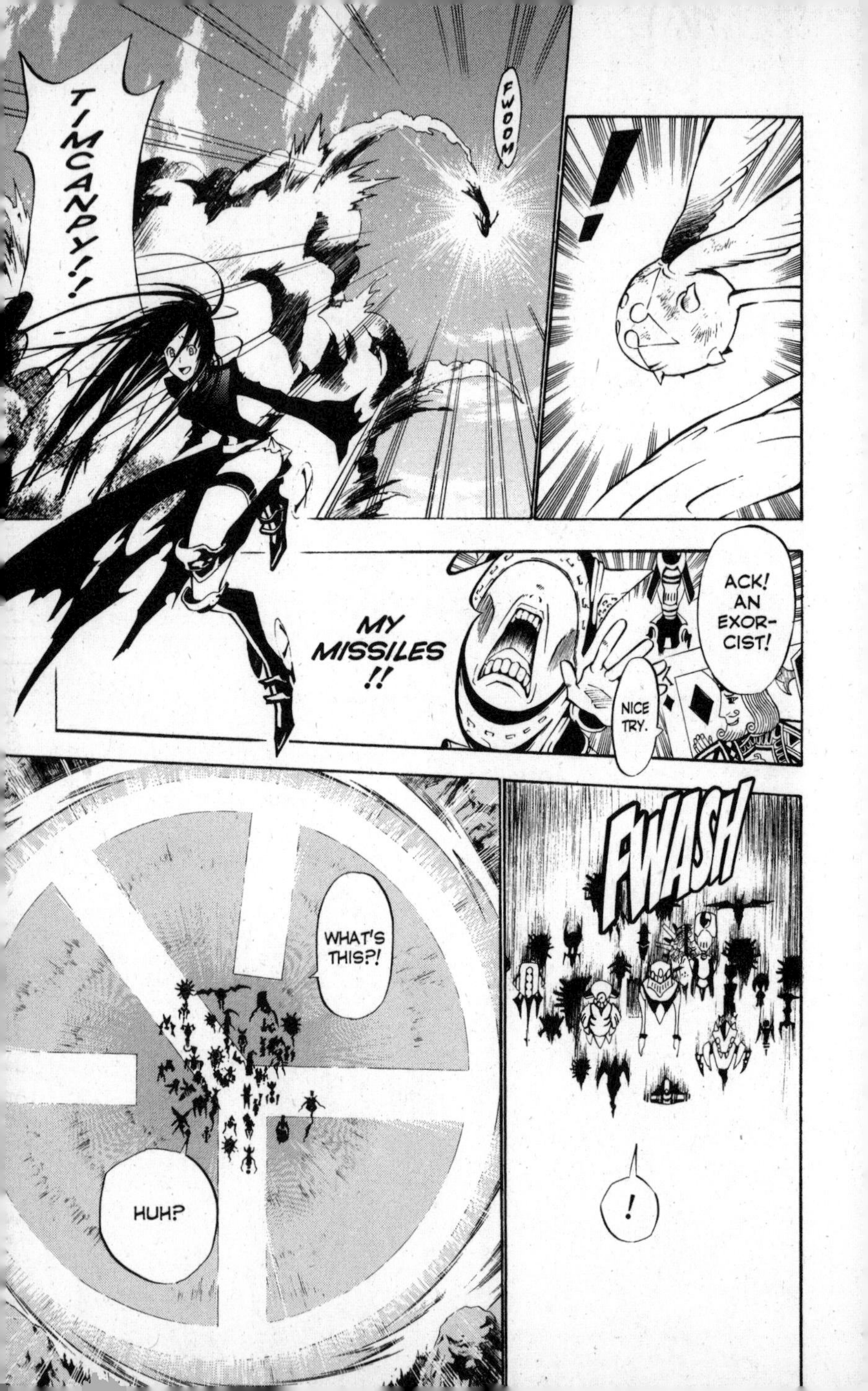
!
FWOOM
TIMCANPY!!
ACK! AN EXOR-CIST!
NICE TRY.
MY MISSILES!!
FWASH
!
WHAT'S THIS?!
HUH?

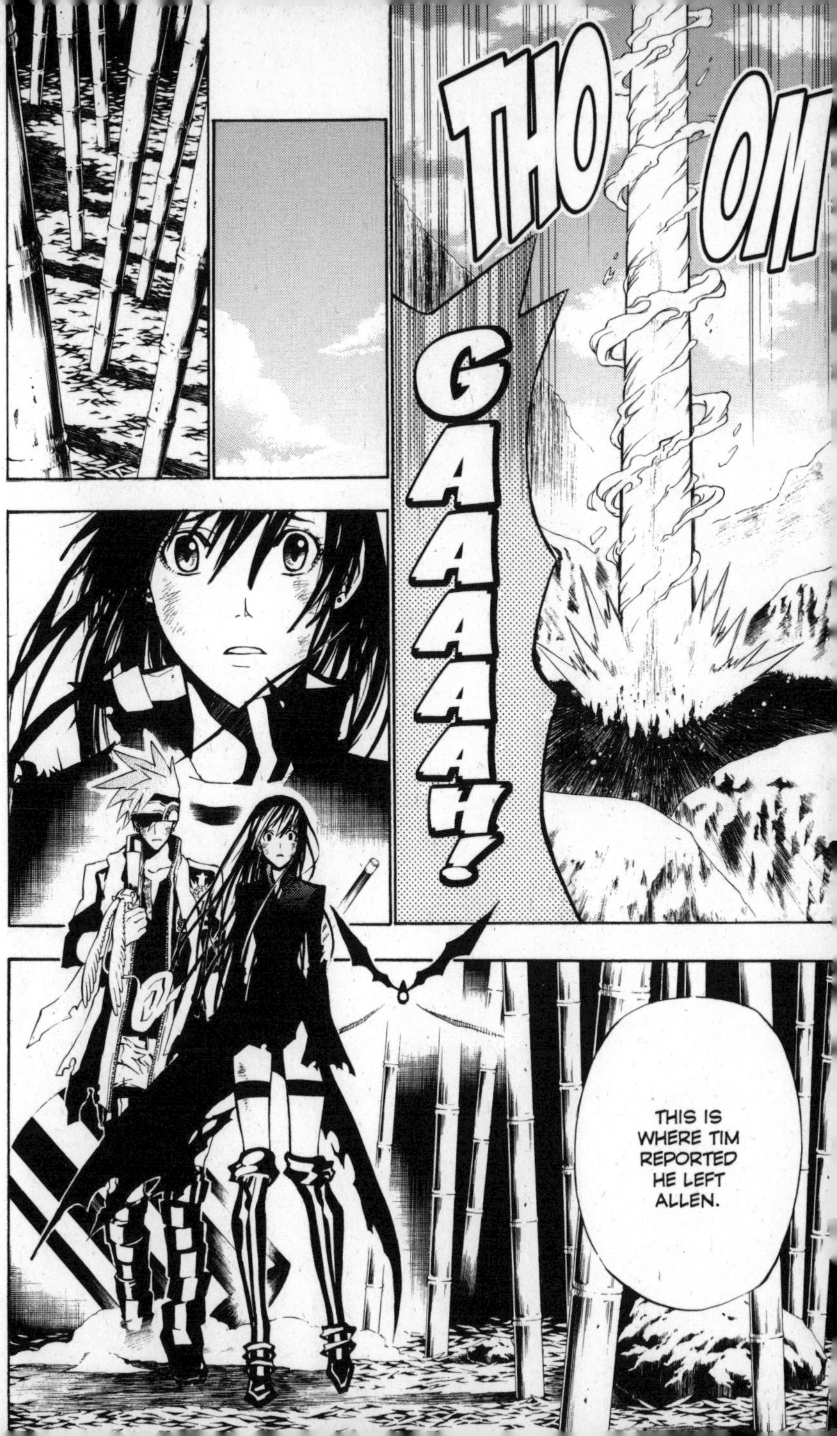
THOOOM
GAAAAAAH!
THIS IS WHERE TIM REPORTED HE LEFT ALLEN.

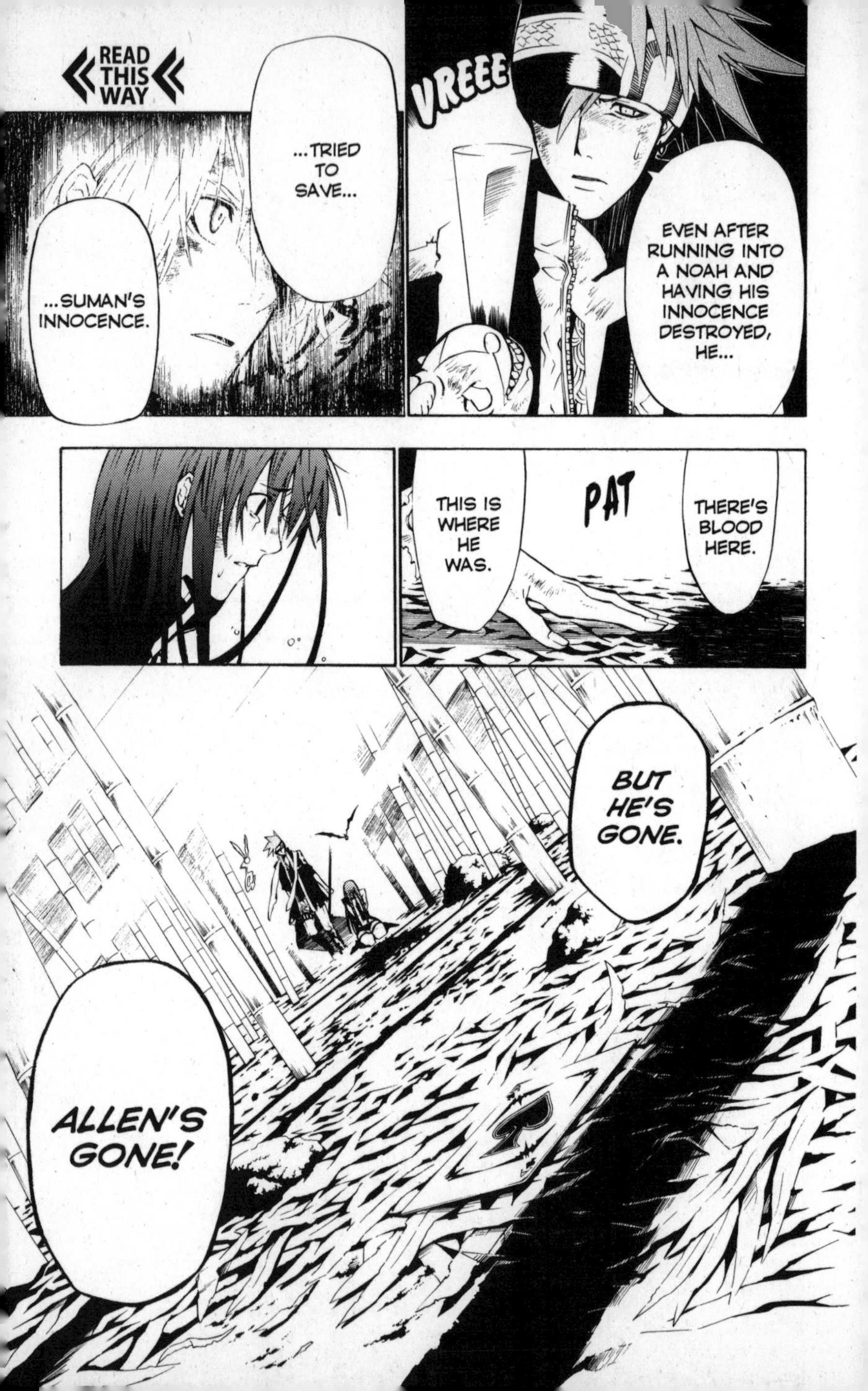
READ THIS WAY
VREEE
EVEN AFTER RUNNING INTO A NOAH AND HAVING HIS INNOCENCE DESTROYED, HE...
...TRIED TO SAVE...
...SUMAN'S INNOCENCE.
THERE'S BLOOD HERE.
PAT
THIS IS WHERE HE WAS.
BUT HE'S GONE.
ALLEN'S GONE!

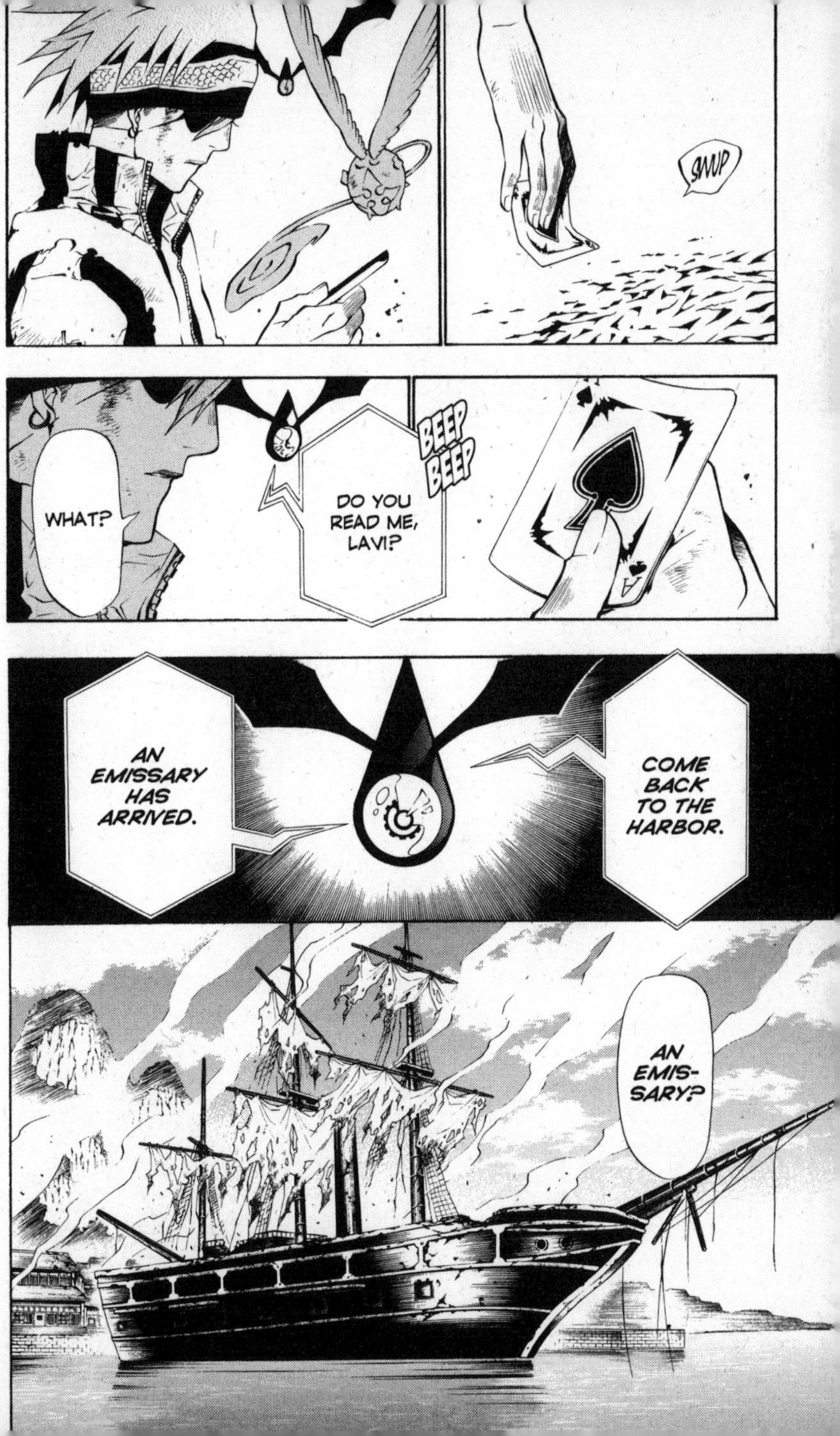
SWUP
BEEP BEEP
DO YOU READ ME, LAVI?
WHAT?
COME BACK TO THE HARBOR.
AN EMISSARY HAS ARRIVED.
AN EMIS-SARY?

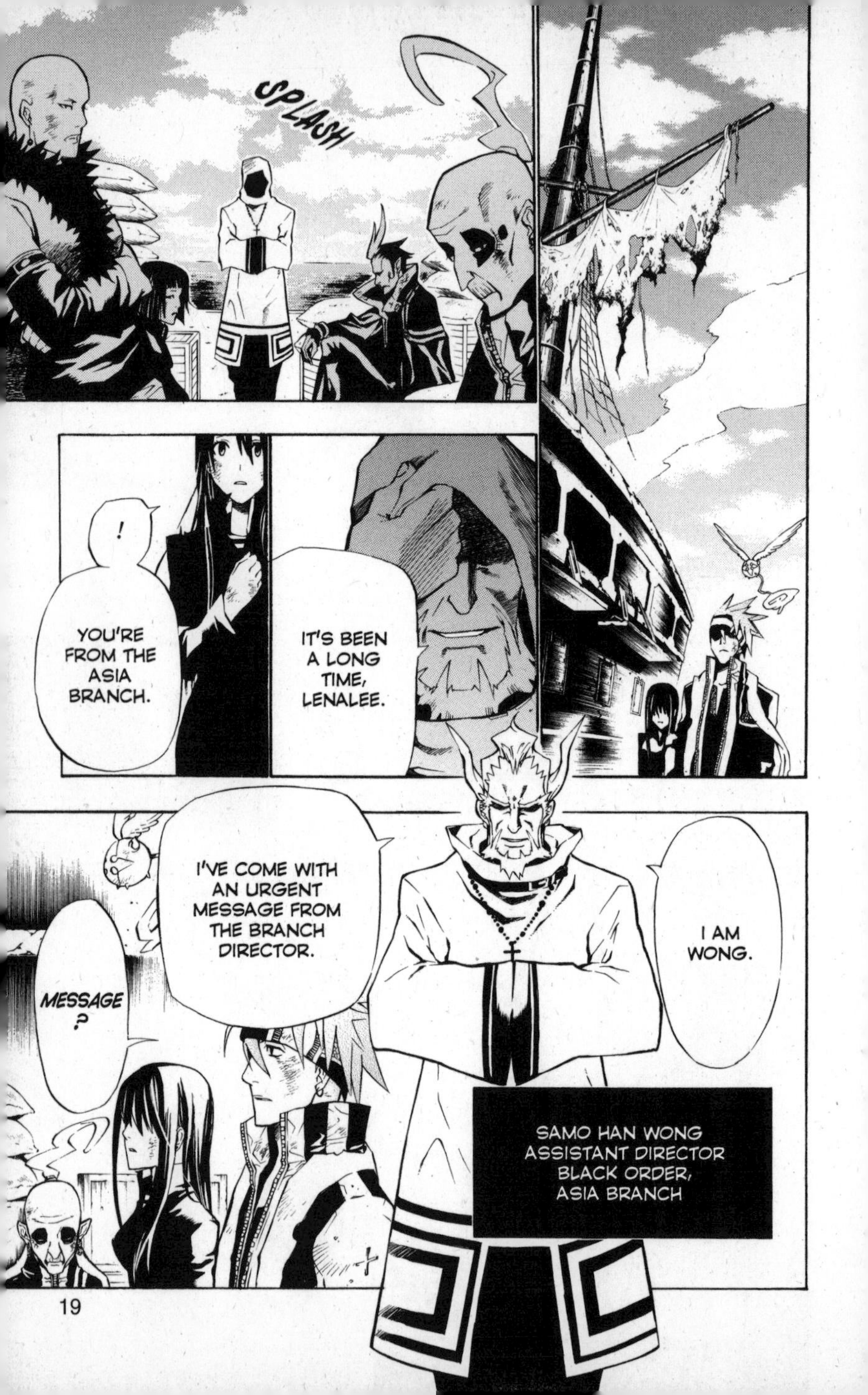
SPLASH
IT'S BEEN A LONG TIME, LENALEE.
!
YOU'RE FROM THE ASIA BRANCH.
I AM WONG.
I'VE COME WITH AN URGENT MESSAGE FROM THE BRANCH DIRECTOR.
SAMO HAN WONG ASSISTANT DIRECTOR BLACK ORDER, ASIA BRANCH
MESSAGE?

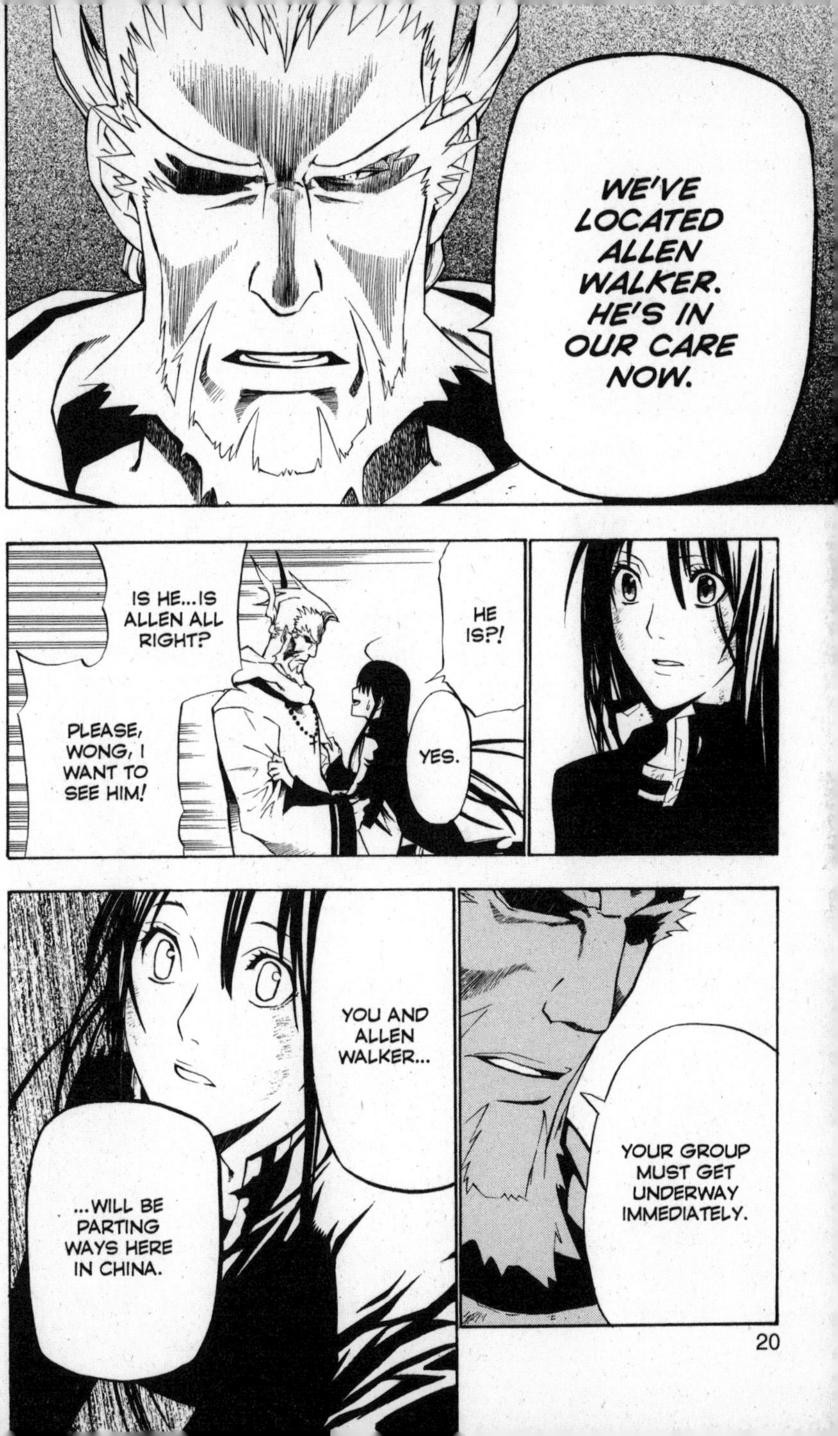
WE'VE LOCATED ALLEN WALKER. HE'S IN OUR CARE NOW.
HE IS?!
YES.
IS HE...IS ALLEN ALL RIGHT?
PLEASE, WONG, I WANT TO SEE HIM!
YOUR GROUP MUST GET UNDERWAY IMMEDIATELY.
YOU AND ALLEN WALKER...
...WILL BE PARTING WAYS HERE IN CHINA.

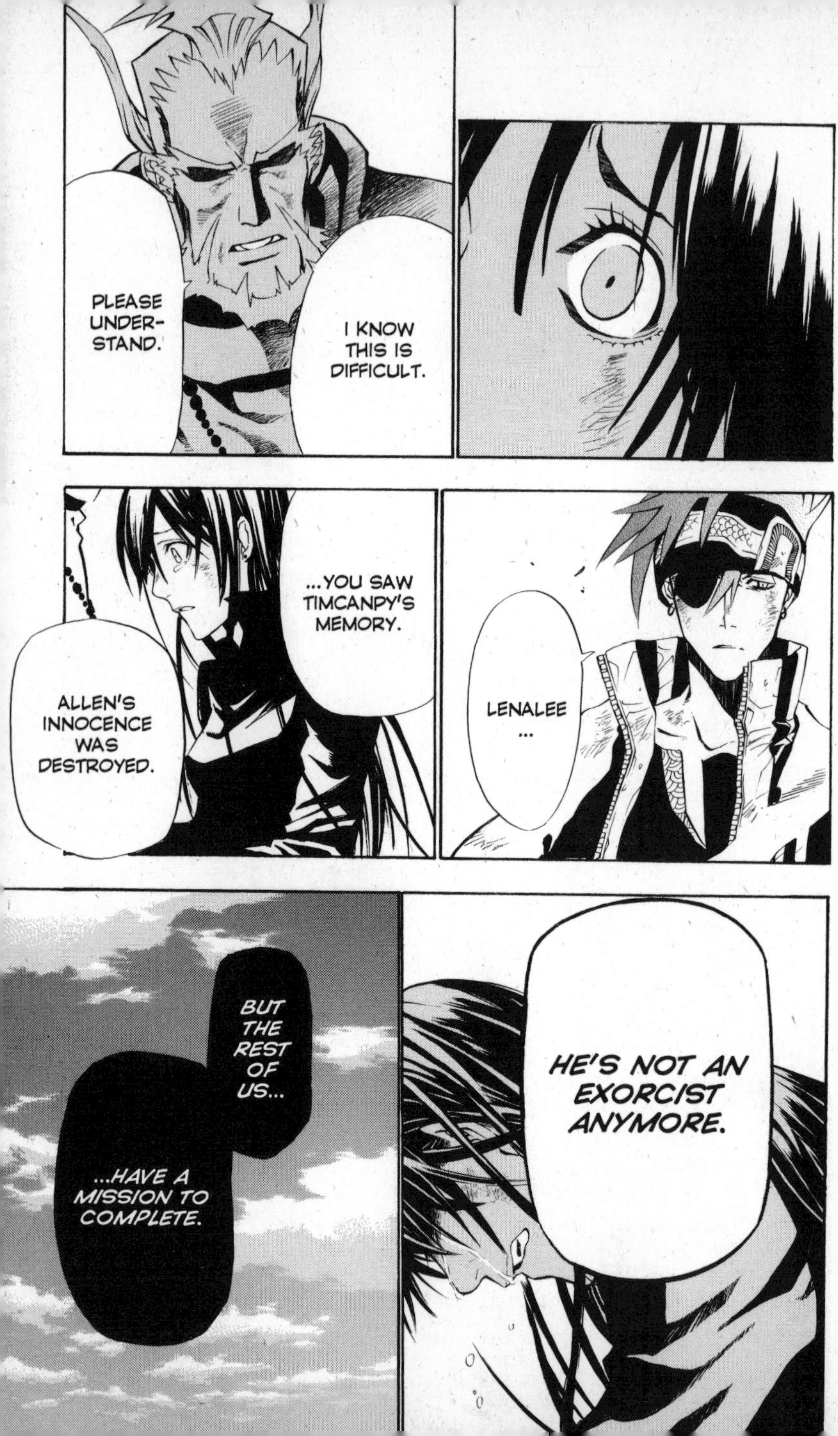
I KNOW THIS IS DIFFICULT.
PLEASE UNDER-STAND.
LENALEE ...
...YOU SAW TIMCANPY'S MEMORY.
ALLEN'S INNOCENCE WAS DESTROYED.
HE'S NOT AN EXORCIST ANYMORE.
BUT THE REST OF US...
...HAVE A MISSION TO COMPLETE.

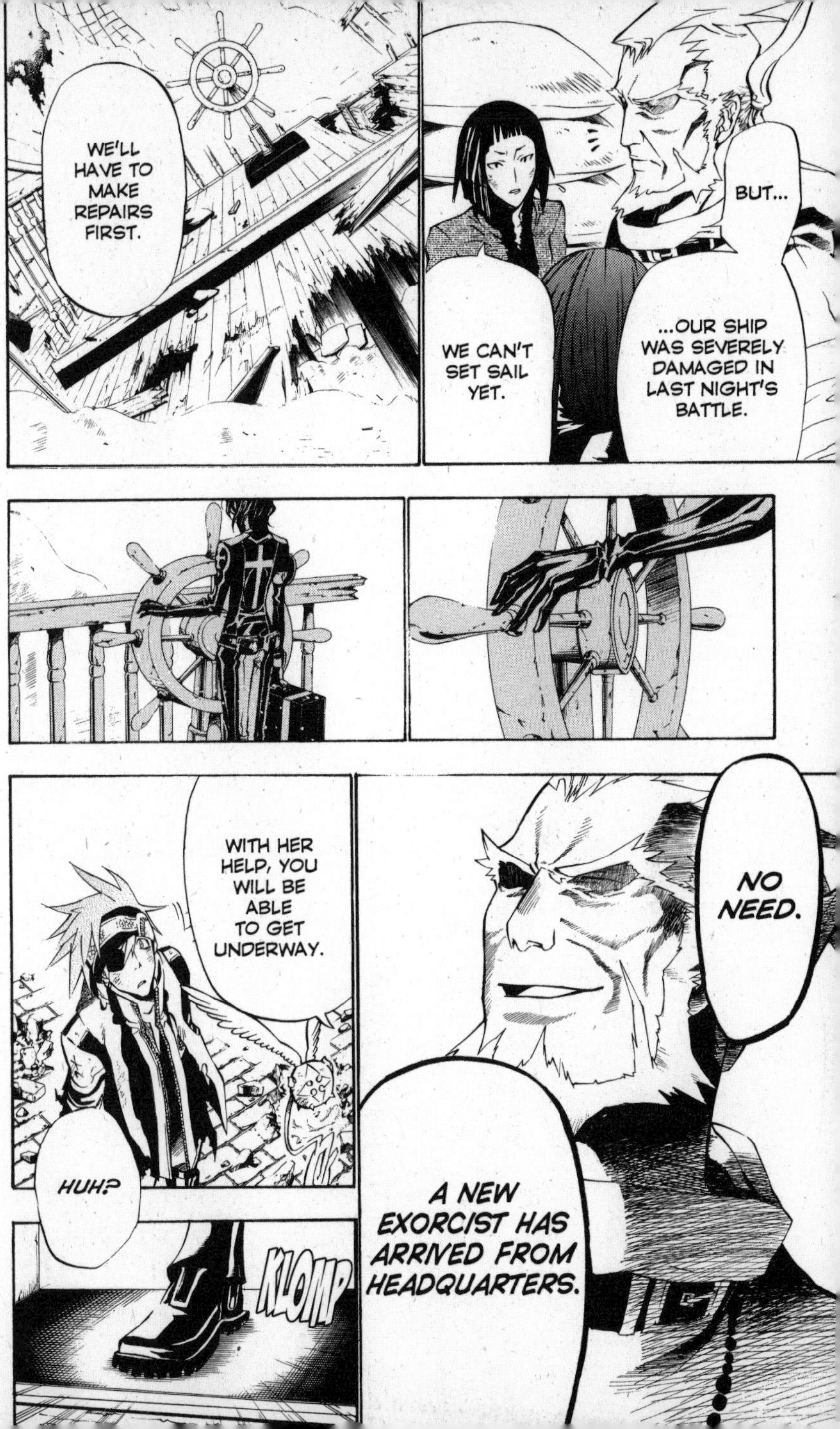
BUT...
...OUR SHIP WAS SEVERELY DAMAGED IN LAST NIGHT'S BATTLE.
WE CAN'T SET SAIL YET.
WE'LL HAVE TO MAKE REPAIRS FIRST.
NO NEED.
A NEW EXORCIST HAS ARRIVED FROM HEADQUARTERS.
WITH HER HELP, YOU WILL BE ABLE TO GET UNDERWAY.
HUH?
KLOMP

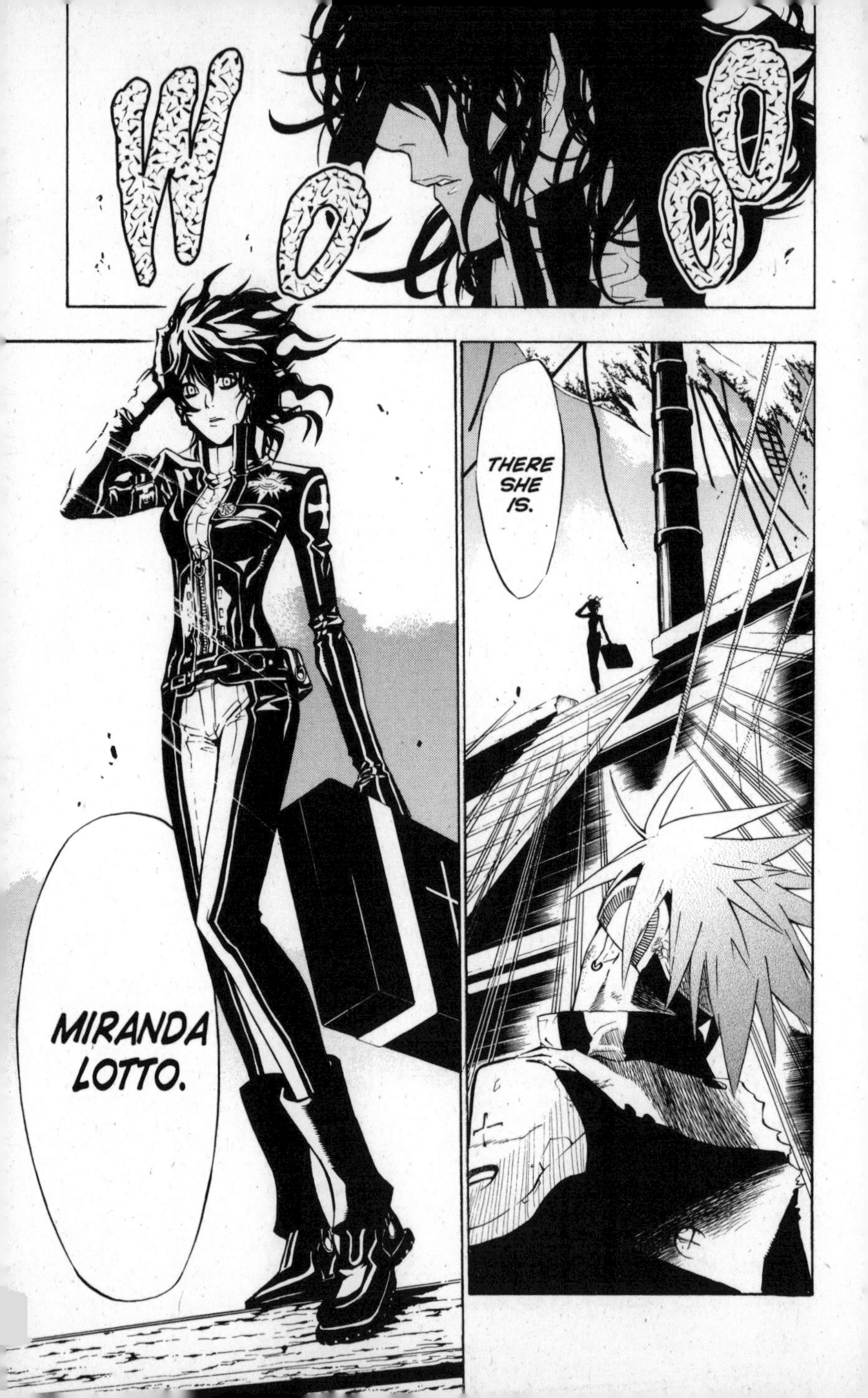
WOOO
THERE SHE IS.
MIRANDA LOTTO.

KOMUI'S DISCUSSION ROOM, VOL. 1

(LAVI) WELL, HERE WE ARE WITH ANOTHER SEGMENT OF THE DISCUSSION ROOM, WHICH KOMUI NEVER SEEMS TO BE AROUND FOR. THIS TIME ALLEN AND I ARE IN CHARGE.
(ALLEN) UM...I DID THIS BACK IN VOL. 4 ALREADY.
(LAVI) WELL, KANDA MADE A MESS OF THINGS WHEN HE DID IT, SO THIS COMIC'S CREATOR HAS ORDERED THE TWO OF US TO DO IT.
(ALLEN) WHAT?! WHY DO I HAVE TO CLEAN UP AFTER KANDA?! (GRRRR!✧)
(LAVI) TAKE IT EASY, ALLEN. HERE, HAVE THIS. (HANDS HIM A DANGO)
(ALLEN) *MITARASHI DANGO! OKAY, I'LL DO IT!
(*RICE DUMPLINGS ON A STICK WITH SWEET SOY SYRUP.)
(LAVI) OKAY THEN, LET'S GO!

Q: DOES LAVI HAVE A THING FOR CUTE GIRLS WITH BIG BREASTS?
A: (LAVI) WHOA BOY! (SWEATING)
(ALLEN) HE'S A MENACE.
(LAVI) HEY, HOLD ON! PEOPLE THINK I ONLY CARE ABOUT LOOKS, BUT I'M PRETTY PICKY ABOUT PERSONALITY, TOO. BUT, HEY, SOMETIMES YOU SEE A GIRL AND IT JUST HITS YOU. I MEAN, I AM A MAN.
(ALLEN) I THINK WE SHOULD MOVE ON.

Q: WHY ISN'T LAVI INTERESTED IN LENALEE?
A: (LAVI) HUH? I AM.
(ALLEN) WHAT?! YOU ARE?! (SWEATING)
(LAVI) YEAH. WHAT'S WITH THE FLOP SWEAT, ALLEN?
(ALLEN) N-NOTHING. (MUNCH, MUNCH)
(LAVI) SURE. (SMIRK)

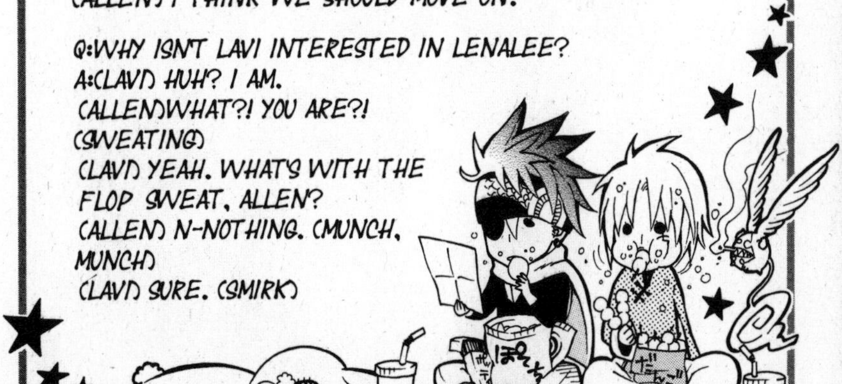

THE 58TH NIGHT: DESTROYER OF TIME

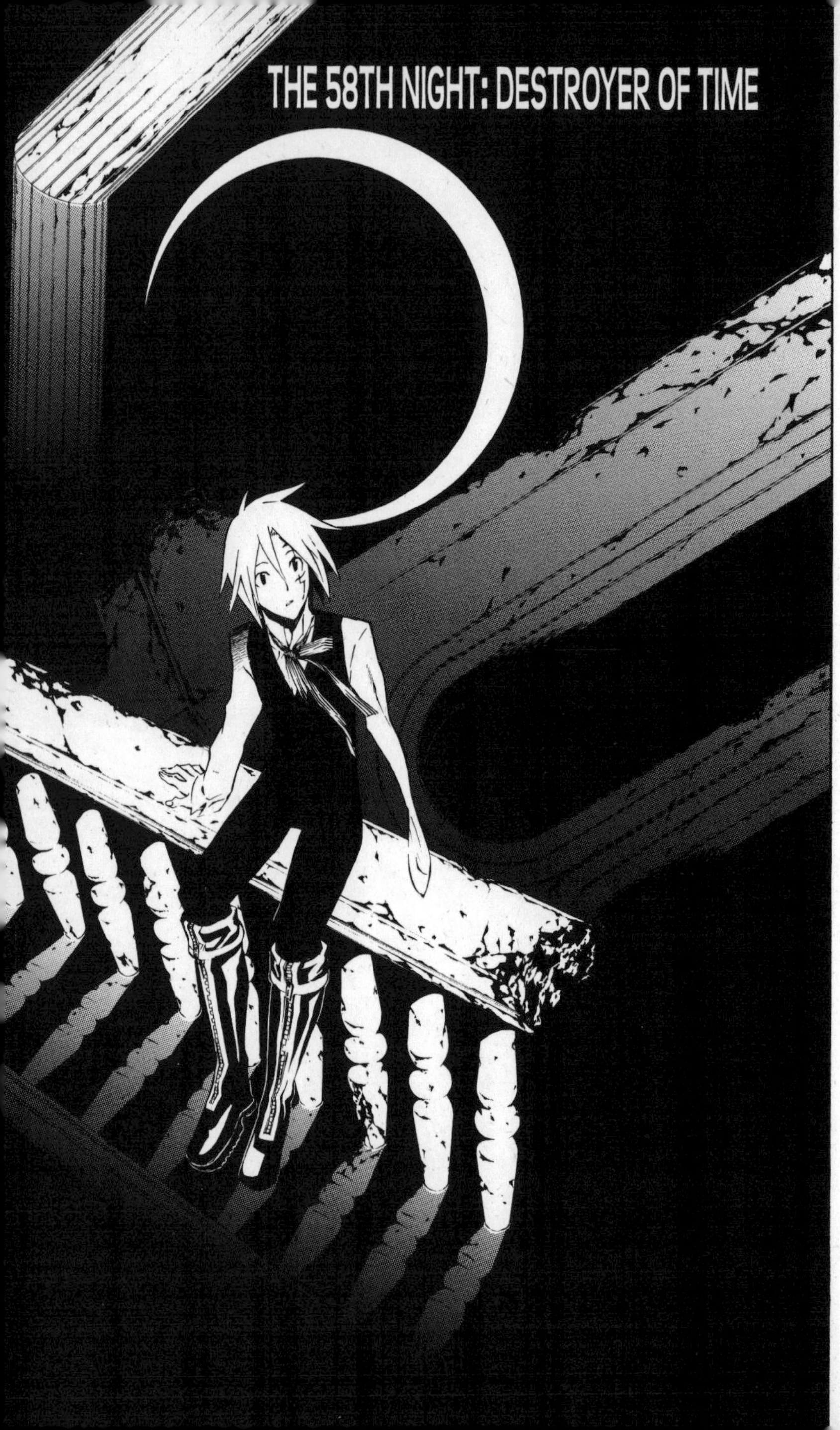

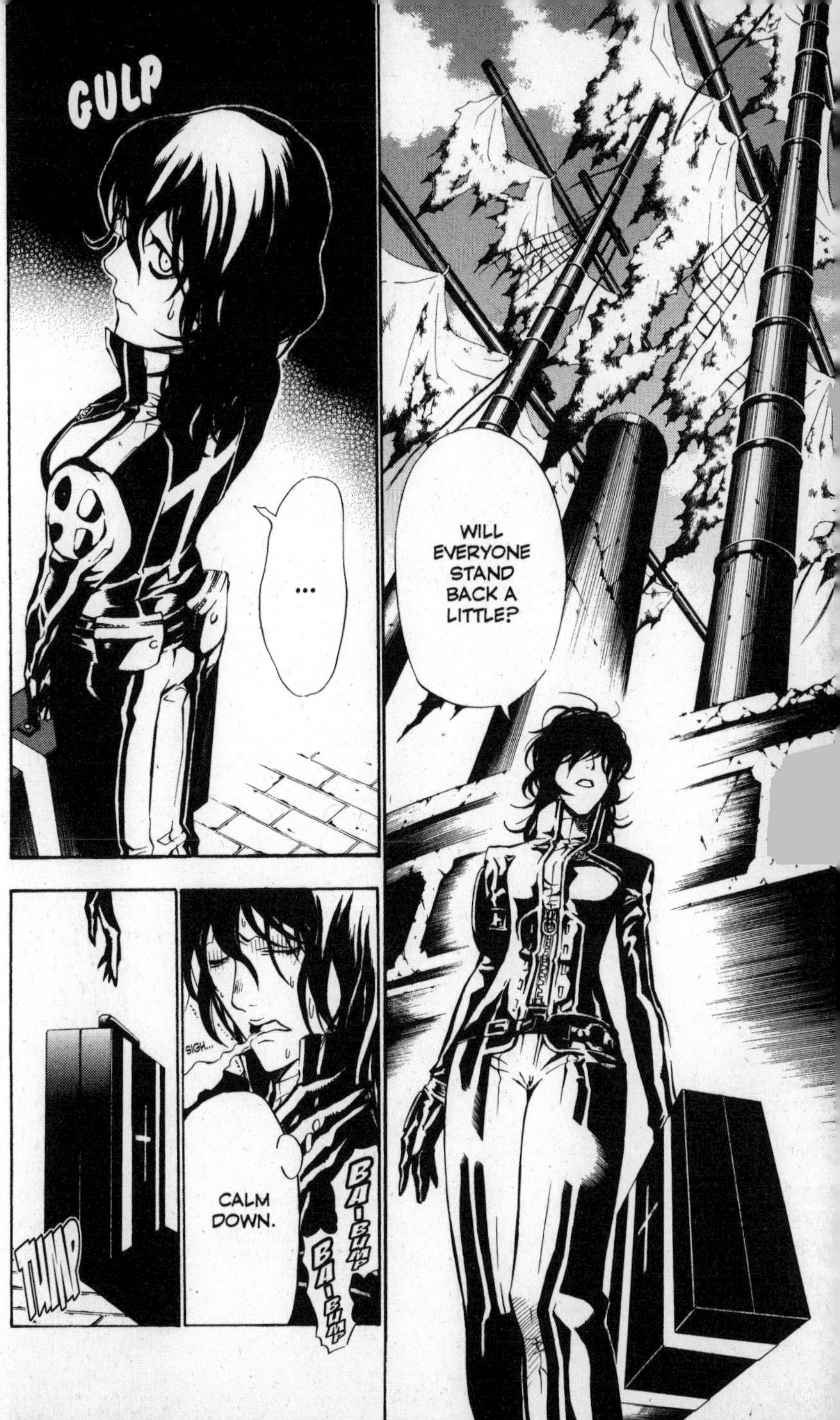
WILL EVERYONE STAND BACK A LITTLE?
GULP
...
SIGH...
CALM DOWN.
BA-BUMP
BA-BUMP
TUMP

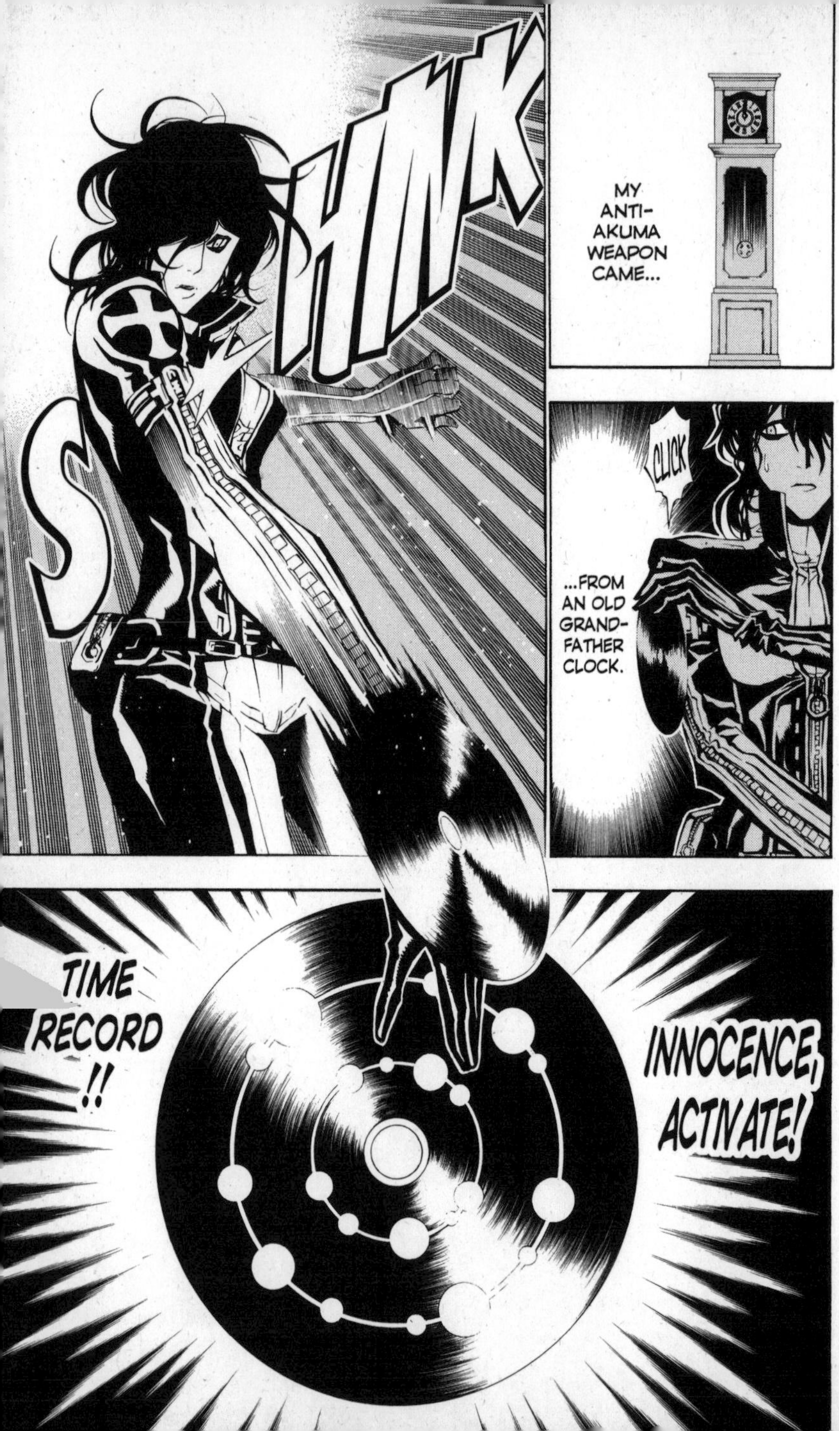
MY ANTI-AKUMA WEAPON CAME...
CLICK
...FROM AN OLD GRANDFATHER CLOCK.
SHINK
INNOCENCE, ACTIVATE!
TIME RECORD!!

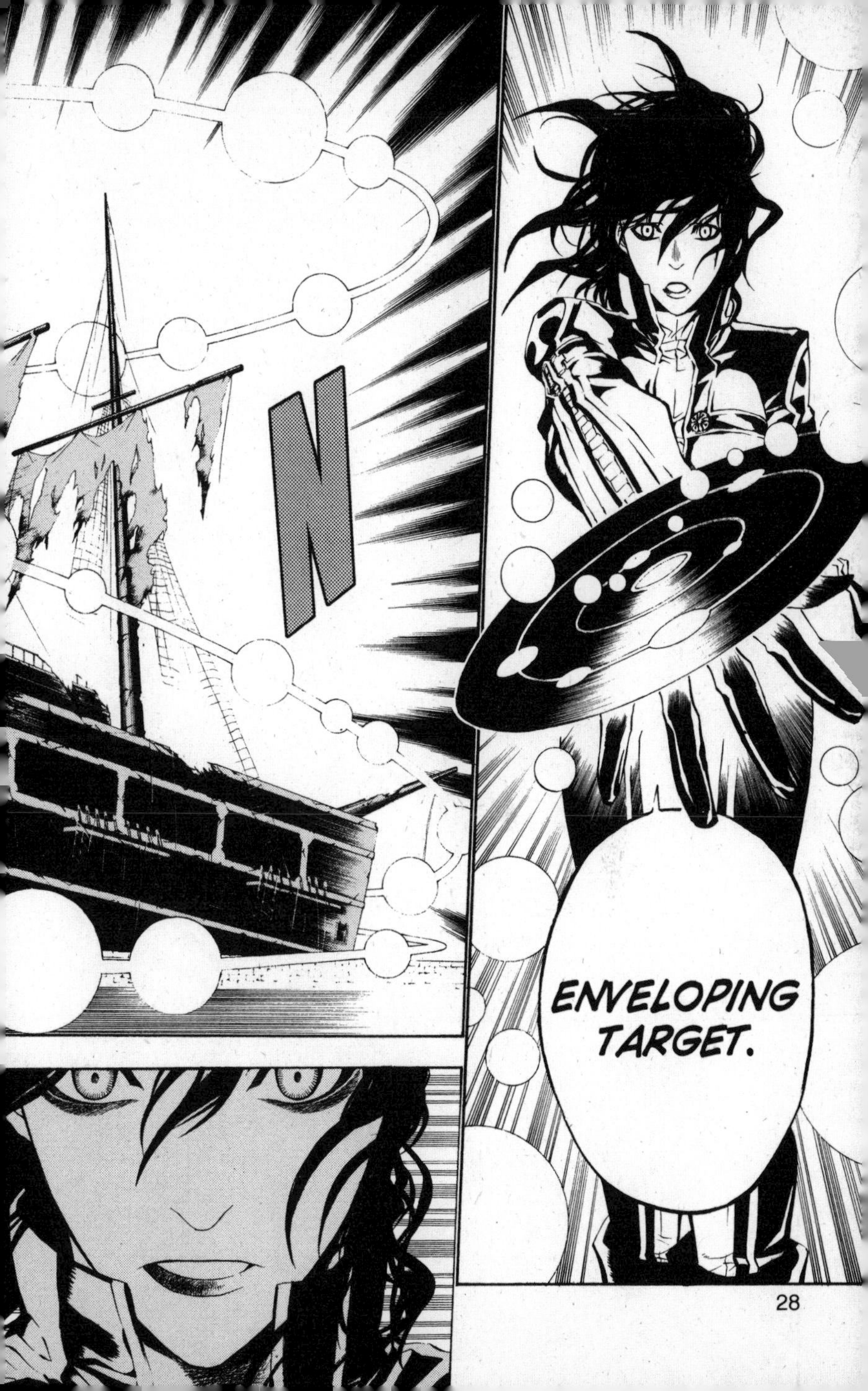
ENVELOPING TARGET.
N

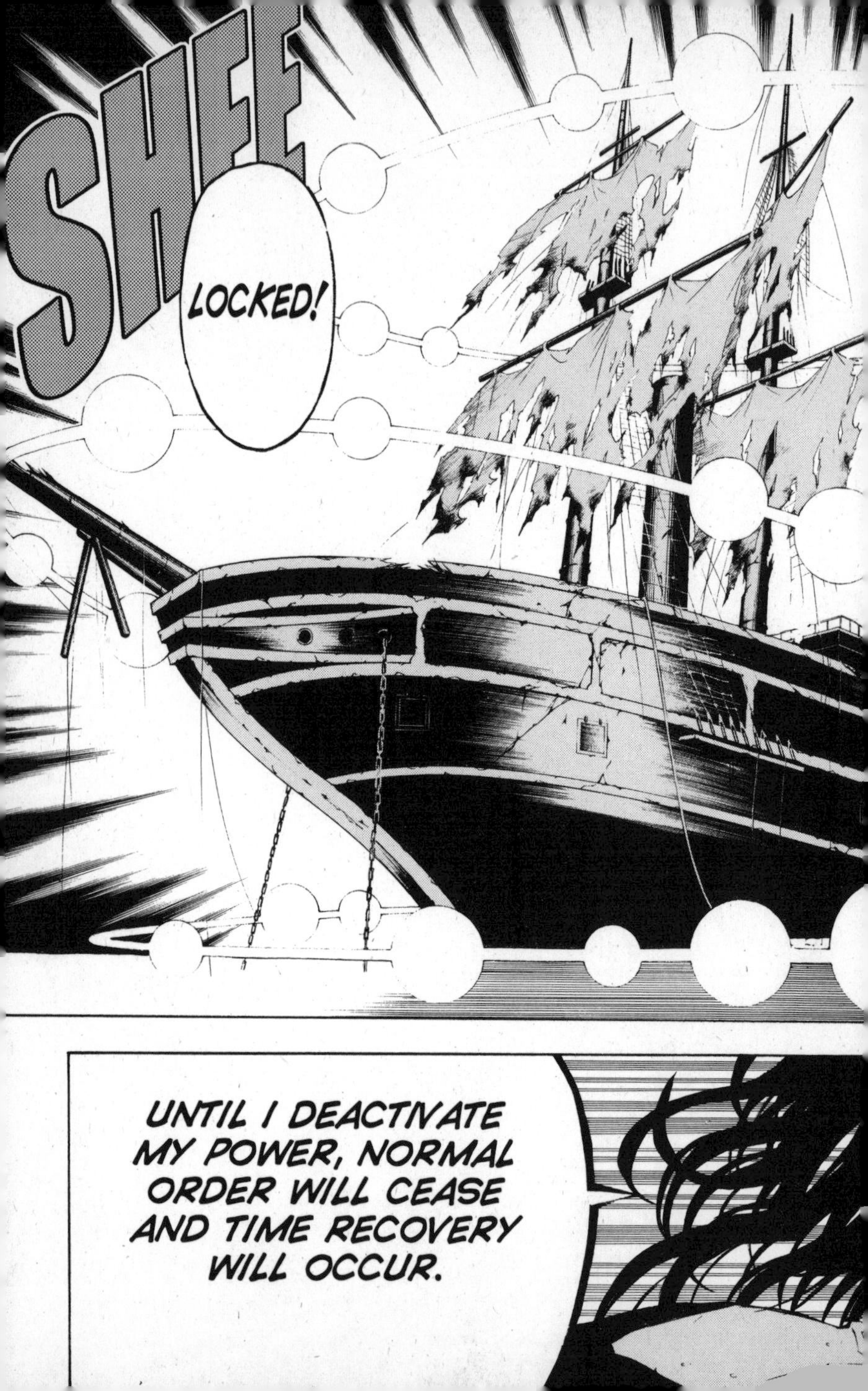
SHEE
LOCKED!
UNTIL I DEACTIVATE MY POWER, NORMAL ORDER WILL CEASE AND TIME RECOVERY WILL OCCUR.

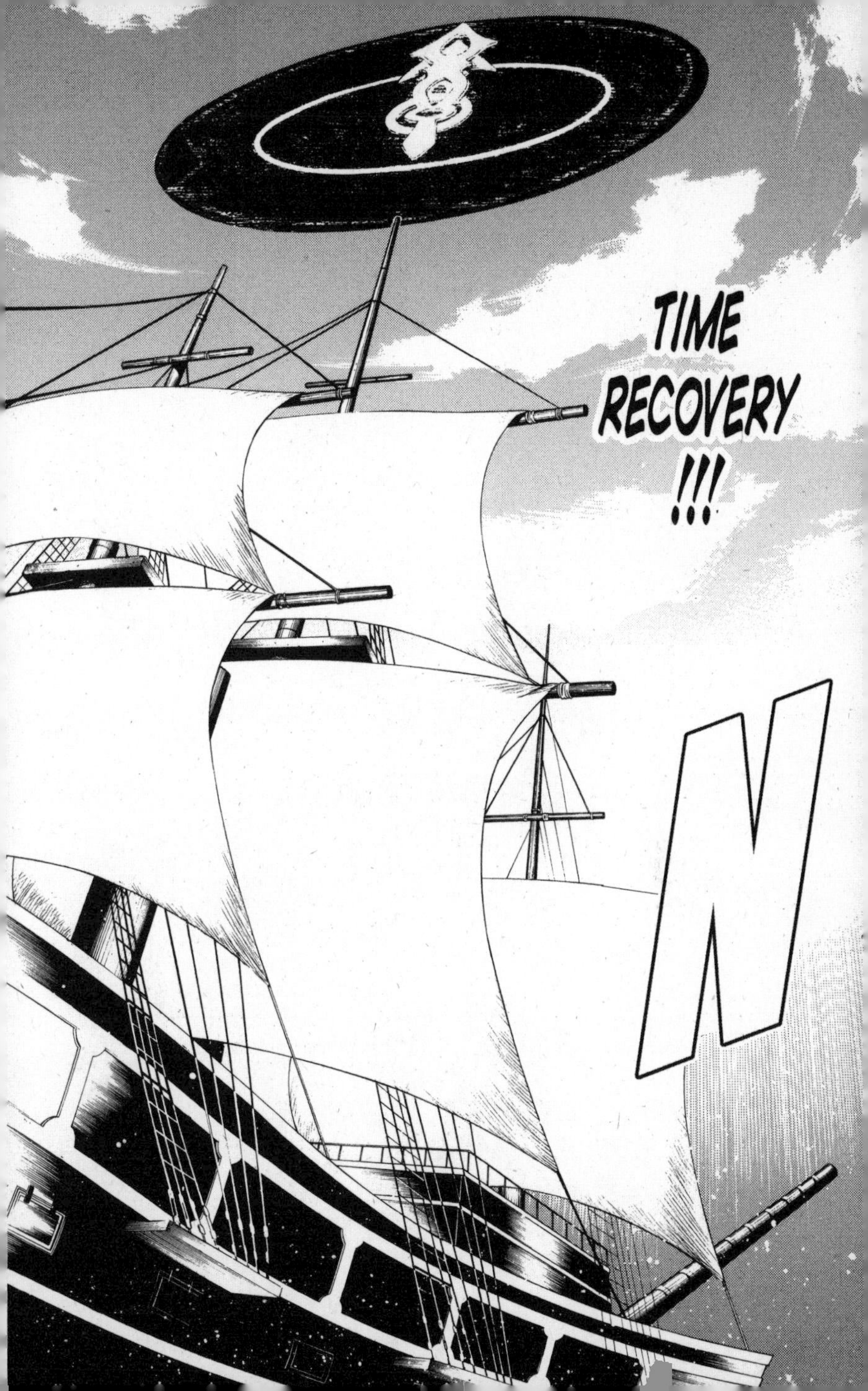
TIME RECOVERY !!!
N

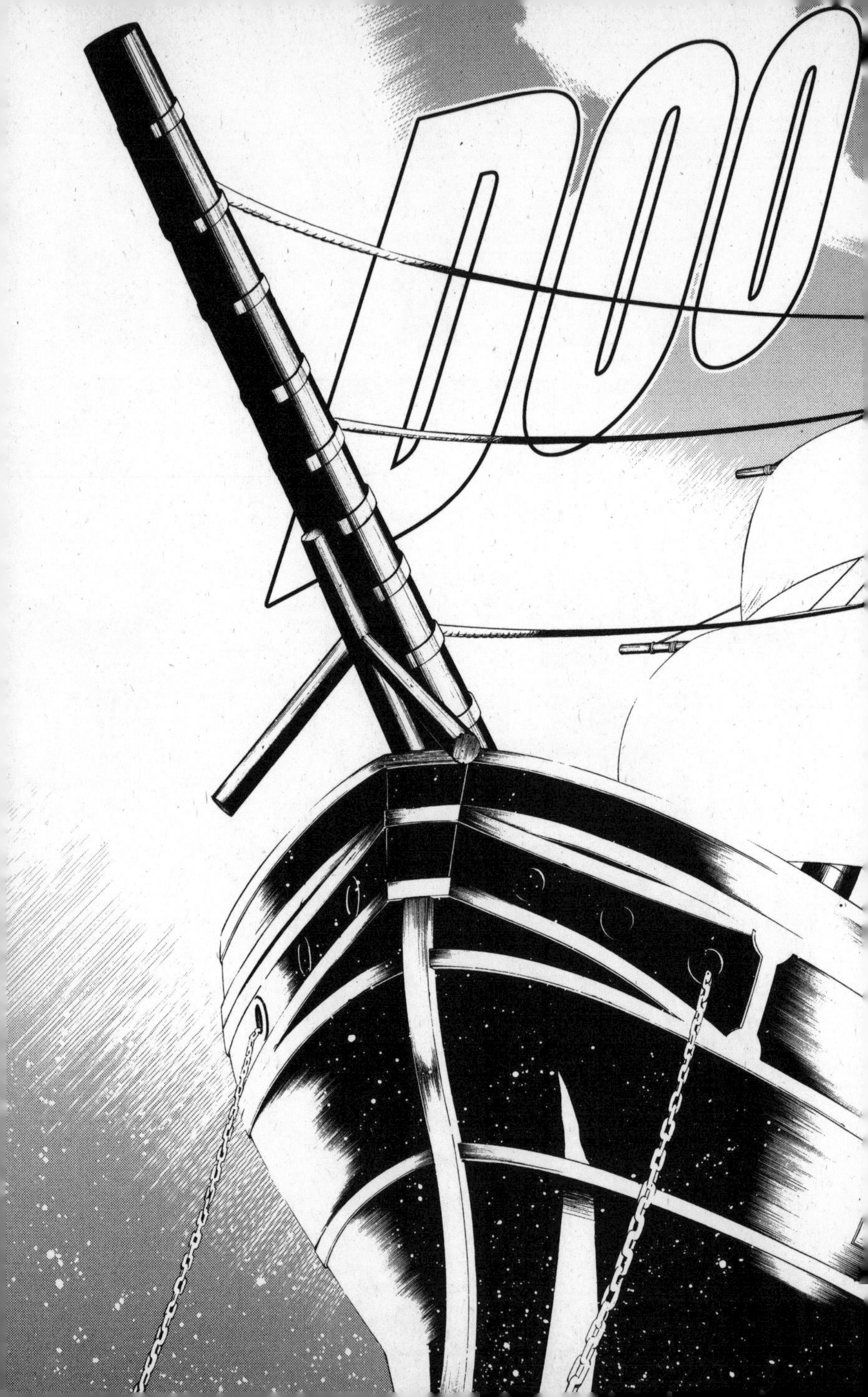
DOOO

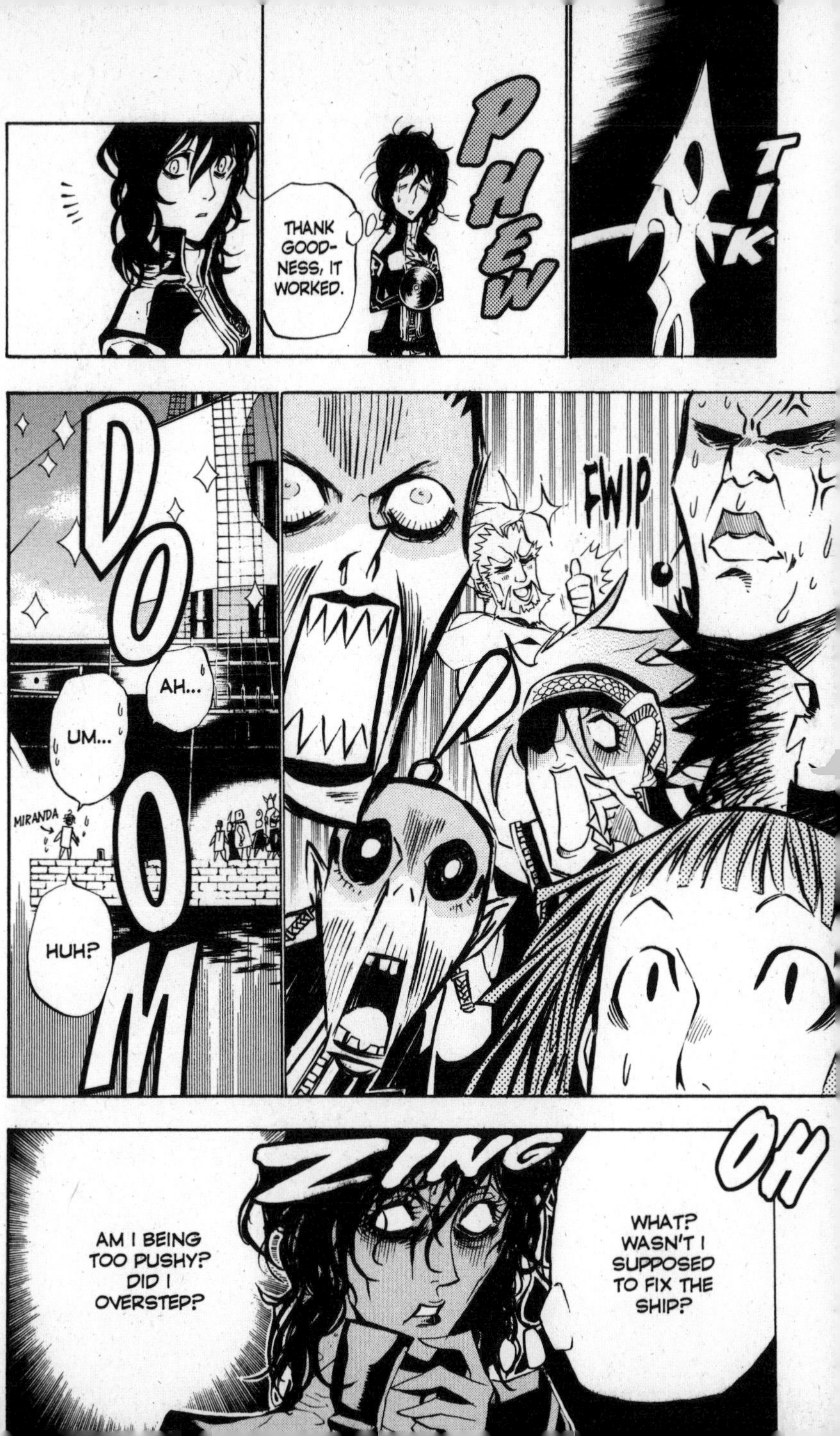
TIK
PHEW
THANK GOODNESS, IT WORKED.
FWIP
DOOM
AH...
UM...
MIRANDA
HUH?
OH
ZING
WHAT? WASN'T I SUPPOSED TO FIX THE SHIP?
AM I BEING TOO PUSHY? DID I OVERSTEP?

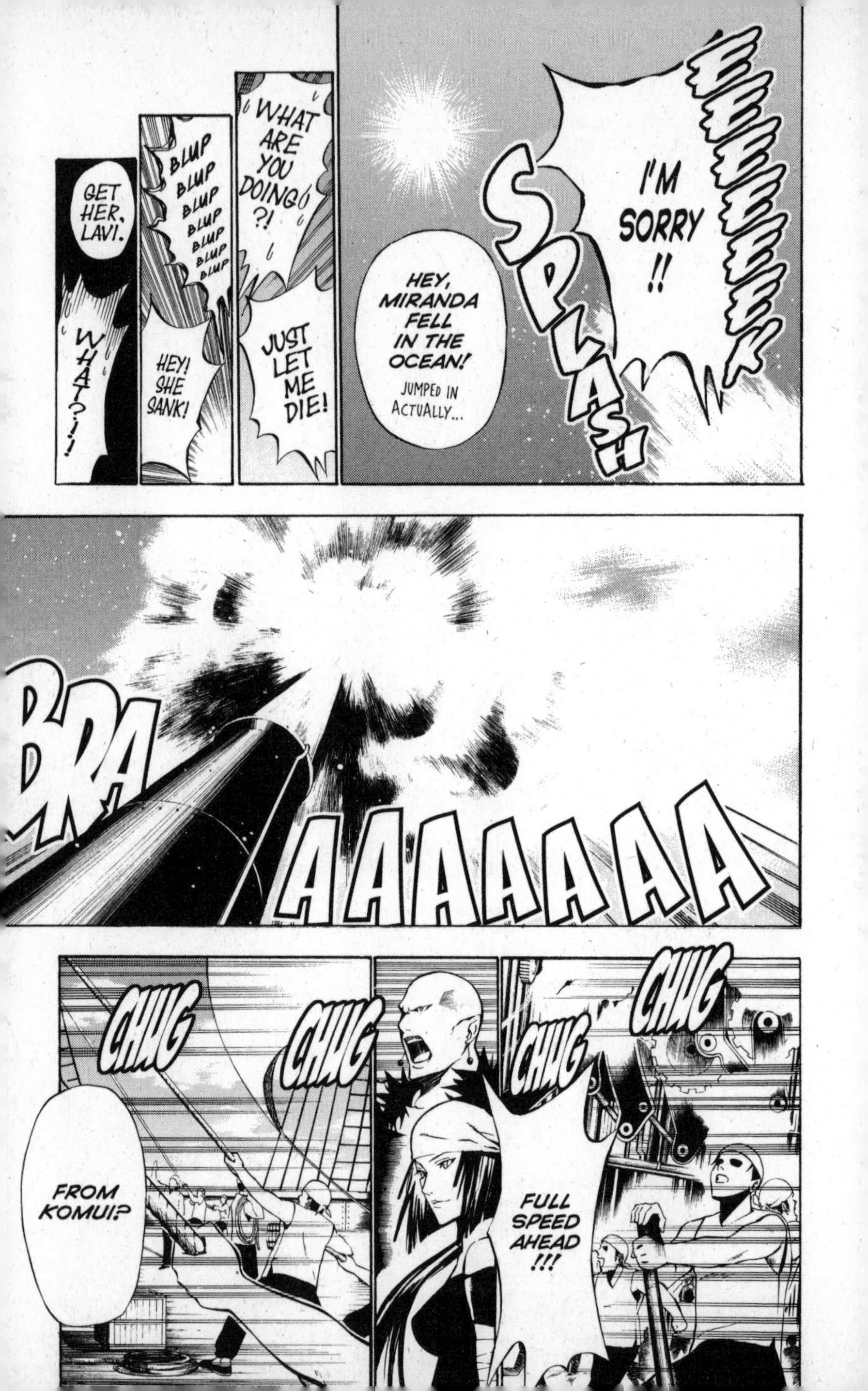
I'M SORRY!!
SPLASH
HEY, MIRANDA FELL IN THE OCEAN!
JUMPED IN ACTUALLY...
WHAT ARE YOU DOING?!
JUST LET ME DIE!
BLUP BLUP BLUP BLUP BLUP BLUP BLUP
HEY! SHE SANK!
GET HER, LAVI.
WHAT?!!
BRAAAAAAAA
CHUG CHUG
CHUG
FULL SPEED AHEAD!!!
CHUG
CHUG
FROM KOMUI?

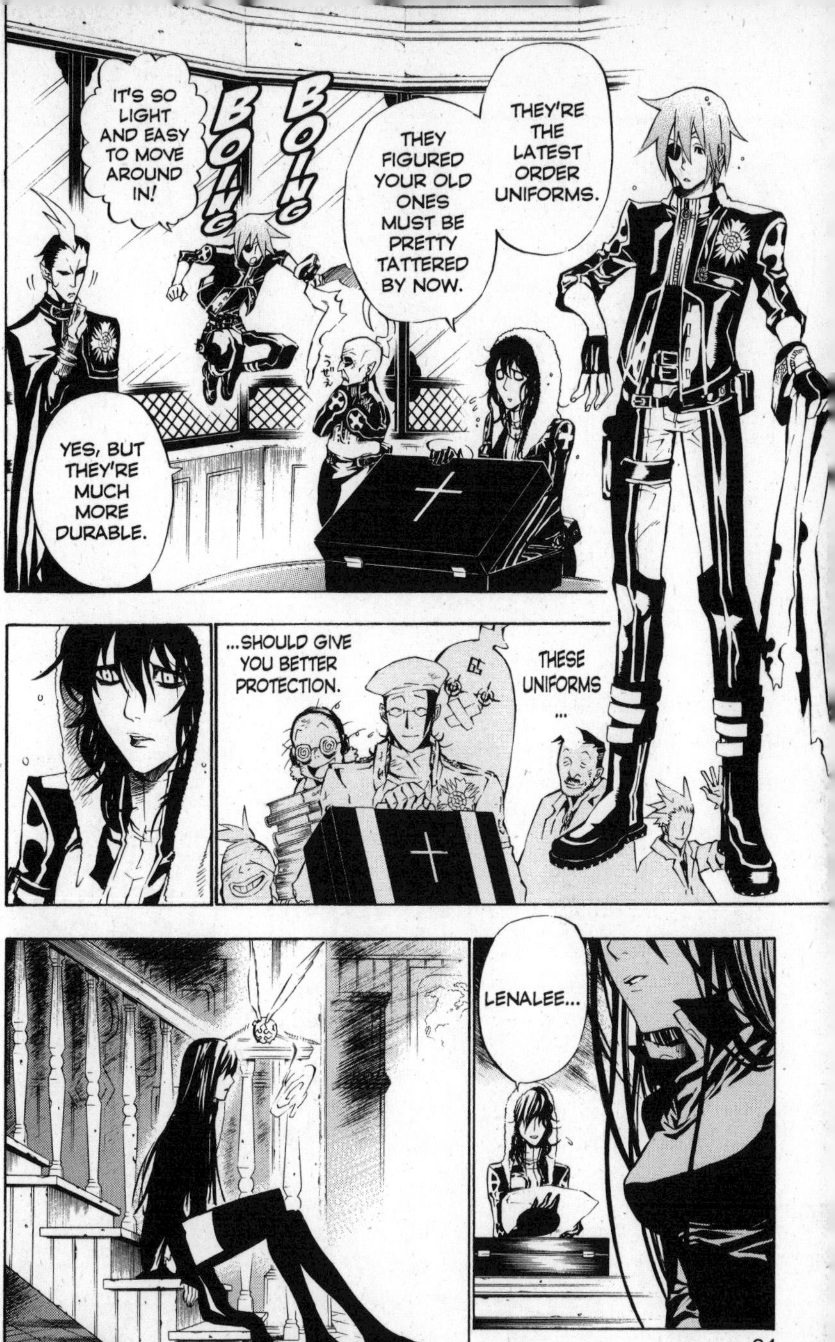
THEY'RE THE LATEST ORDER UNIFORMS.
THEY FIGURED YOUR OLD ONES MUST BE PRETTY TATTERED BY NOW.
BOING
BOING
IT'S SO LIGHT AND EASY TO MOVE AROUND IN!
YES, BUT THEY'RE MUCH MORE DURABLE.
THESE UNIFORMS ...
...SHOULD GIVE YOU BETTER PROTECTION.
LENALEE...

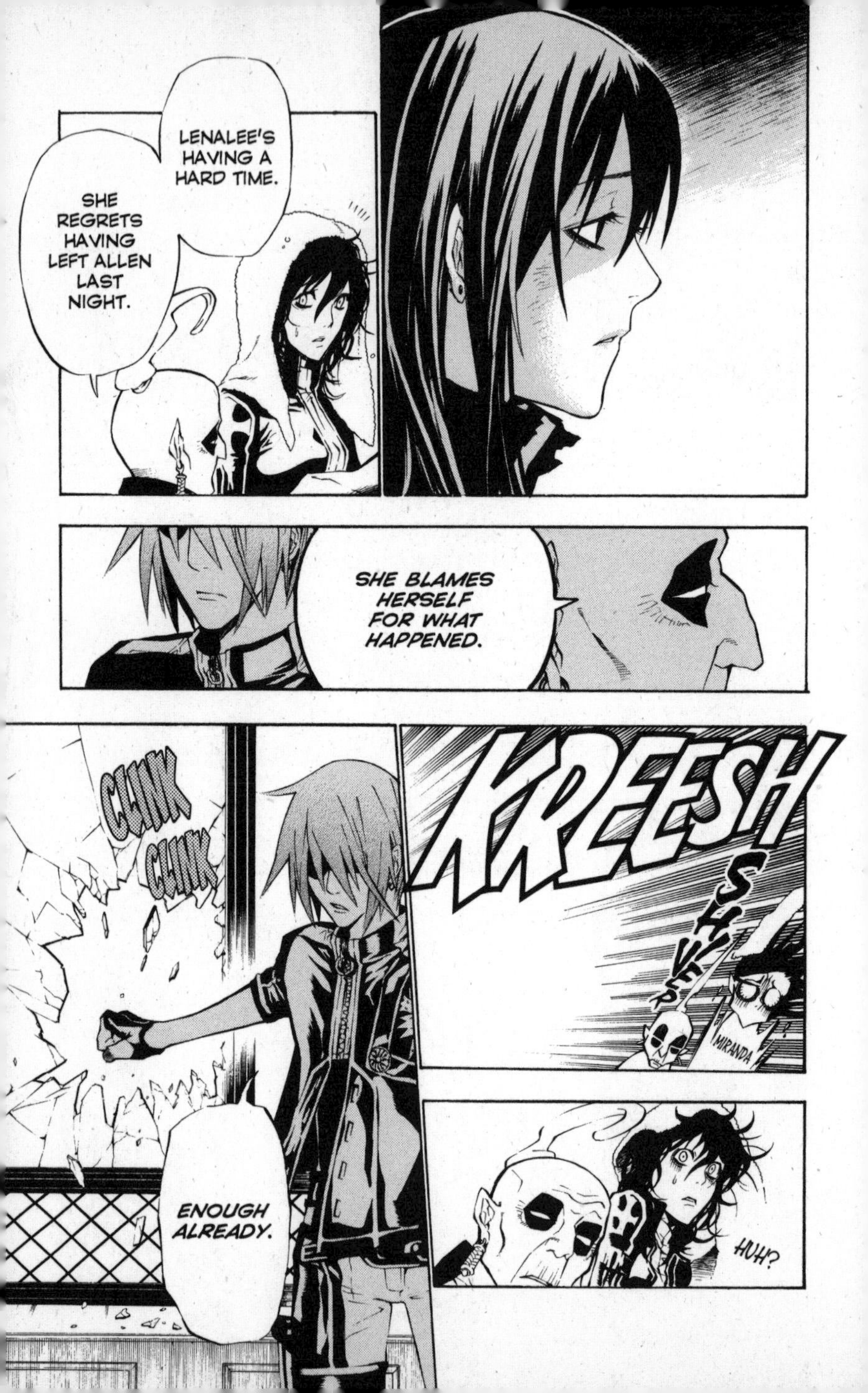
LENALEE'S HAVING A HARD TIME.
SHE REGRETS HAVING LEFT ALLEN LAST NIGHT.
SHE BLAMES HERSELF FOR WHAT HAPPENED.
KREESH
SHIVER
MIRANDA
HUH?
CLINK
CLINK
ENOUGH ALREADY.

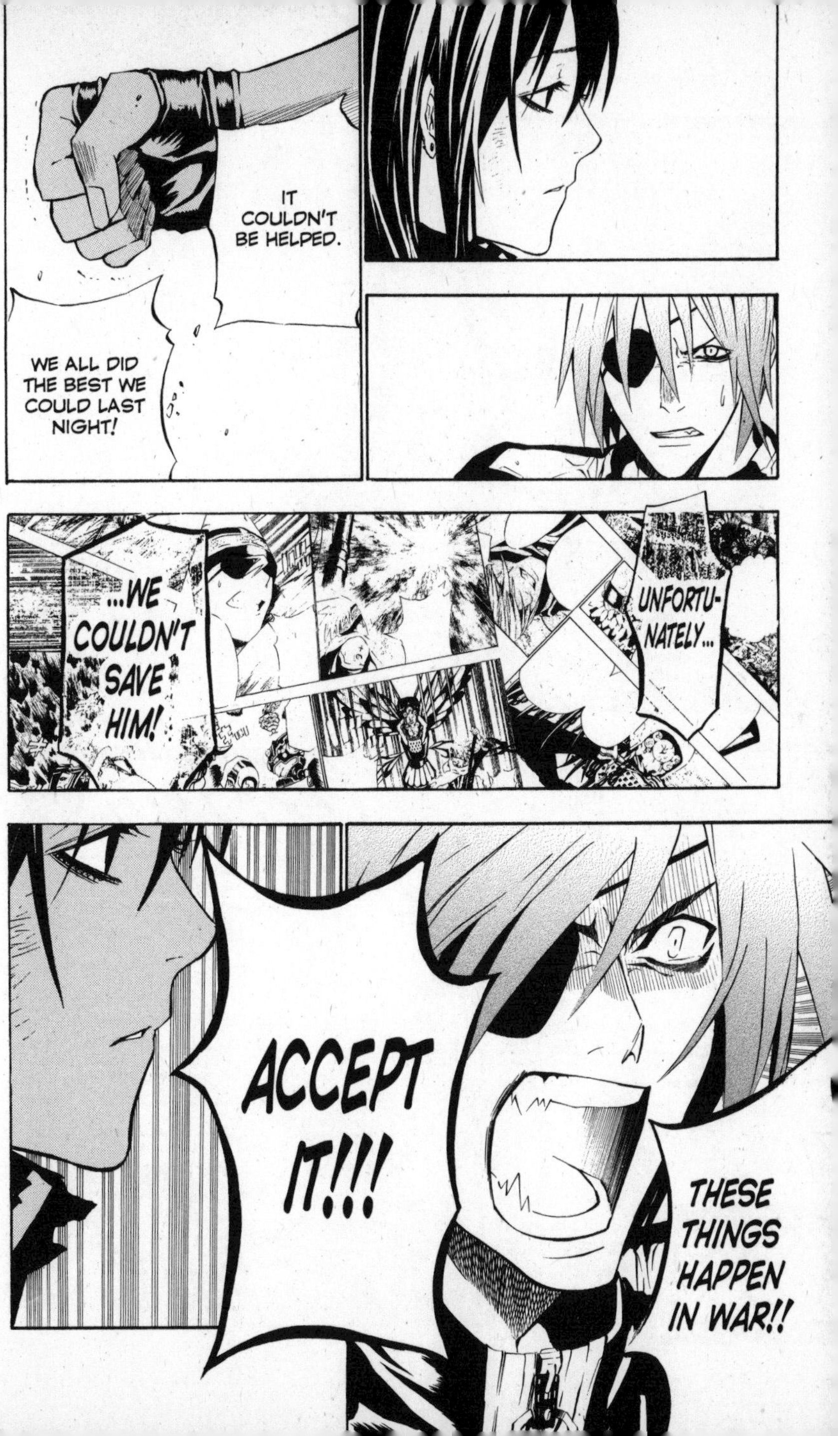
IT COULDN'T BE HELPED.
WE ALL DID THE BEST WE COULD LAST NIGHT!
UNFORTU-NATELY...
...WE COULDN'T SAVE HIM!
ACCEPT IT!!!
THESE THINGS HAPPEN IN WAR!!

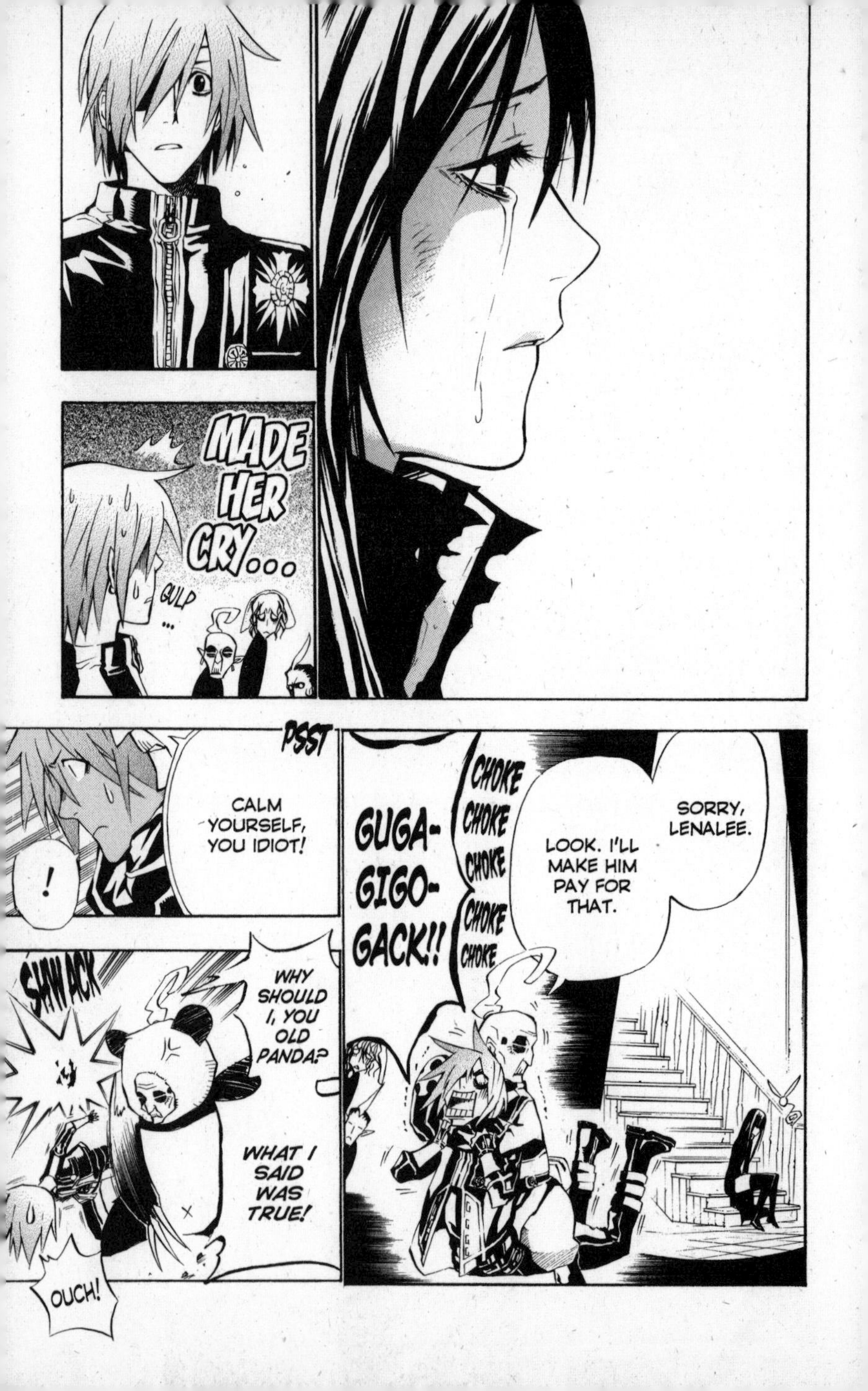
MADE HER CRY...
GULP ...
SORRY, LENALEE.
LOOK. I'LL MAKE HIM PAY FOR THAT.
CHOKE CHOKE CHOKE CHOKE CHOKE
GUGA-GIGO-GACK!!
PSST
CALM YOURSELF, YOU IDIOT!
!
WHY SHOULD I, YOU OLD PANDA?
SHWACK
WHAT I SAID WAS TRUE!
OUCH!

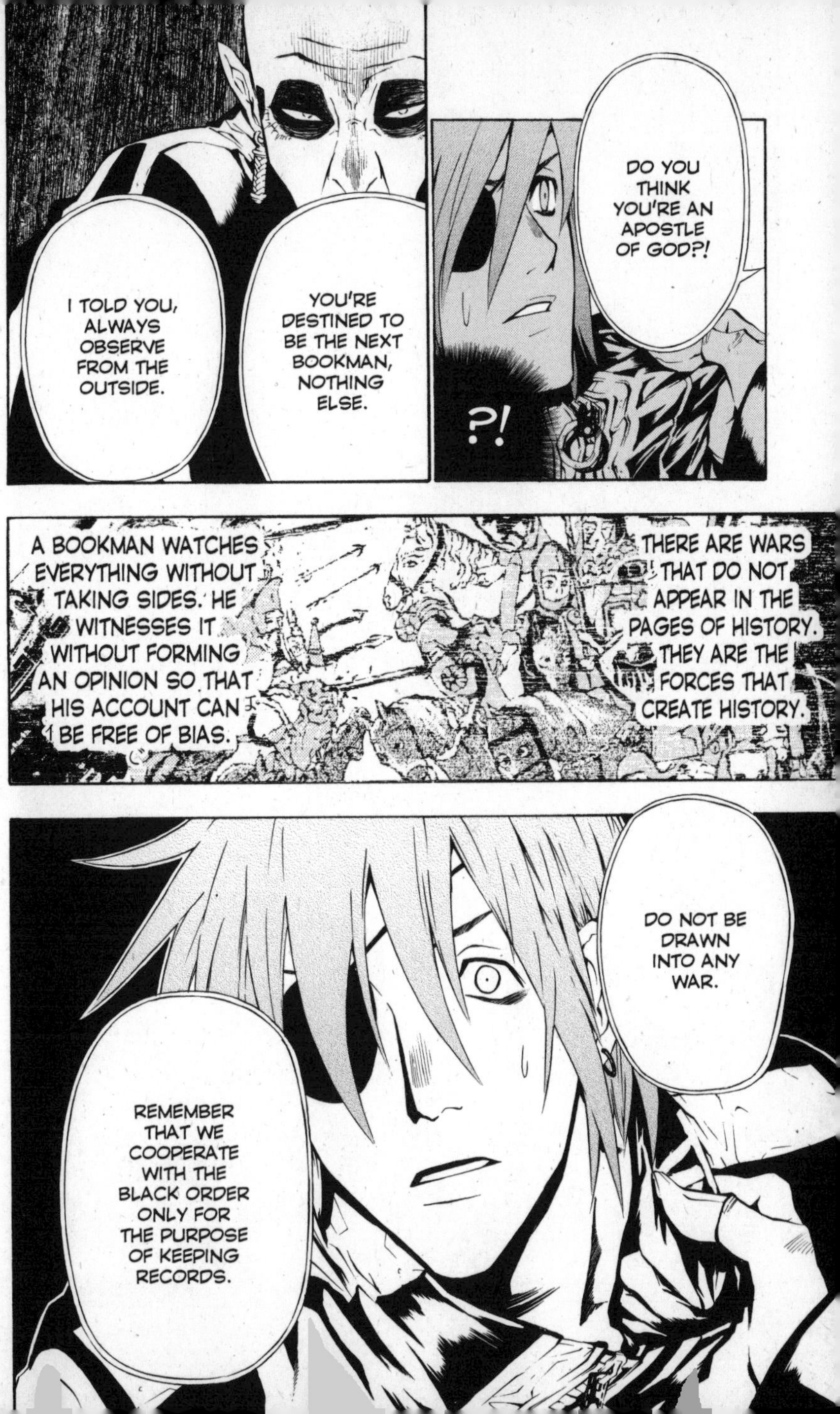
DO YOU THINK YOU'RE AN APOSTLE OF GOD?!
?!
YOU'RE DESTINED TO BE THE NEXT BOOKMAN, NOTHING ELSE.
I TOLD YOU, ALWAYS OBSERVE FROM THE OUTSIDE.
THERE ARE WARS THAT DO NOT APPEAR IN THE PAGES OF HISTORY. THEY ARE THE FORCES THAT CREATE HISTORY.
A BOOKMAN WATCHES EVERYTHING WITHOUT TAKING SIDES. HE WITNESSES IT WITHOUT FORMING AN OPINION SO THAT HIS ACCOUNT CAN BE FREE OF BIAS.
DO NOT BE DRAWN INTO ANY WAR.
REMEMBER THAT WE COOPERATE WITH THE BLACK ORDER ONLY FOR THE PURPOSE OF KEEPING RECORDS.

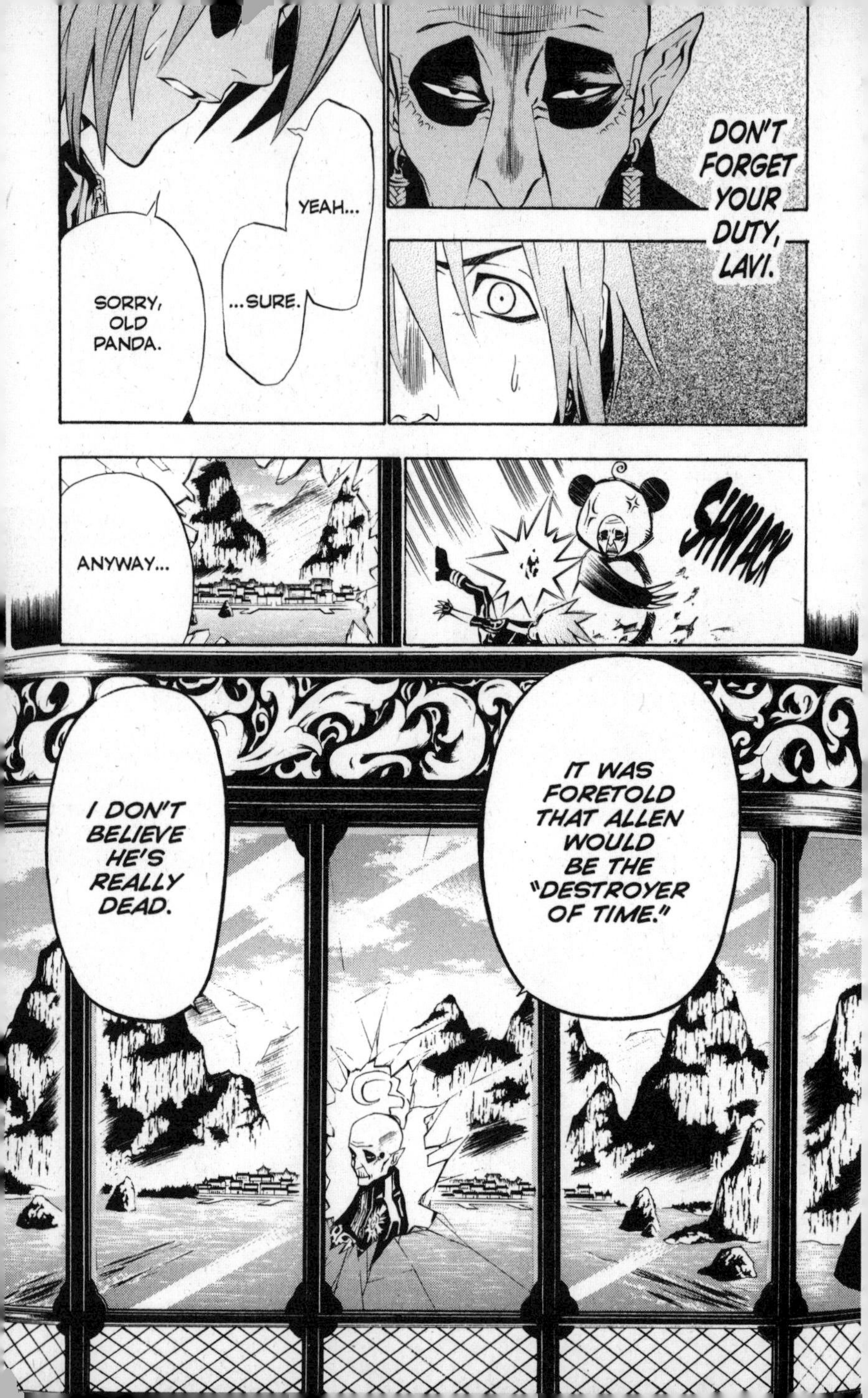
DON'T FORGET YOUR DUTY, LAVI.
YEAH... ...SURE.
SORRY, OLD PANDA.
SHWACK
ANYWAY...
IT WAS FORETOLD THAT ALLEN WOULD BE THE "DESTROYER OF TIME."
I DON'T BELIEVE HE'S REALLY DEAD.

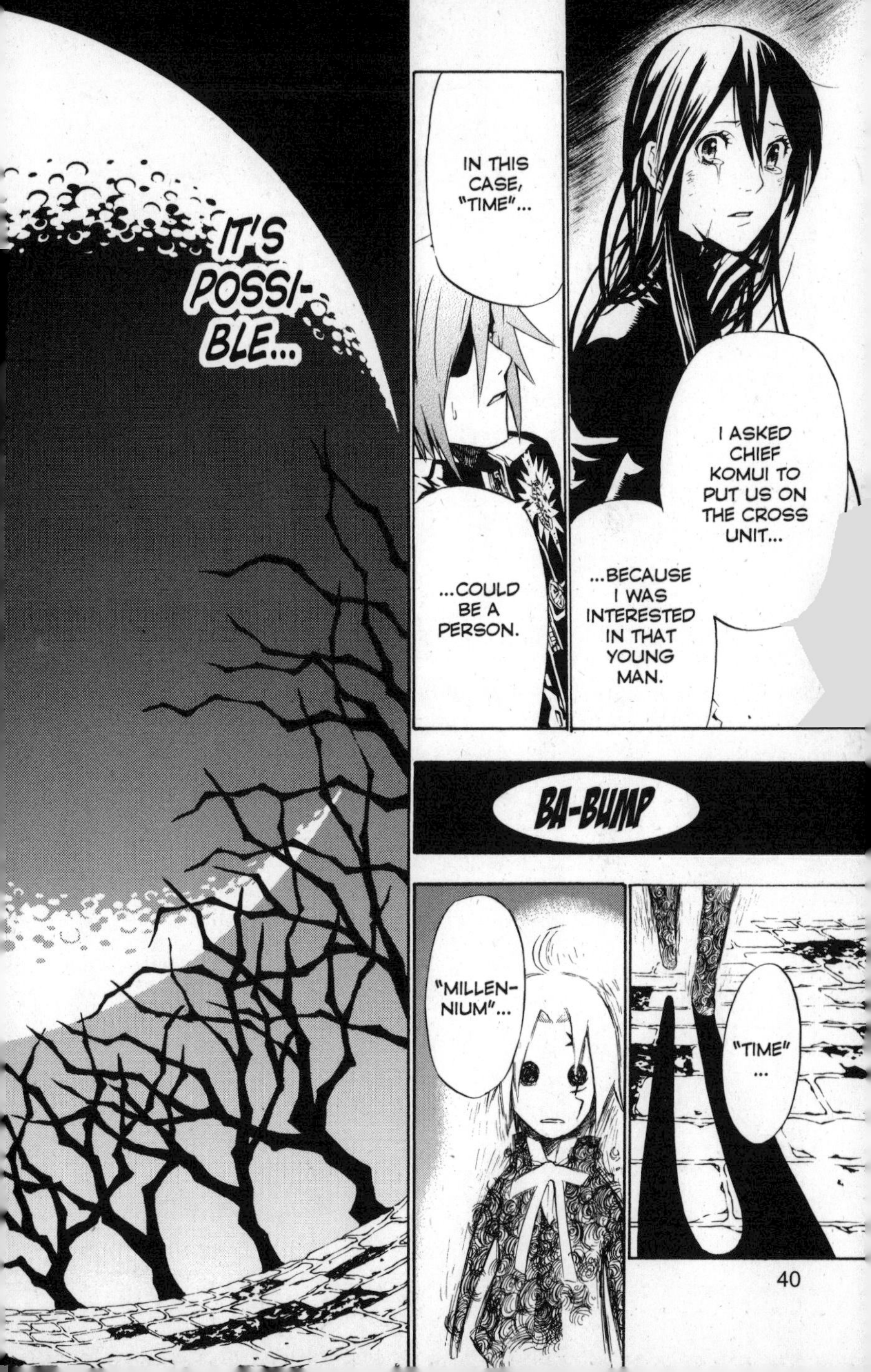
I ASKED CHIEF KOMUI TO PUT US ON THE CROSS UNIT...
...BECAUSE I WAS INTERESTED IN THAT YOUNG MAN.
IN THIS CASE, "TIME"...
...COULD BE A PERSON.
BA-BUMP
"TIME" ...
"MILLEN-NIUM"...
IT'S POSSI-BLE...

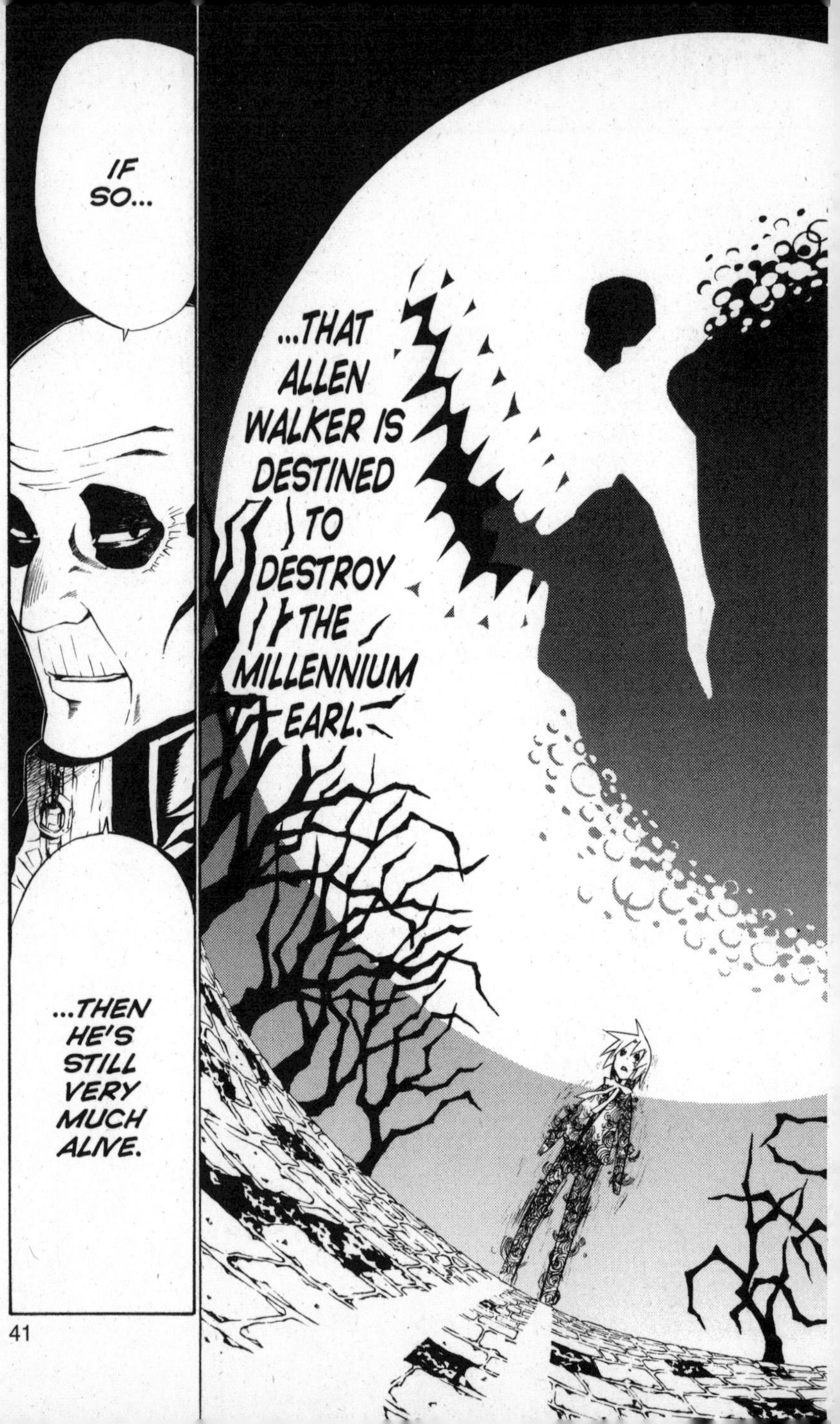
...THAT ALLEN WALKER IS DESTINED TO DESTROY THE MILLENNIUM EARL.
IF SO...
...THEN HE'S STILL VERY MUCH ALIVE.

KOMUI'S DISCUSSION ROOM, VOL. 2

Q: IN THE DISCUSSION ROOM IN VOL. 4, IN RESPONSE TO THE QUESTION ABOUT VALENTINE'S DAY CHOCOLATES, ALLEN SAID, "THANK YOU VERY MUCH," BUT IN VOL. 5, REEVER SAID THAT ALLEN DOESN'T LIKE CHOCOLATE. WHICH IS IT?

A: (ALLEN) HEY, THIS IS FROM THE SAME PERSON WHO SENT THE QUESTION ABOUT THE VALENTINE'S CHOCOLATES.

(LAVI) YEAH, BUT WE GET THIS QUESTION A LOT. SO, WHAT'S THE ANSWER?

(ALLEN) HMM...I THINK THE MISUNDERSTANDING HAPPENED WHEN LENALEE WAS PRACTICING MAKING A BIRTHDAY CAKE FOR KOMUI. I SAW THAT IT WAS A CHOCOLATE CAKE SO I TASTED IT ONLY TO DISCOVER THAT IT TASTED LIKE LIQUOR!

(LAVI) SO IT WAS A CAKE WITH LIQUOR IN IT. I GUESS CAKES ARE FOR GROWN UPS IN THE WEST.

(ALLEN) I FELT BAD FOR LENALEE, BUT I JUST COULDN'T EAT IT. I DON'T LIKE LIQUOR.

(LAVI) WHAT? YOU DON'T DRINK? (WHAT A CHILD.)

(ALLEN) DURING MY TRAVELS WHILE I WAS TRAINING, I WAS SO HUNGRY THAT I ATE SOME LIQUOR-FILLED CHOCOLATES THAT MY MASTER HAD HIDDEN. WHEN HE CAUGHT ME, HE MADE ME SWEAR I'D NEVER DO IT AGAIN. IT'S NOT LIKE I CAN'T DRINK IT, BUT IT MAKES ME REMEMBER THE PUNISHMENT MY MASTER INFLICTED ON ME. NOW IF I EVEN SMELL LIQUOR I FEEL SICK. BUT IT WAS A BEAUTIFUL CAKE.

(LAVI) (HMM...I WONDER WHAT GENERAL CROSS DID TO HIM?)

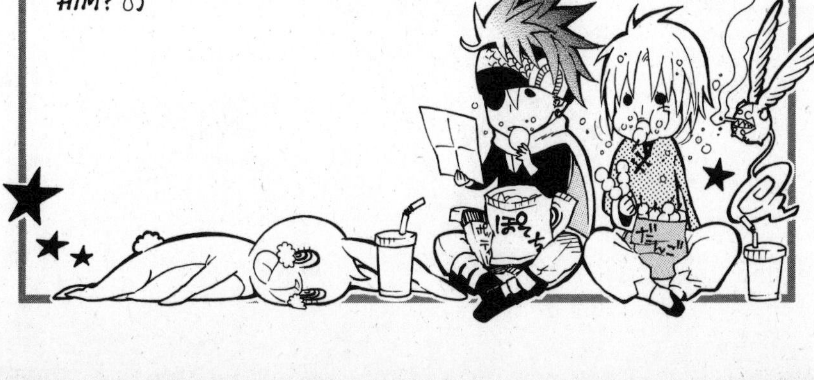

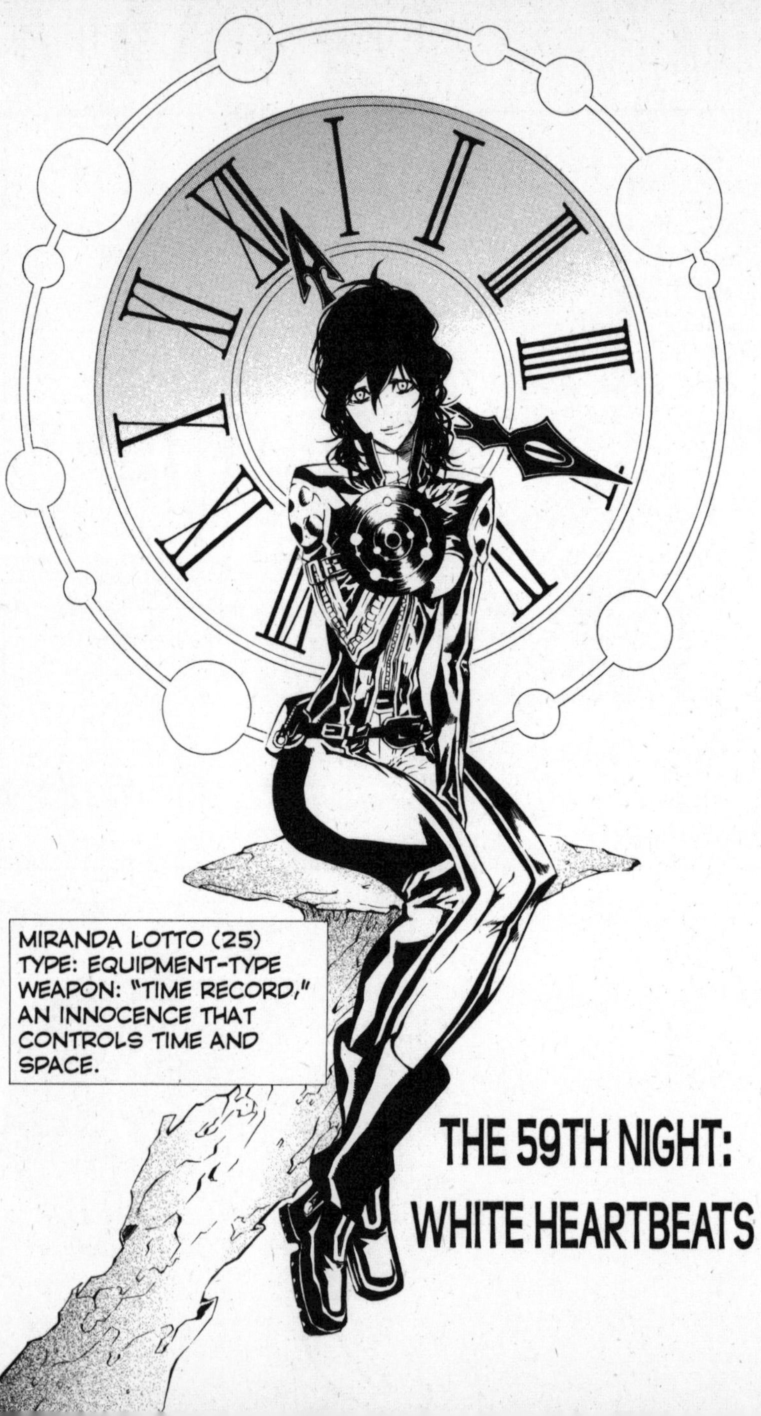
MIRANDA LOTTO (25)
TYPE: EQUIPMENT-TYPE
WEAPON: "TIME RECORD," AN INNOCENCE THAT CONTROLS TIME AND SPACE.
THE 59TH NIGHT: WHITE HEARTBEATS

KSHHHH

H

WHOO

M

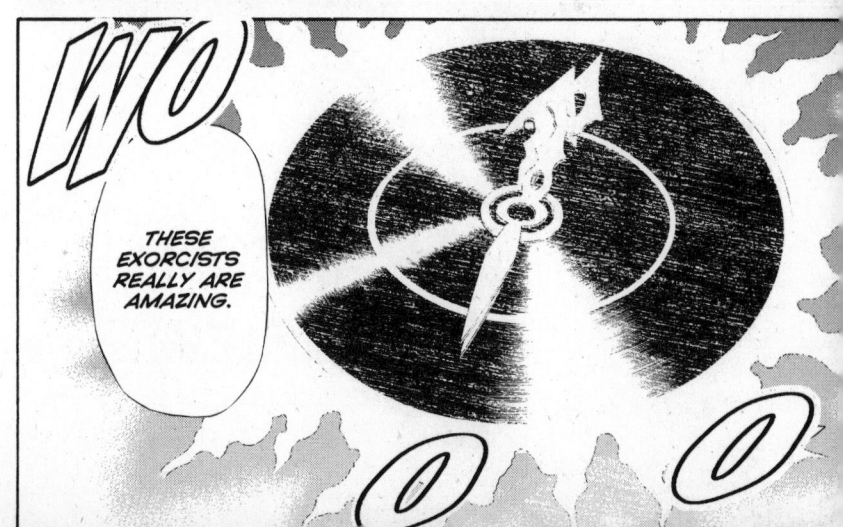

WO

THESE
EXORCISTS
REALLY ARE
AMAZING.

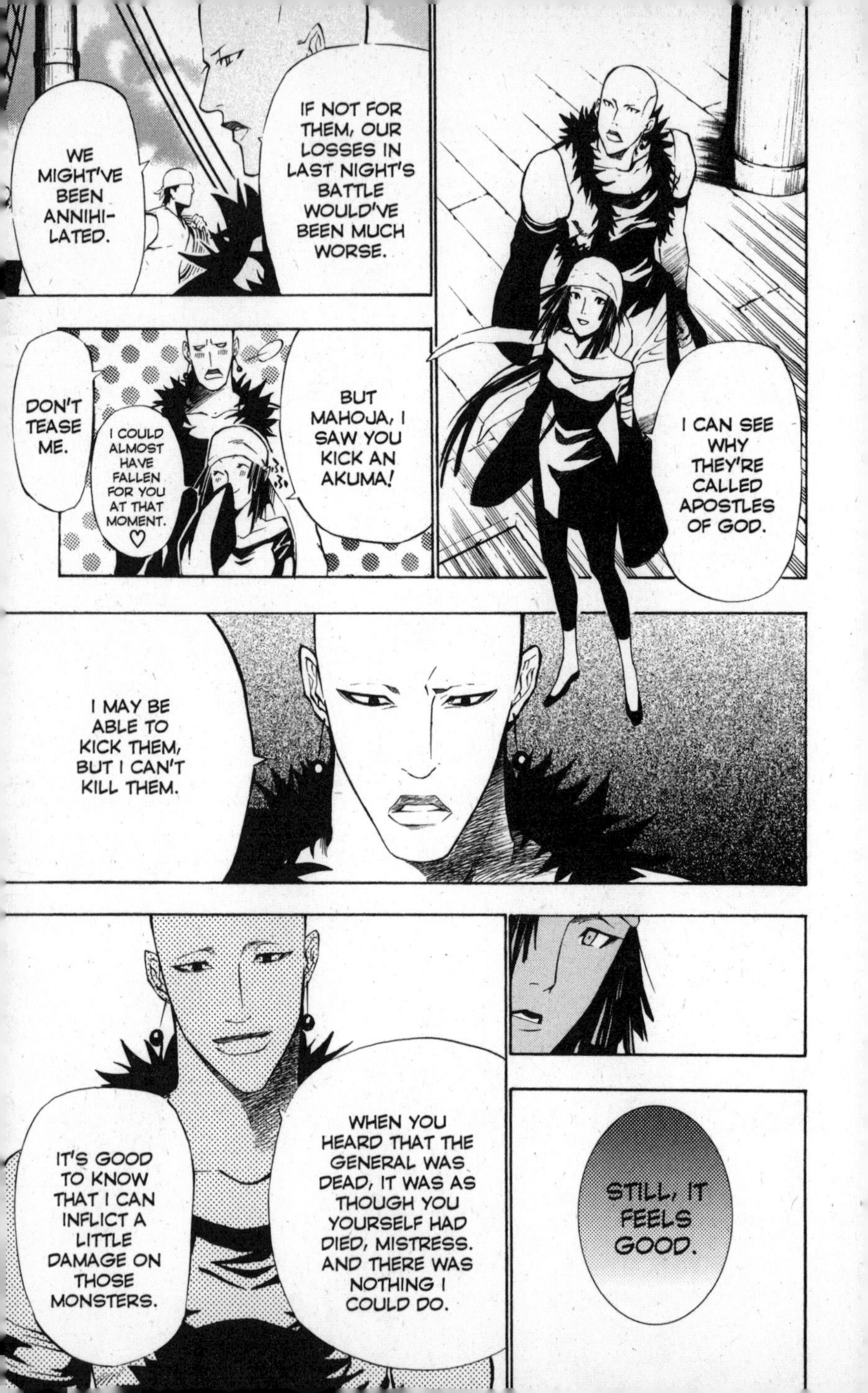
I CAN SEE WHY THEY'RE CALLED APOSTLES OF GOD.
IF NOT FOR THEM, OUR LOSSES IN LAST NIGHT'S BATTLE WOULD'VE BEEN MUCH WORSE.
WE MIGHT'VE BEEN ANNIHI-LATED.
BUT MAHOJA, I SAW YOU KICK AN AKUMA!
I COULD ALMOST HAVE FALLEN FOR YOU AT THAT MOMENT. ♡
DON'T TEASE ME.
I MAY BE ABLE TO KICK THEM, BUT I CAN'T KILL THEM.
STILL, IT FEELS GOOD.
WHEN YOU HEARD THAT THE GENERAL WAS DEAD, IT WAS AS THOUGH YOU YOURSELF HAD DIED, MISTRESS. AND THERE WAS NOTHING I COULD DO.
IT'S GOOD TO KNOW THAT I CAN INFLICT A LITTLE DAMAGE ON THOSE MONSTERS.

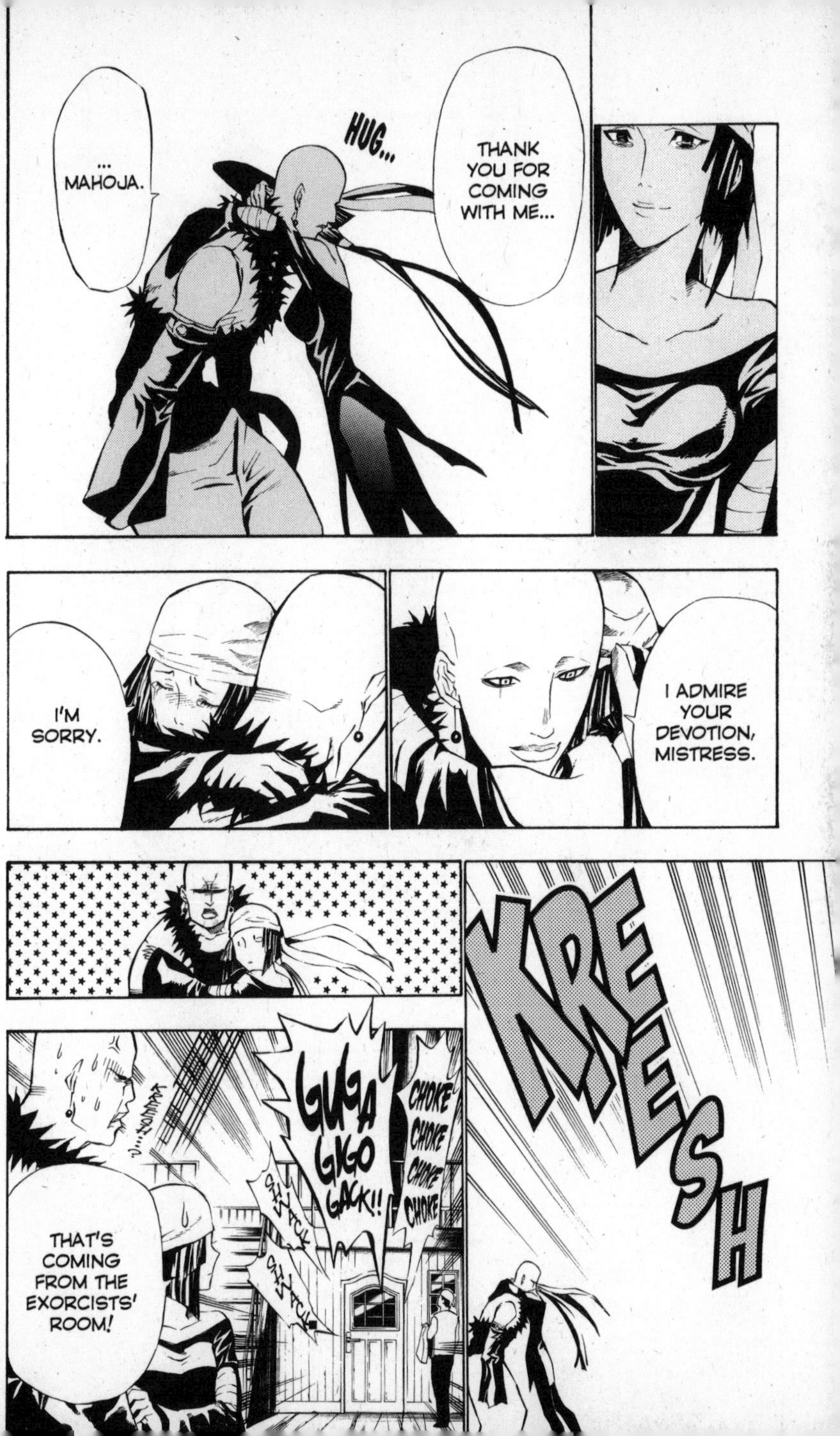

THANK YOU FOR COMING WITH ME...
HUG...
... MAHOJA.
I ADMIRE YOUR DEVOTION, MISTRESS.
I'M SORRY.
KREESH
CHOKE CHOKE CHOKE CHOKE
GUGA GIGO GACK!!
THAT'S COMING FROM THE EXORCISTS' ROOM!

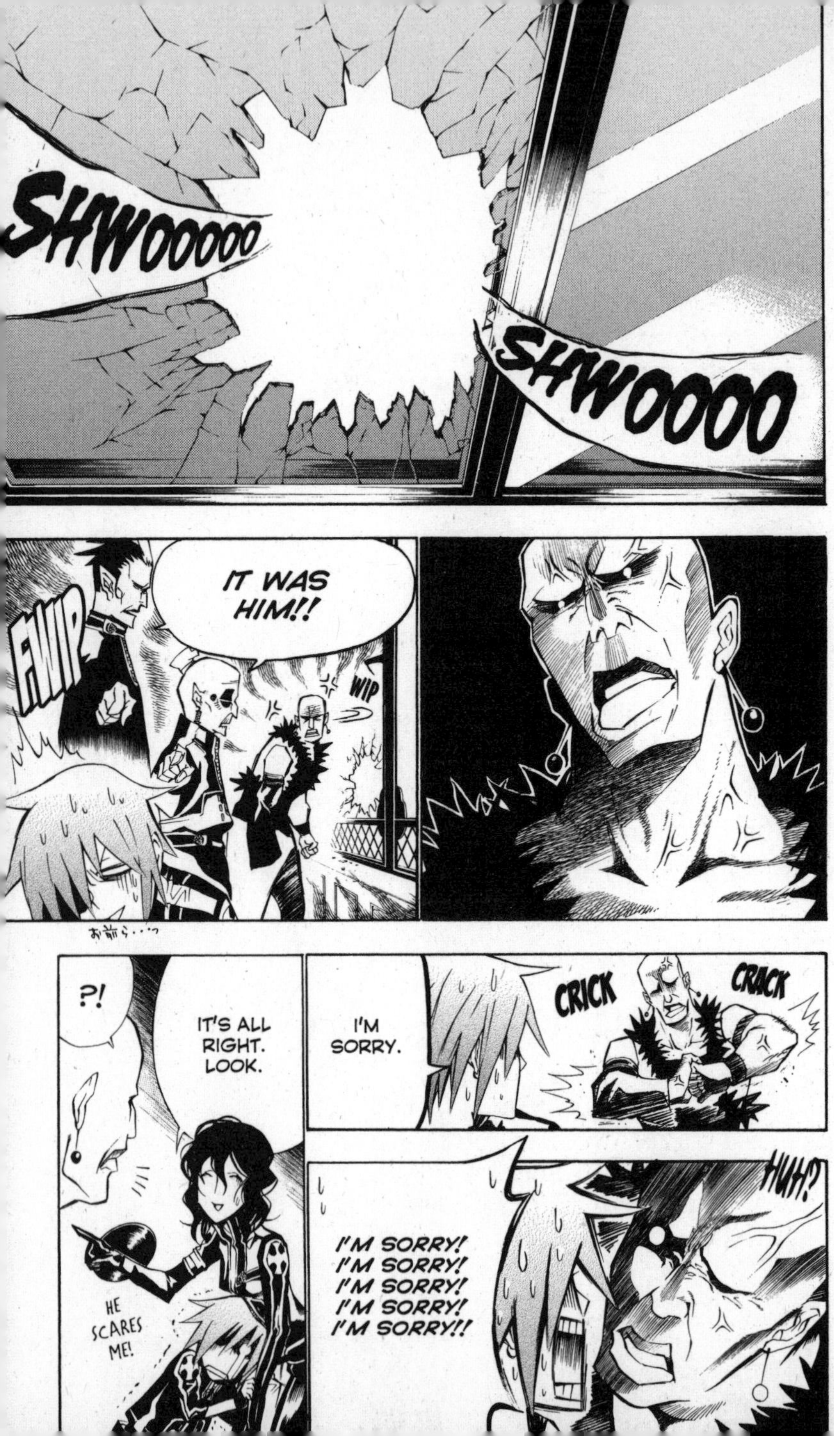
SHWOOOO
SHWOOOOO
IT WAS HIM!!
WIP
FWIP
お前ら・・・っ
CRACK
CRICK
I'M SORRY.
HUH!?
I'M SORRY! I'M SORRY! I'M SORRY! I'M SORRY! I'M SORRY!!
IT'S ALL RIGHT. LOOK.
?!
HE SCARES ME!

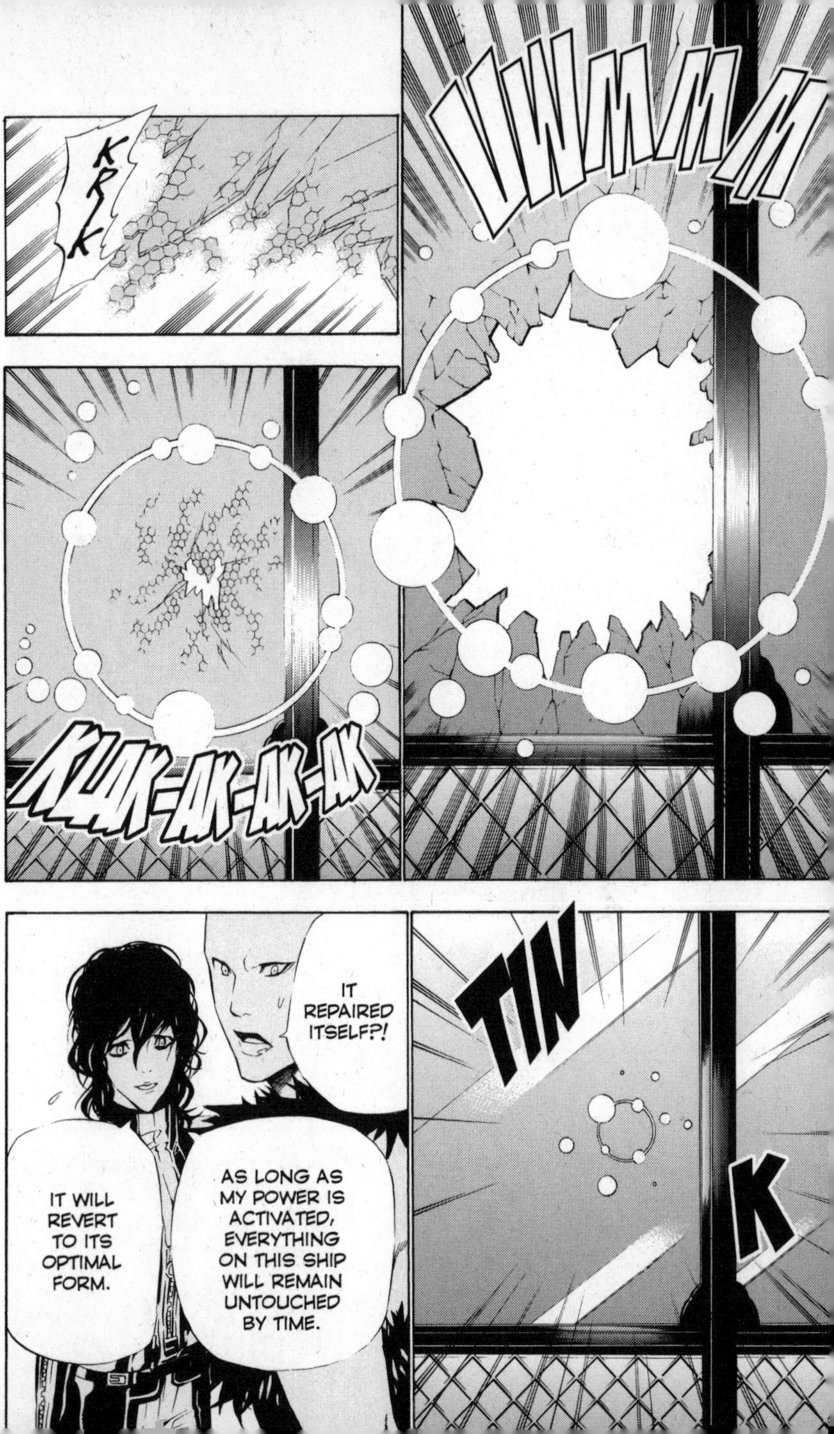
VWMMMM
KRIK
KLAK-AK-AK-AK
TIN
K
IT REPAIRED ITSELF?!
AS LONG AS MY POWER IS ACTIVATED, EVERYTHING ON THIS SHIP WILL REMAIN UNTOUCHED BY TIME.
IT WILL REVERT TO ITS OPTIMAL FORM.

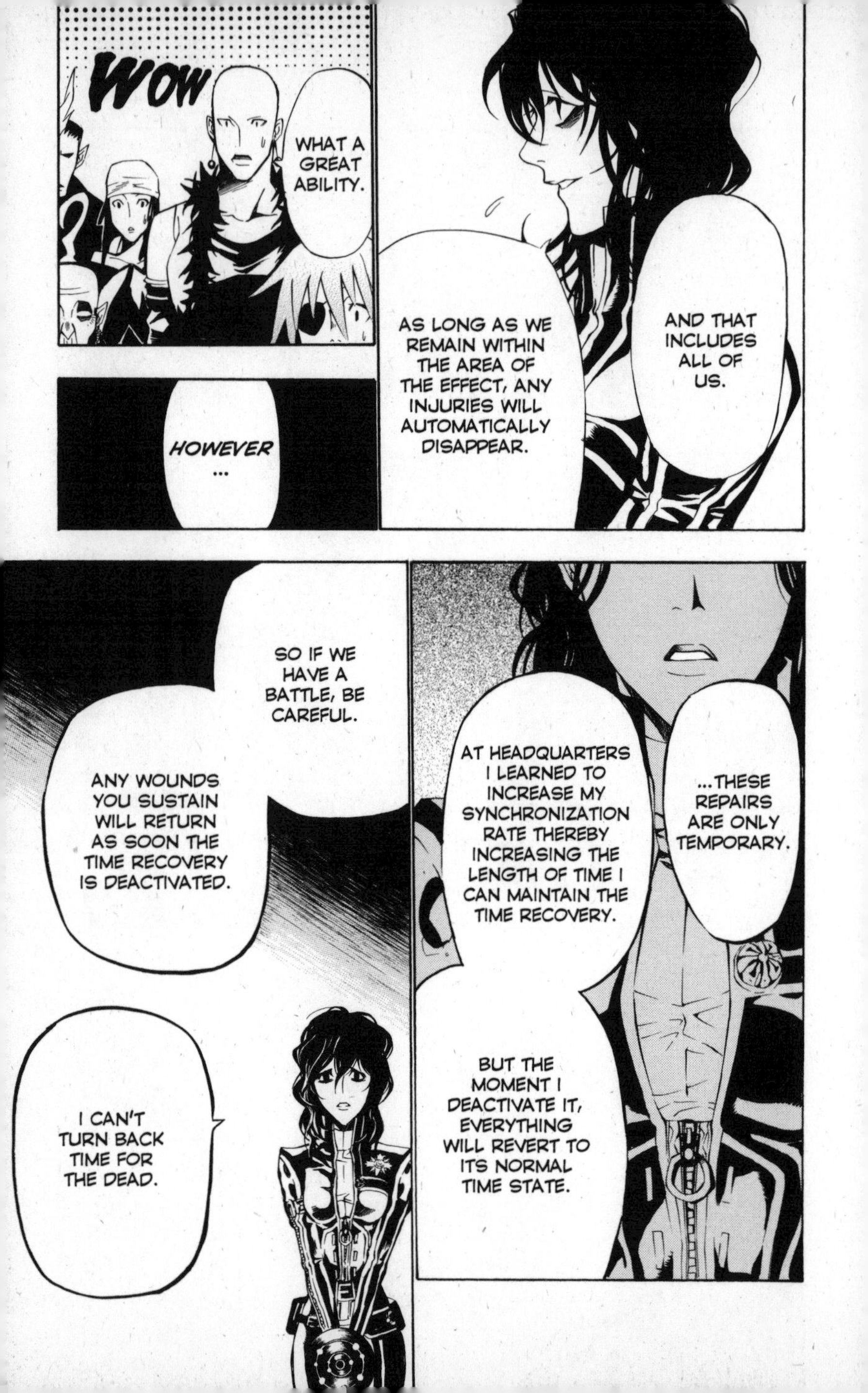
AND THAT INCLUDES ALL OF US.
AS LONG AS WE REMAIN WITHIN THE AREA OF THE EFFECT, ANY INJURIES WILL AUTOMATICALLY DISAPPEAR.
WOW
WHAT A GREAT ABILITY.
HOWEVER ...
...THESE REPAIRS ARE ONLY TEMPORARY.
AT HEADQUARTERS I LEARNED TO INCREASE MY SYNCHRONIZATION RATE THEREBY INCREASING THE LENGTH OF TIME I CAN MAINTAIN THE TIME RECOVERY.
BUT THE MOMENT I DEACTIVATE IT, EVERYTHING WILL REVERT TO ITS NORMAL TIME STATE.
SO IF WE HAVE A BATTLE, BE CAREFUL.
ANY WOUNDS YOU SUSTAIN WILL RETURN AS SOON THE TIME RECOVERY IS DEACTIVATED.
I CAN'T TURN BACK TIME FOR THE DEAD.

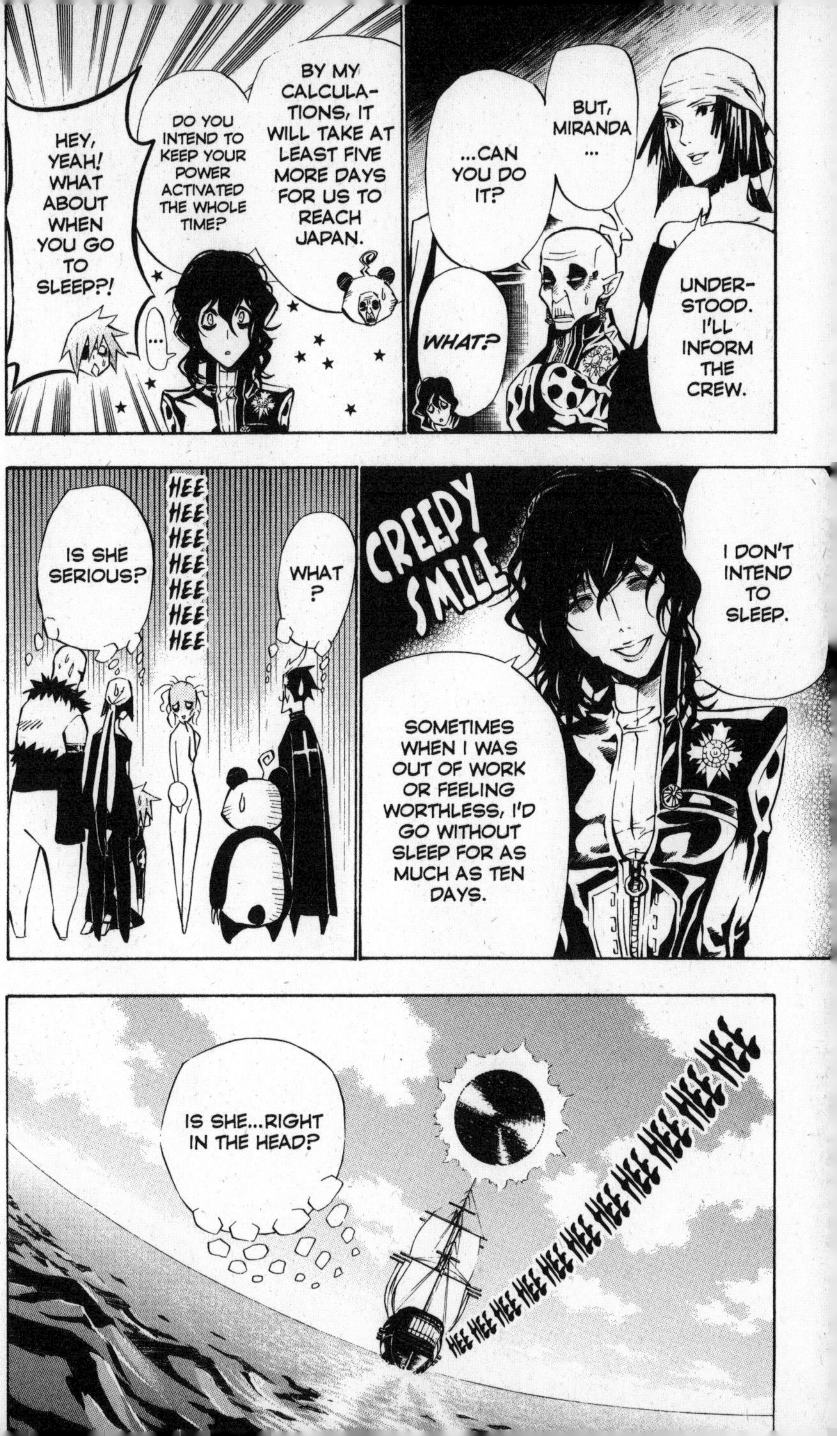
BUT, MIRANDA...
...CAN YOU DO IT?
UNDERSTOOD. I'LL INFORM THE CREW.
WHAT?
BY MY CALCULATIONS, IT WILL TAKE AT LEAST FIVE MORE DAYS FOR US TO REACH JAPAN.
DO YOU INTEND TO KEEP YOUR POWER ACTIVATED THE WHOLE TIME?
HEY, YEAH! WHAT ABOUT WHEN YOU GO TO SLEEP?!
...
I DON'T INTEND TO SLEEP.
CREEPY SMILE
SOMETIMES WHEN I WAS OUT OF WORK OR FEELING WORTHLESS, I'D GO WITHOUT SLEEP FOR AS MUCH AS TEN DAYS.
WHAT?
HEE HEE HEE HEE HEE HEE HEE
IS SHE SERIOUS?
IS SHE...RIGHT IN THE HEAD?
HEE HEE HEE HEE HEE HEE HEE HEE HEE HEE HEE HEE

READ THIS WAY

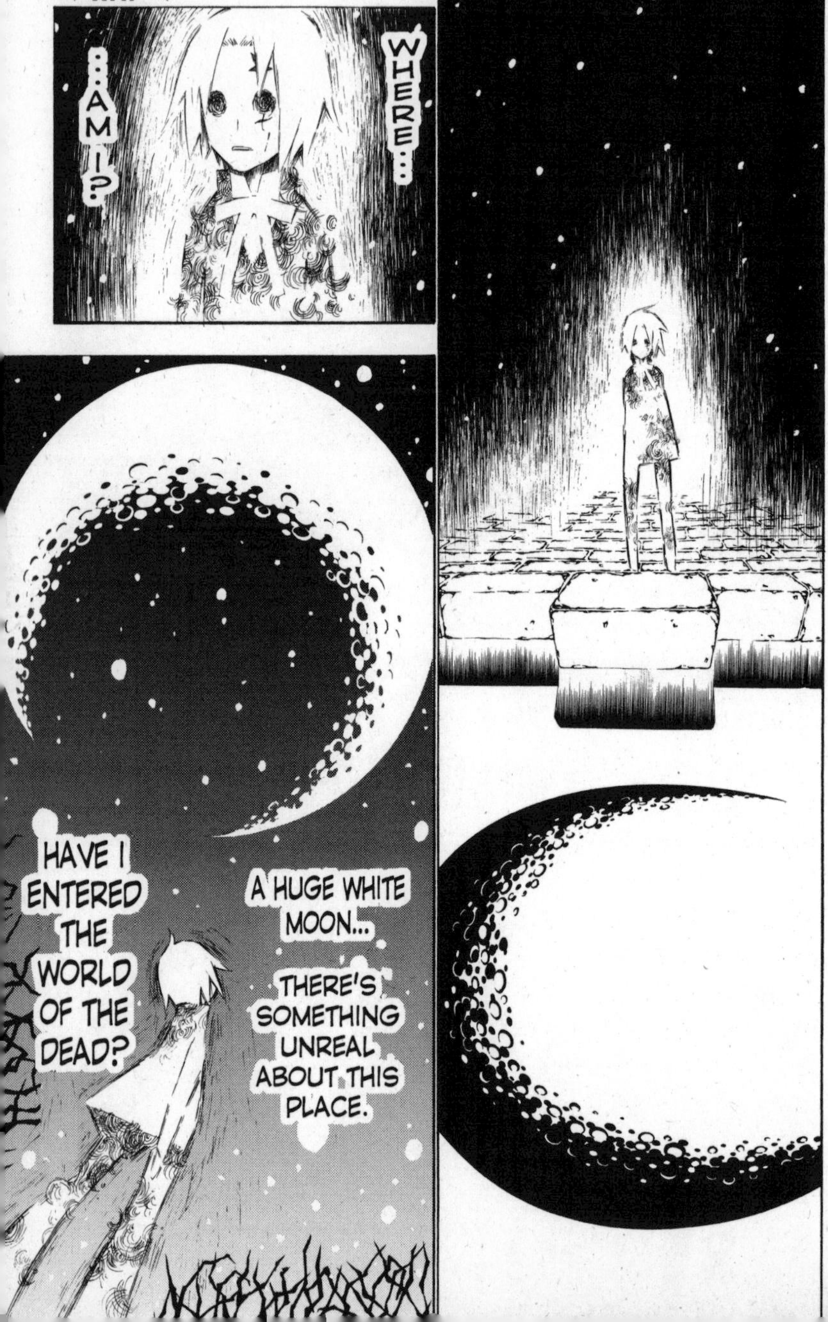
WHERE...
...AM I?
A HUGE WHITE MOON...
THERE'S SOMETHING UNREAL ABOUT THIS PLACE.
HAVE I ENTERED THE WORLD OF THE DEAD?

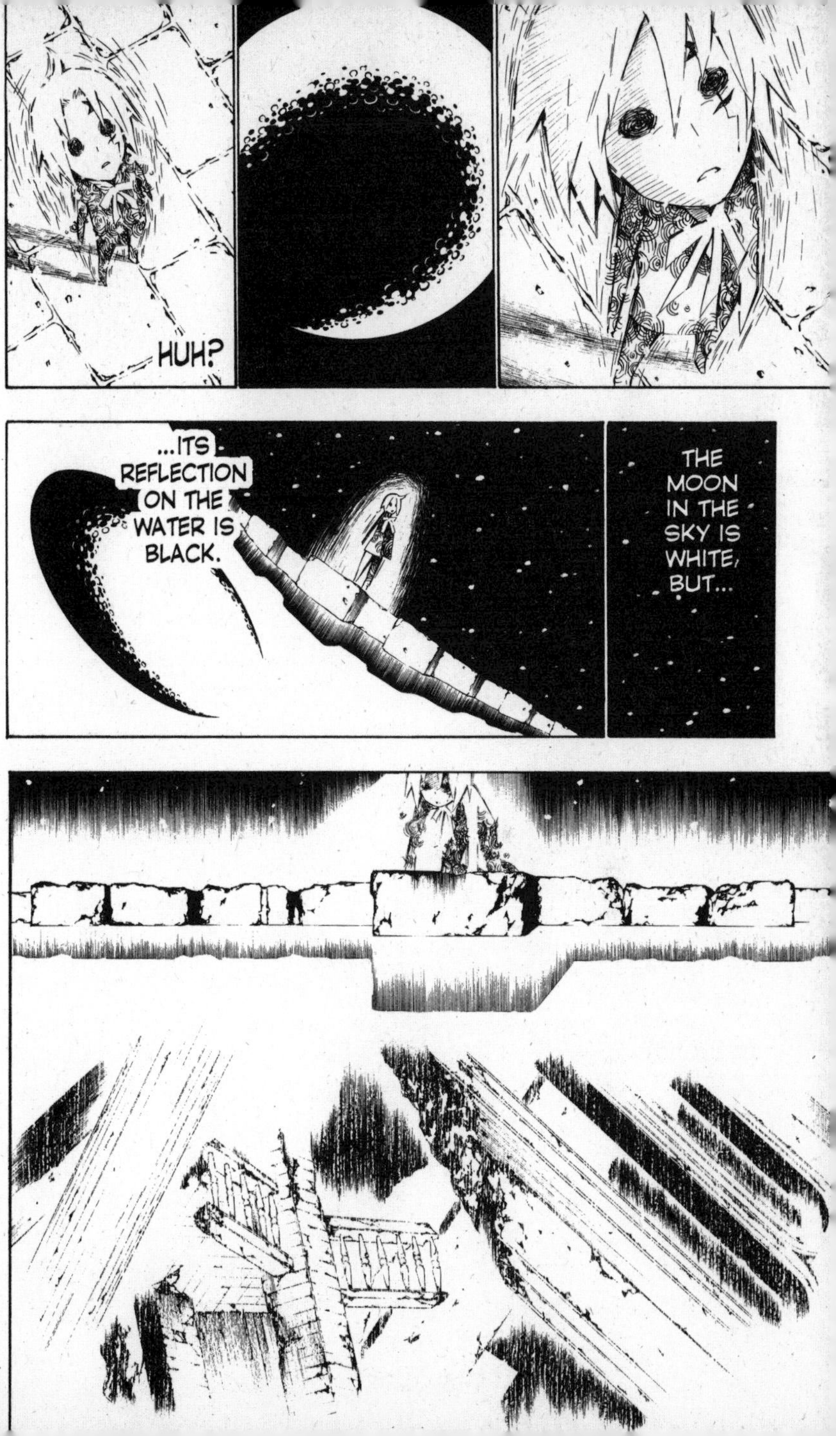
HUH?
THE MOON IN THE SKY IS WHITE, BUT...
...ITS REFLECTION ON THE WATER IS BLACK.

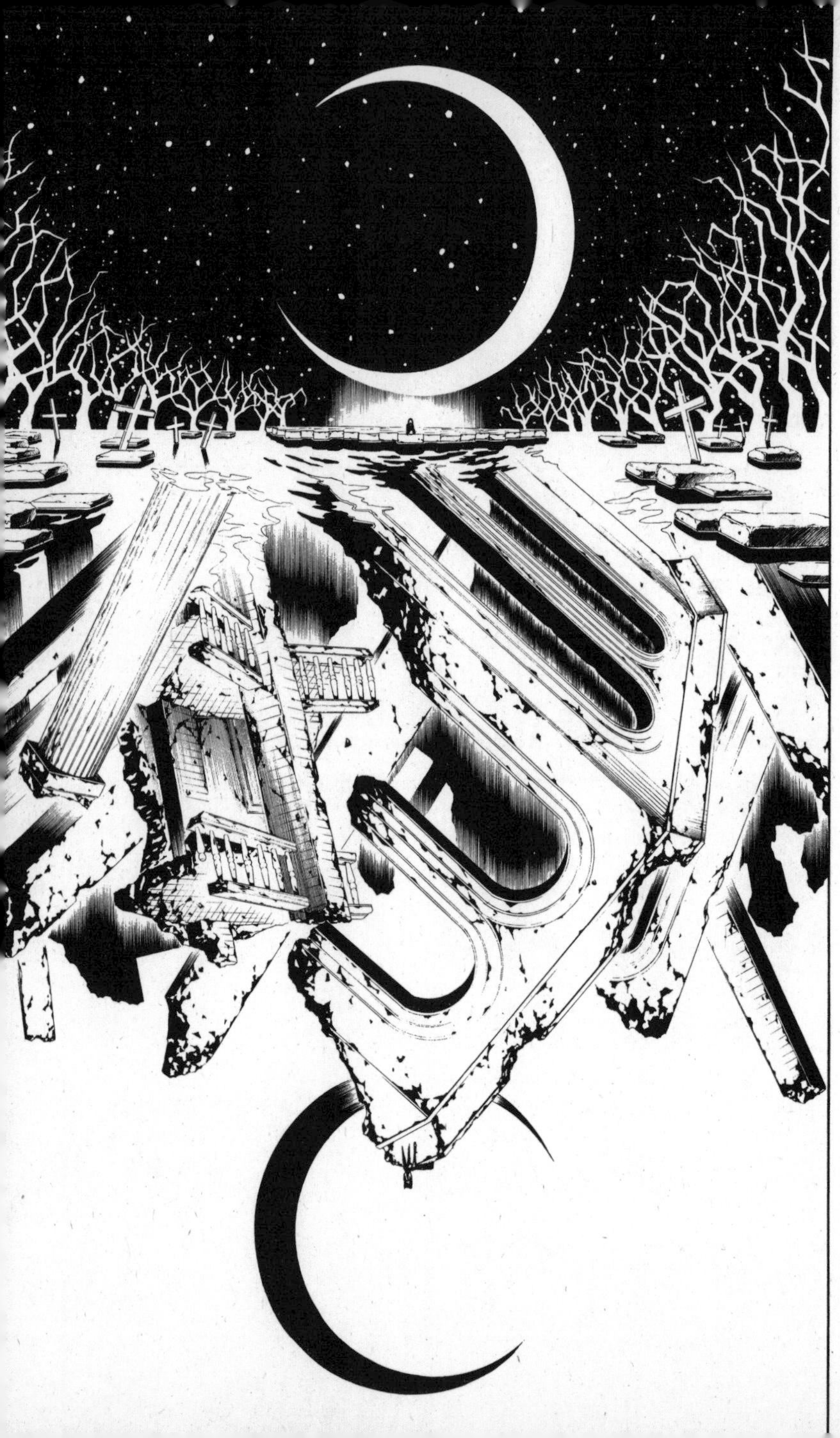

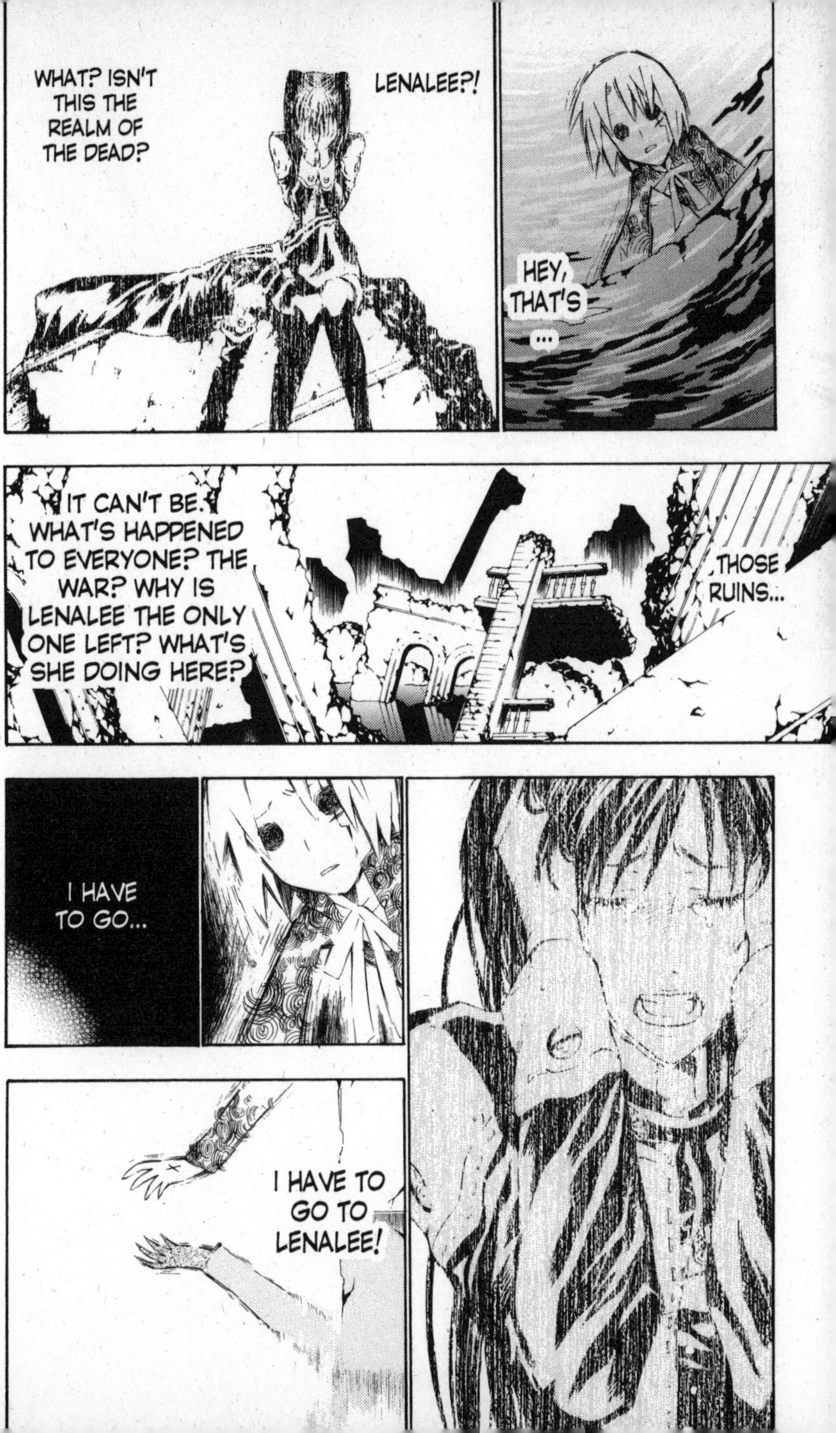
HEY, THAT'S ...
LENALEE?!
WHAT? ISN'T THIS THE REALM OF THE DEAD?
THOSE RUINS...
IT CAN'T BE. WHAT'S HAPPENED TO EVERYONE? THE WAR? WHY IS LENALEE THE ONLY ONE LEFT? WHAT'S SHE DOING HERE?
I HAVE TO GO...
I HAVE TO GO TO LENALEE!

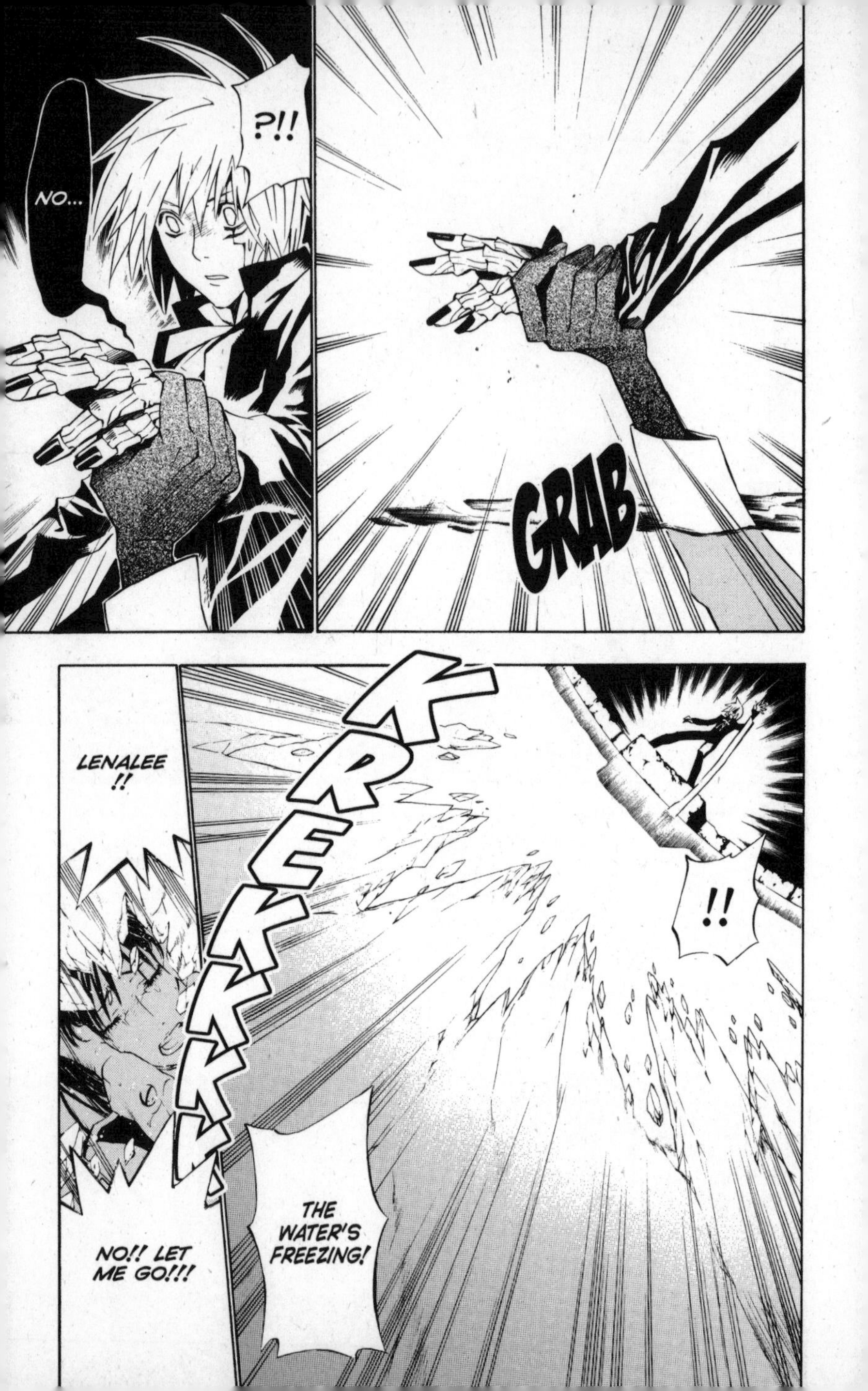
GRAB
?!!
NO...
!!
KREKKKKK
LENALEE !!
THE WATER'S FREEZING!
NO!! LET ME GO!!!

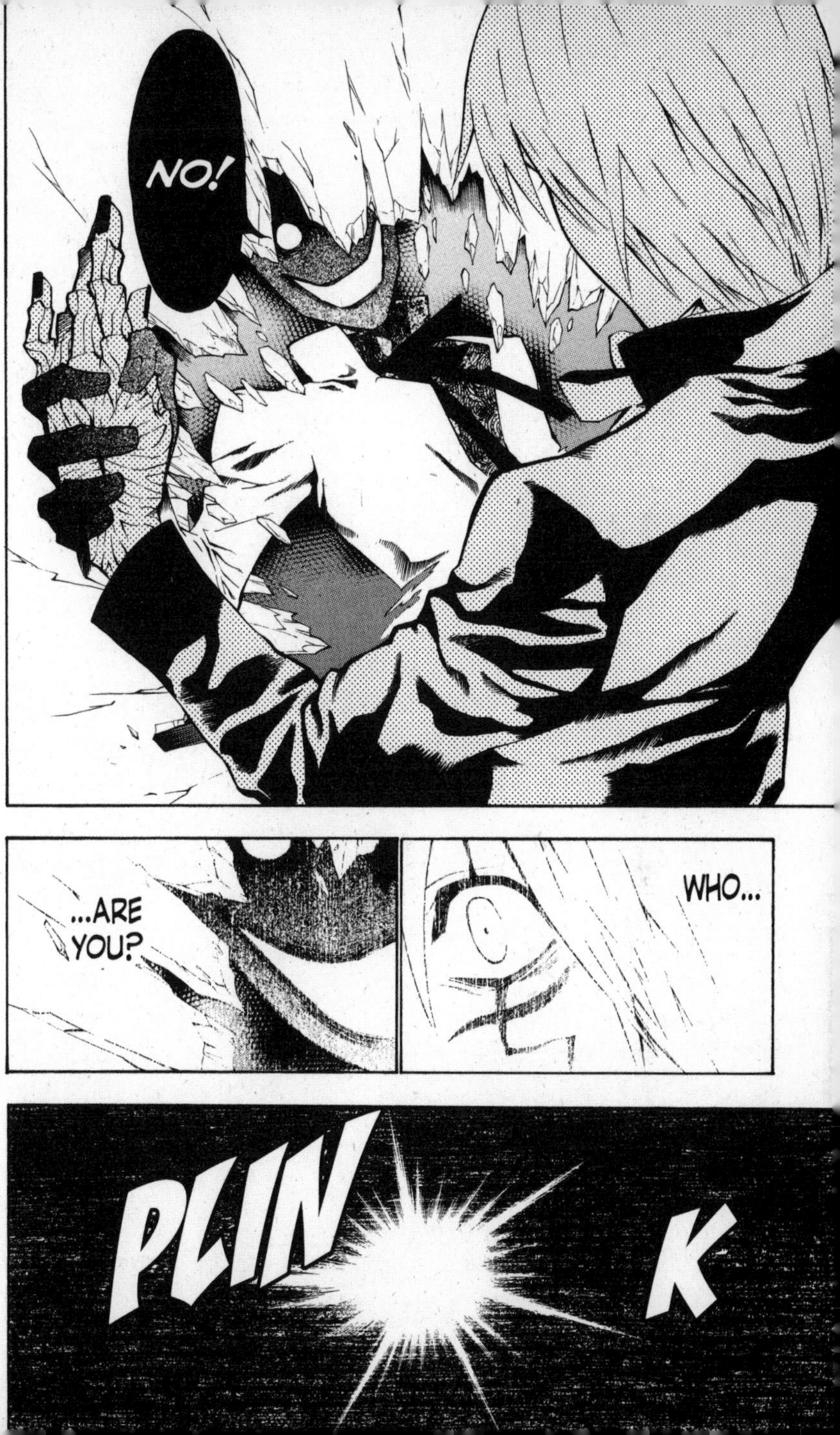
NO!
WHO...
...ARE YOU?
PLIN K

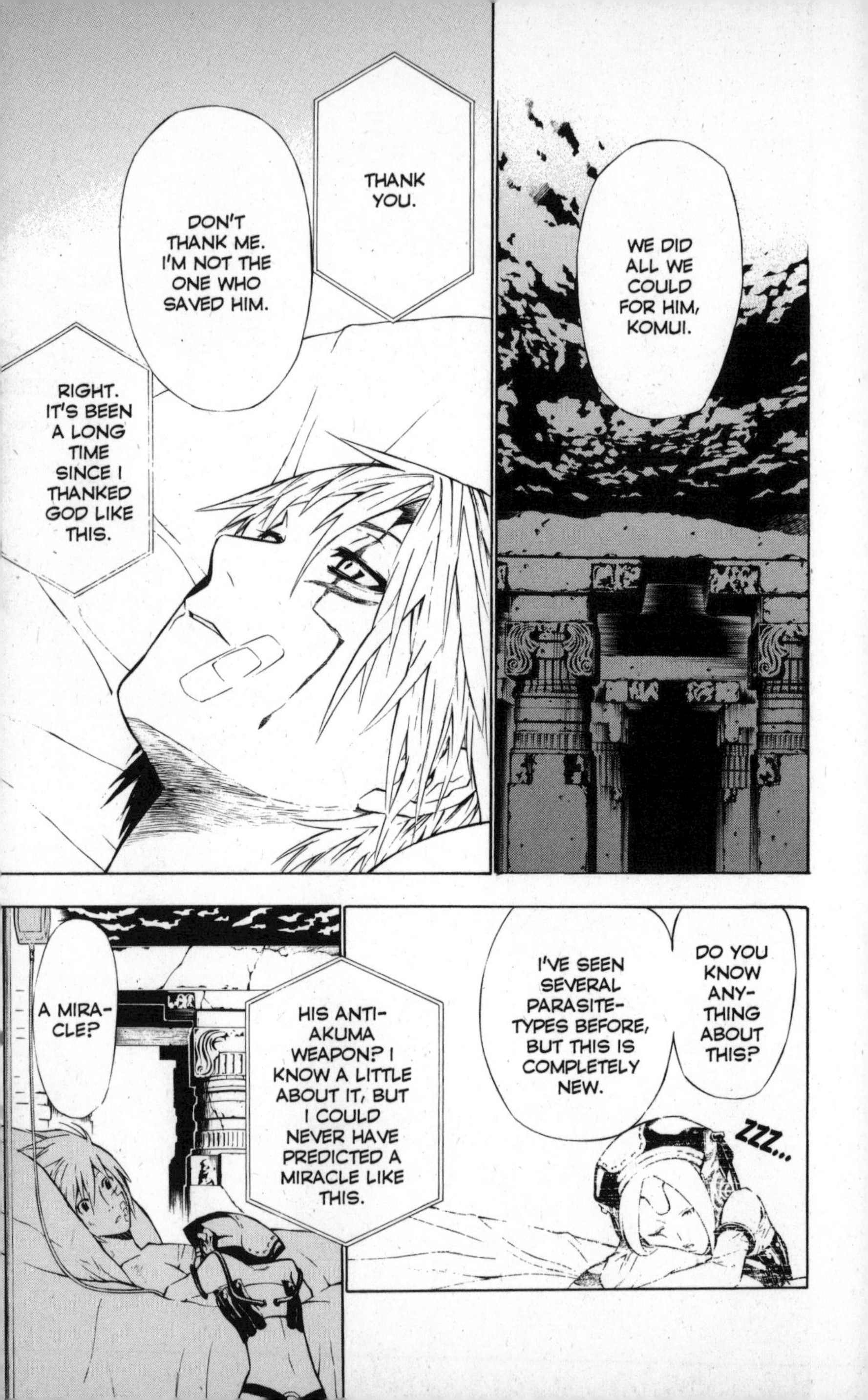
WE DID ALL WE COULD FOR HIM, KOMUI.
THANK YOU.
DON'T THANK ME. I'M NOT THE ONE WHO SAVED HIM.
RIGHT. IT'S BEEN A LONG TIME SINCE I THANKED GOD LIKE THIS.
DO YOU KNOW ANY-THING ABOUT THIS?
I'VE SEEN SEVERAL PARASITE-TYPES BEFORE, BUT THIS IS COMPLETELY NEW.
ZZZ...
HIS ANTI-AKUMA WEAPON? I KNOW A LITTLE ABOUT IT, BUT I COULD NEVER HAVE PREDICTED A MIRACLE LIKE THIS.
A MIRA-CLE?

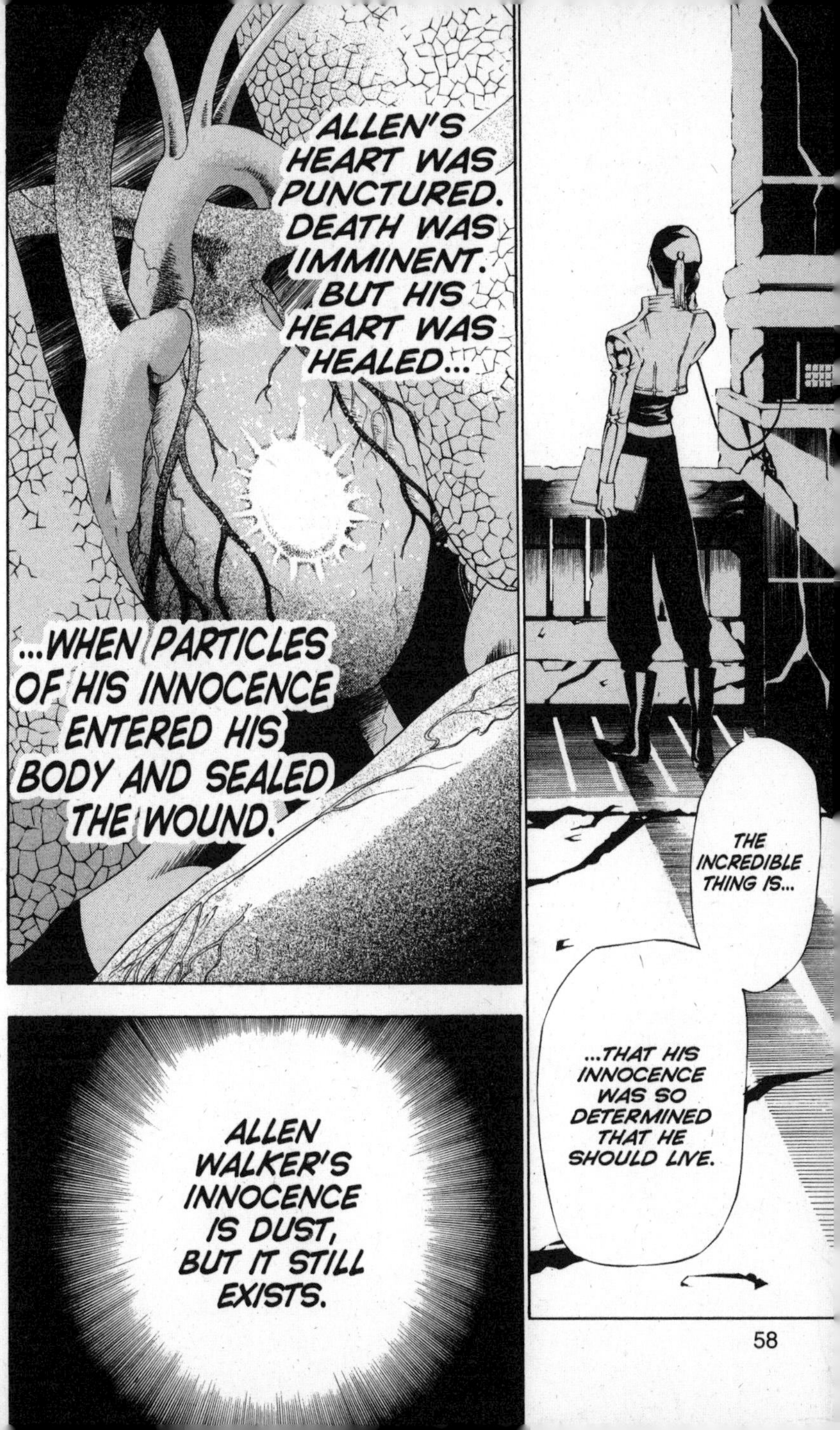

THE INCREDIBLE THING IS...
...THAT HIS INNOCENCE WAS SO DETERMINED THAT HE SHOULD LIVE.
ALLEN'S HEART WAS PUNCTURED. DEATH WAS IMMINENT. BUT HIS HEART WAS HEALED...
...WHEN PARTICLES OF HIS INNOCENCE ENTERED HIS BODY AND SEALED THE WOUND.
ALLEN WALKER'S INNOCENCE IS DUST, BUT IT STILL EXISTS.

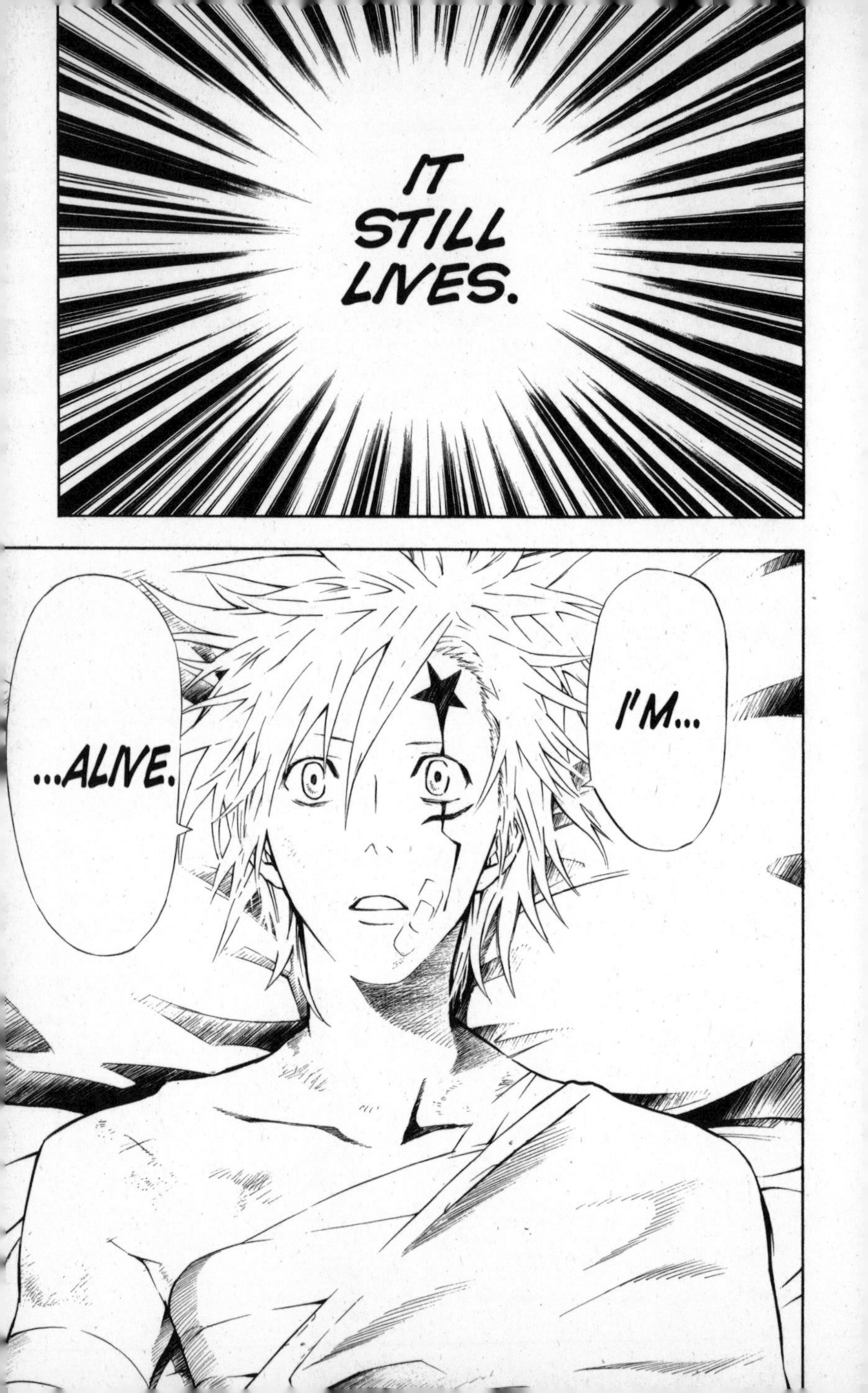
IT STILL LIVES.
I'M...
...ALIVE.

KOMUI'S DISCUSSION ROOM, VOL. 3

Q: IF ALLEN, KANDA, LAVI, AND LENALEE WEREN'T EXORCISTS, WHAT WOULD THEY BE?

A: (LAVI) I'D BE A BOOKMAN. I HAVE NO INTEREST IN BEING ANYTHING ELSE.

(ALLEN) I'D BE...A TRAVELING ENTERTAINER. I USED TO LIKE BEING A CLOWN AND MAKING PEOPLE LAUGH.

(LAVI) LENALEE WOULD BE A...HOUSEWIFE?

(ALLEN) AS LONG AS KOMUI'S AROUND, I DON'T SEE THAT HAPPENING.

(LAVI) AS FOR YU?

(ALLEN) ...

(LAVI & ALLEN) A NOODLE MAKER?

Q: DOES THE WEIGHT OF LAVI'S HAMMER CHANGE WHEN IT CHANGES SIZE?

A: (ALLEN) I WAS WONDERING ABOUT THAT MYSELF. I'M SURPRISED HE CAN SWING IT AROUND WHEN IT'S SO BIG.

(LAVI) OF COURSE ITS WEIGHT CHANGES WITH ITS SIZE. THE BIGGER IT IS, THE MORE DAMAGE IT CAUSES. BUT I DON'T FEEL THE WEIGHT BECAUSE I'M ITS ACCOMMODATOR. IT WOULD BE TOO HEAVY FOR ANYONE ELSE, THOUGH.

(ALLEN) WOW...

Q: TIMCANPY IS OFTEN SEEN CHEWING ON SOMETHING, BUT WHAT IS ITS NORMAL FOOD?

A: (ALLEN) TIM DOESN'T EAT. GOLEMS AREN'T REALLY ALIVE.

(LAVI) THEN WHY IS IT ALWAYS BITING THINGS?

(ALLEN) ITCHY TEETH?

Q: IS 65 HUMAN?

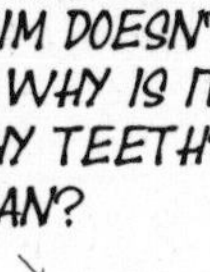

A: (LAVI & ALLEN) OF COURSE NOT!

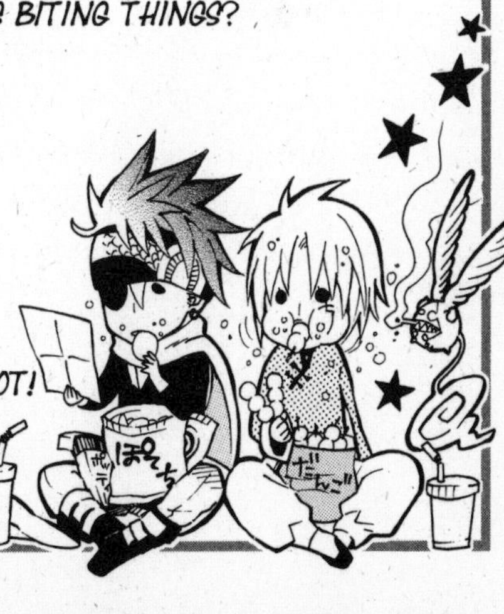

THE 60TH NIGHT: THE SWORN PATH

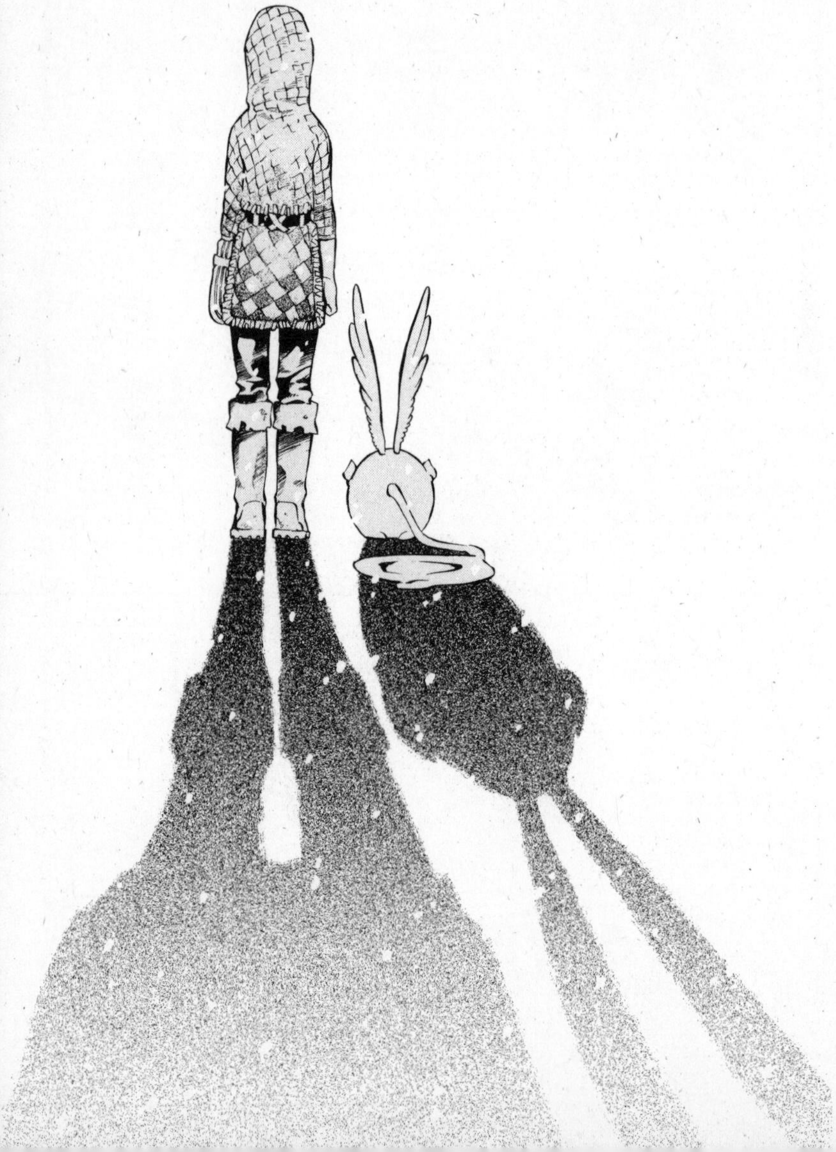

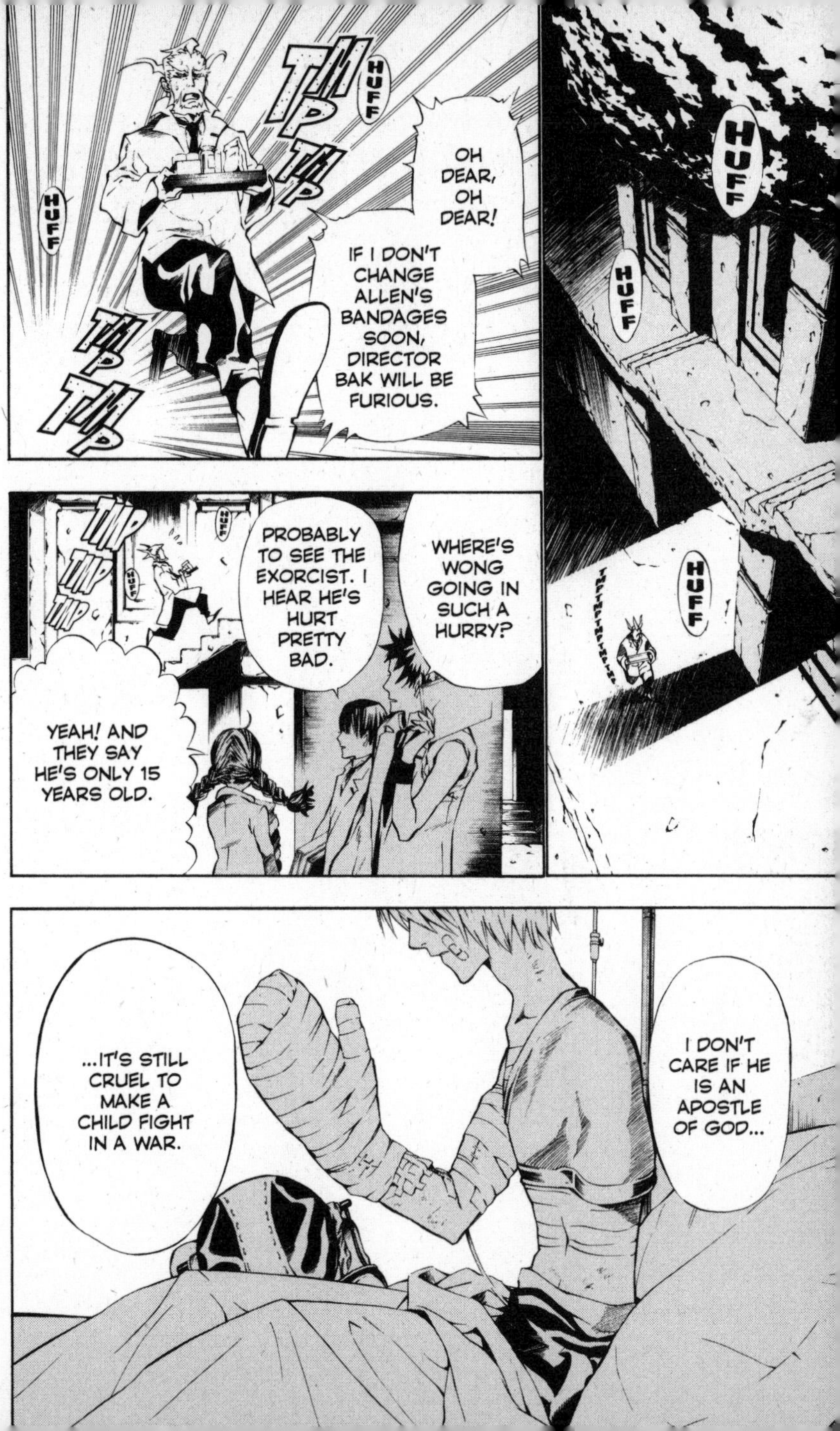
HUFF
HUFF
HUFF
HUFF
HUFF
OH DEAR, OH DEAR!
IF I DON'T CHANGE ALLEN'S BANDAGES SOON, DIRECTOR BAK WILL BE FURIOUS.
WHERE'S WONG GOING IN SUCH A HURRY?
PROBABLY TO SEE THE EXORCIST. I HEAR HE'S HURT PRETTY BAD.
YEAH! AND THEY SAY HE'S ONLY 15 YEARS OLD.
I DON'T CARE IF HE IS AN APOSTLE OF GOD...
...IT'S STILL CRUEL TO MAKE A CHILD FIGHT IN A WAR.

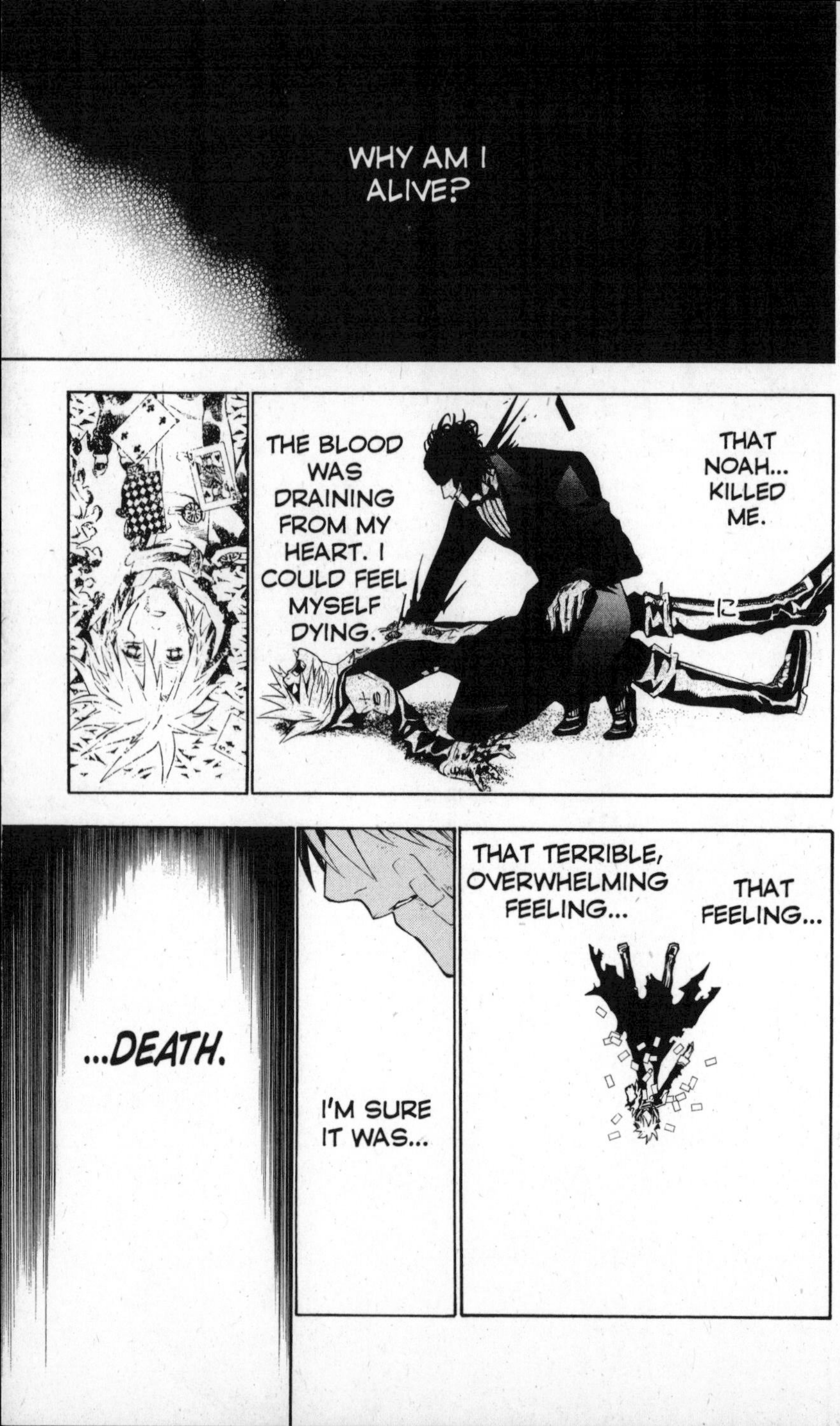
WHY AM I ALIVE?
THAT NOAH... KILLED ME.
THE BLOOD WAS DRAINING FROM MY HEART. I COULD FEEL MYSELF DYING.
THAT FEELING...
THAT TERRIBLE, OVERWHELMING FEELING...
I'M SURE IT WAS...
...DEATH.

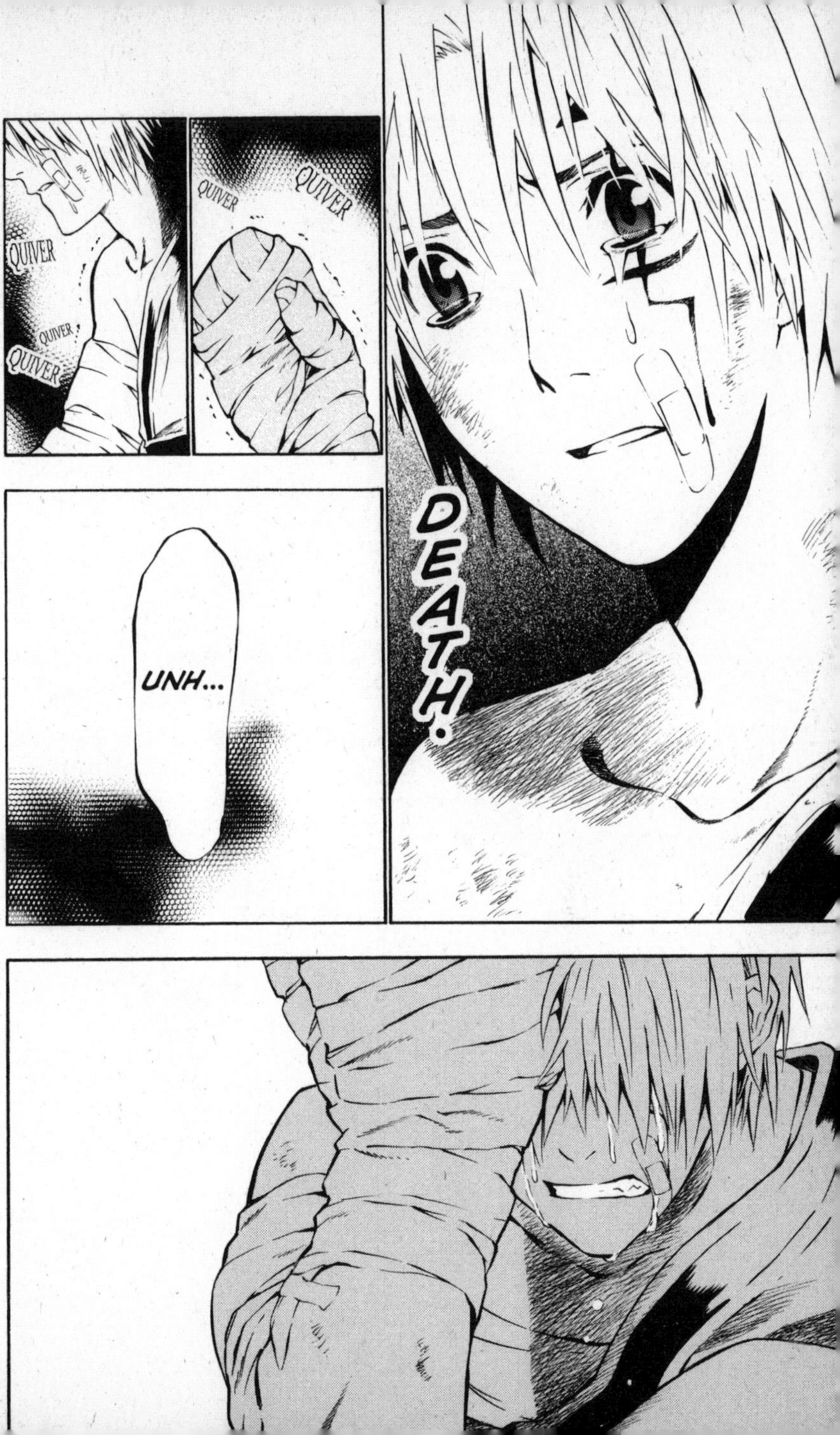
DEATH.
QUIVER
QUIVER
QUIVER
QUIVER
QUIVER
UNH...

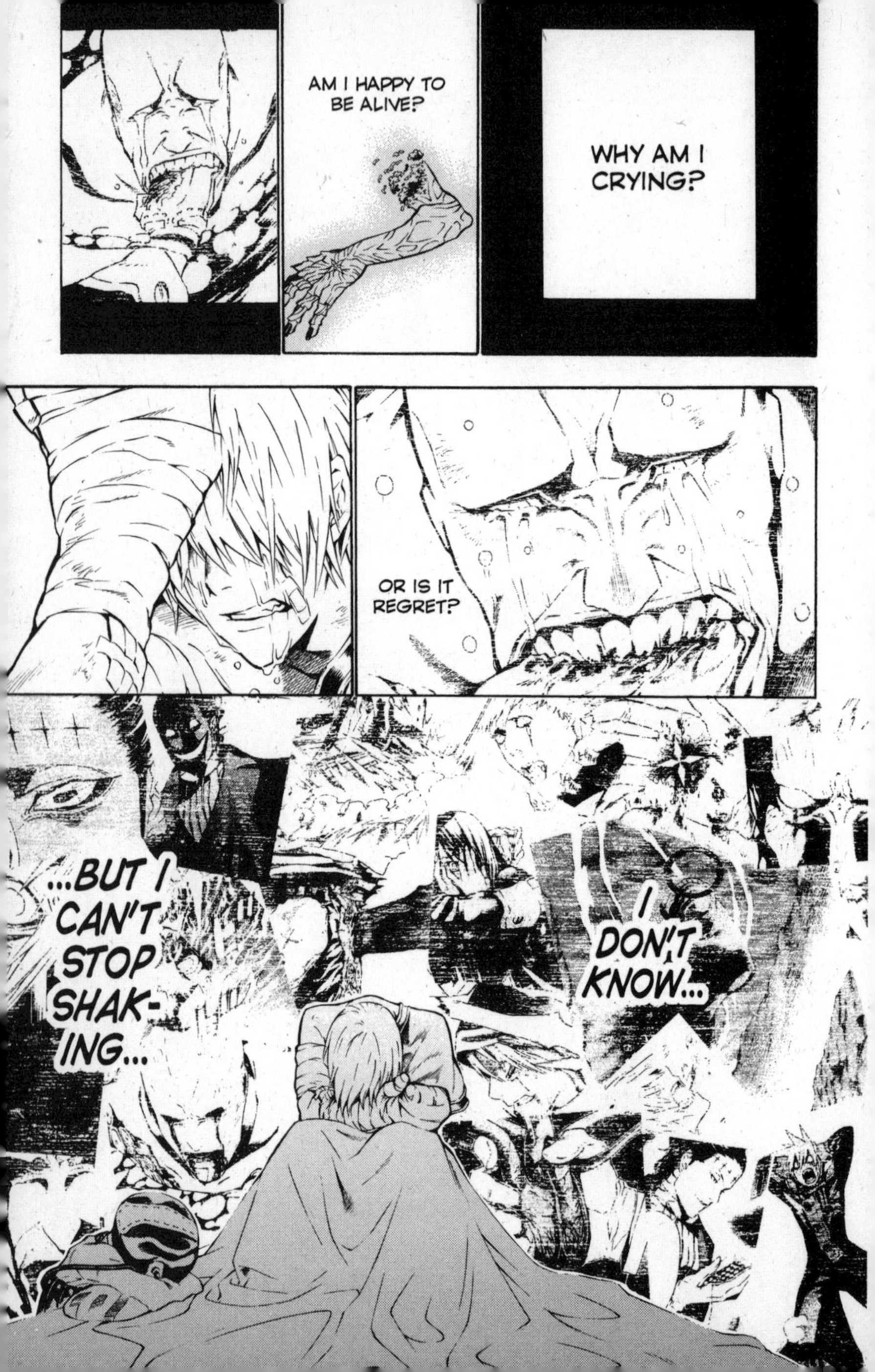
WHY AM I CRYING?
AM I HAPPY TO BE ALIVE?
OR IS IT REGRET?
I DON'T KNOW...
...BUT I CAN'T STOP SHAK-ING...

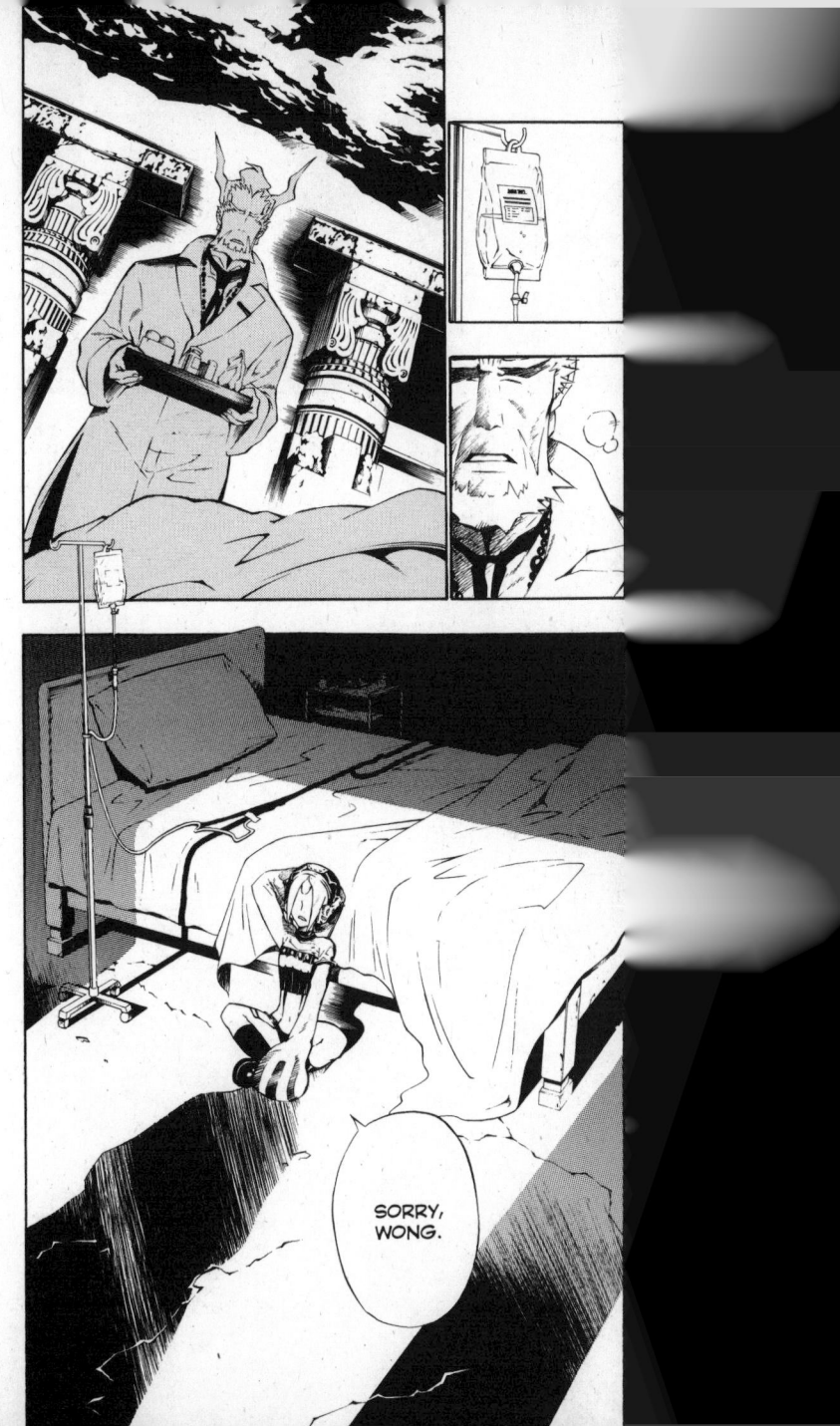

SORRY,
WONG.

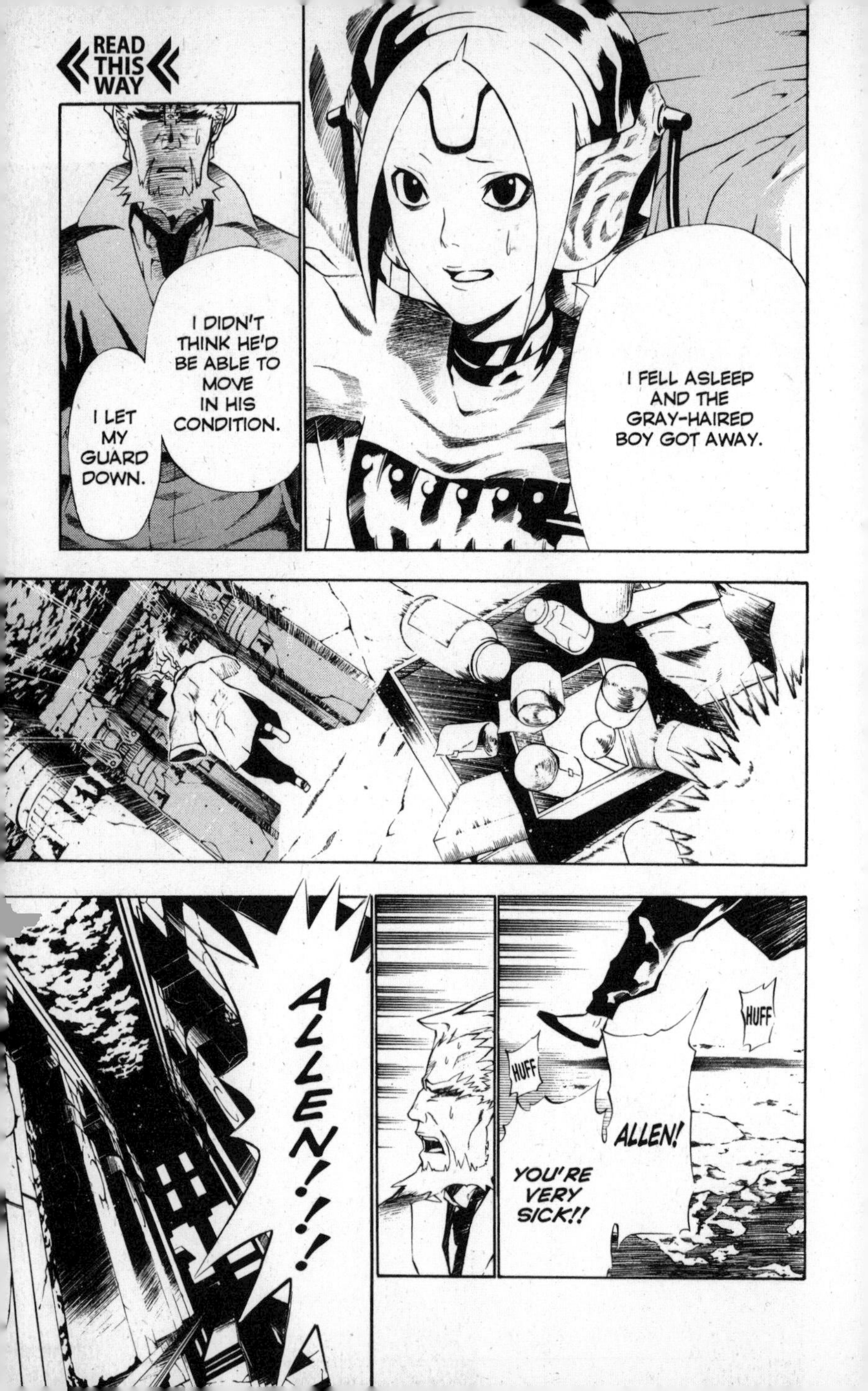
READ THIS WAY
I FELL ASLEEP AND THE GRAY-HAIRED BOY GOT AWAY.
I DIDN'T THINK HE'D BE ABLE TO MOVE IN HIS CONDITION.
I LET MY GUARD DOWN.
HUFF
HUFF
ALLEN!
YOU'RE VERY SICK!!
ALLEN!!!!

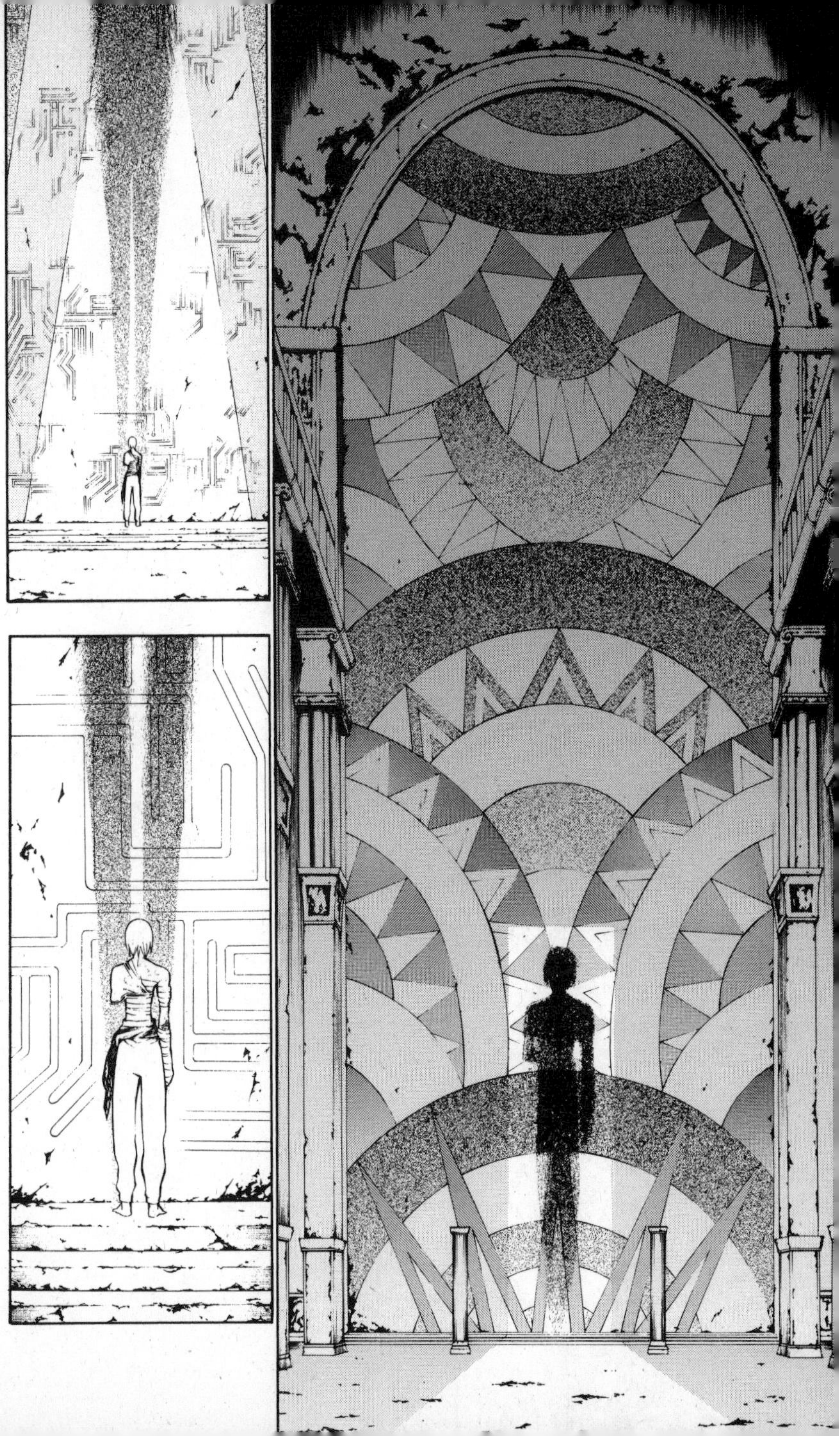

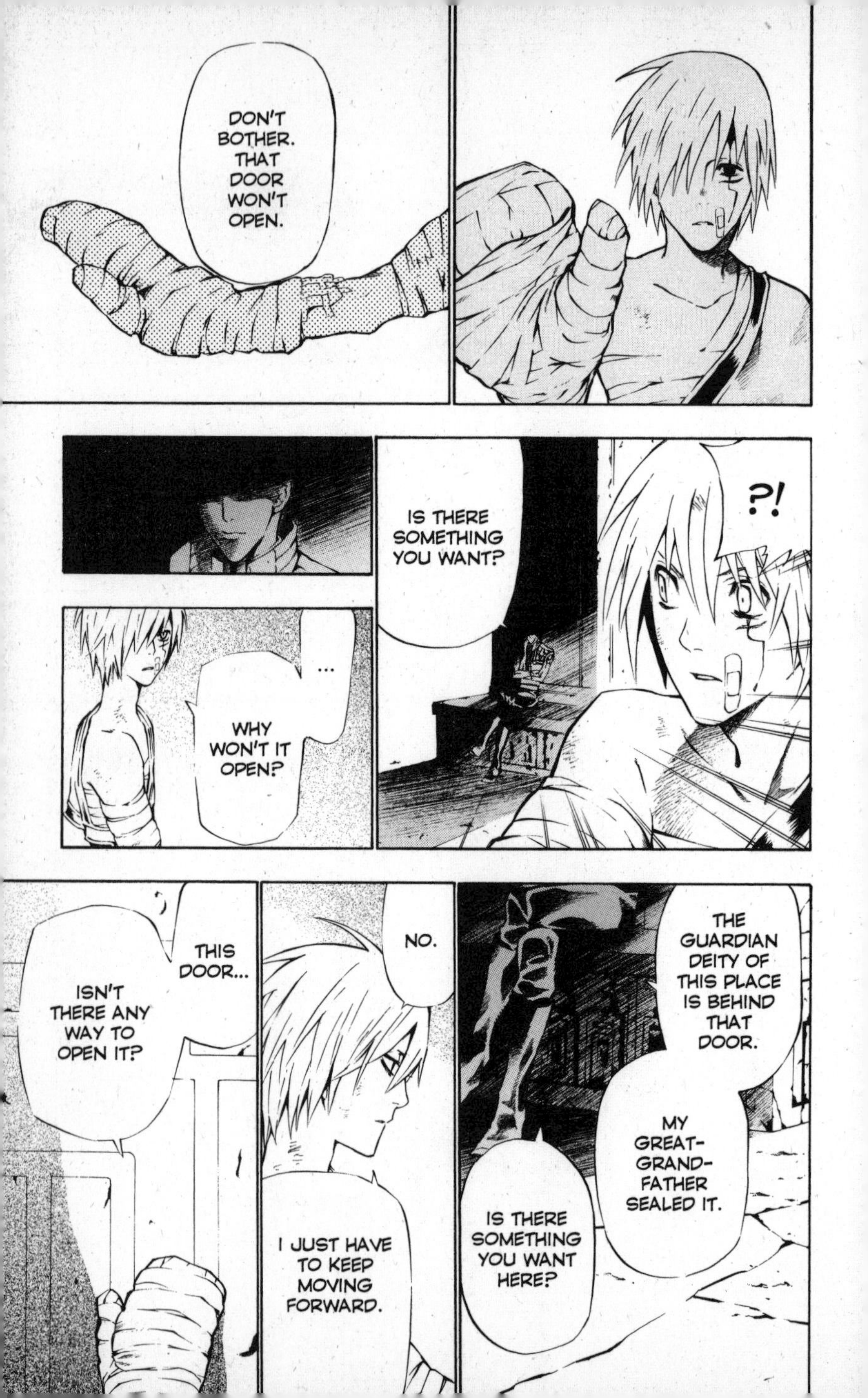
DON'T BOTHER. THAT DOOR WON'T OPEN.
IS THERE SOMETHING YOU WANT?
?!
...
WHY WON'T IT OPEN?
THE GUARDIAN DEITY OF THIS PLACE IS BEHIND THAT DOOR.
MY GREAT-GRAND-FATHER SEALED IT.
IS THERE SOMETHING YOU WANT HERE?
NO.
I JUST HAVE TO KEEP MOVING FORWARD.
THIS DOOR...
ISN'T THERE ANY WAY TO OPEN IT?

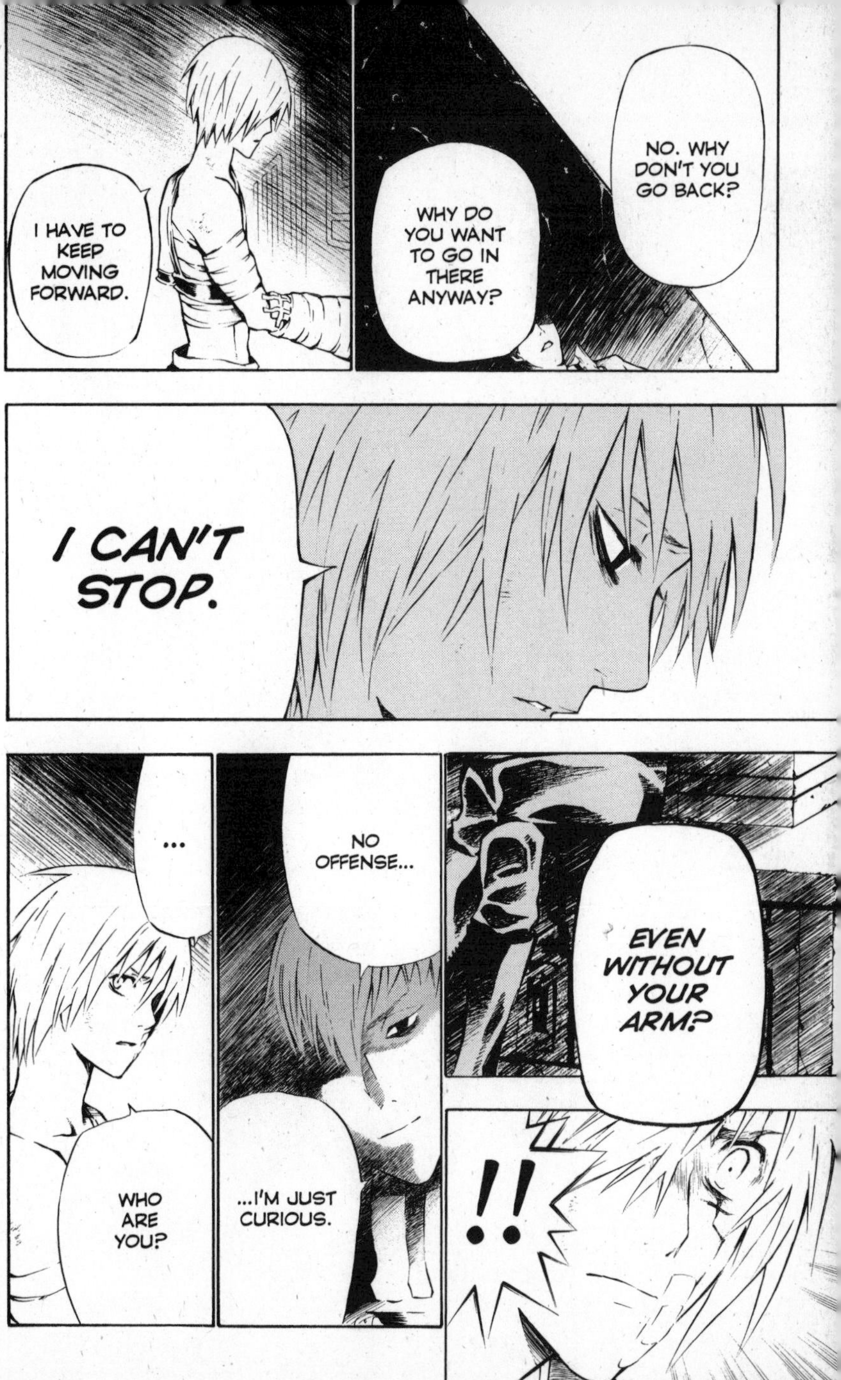
NO. WHY DON'T YOU GO BACK?
WHY DO YOU WANT TO GO IN THERE ANYWAY?
I HAVE TO KEEP MOVING FORWARD.
I CAN'T STOP.
EVEN WITHOUT YOUR ARM?
!!
NO OFFENSE...
...I'M JUST CURIOUS.
...
WHO ARE YOU?

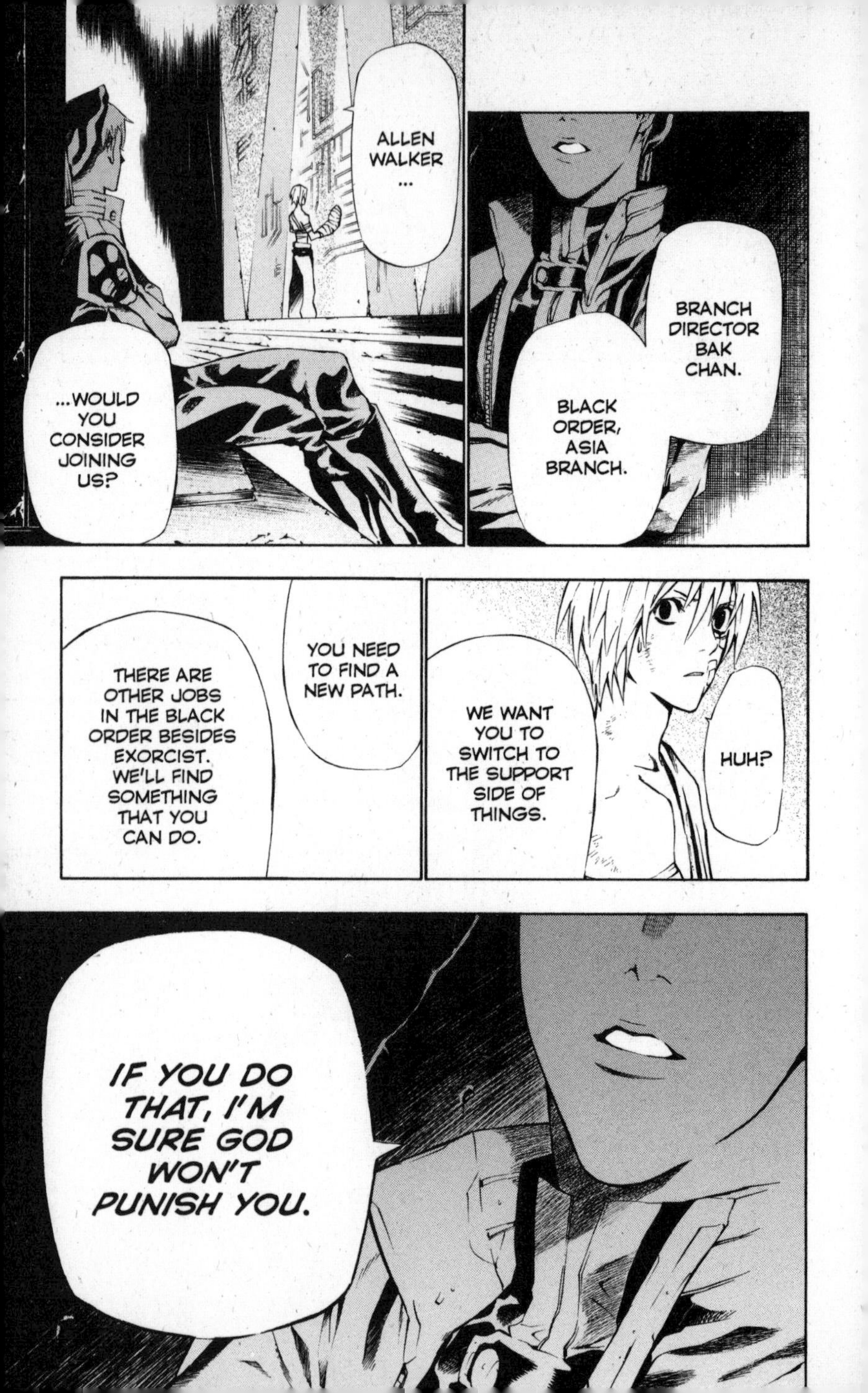
BRANCH DIRECTOR BAK CHAN.
BLACK ORDER, ASIA BRANCH.
ALLEN WALKER ...
...WOULD YOU CONSIDER JOINING US?
HUH?
WE WANT YOU TO SWITCH TO THE SUPPORT SIDE OF THINGS.
YOU NEED TO FIND A NEW PATH.
THERE ARE OTHER JOBS IN THE BLACK ORDER BESIDES EXORCIST. WE'LL FIND SOMETHING THAT YOU CAN DO.
IF YOU DO THAT, I'M SURE GOD WON'T PUNISH YOU.

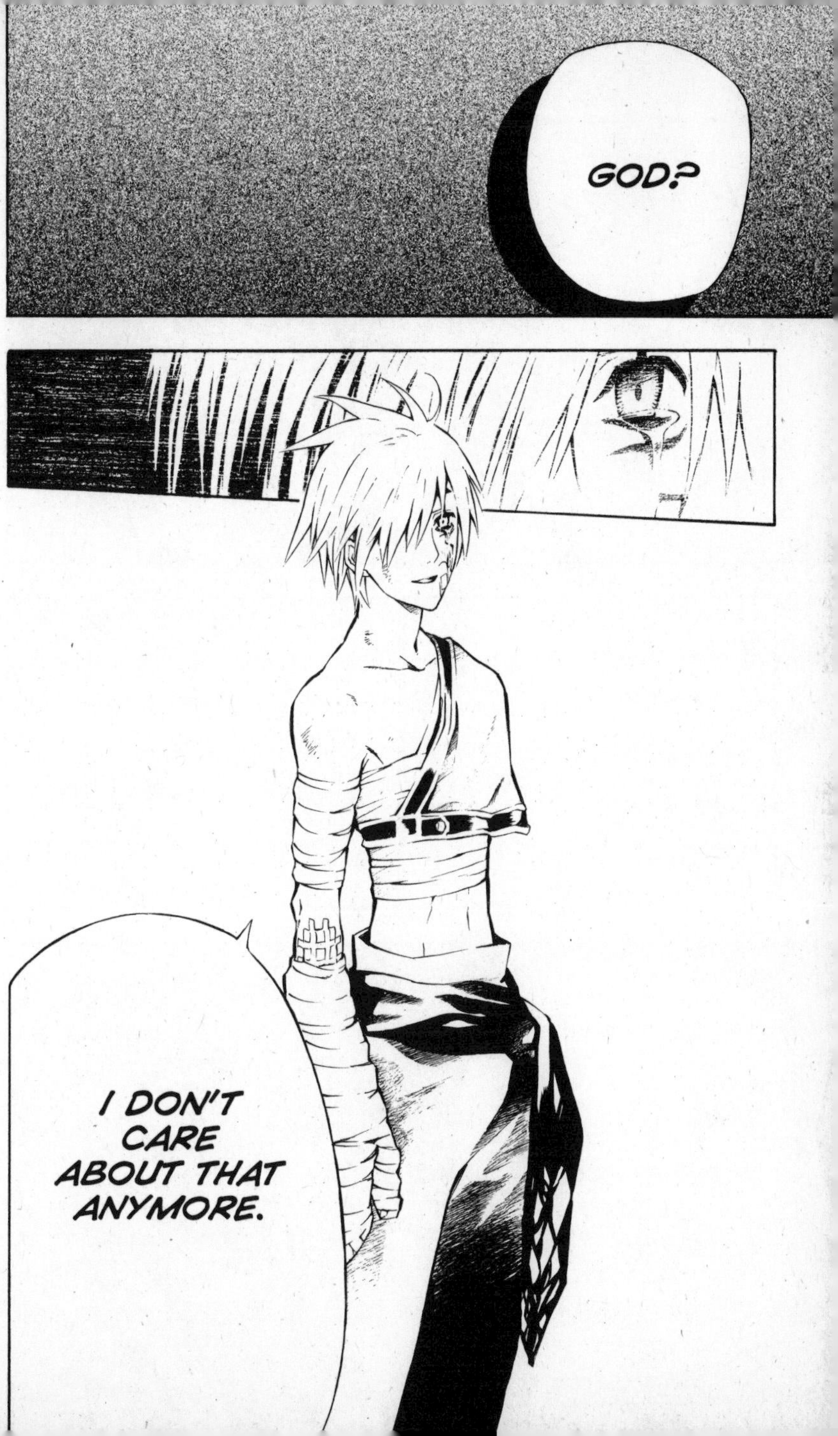
GOD?
I DON'T CARE ABOUT THAT ANYMORE.

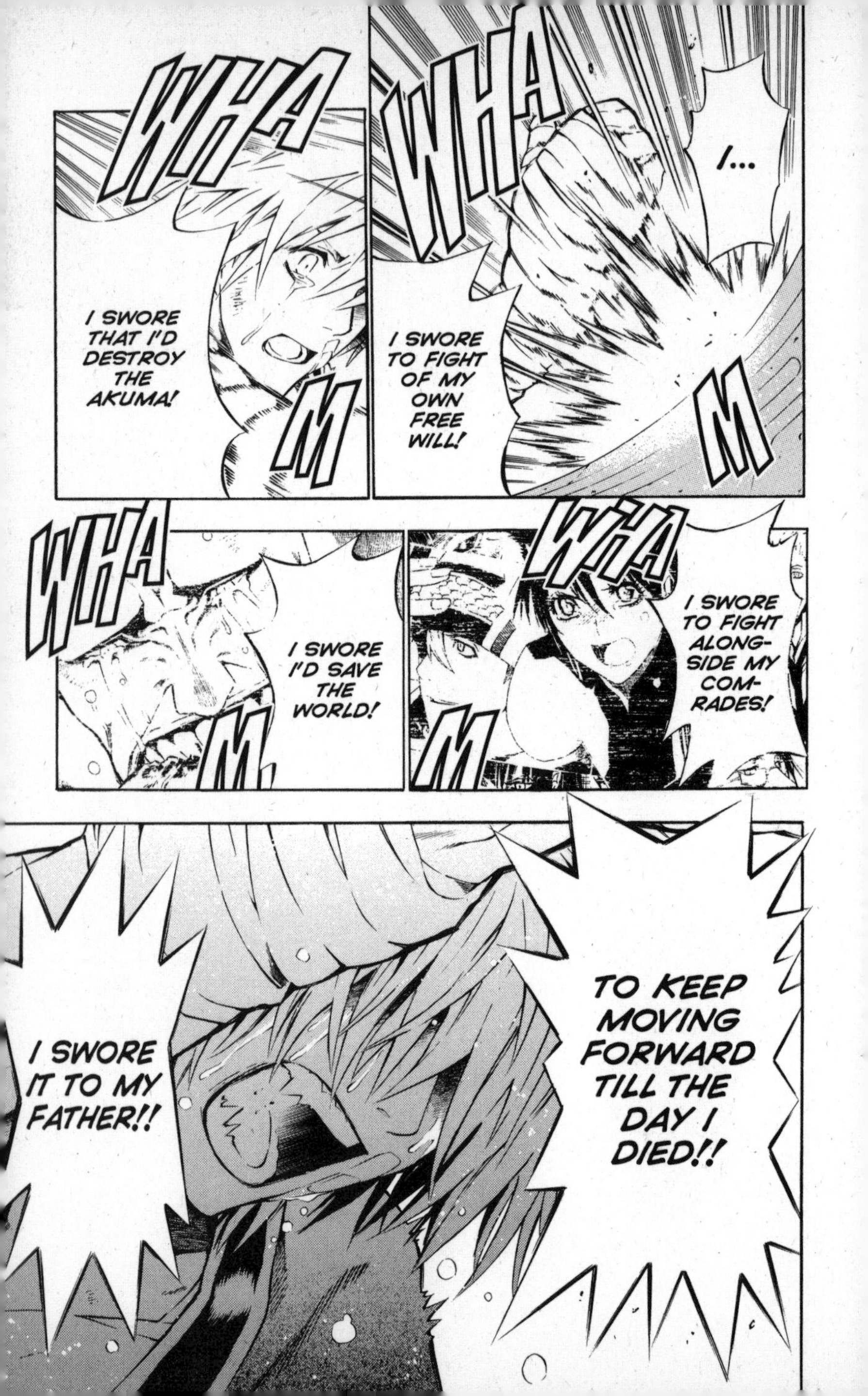
I...
WHAM
I SWORE TO FIGHT OF MY OWN FREE WILL!
WHAM
I SWORE THAT I'D DESTROY THE AKUMA!
WHAM
I SWORE TO FIGHT ALONG-SIDE MY COM-RADES!
WHAM
I SWORE I'D SAVE THE WORLD!
TO KEEP MOVING FORWARD TILL THE DAY I DIED!!
I SWORE IT TO MY FATHER!!

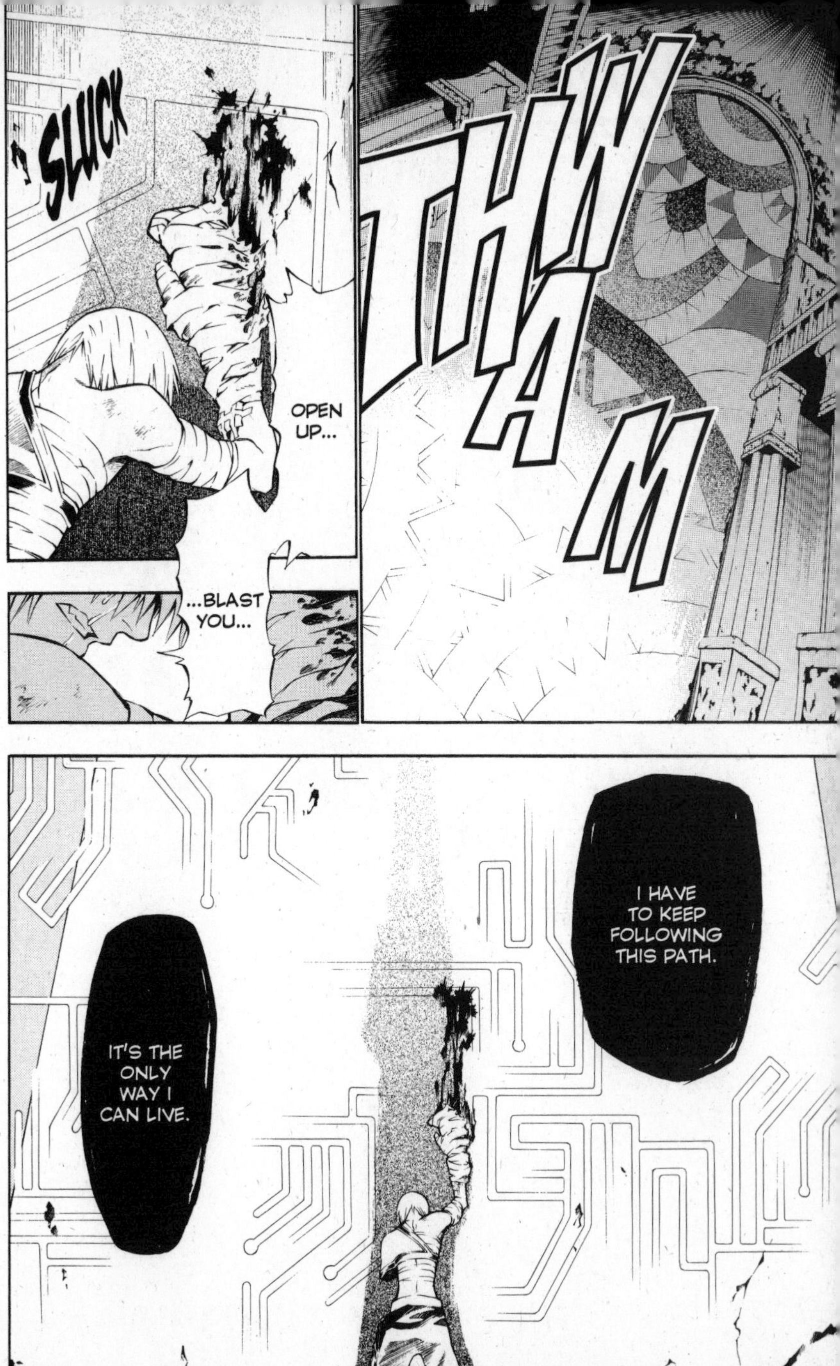
THWAM
SLUCK
OPEN UP...
...BLAST YOU...
I HAVE TO KEEP FOLLOWING THIS PATH.
IT'S THE ONLY WAY I CAN LIVE.

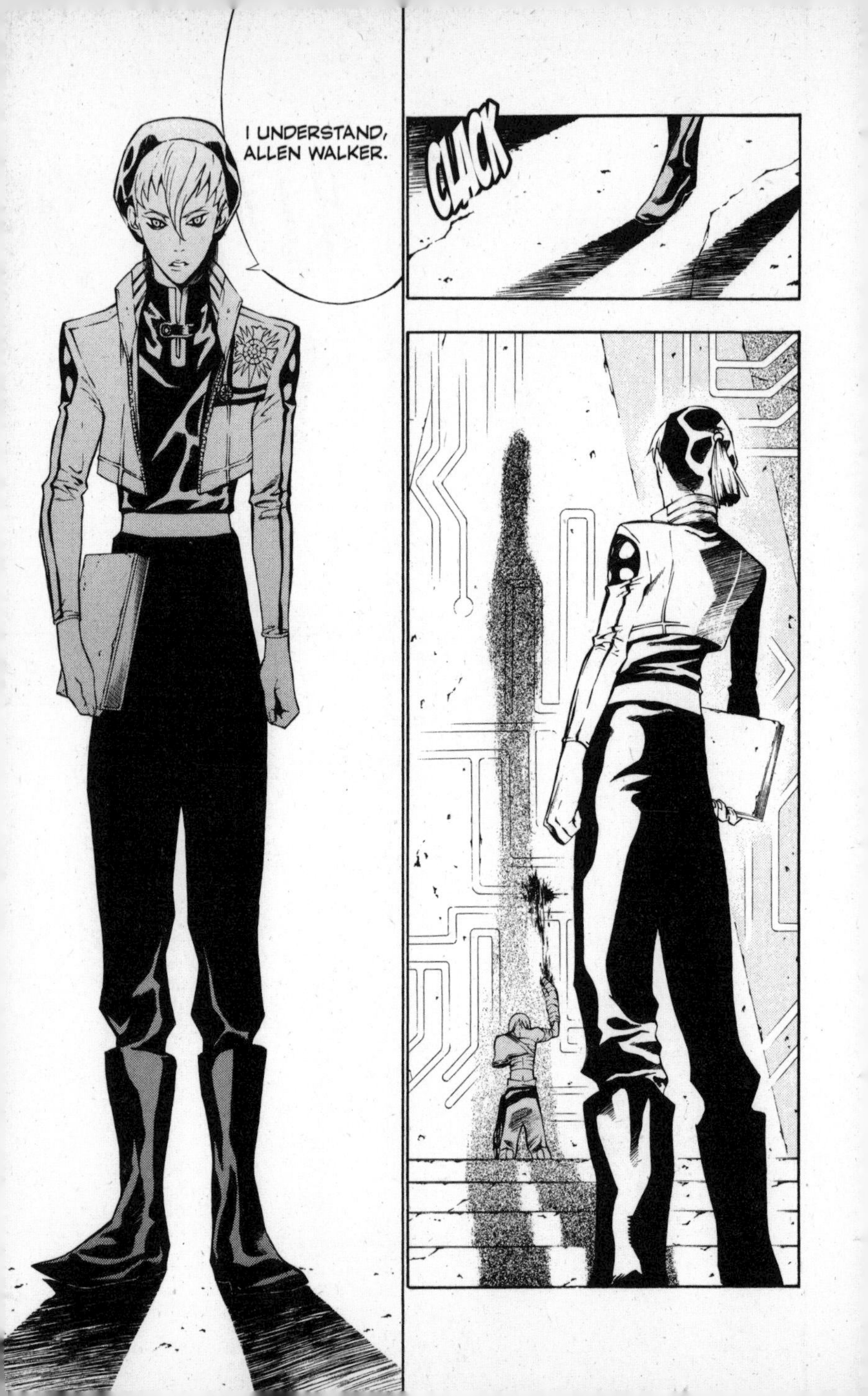
CLACK
I UNDERSTAND, ALLEN WALKER.

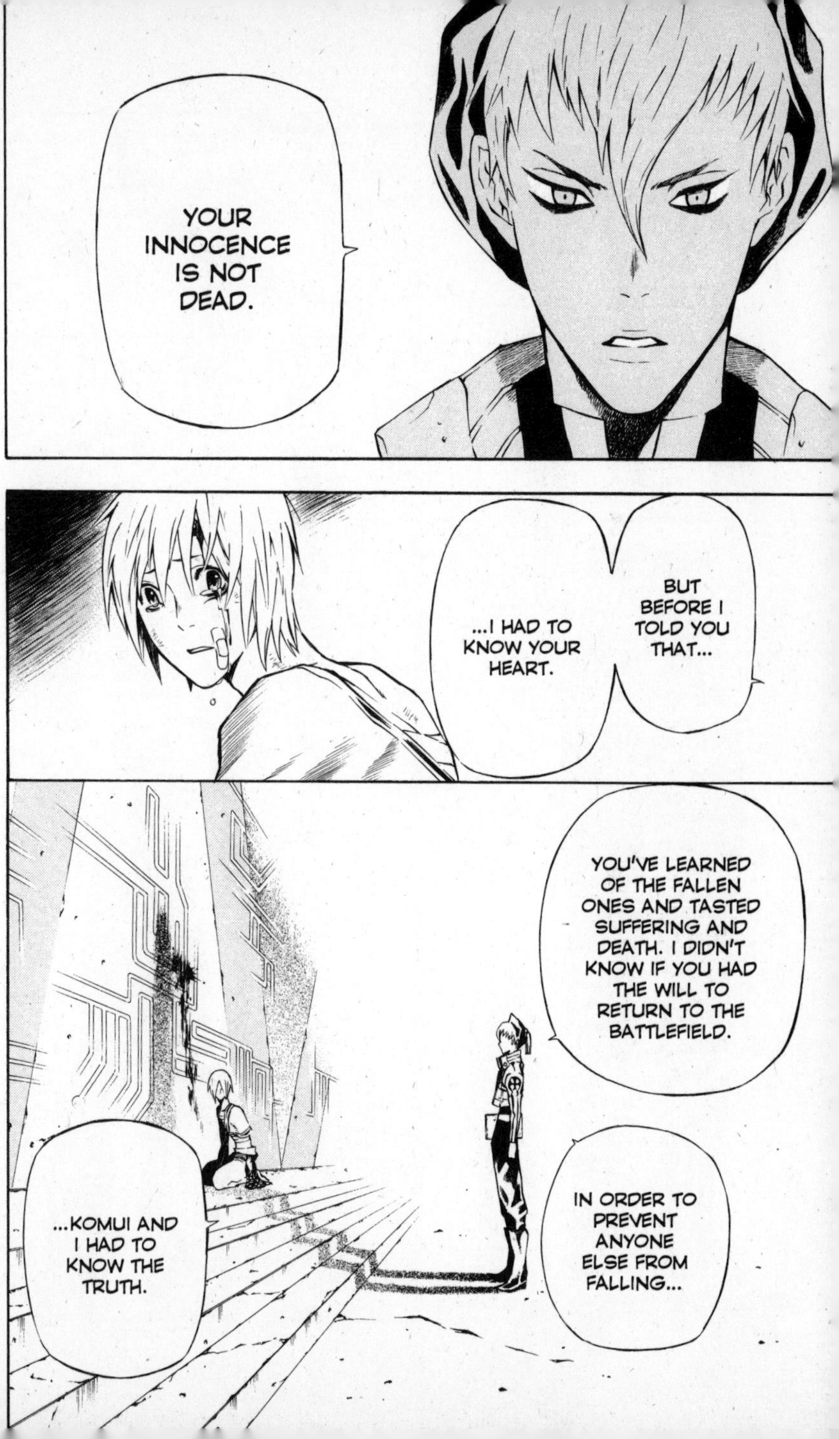
YOUR INNOCENCE IS NOT DEAD.
BUT BEFORE I TOLD YOU THAT...
...I HAD TO KNOW YOUR HEART.
YOU'VE LEARNED OF THE FALLEN ONES AND TASTED SUFFERING AND DEATH. I DIDN'T KNOW IF YOU HAD THE WILL TO RETURN TO THE BATTLEFIELD.
IN ORDER TO PREVENT ANYONE ELSE FROM FALLING...
...KOMUI AND I HAD TO KNOW THE TRUTH.

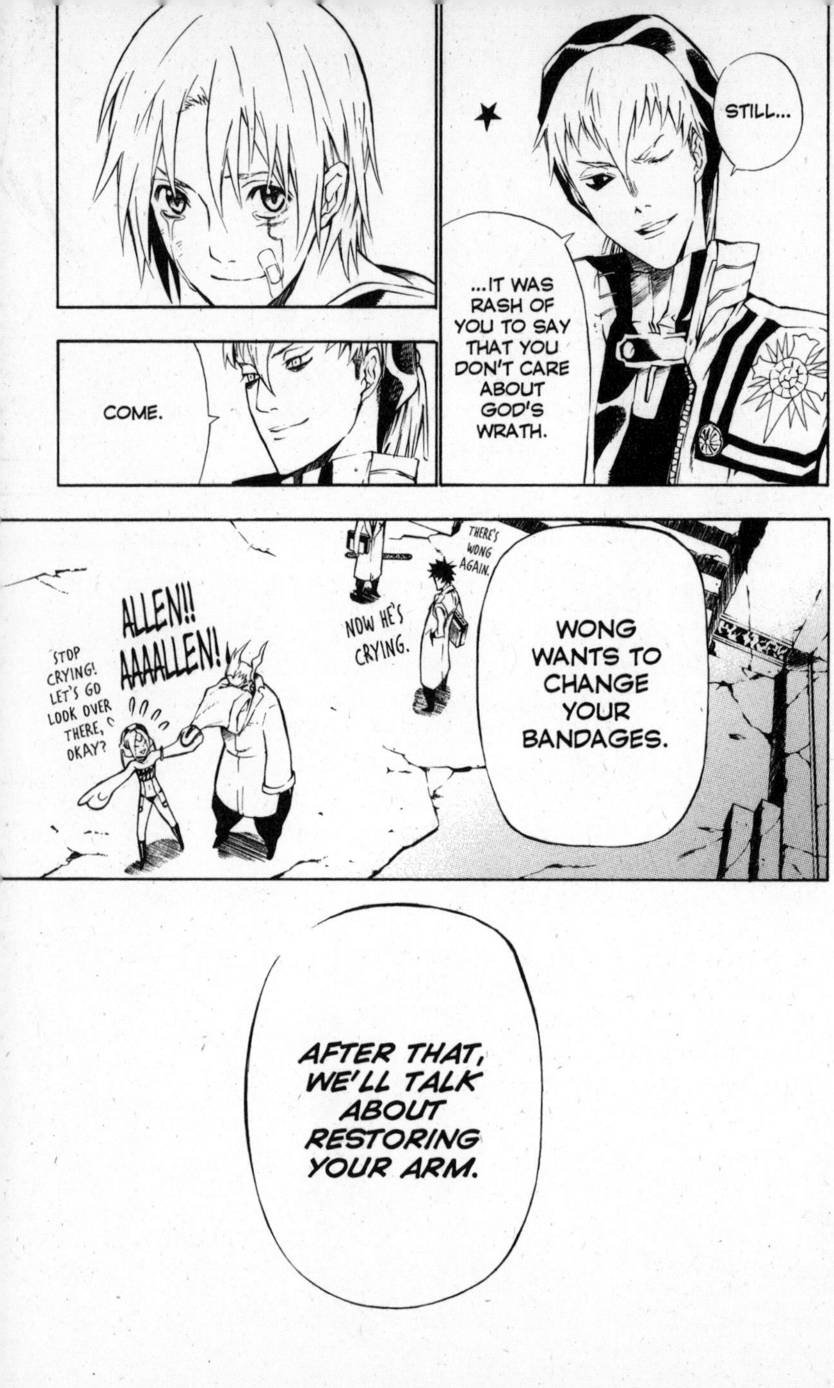
STILL...
...IT WAS RASH OF YOU TO SAY THAT YOU DON'T CARE ABOUT GOD'S WRATH.
COME.
THERE'S WONG AGAIN.
WONG WANTS TO CHANGE YOUR BANDAGES.
NOW HE'S CRYING.
ALLEN!! AAAALLEN!
STOP CRYING! LET'S GO LOOK OVER THERE, OKAY?
AFTER THAT, WE'LL TALK ABOUT RESTORING YOUR ARM.

KOMUI'S DISCUSSION ROOM, VOL. 4

Q: ARE THE PEOPLE IN THE SCIENCE SECTION MARRIED, OR DO THEY HAVE GIRLFRIENDS?
A: (LAVI) I THINK MOST OF THEM ARE SINGLE.
(ALLEN) THE WORK BEING WHAT IT IS, AFTER ALL.
Q: IN THE "DISCUSSION ROOM" IN VOL. 6, KANDA SAID THAT REEVER'S DRINK WAS LEMON SODA, BUT IN THE PROFILE IN VOL. 2, IT JUST SAYS IT'S A SODA. DOES HE DRINK OTHER FLAVORS OF SODA IN THAT CUP, OR WAS KANDA MISTAKEN?
A: (ALLEN) KANDA WAS WRONG.
(LAVI) NOW DON'T TELL LIES. (SWEATING) I HEARD THAT KOMUI KEPT MISTAKING REEVER'S COLA FOR COFFEE, SO REEVER HAD TO SWITCH TO LEMON SODA. ACTUALLY, REEVER SEEMS TO LIKE ANYTHING THAT'S CARBONATED.
Q: WHAT ARE ALLEN, KANDA, AND LAVI'S ROOMS LIKE?
A: (ALLEN) I DON'T KNOW ABOUT KANDA'S, BUT I GOT A NEW ROOM AFTER KOMLIN DESTROYED MY FIRST ONE. IT USED TO BE A STORAGE ROOM, BUT IT'S NICE AND BIG---ABOUT 80 SQUARE FEET. OH, AND IT'S THE CLOSEST ROOM TO THE DINING HALL! ♬
(LAVI) CLOSEST TO THE DINING HALL? YOU MEAN THAT CREEPY ROOM THAT YOU FOUND AT THE END OF VOL. 1?
(ALLEN) I DON'T CARE HOW CREEPY IT IS! LOCATION, LOCATION, LOCATION! (EYES SHINING)
(LAVI) I SHARE A ROOM WITH THE OLD PANDA. IT'S ABOUT 120 SQUARE FEET.
Q: WHEN ALLEN ACTIVATES HIS INNOCENCE, HIS SLEEVE SEEMS TO DISAPPEAR. WHERE DOES IT GO?
A: (ALLEN) HMM...I HAVE NO IDEA.
(LAVI) YOU DON'T?
(ALLEN) I'M JUST GLAD IT DOESN'T RIP.

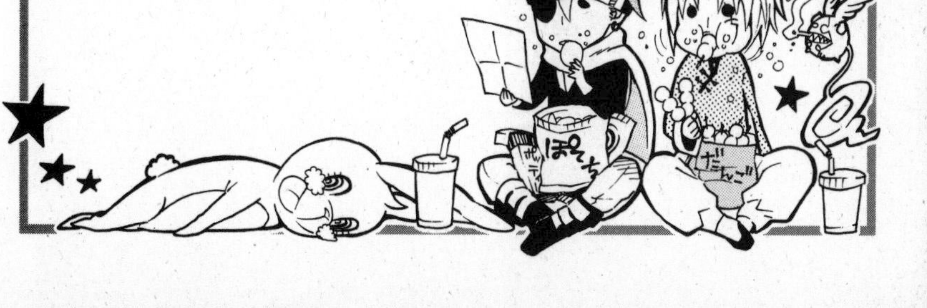

THE 61ST NIGHT: LEFT ARM

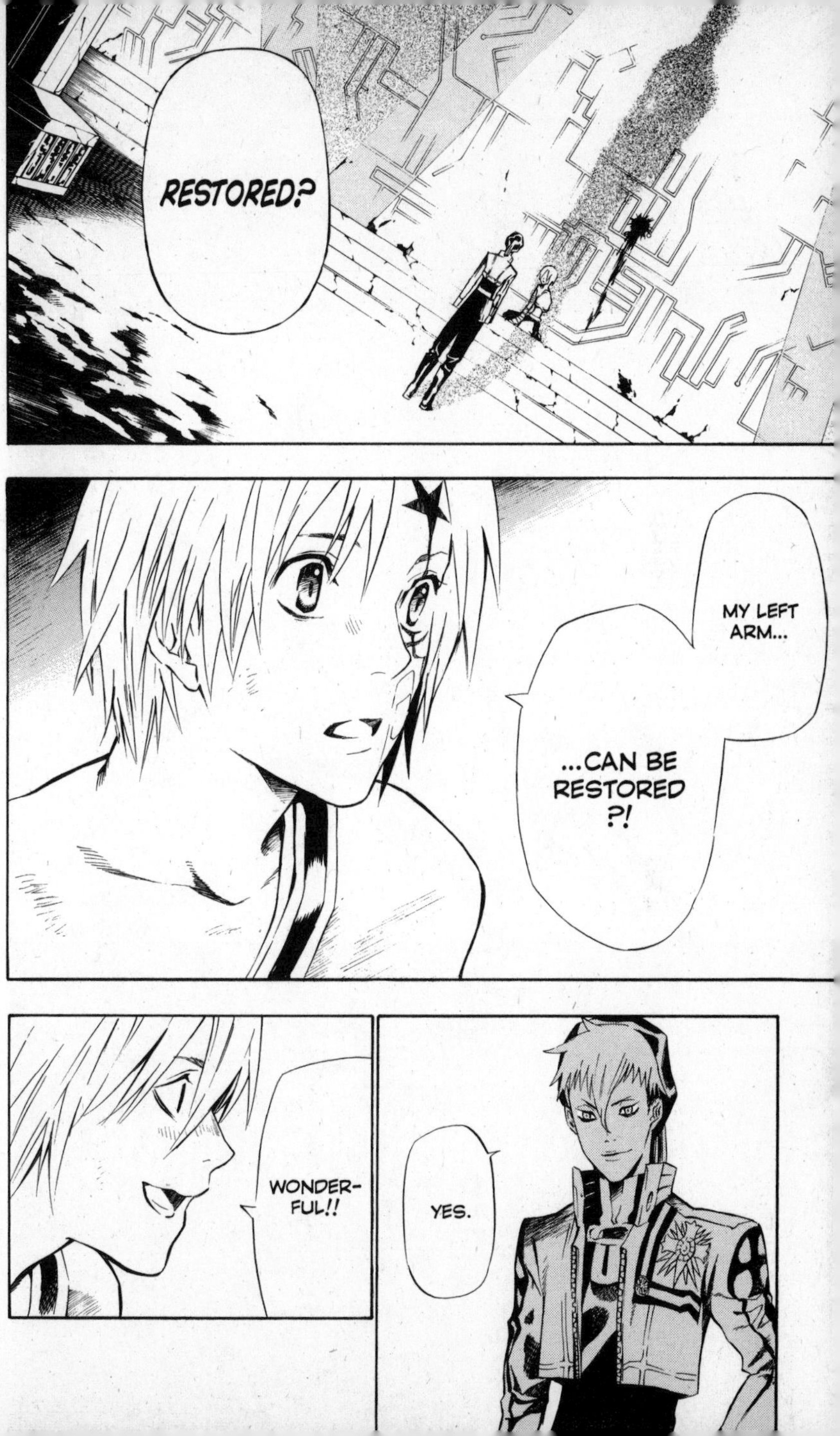
RESTORED?
MY LEFT ARM...
...CAN BE RESTORED ?!
YES.
WONDER-FUL!!

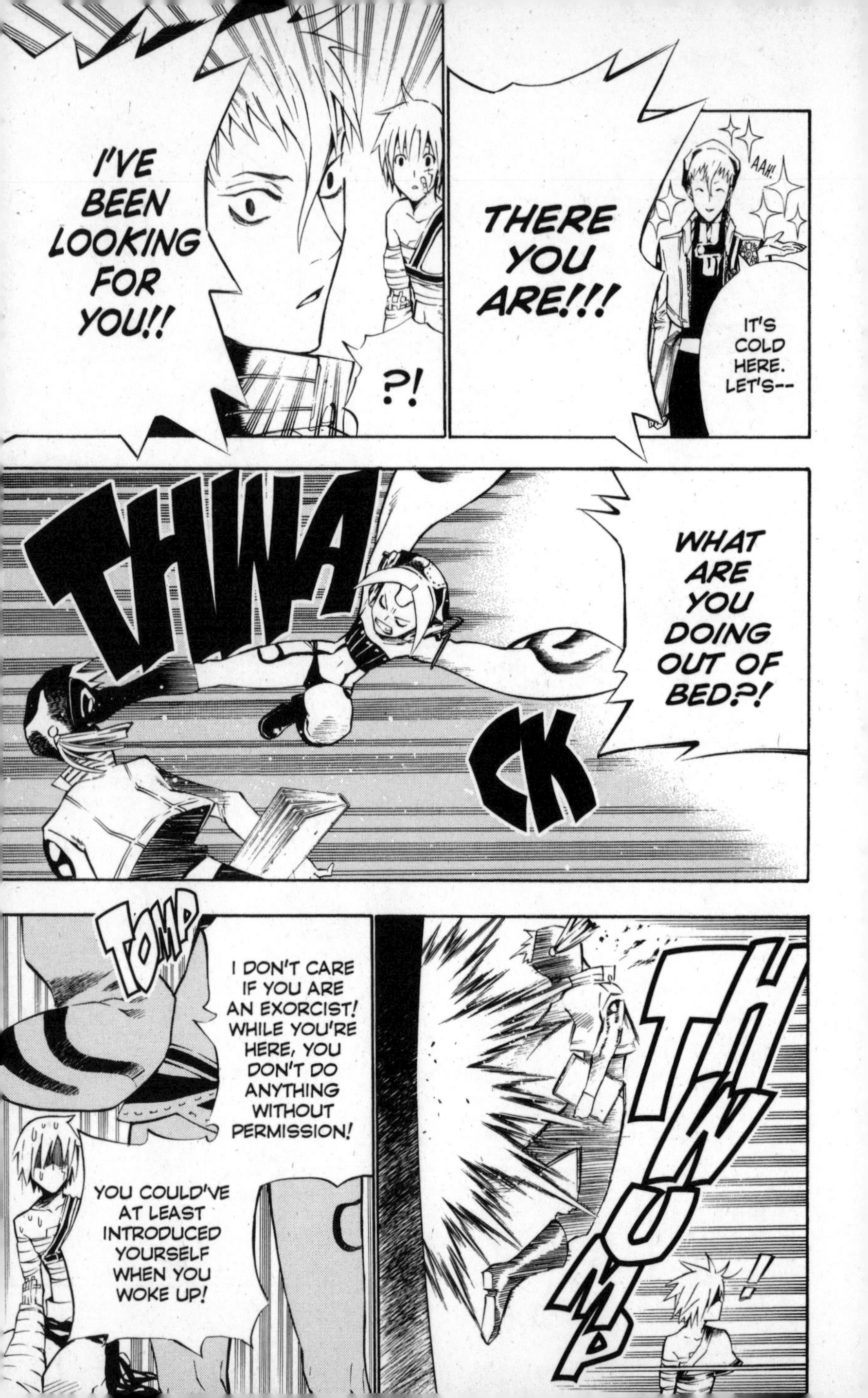
AAH!
IT'S COLD HERE. LET'S--
THERE YOU ARE!!!
I'VE BEEN LOOKING FOR YOU!!
?!
WHAT ARE YOU DOING OUT OF BED?!
THWACK
THUMP!
TOMP
I DON'T CARE IF YOU ARE AN EXORCIST! WHILE YOU'RE HERE, YOU DON'T DO ANYTHING WITHOUT PERMISSION!
YOU COULD'VE AT LEAST INTRODUCED YOURSELF WHEN YOU WOKE UP!

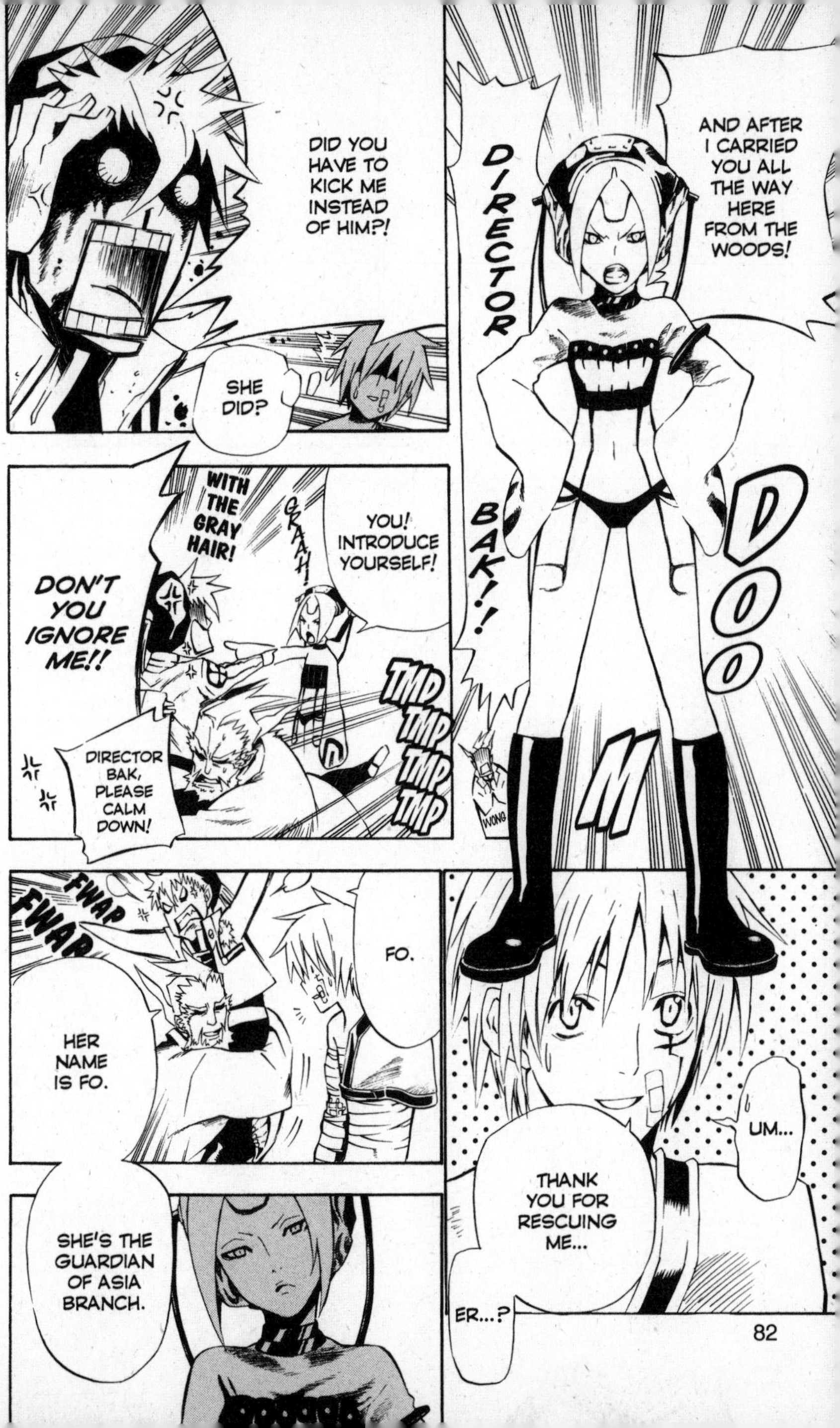
AND AFTER I CARRIED YOU ALL THE WAY HERE FROM THE WOODS!
DIRECTOR BAK!!
DOOOM
WONG
DID YOU HAVE TO KICK ME INSTEAD OF HIM?!
SHE DID?
YOU! INTRODUCE YOURSELF!
GRAAH!
WITH THE GRAY HAIR!
DON'T YOU IGNORE ME!!
TMP TMP TMP TMP
DIRECTOR BAK, PLEASE CALM DOWN!
UM...
THANK YOU FOR RESCUING ME...
ER...?
FO.
FWAP FWAP
HER NAME IS FO.
SHE'S THE GUARDIAN OF ASIA BRANCH.

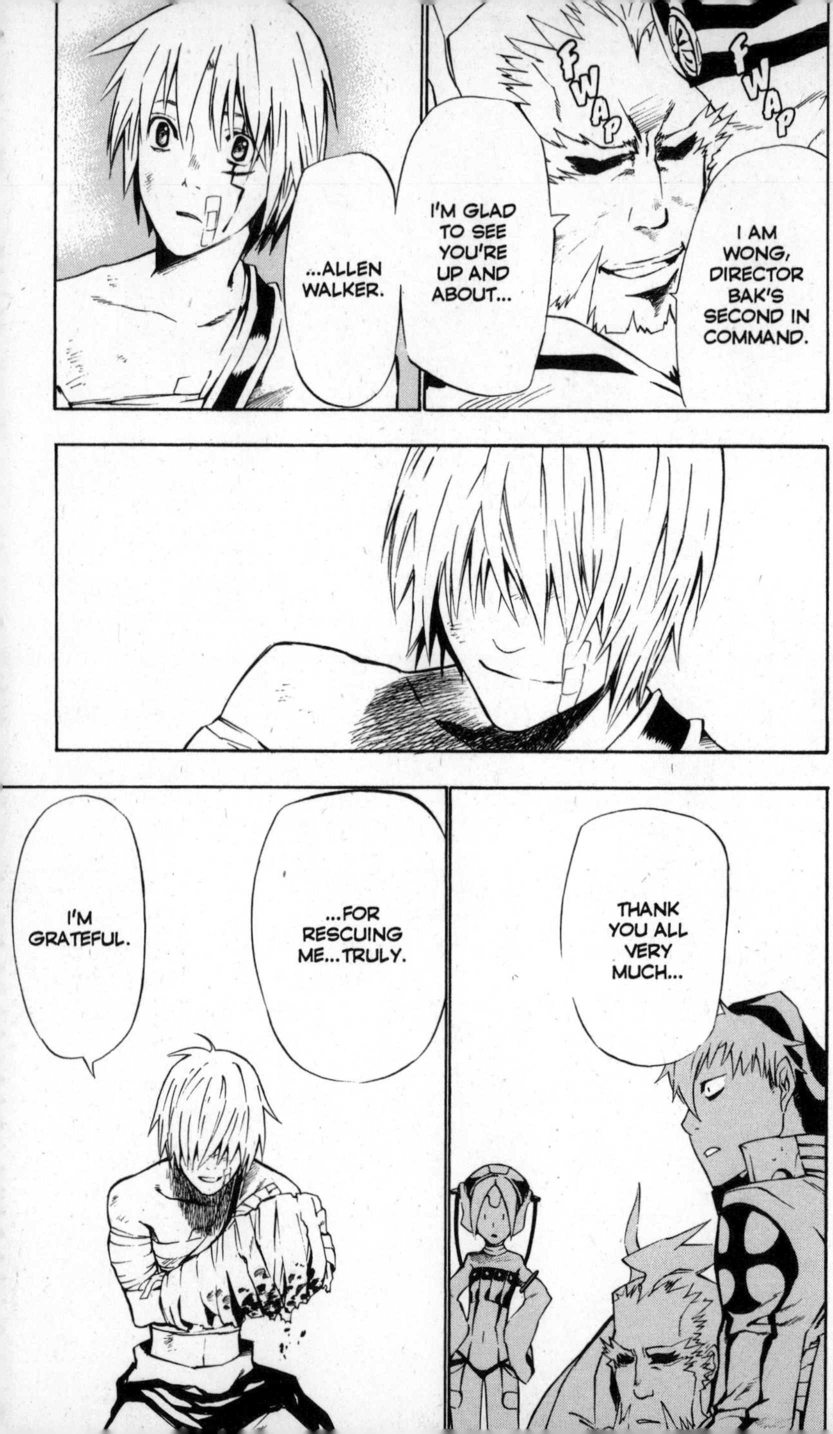
FWAP
FWAP
I AM WONG, DIRECTOR BAK'S SECOND IN COMMAND.
I'M GLAD TO SEE YOU'RE UP AND ABOUT...
...ALLEN WALKER.
THANK YOU ALL VERY MUCH...
...FOR RESCUING ME...TRULY.
I'M GRATEFUL.

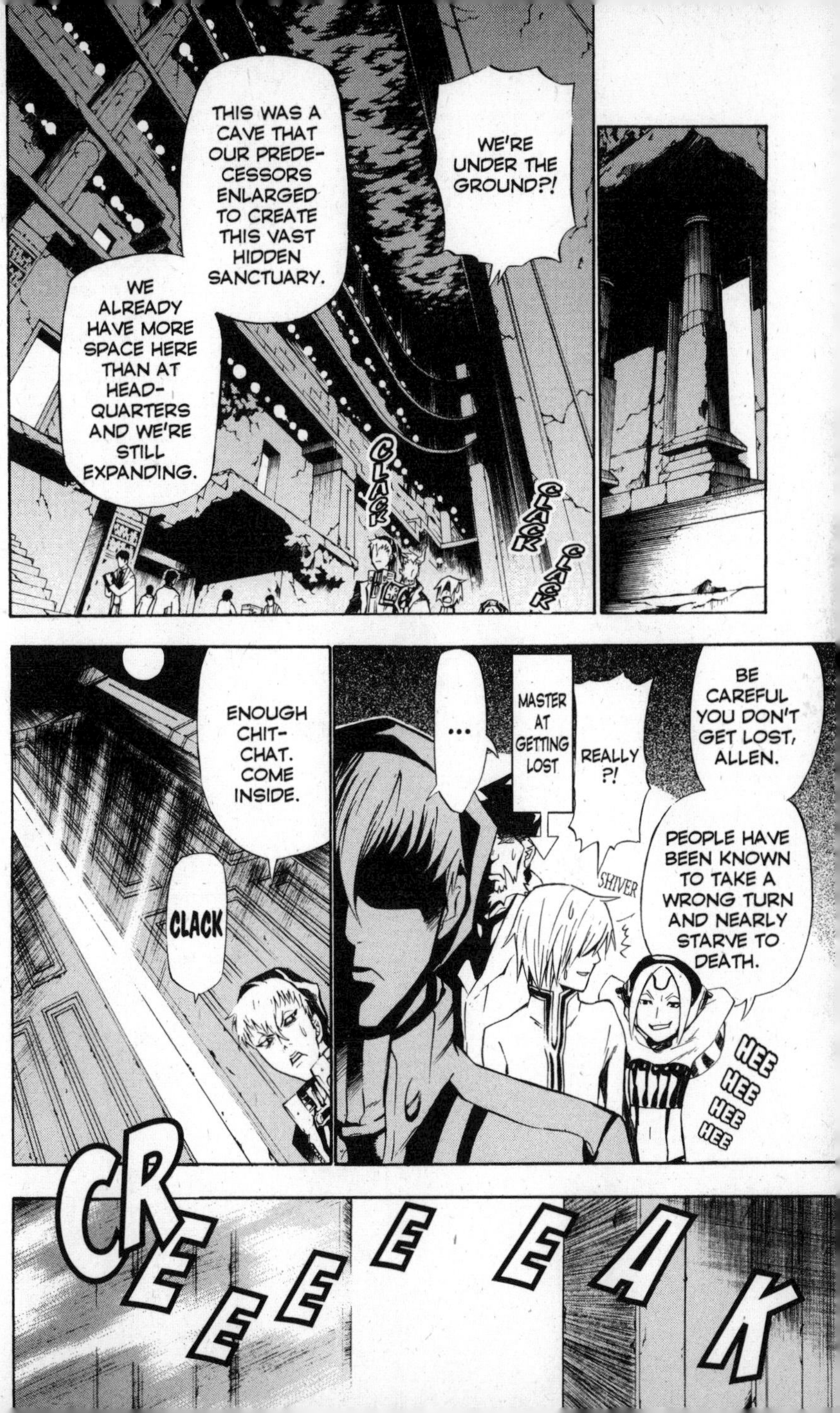
WE'RE UNDER THE GROUND?!
THIS WAS A CAVE THAT OUR PREDE-CESSORS ENLARGED TO CREATE THIS VAST HIDDEN SANCTUARY.
WE ALREADY HAVE MORE SPACE HERE THAN AT HEAD-QUARTERS AND WE'RE STILL EXPANDING.
CLACK
CLACK
CLACK
BE CAREFUL YOU DON'T GET LOST, ALLEN.
PEOPLE HAVE BEEN KNOWN TO TAKE A WRONG TURN AND NEARLY STARVE TO DEATH.
HEE HEE HEE HEE
REALLY ?!
SHIVER
MASTER AT GETTING LOST
...
ENOUGH CHIT-CHAT. COME INSIDE.
CLACK
CREEEEEEAK

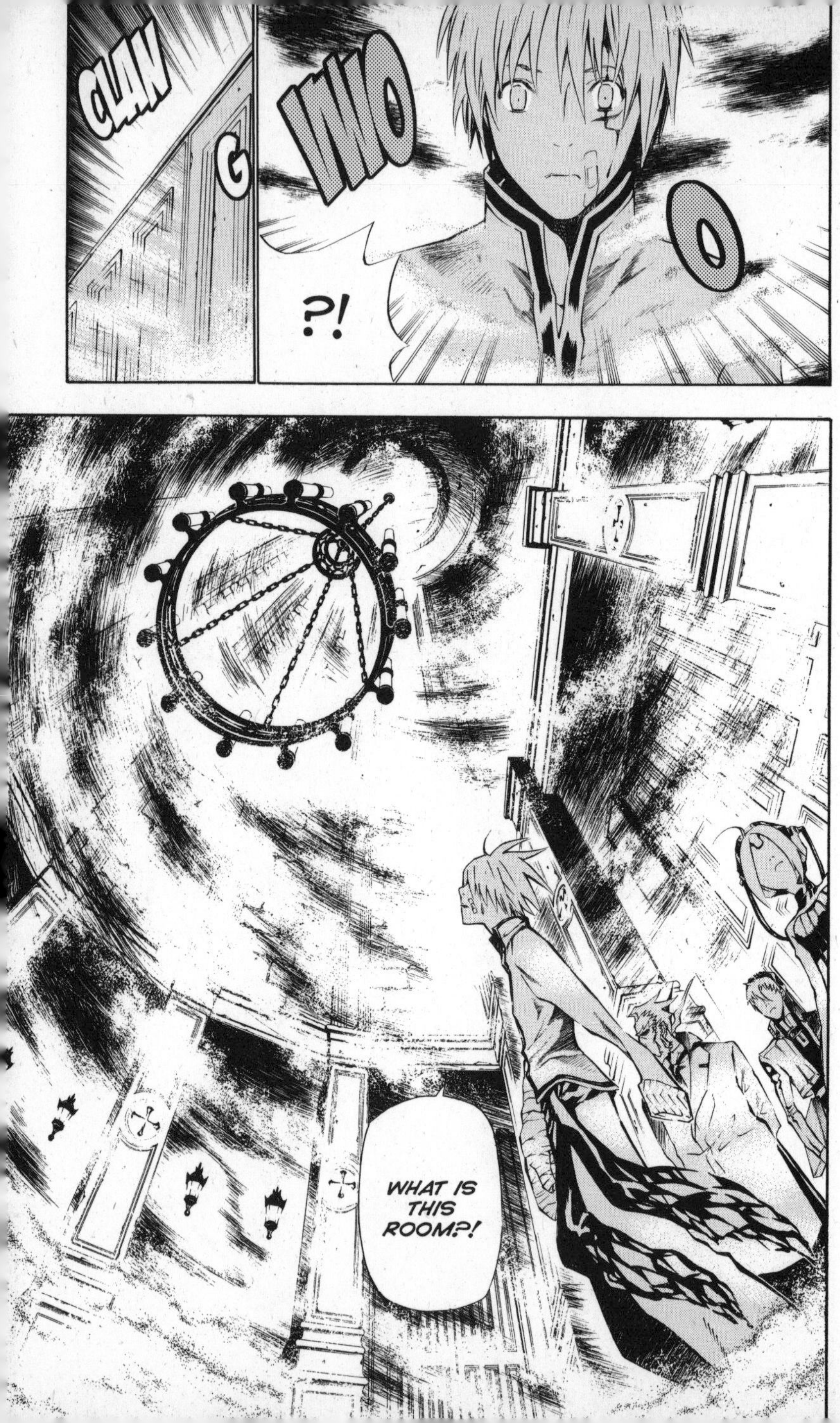
?!
CLANG
WHAT IS THIS ROOM?!

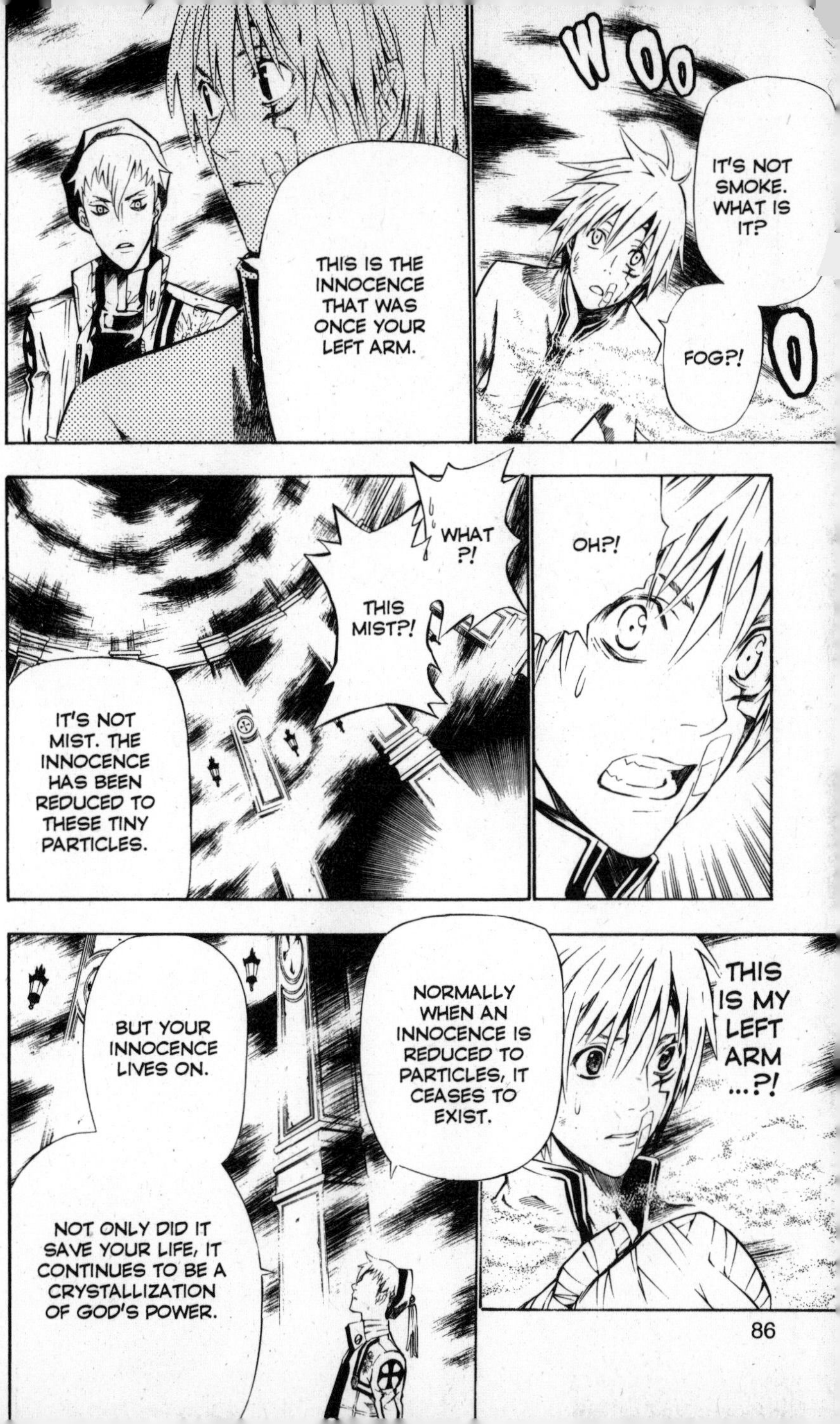
WOO
IT'S NOT SMOKE. WHAT IS IT?
FOG?!
O
THIS IS THE INNOCENCE THAT WAS ONCE YOUR LEFT ARM.
OH?!
WHAT ?!
THIS MIST?!
IT'S NOT MIST. THE INNOCENCE HAS BEEN REDUCED TO THESE TINY PARTICLES.
THIS IS MY LEFT ARM ...?!
NORMALLY WHEN AN INNOCENCE IS REDUCED TO PARTICLES, IT CEASES TO EXIST.
BUT YOUR INNOCENCE LIVES ON.
NOT ONLY DID IT SAVE YOUR LIFE, IT CONTINUES TO BE A CRYSTALLIZATION OF GOD'S POWER.

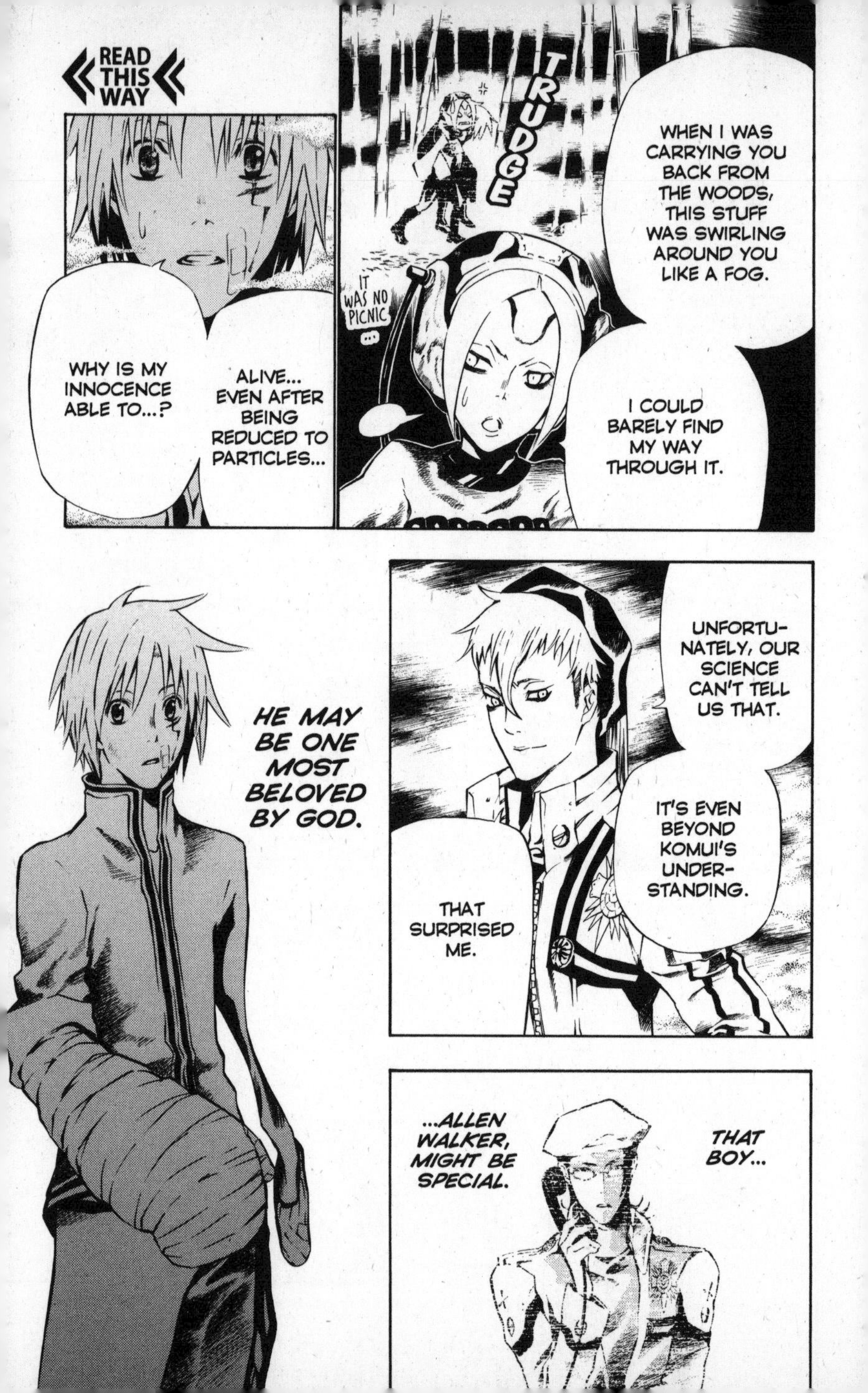
READ THIS WAY
WHEN I WAS CARRYING YOU BACK FROM THE WOODS, THIS STUFF WAS SWIRLING AROUND YOU LIKE A FOG.
TRUDGE
IT WAS NO PICNIC...
I COULD BARELY FIND MY WAY THROUGH IT.
ALIVE... EVEN AFTER BEING REDUCED TO PARTICLES...
WHY IS MY INNOCENCE ABLE TO...?
UNFORTU-NATELY, OUR SCIENCE CAN'T TELL US THAT.
IT'S EVEN BEYOND KOMUI'S UNDER-STANDING.
THAT SURPRISED ME.
THAT BOY...
...ALLEN WALKER, MIGHT BE SPECIAL.
HE MAY BE ONE MOST BELOVED BY GOD.

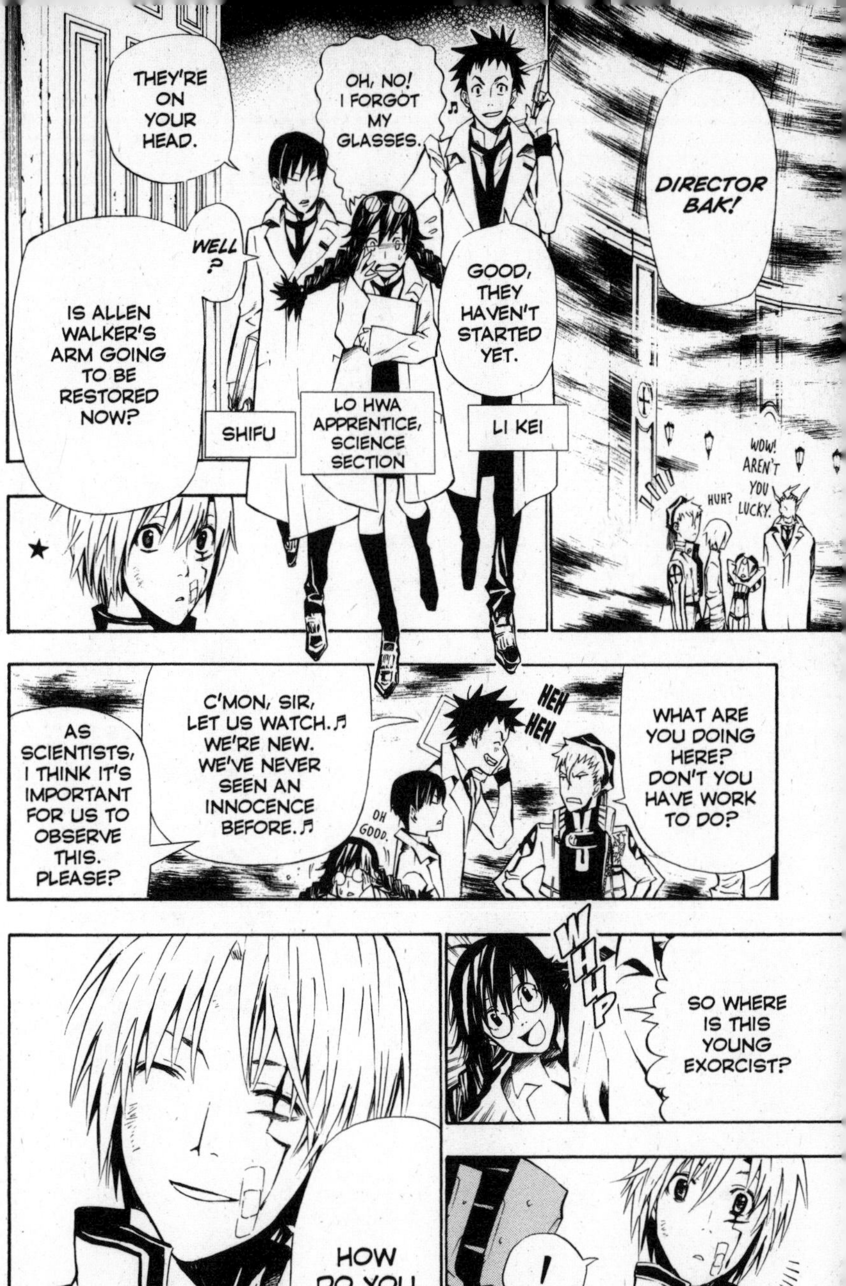
DIRECTOR BAK!
WOW! AREN'T YOU LUCKY.
HUH?
GOOD, THEY HAVEN'T STARTED YET.
OH, NO! I FORGOT MY GLASSES.
THEY'RE ON YOUR HEAD.
LI KEI
LO HWA APPRENTICE, SCIENCE SECTION
SHIFU
WELL?
IS ALLEN WALKER'S ARM GOING TO BE RESTORED NOW?
WHAT ARE YOU DOING HERE? DON'T YOU HAVE WORK TO DO?
HEH HEH
C'MON, SIR, LET US WATCH.♬ WE'RE NEW. WE'VE NEVER SEEN AN INNOCENCE BEFORE.♬
OH GOOD.
AS SCIENTISTS, I THINK IT'S IMPORTANT FOR US TO OBSERVE THIS. PLEASE?
SO WHERE IS THIS YOUNG EXORCIST?
WHUP
!
HOW DO YOU DO?

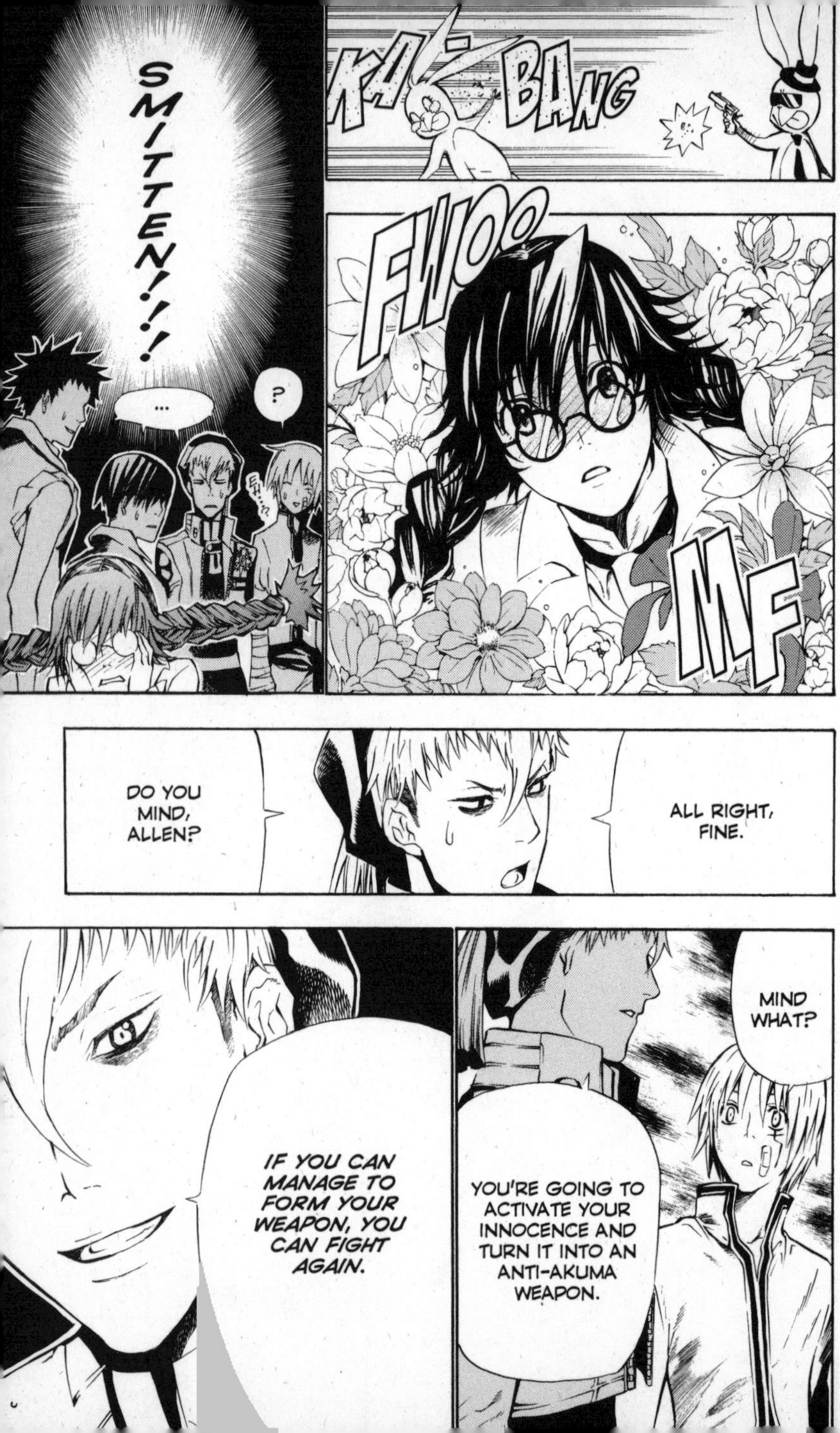
KA-BANG
FWOO
MF
SMITTEN!!!
...
?
EH...?
ALL RIGHT, FINE.
DO YOU MIND, ALLEN?
MIND WHAT?
YOU'RE GOING TO ACTIVATE YOUR INNOCENCE AND TURN IT INTO AN ANTI-AKUMA WEAPON.
IF YOU CAN MANAGE TO FORM YOUR WEAPON, YOU CAN FIGHT AGAIN.

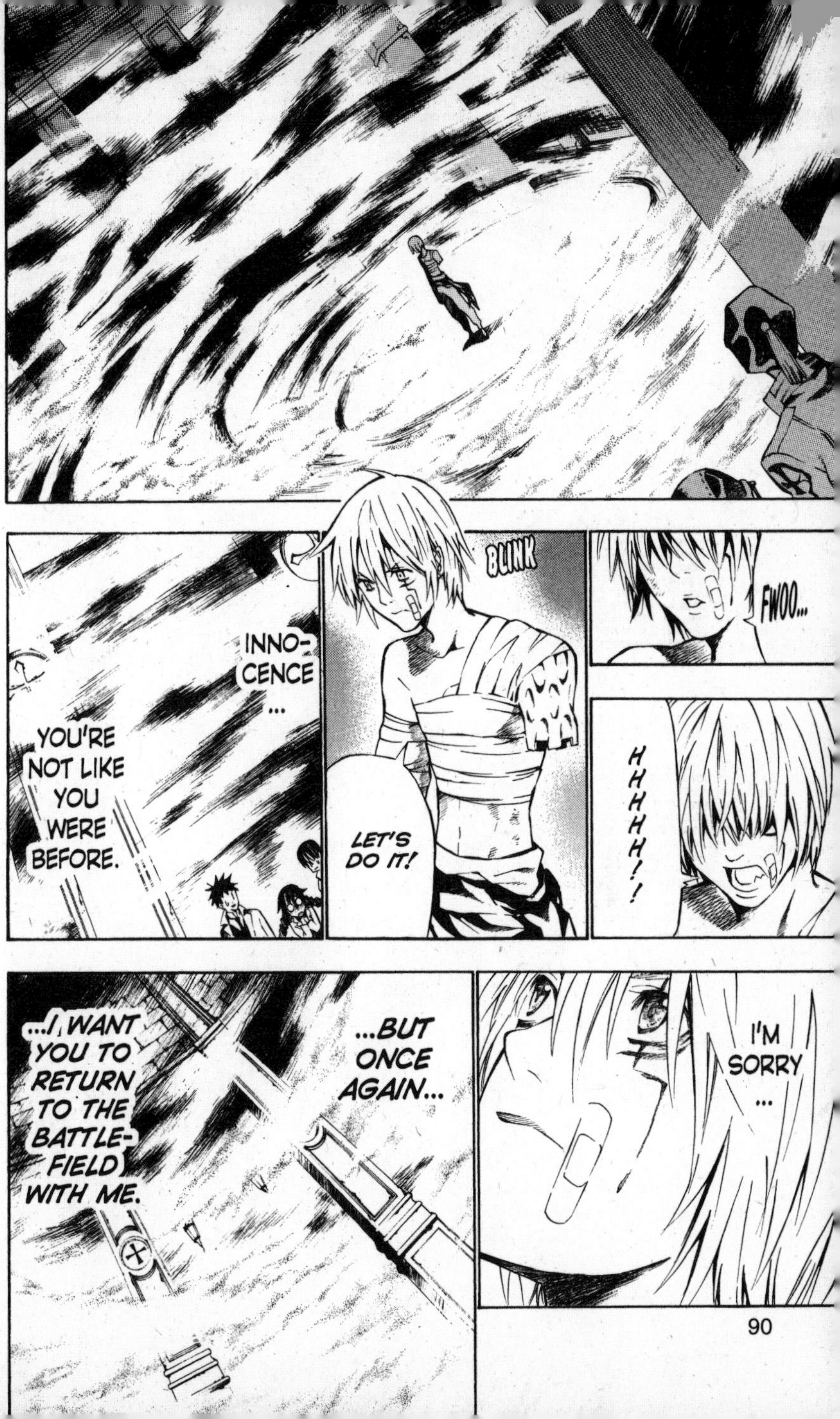
FWOO...
HHHHH!!
BLINK
LET'S DO IT!
INNO-CENCE...
YOU'RE NOT LIKE YOU WERE BEFORE.
I'M SORRY...
...BUT ONCE AGAIN...
...I WANT YOU TO RETURN TO THE BATTLE-FIELD WITH ME.

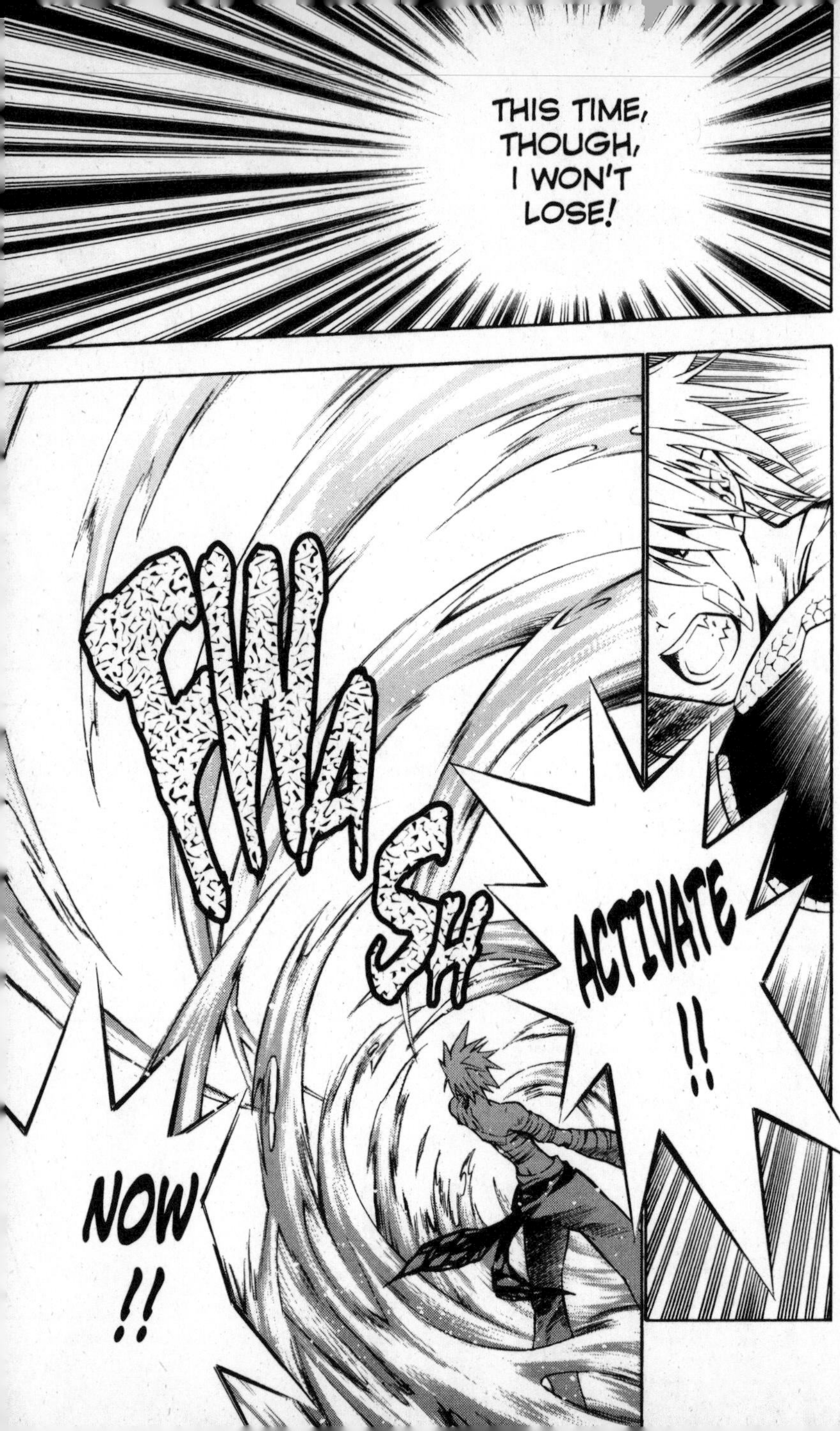
THIS TIME, THOUGH, I WON'T LOSE!
ACTIVATE !!
CWASH
NOW !!

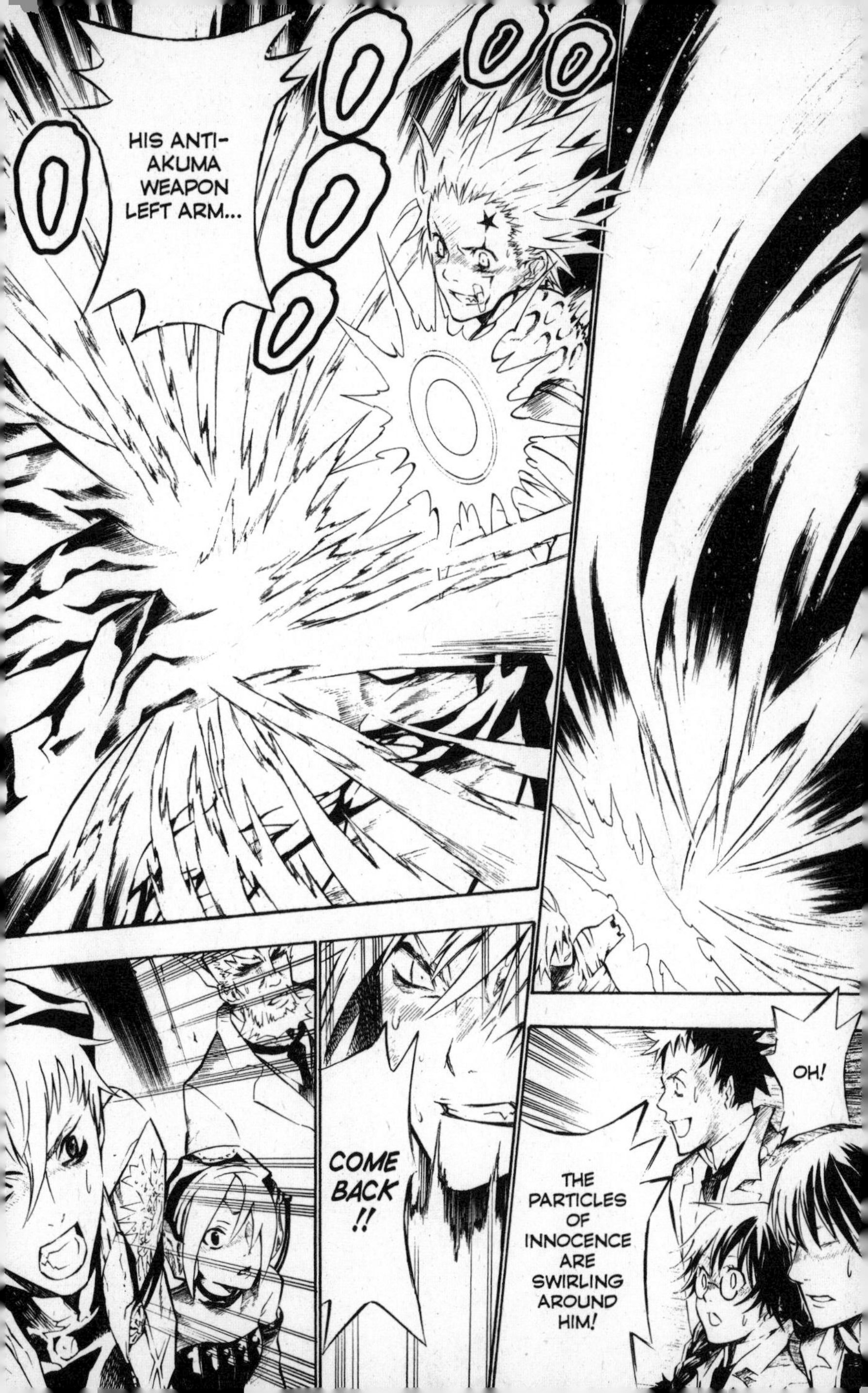
HIS ANTI-AKUMA WEAPON LEFT ARM...
OH!
THE PARTICLES OF INNOCENCE ARE SWIRLING AROUND HIM!
COME BACK !!

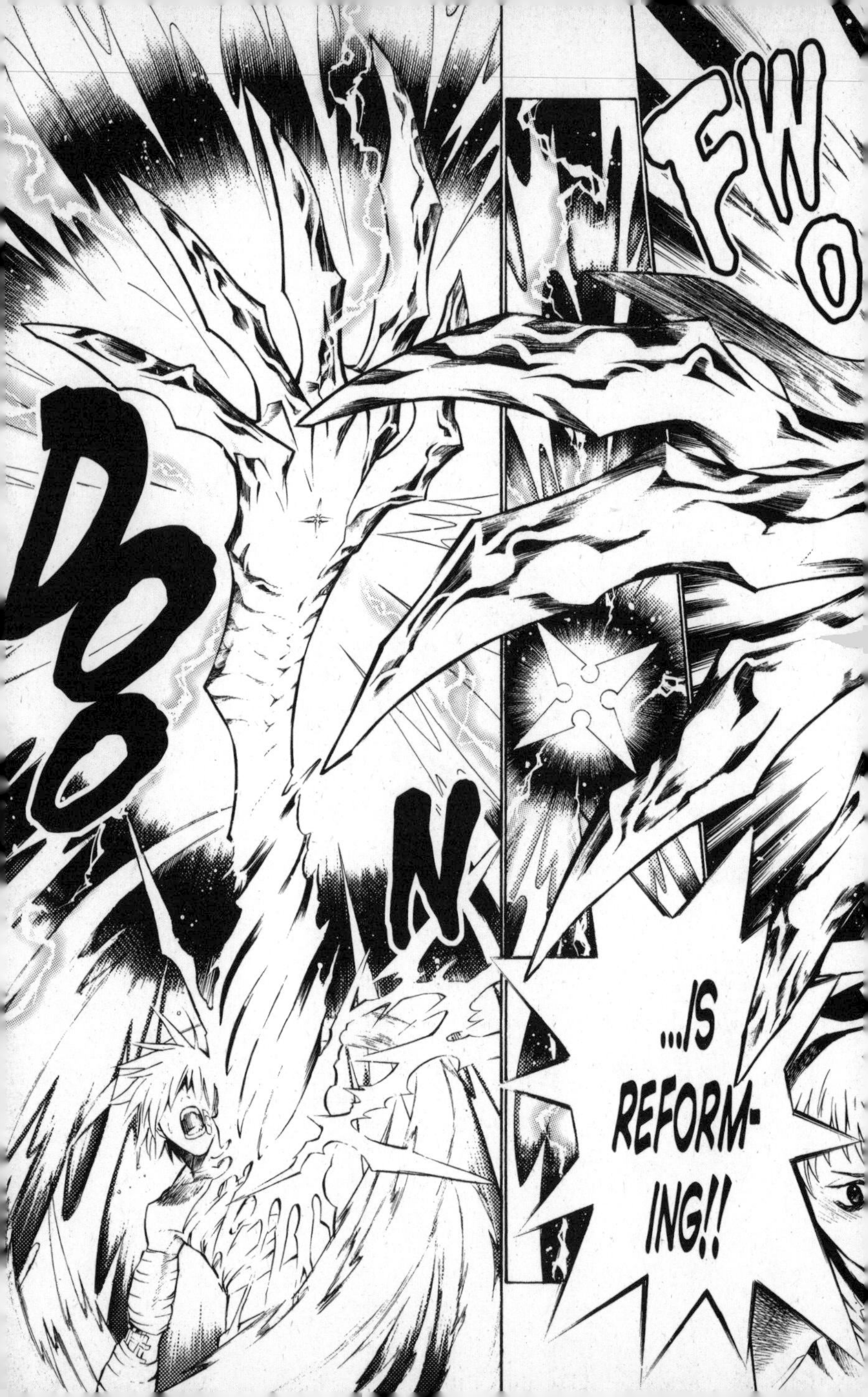
FWO
...IS REFORM-ING!!
DOOON

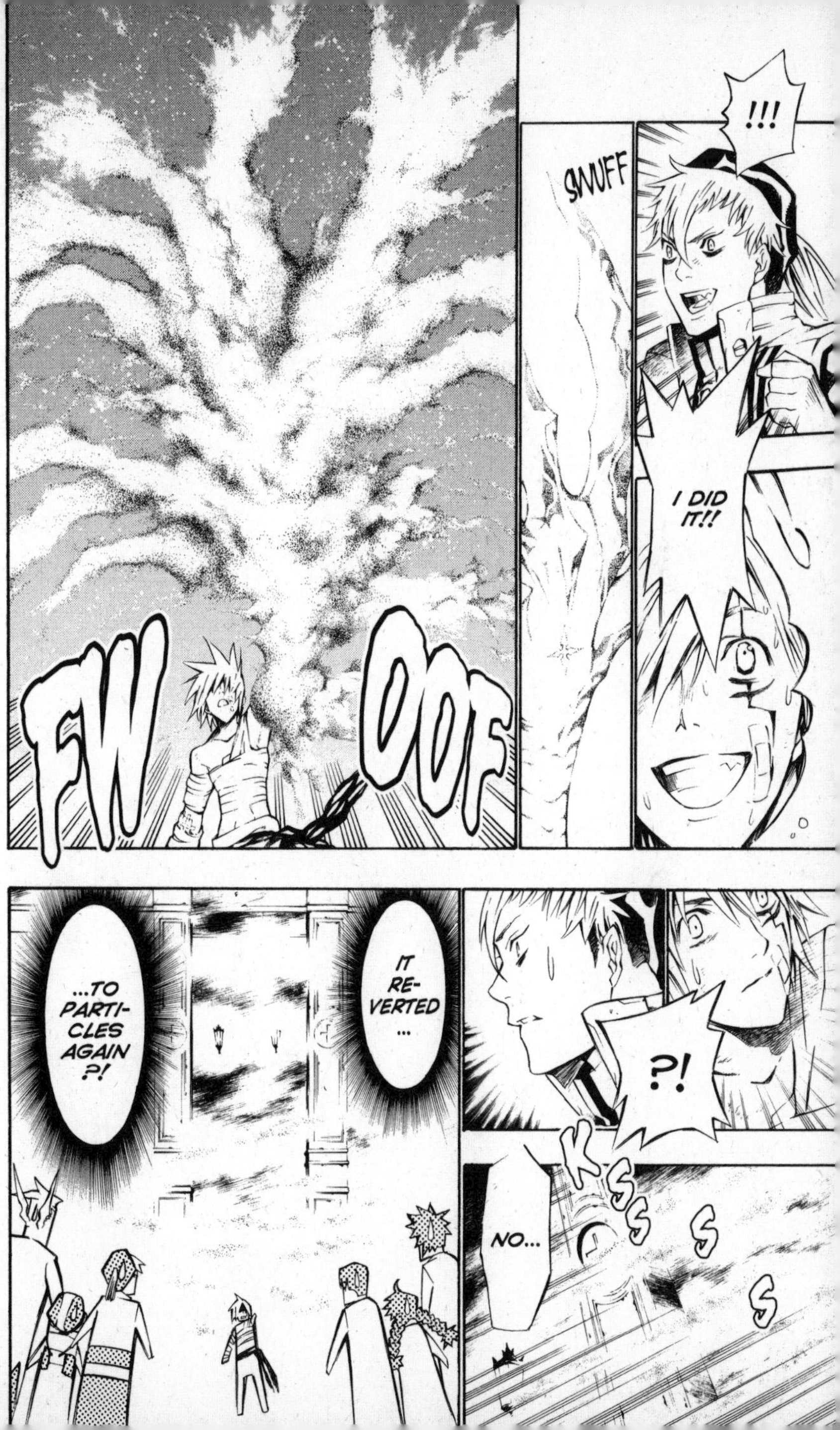
!!!
I DID IT!!
SNUFF
FW
OOF
?!
KSSS
S
S
NO...
IT RE-VERTED...
...TO PARTI-CLES AGAIN?!

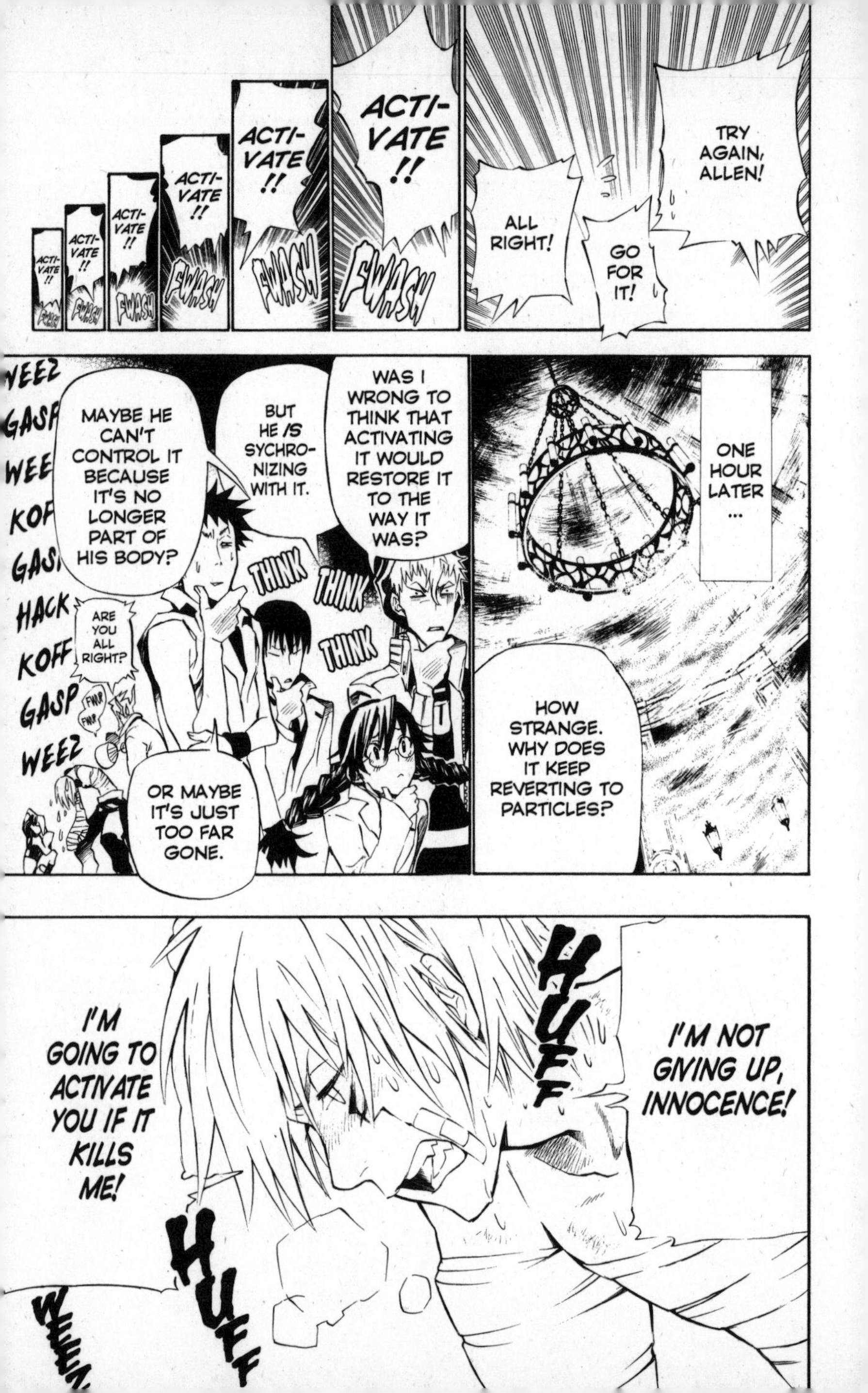

TRY AGAIN, ALLEN!
GO FOR IT!
ALL RIGHT!
ACTIVATE!!
FWASH
ACTIVATE!!
FWASH
ACTIVATE!!
FWASH
ACTIVATE!!
FWASH
ACTIVATE!!
FWASH
ACTIVATE!!
ONE HOUR LATER...
HOW STRANGE. WHY DOES IT KEEP REVERTING TO PARTICLES?
WAS I WRONG TO THINK THAT ACTIVATING IT WOULD RESTORE IT TO THE WAY IT WAS?
BUT HE IS SYCHRONIZING WITH IT.
MAYBE HE CAN'T CONTROL IT BECAUSE IT'S NO LONGER PART OF HIS BODY?
THINK
THINK
THINK
OR MAYBE IT'S JUST TOO FAR GONE.
ARE YOU ALL RIGHT?
WEEZ
HACK
KOFF
GASP
WEEZ
I'M NOT GIVING UP, INNOCENCE!
HUFF
I'M GOING TO ACTIVATE YOU IF IT KILLS ME!
HUFF

Komui's Discussion Room, Vol. 5

Q: IF YOU WERE TO WHISPER INTO KOMUI'S EAR, "ALLEN AND LENALEE ARE GETTING MARRIED," OR, "LAVI GROPED LENALEE," WHAT WOULD HE DO? WOULD HE KILL ALLEN AND LAVI? WOULD YOU GIVE IT A TRY?

A: (LAVI) WHOA! HERE IT COMES... (SWEATING)

(ALLEN) I KNEW WE'D GET SOMETHING LIKE THIS EVENTUALLY.

(LAVI) I CAN'T TAKE IT?

(ALLEN) I DON'T WANT TO DIE FOR A SILLY EXPERIMENT.

Q: AFTER THE PHONE CALL IN VOL. 5, THE PICTURE OF YOSHI THAT KOMUI STARTS TO DRAW IS HOLDING A BALL. IS THAT A DRAGON BALL?

A: (LAVI) WHAT WOULD YOU WISH FOR ONCE YOU FOUND ALL SEVEN?

(ALLEN) HMM...I'D WISH THAT ALL THE DEBTS MY MASTER TRANSFERRED TO ME WOULD GO AWAY.

(LAVI) YOU'RE STILL PAYING HIS DEBTS?!

(ALLEN) HEY, IS THIS DRAGON BALL THE ONE THAT LETS YOU HAVE THREE WISHES?

Q: HOW DO THEY CHANGE GATEKEEPERS WHEN THE TIME COMES?

A: (LAVI) OH, THIS IS SOMETHING I'VE WANTED TO SEE! IT SOUNDS REALLY INTERESTING.

(ALLEN) YES, I WONDER HOW IT'S DONE? THEN AGAIN, ALESTINA (THE GATEKEEPER) DOESN'T SEEM TO LIKE ME VERY MUCH.

(LAVI) HE'S GROUCHY AND HE HOLDS A GRUDGE.

(ALLEN) THE BLACK ORDER IS FULL OF STRANGE THINGS THE READERS HAVE NEVER SEEN. I'D LIKE TO TAKE THEM ON A TOUR ONE DAY.

(LAVI) ALLEN, DID YOU KNOW THERE ARE GHOSTS IN HERE?

(ALLEN) R-REALLY?

(FACE GOING PALE)

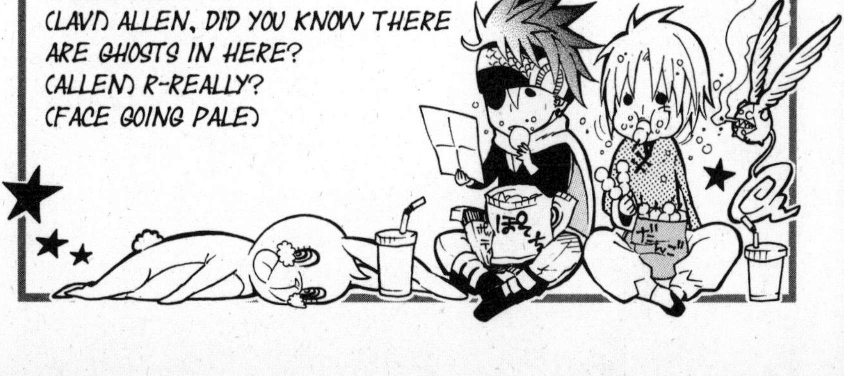

THE 62ND NIGHT: OPERATION

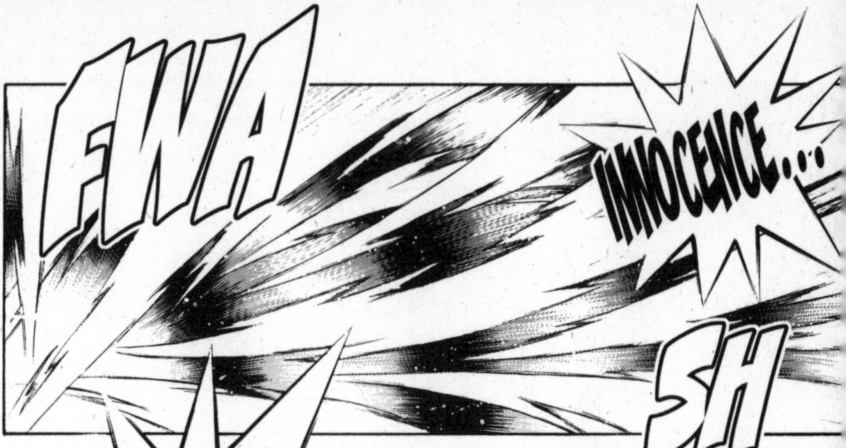
INNOCENCE...
SH
FWA
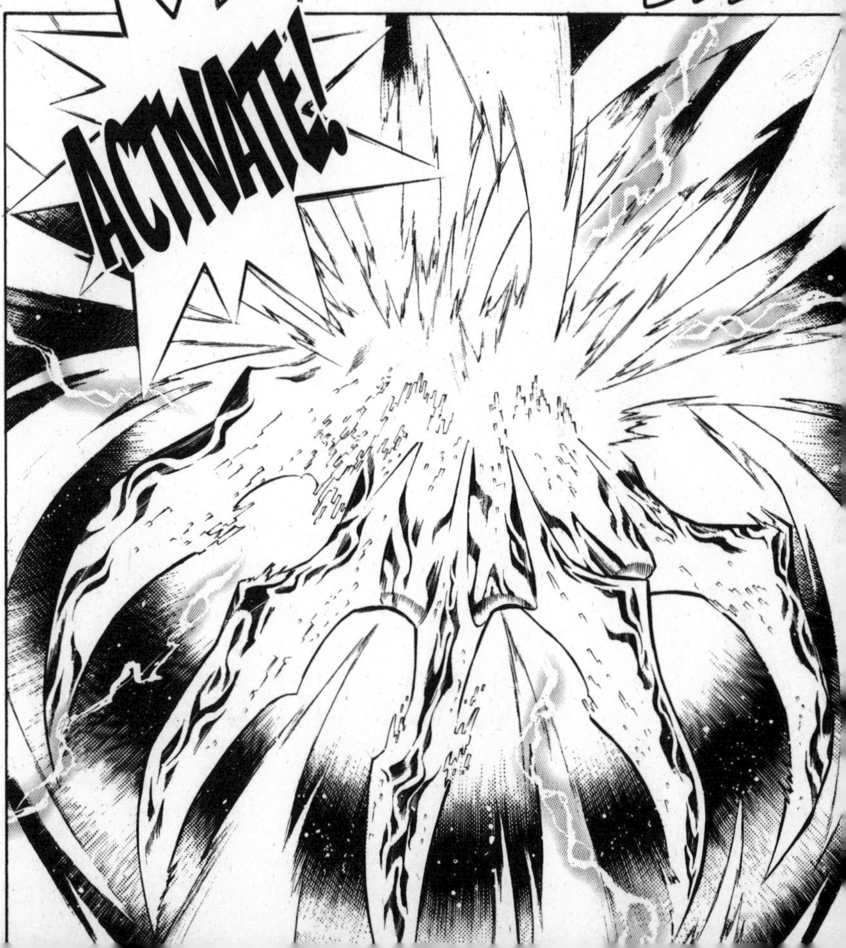
ACTIVATE!

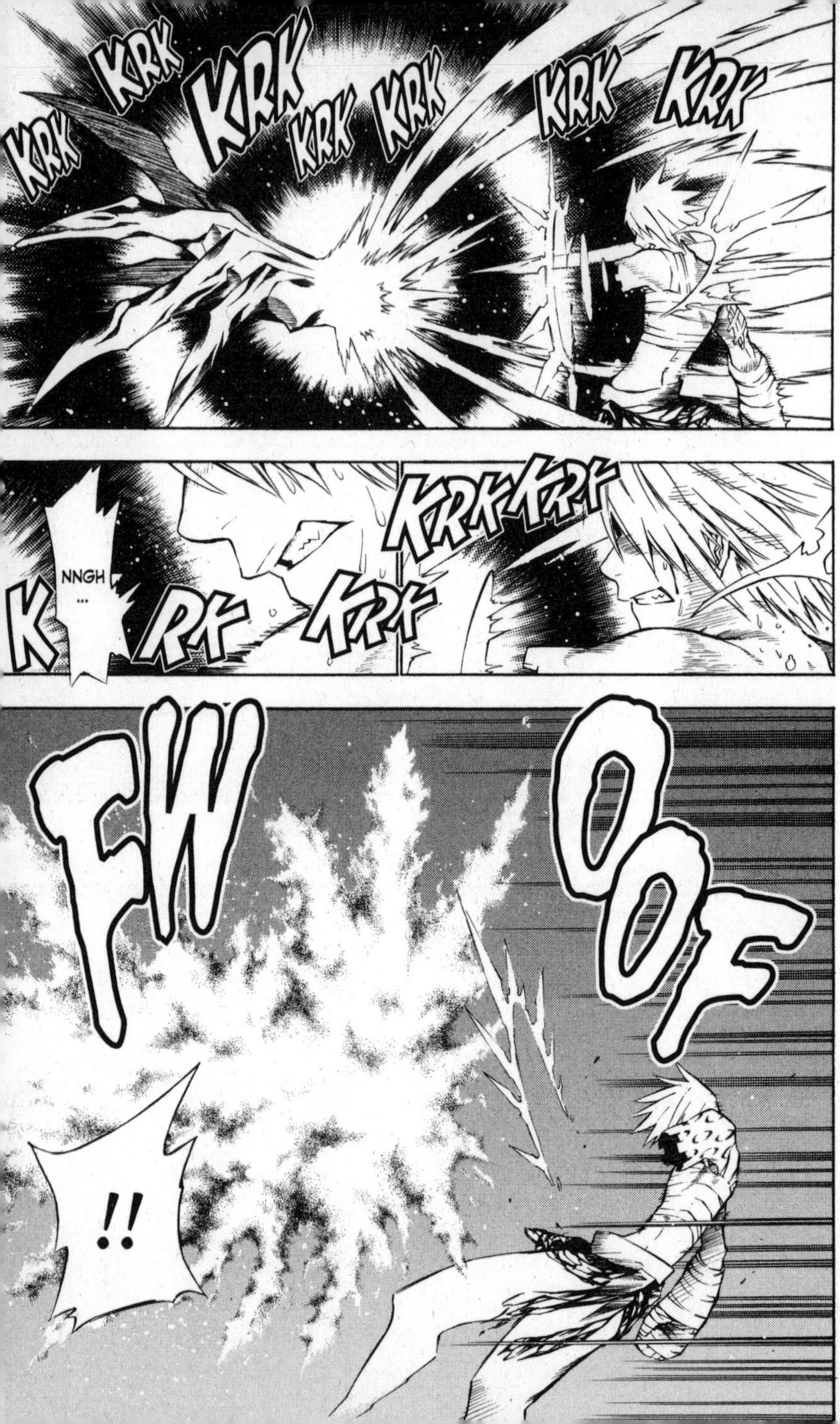
KRK
KRK
KRK
KRK
KRK
KRK
KRK
KRKKRK
KRK
NNGH ...
K RK
FWOOF
!!

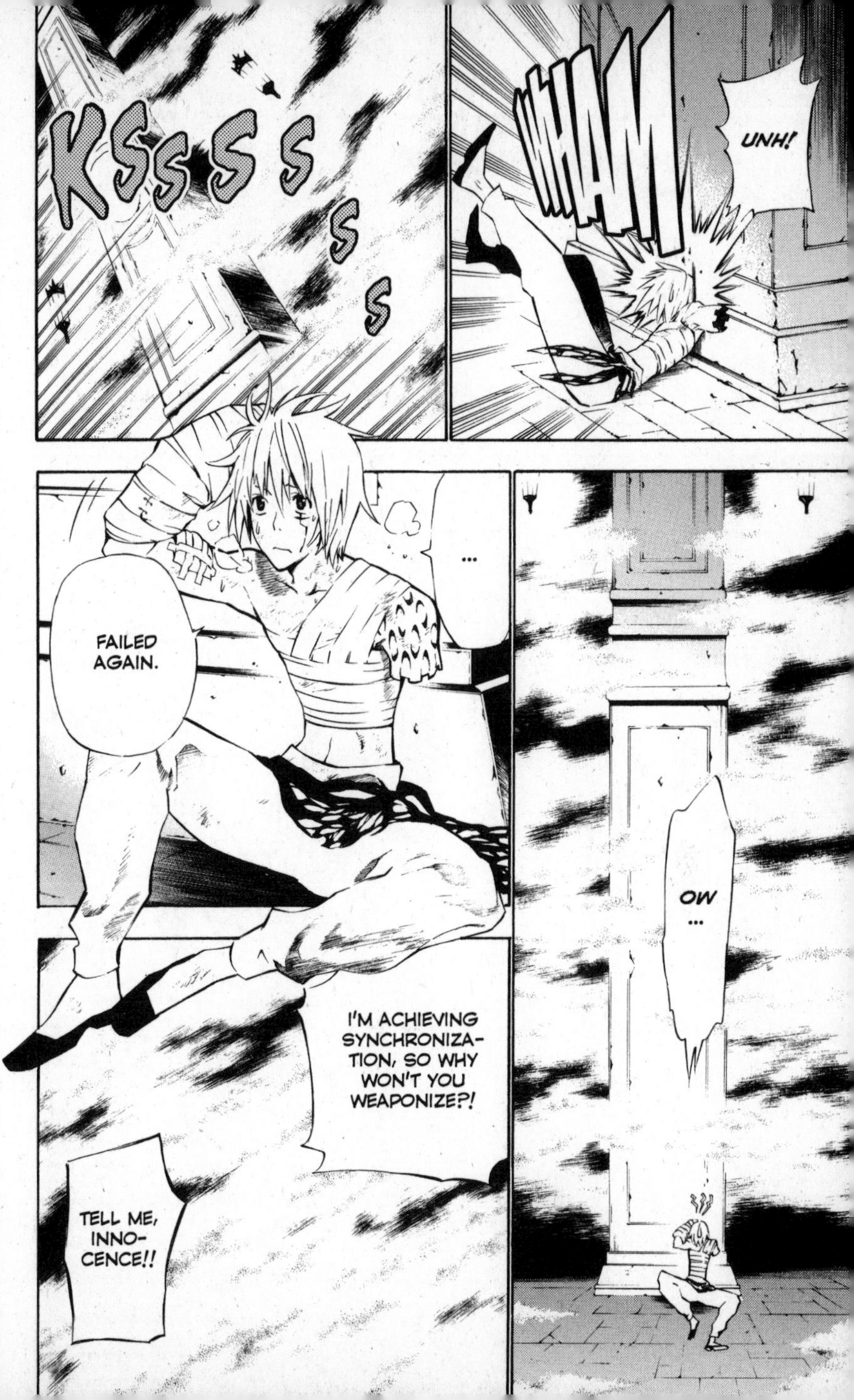
WHAM
UNH!
KSSSSSSS
OW...
...
FAILED AGAIN.
I'M ACHIEVING SYNCHRONIZATION, SO WHY WON'T YOU WEAPONIZE?!
TELL ME, INNOCENCE!!

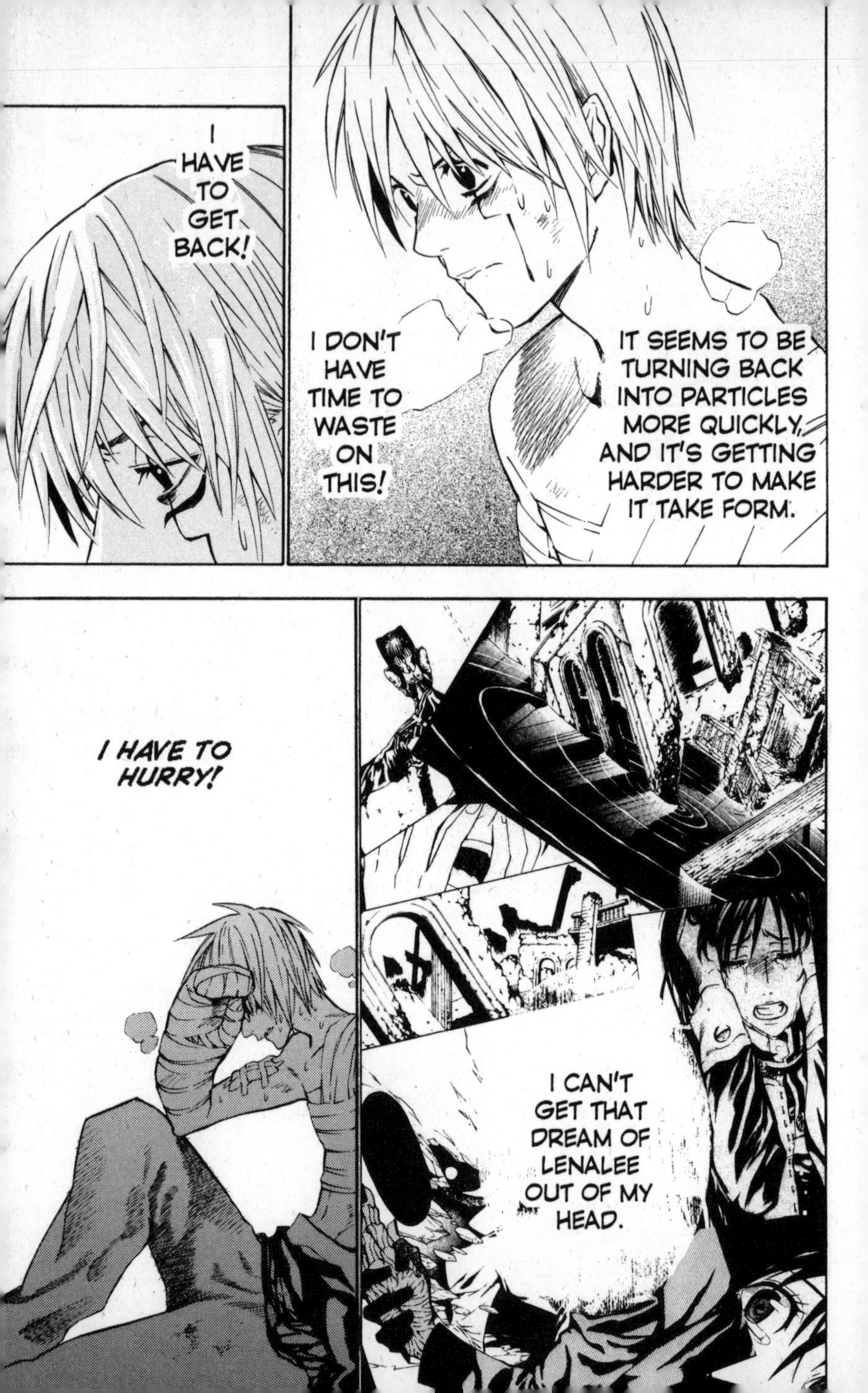
IT SEEMS TO BE TURNING BACK INTO PARTICLES MORE QUICKLY, AND IT'S GETTING HARDER TO MAKE IT TAKE FORM.
I DON'T HAVE TIME TO WASTE ON THIS!
I HAVE TO GET BACK!
I CAN'T GET THAT DREAM OF LENALEE OUT OF MY HEAD.
I HAVE TO HURRY!

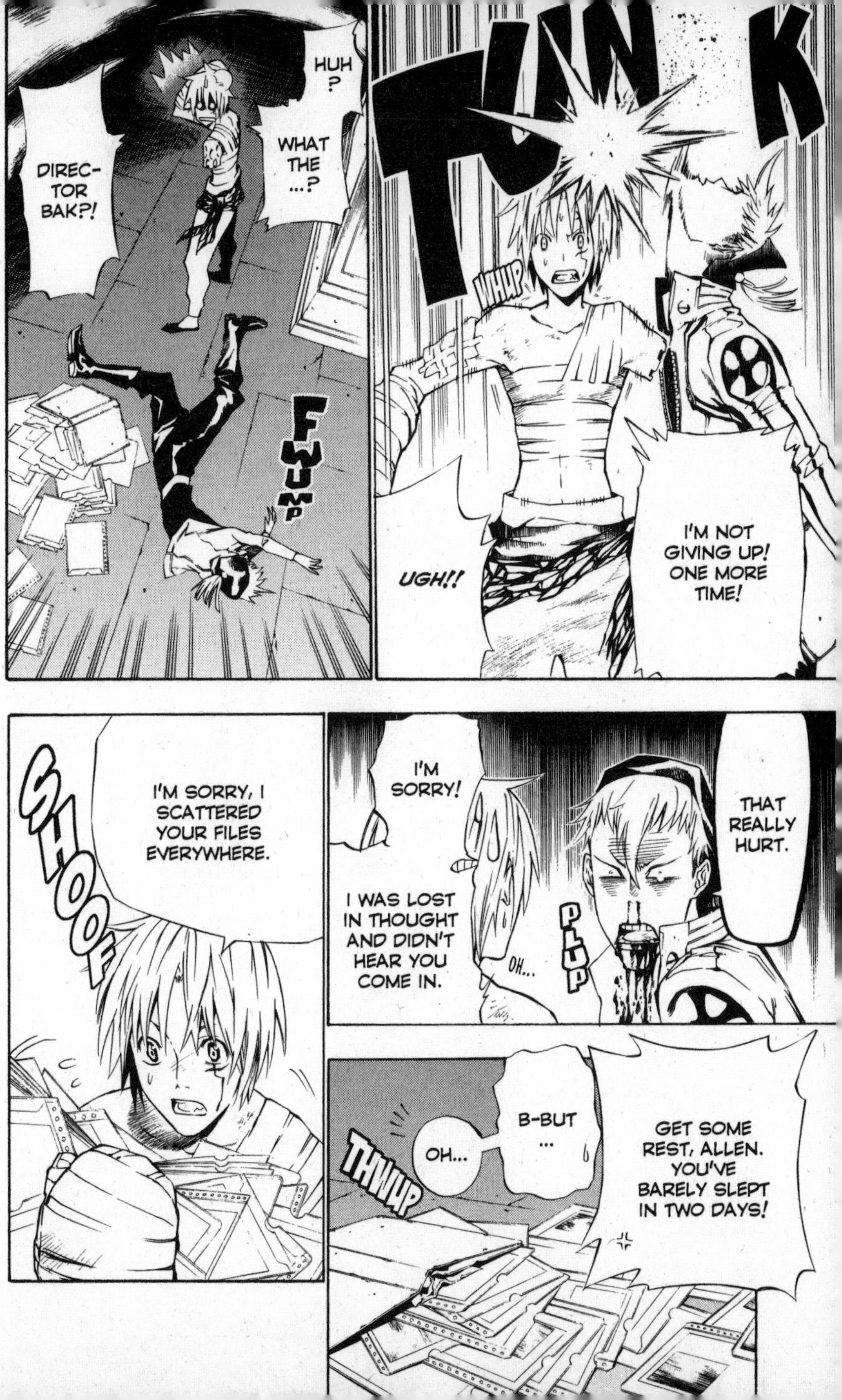
TUNK
WHUP
UGH!!
I'M NOT GIVING UP! ONE MORE TIME!
HUH?
WHAT THE ...?
DIRECTOR BAK?!
FWUMP
THAT REALLY HURT.
PLUP
I'M SORRY!
OH...
I WAS LOST IN THOUGHT AND DIDN'T HEAR YOU COME IN.
GET SOME REST, ALLEN. YOU'VE BARELY SLEPT IN TWO DAYS!
B-BUT ...
OH...
THWUP
SHOOF
I'M SORRY, I SCATTERED YOUR FILES EVERYWHERE.

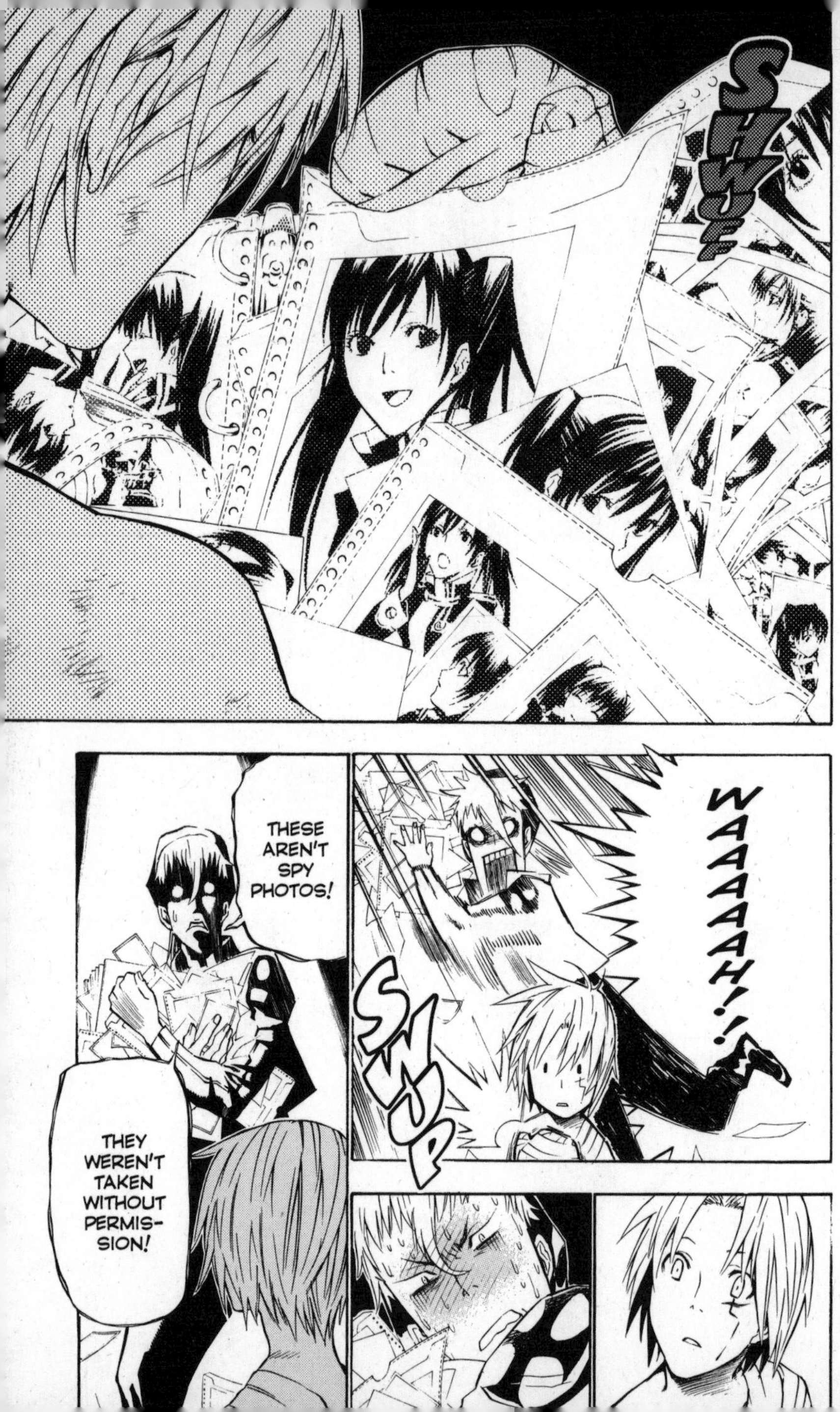
SHWUF
WAAAAAH!!
SWUP
THESE AREN'T SPY PHOTOS!
THEY WEREN'T TAKEN WITHOUT PERMISSION!

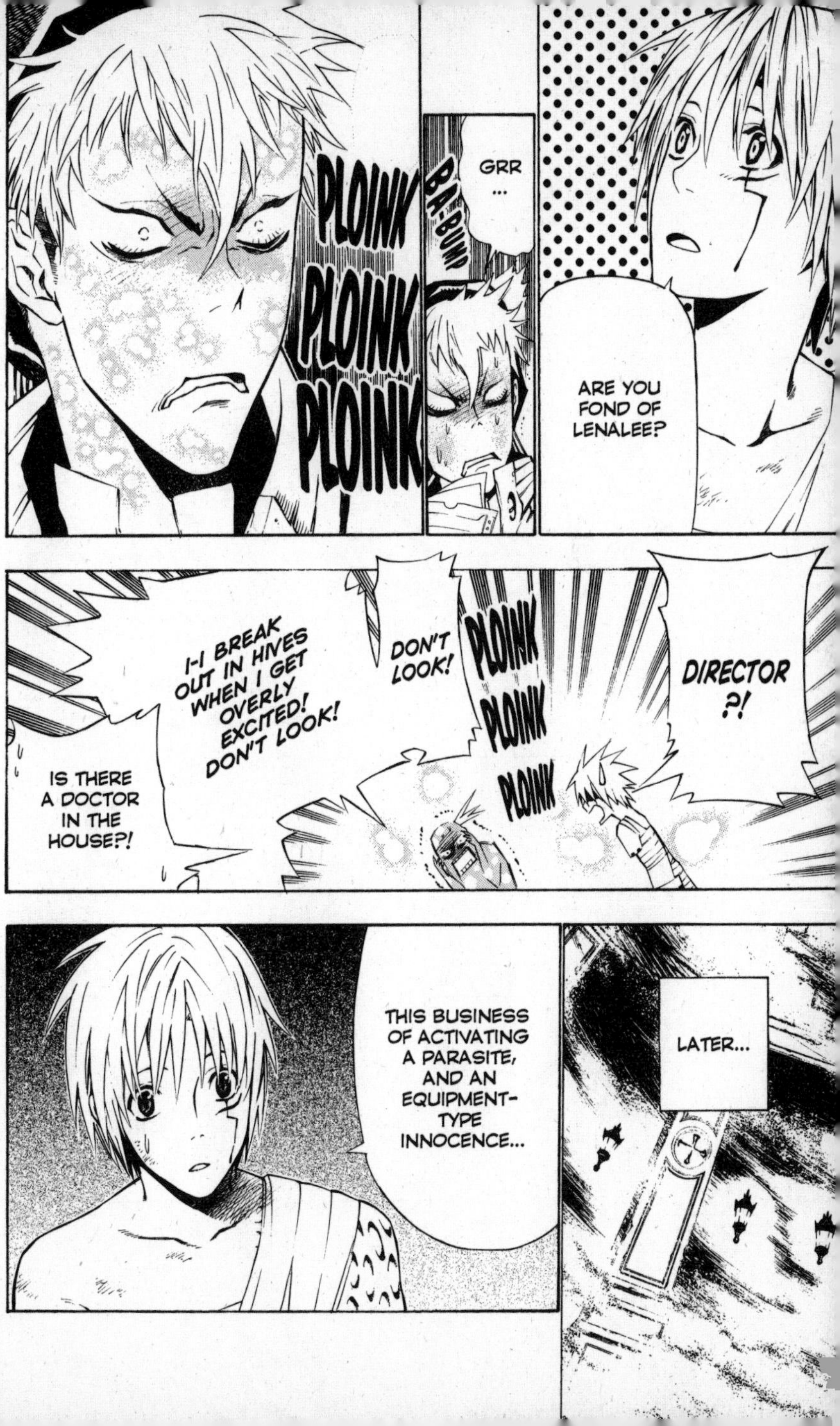
ARE YOU FOND OF LENALEE?
GRR ...
BA-BUMP
PLOINK PLOINK PLOINK
DIRECTOR ?!
DON'T LOOK!
PLOINK PLOINK PLOINK
I-I BREAK OUT IN HIVES WHEN I GET OVERLY EXCITED! DON'T LOOK!
IS THERE A DOCTOR IN THE HOUSE?!
LATER...
THIS BUSINESS OF ACTIVATING A PARASITE, AND AN EQUIPMENT-TYPE INNOCENCE...

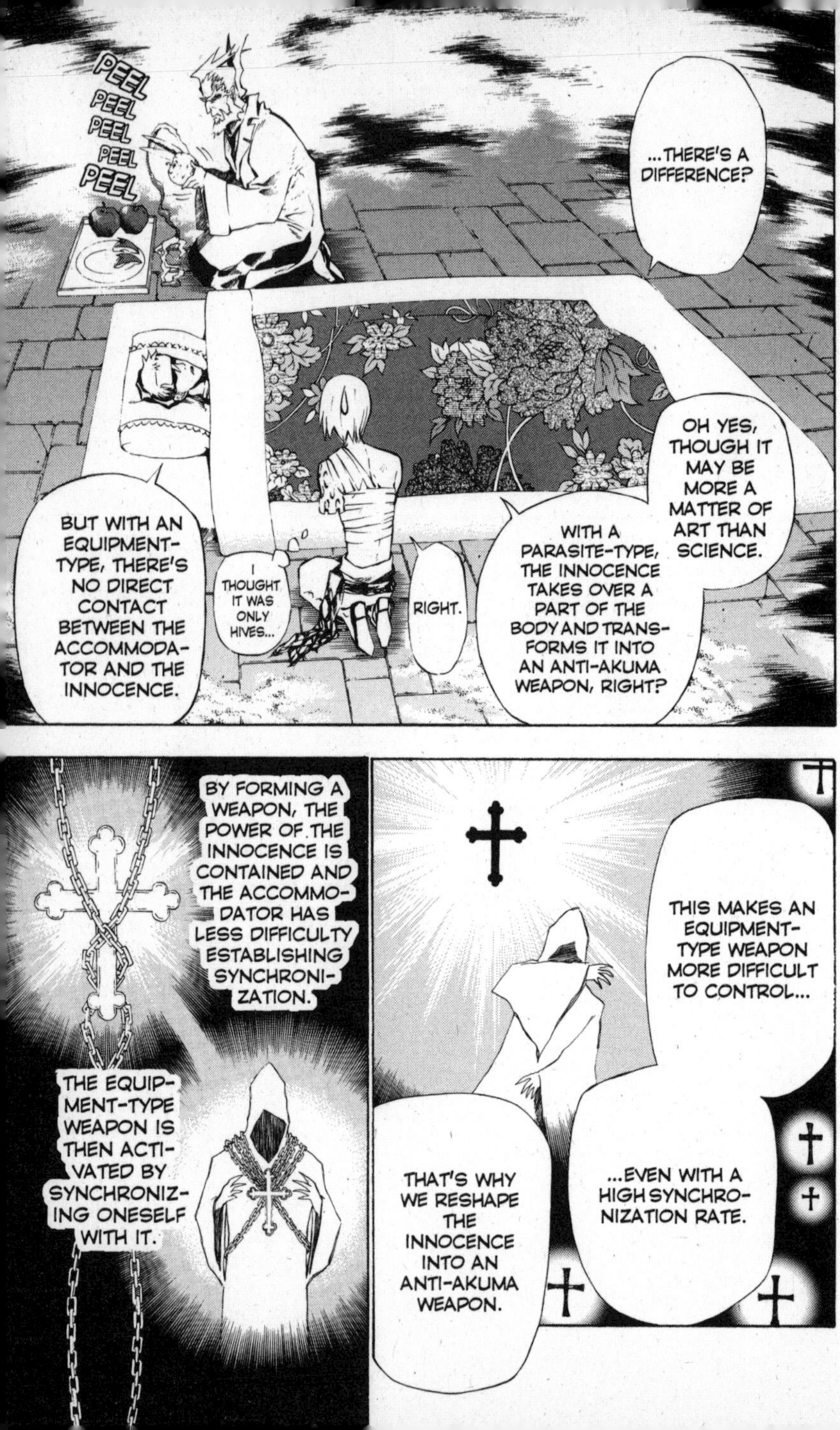
...THERE'S A DIFFERENCE?
PEEL PEEL PEEL PEEL PEEL
OH YES, THOUGH IT MAY BE MORE A MATTER OF ART THAN SCIENCE.
WITH A PARASITE-TYPE, THE INNOCENCE TAKES OVER A PART OF THE BODY AND TRANSFORMS IT INTO AN ANTI-AKUMA WEAPON, RIGHT?
RIGHT.
I THOUGHT IT WAS ONLY HIVES...
BUT WITH AN EQUIPMENT-TYPE, THERE'S NO DIRECT CONTACT BETWEEN THE ACCOMMODATOR AND THE INNOCENCE.
THIS MAKES AN EQUIPMENT-TYPE WEAPON MORE DIFFICULT TO CONTROL...
...EVEN WITH A HIGH SYNCHRONIZATION RATE.
THAT'S WHY WE RESHAPE THE INNOCENCE INTO AN ANTI-AKUMA WEAPON.
BY FORMING A WEAPON, THE POWER OF THE INNOCENCE IS CONTAINED AND THE ACCOMMODATOR HAS LESS DIFFICULTY ESTABLISHING SYNCHRONIZATION.
THE EQUIPMENT-TYPE WEAPON IS THEN ACTIVATED BY SYNCHRONIZING ONESELF WITH IT.

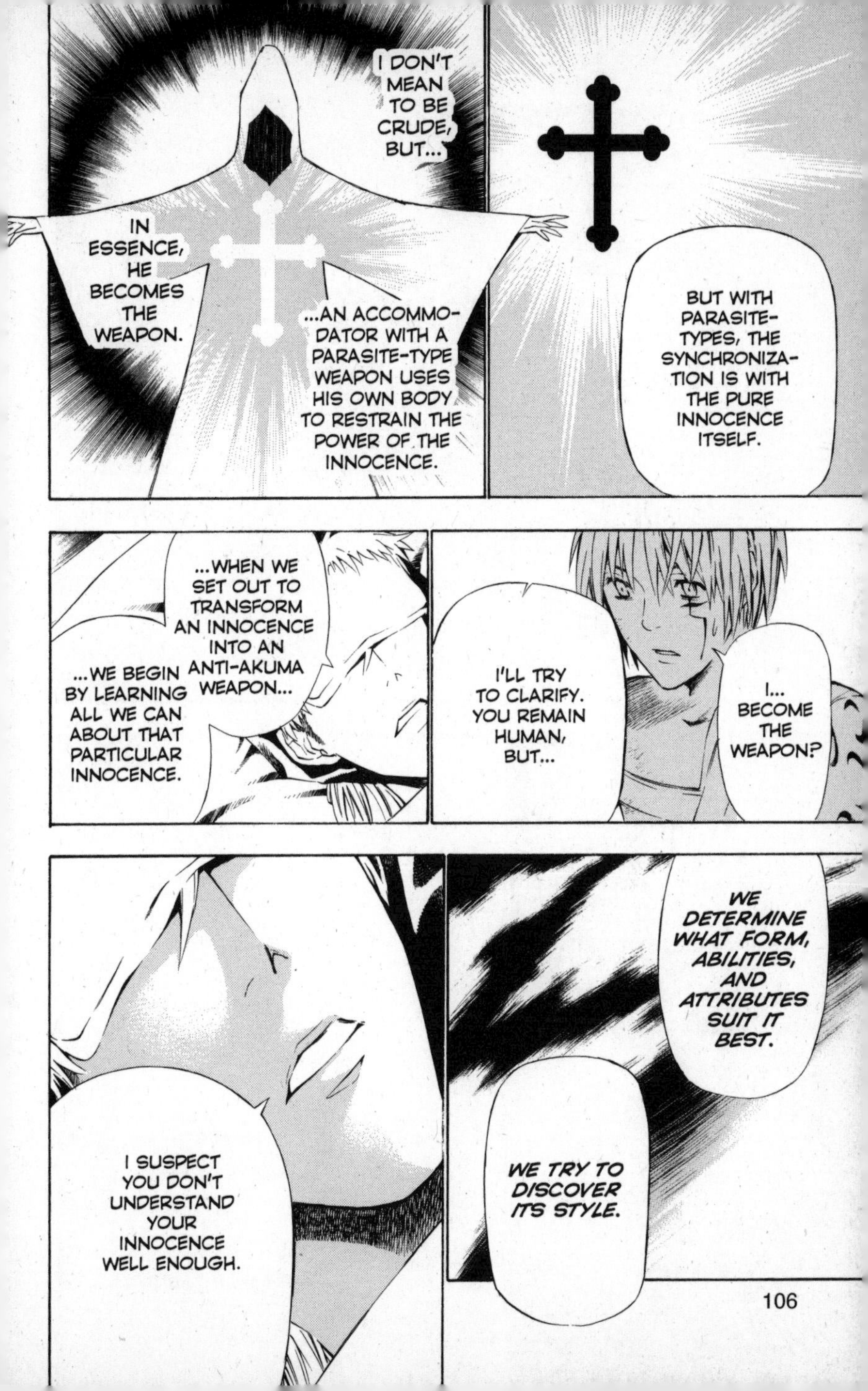
BUT WITH PARASITE-TYPES, THE SYNCHRONIZATION IS WITH THE PURE INNOCENCE ITSELF.
I DON'T MEAN TO BE CRUDE, BUT...
...AN ACCOMMODATOR WITH A PARASITE-TYPE WEAPON USES HIS OWN BODY TO RESTRAIN THE POWER OF THE INNOCENCE.
IN ESSENCE, HE BECOMES THE WEAPON.
I... BECOME THE WEAPON?
I'LL TRY TO CLARIFY. YOU REMAIN HUMAN, BUT...
...WHEN WE SET OUT TO TRANSFORM AN INNOCENCE INTO AN ANTI-AKUMA WEAPON...
...WE BEGIN BY LEARNING ALL WE CAN ABOUT THAT PARTICULAR INNOCENCE.
WE DETERMINE WHAT FORM, ABILITIES, AND ATTRIBUTES SUIT IT BEST.
WE TRY TO DISCOVER ITS STYLE.
I SUSPECT YOU DON'T UNDERSTAND YOUR INNOCENCE WELL ENOUGH.

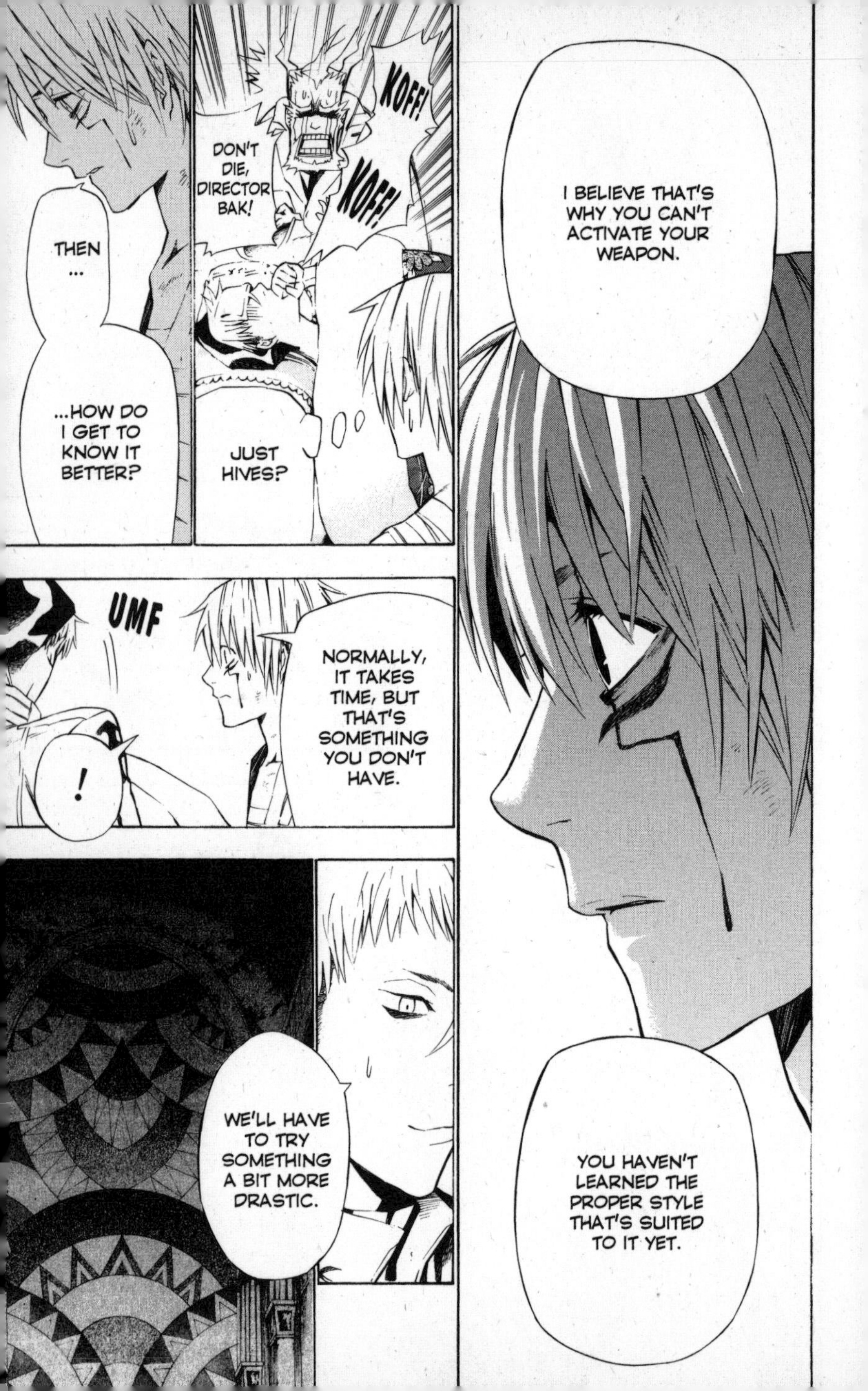
I BELIEVE THAT'S WHY YOU CAN'T ACTIVATE YOUR WEAPON.
YOU HAVEN'T LEARNED THE PROPER STYLE THAT'S SUITED TO IT YET.
KOFF!
KOFF!
DON'T DIE, DIRECTOR BAK!
JUST HIVES?
THEN ...
...HOW DO I GET TO KNOW IT BETTER?
NORMALLY, IT TAKES TIME, BUT THAT'S SOMETHING YOU DON'T HAVE.
UMF
!
WE'LL HAVE TO TRY SOMETHING A BIT MORE DRASTIC.

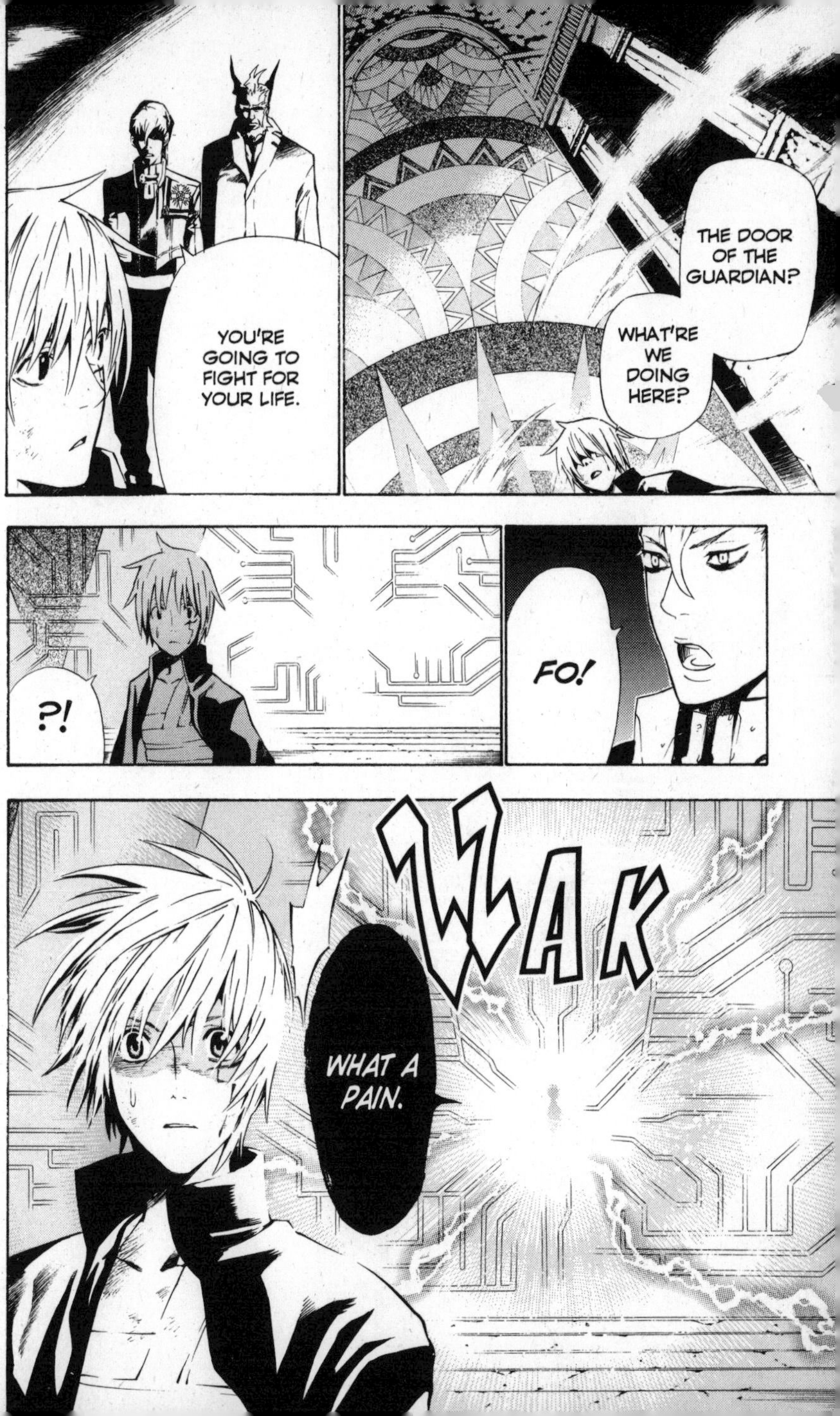
THE DOOR OF THE GUARDIAN?
WHAT'RE WE DOING HERE?
YOU'RE GOING TO FIGHT FOR YOUR LIFE.
FO!
?!
WAK
WHAT A PAIN.

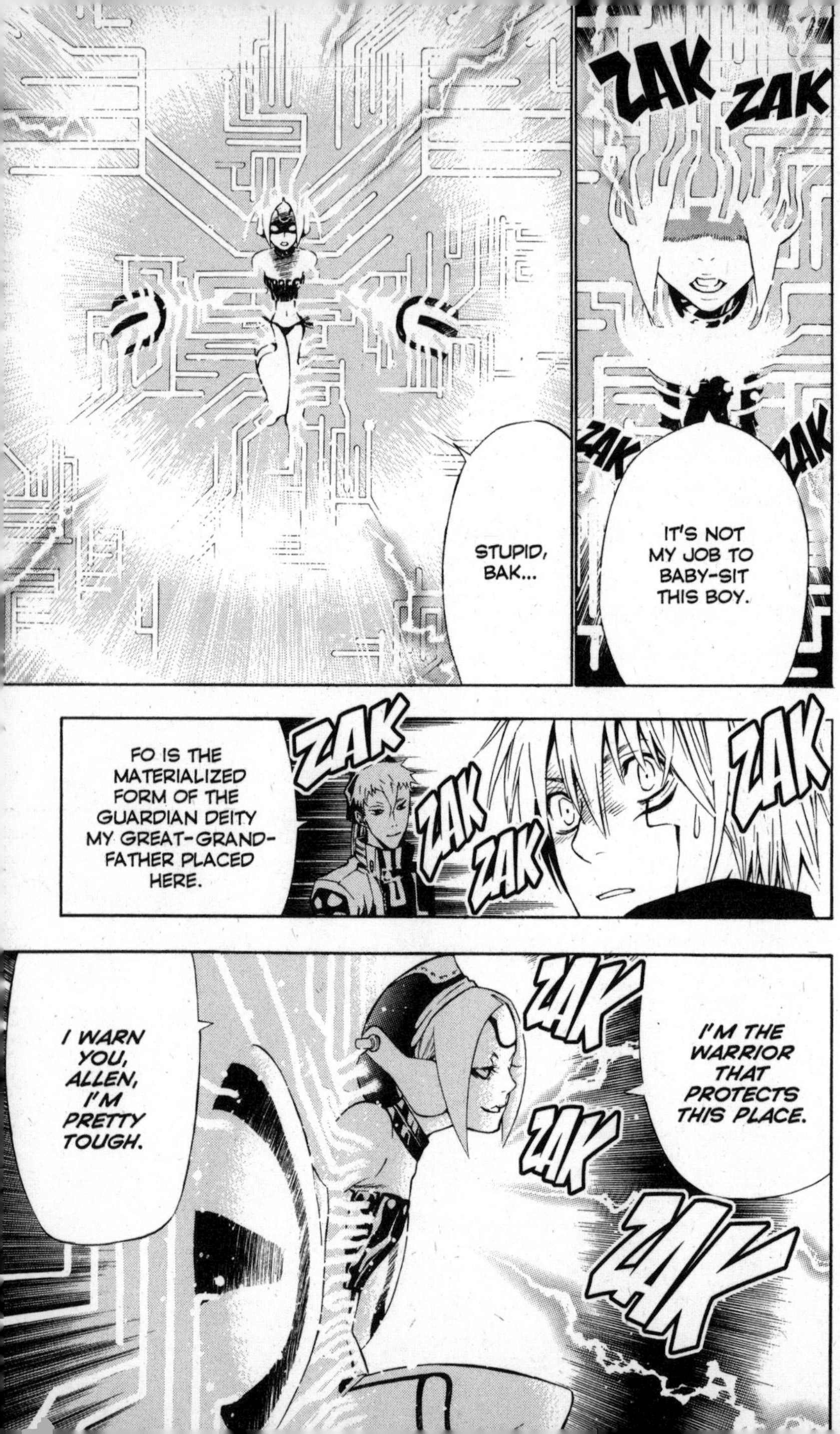
ZAK ZAK
ZAK ZAK
IT'S NOT MY JOB TO BABY-SIT THIS BOY.
STUPID, BAK...
ZAK
ZAK ZAK
ZAK
FO IS THE MATERIALIZED FORM OF THE GUARDIAN DEITY MY GREAT-GRAND-FATHER PLACED HERE.
I'M THE WARRIOR THAT PROTECTS THIS PLACE.
ZAK
ZAK
ZAK
I WARN YOU, ALLEN, I'M PRETTY TOUGH.

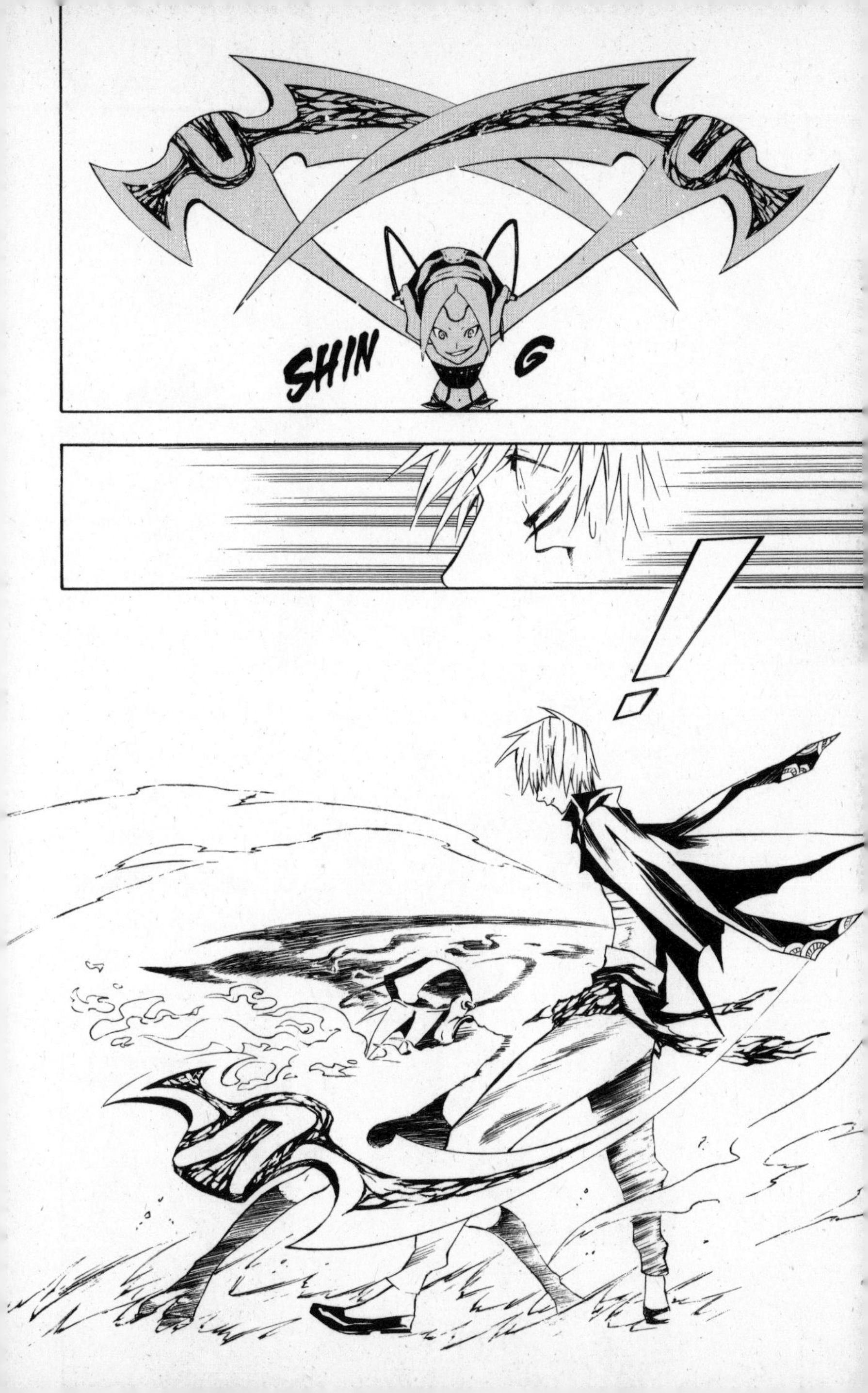
SHIN G
!

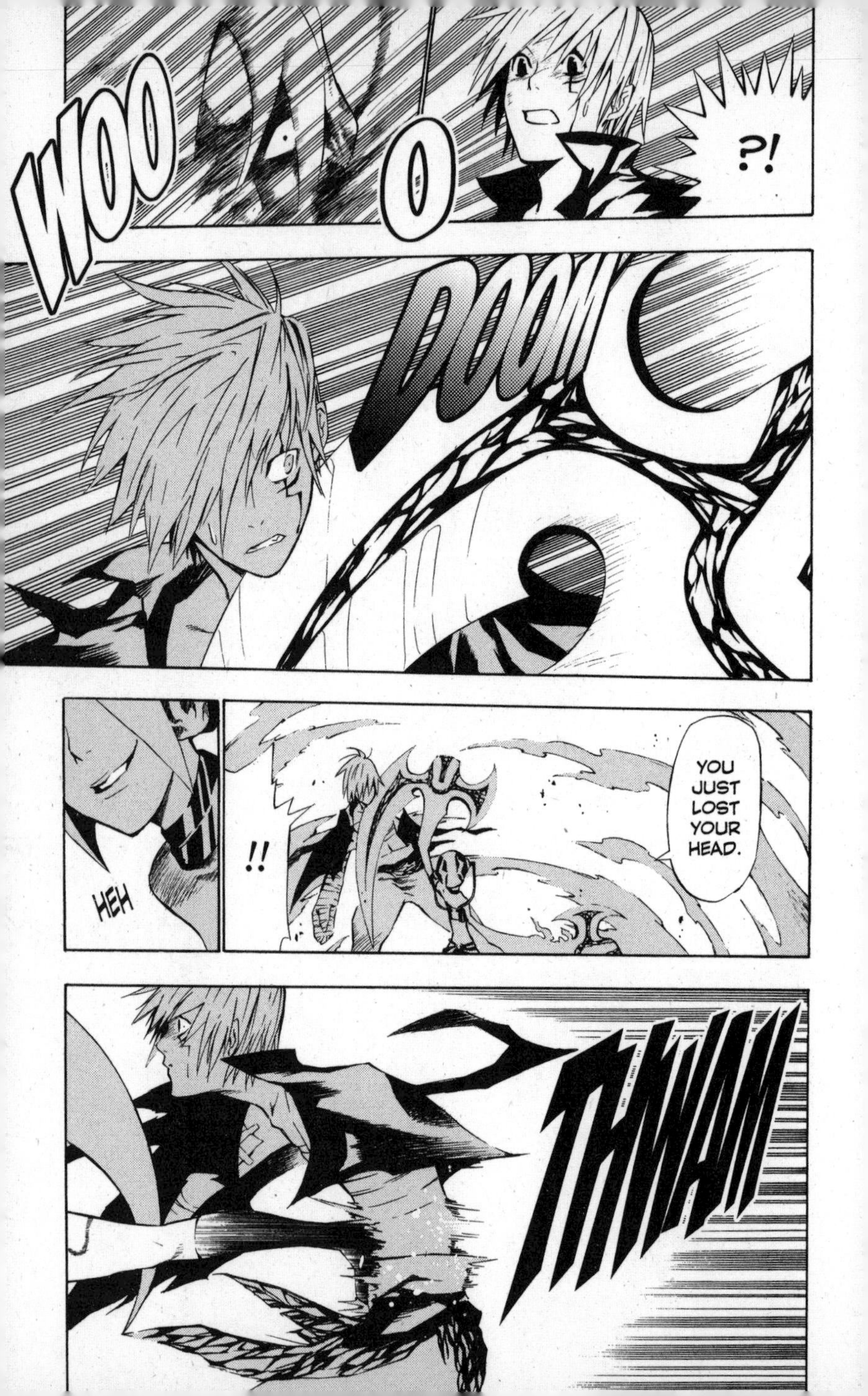

?!
WOOO
DOOM
YOU JUST LOST YOUR HEAD.
!!
HEH
THWAM

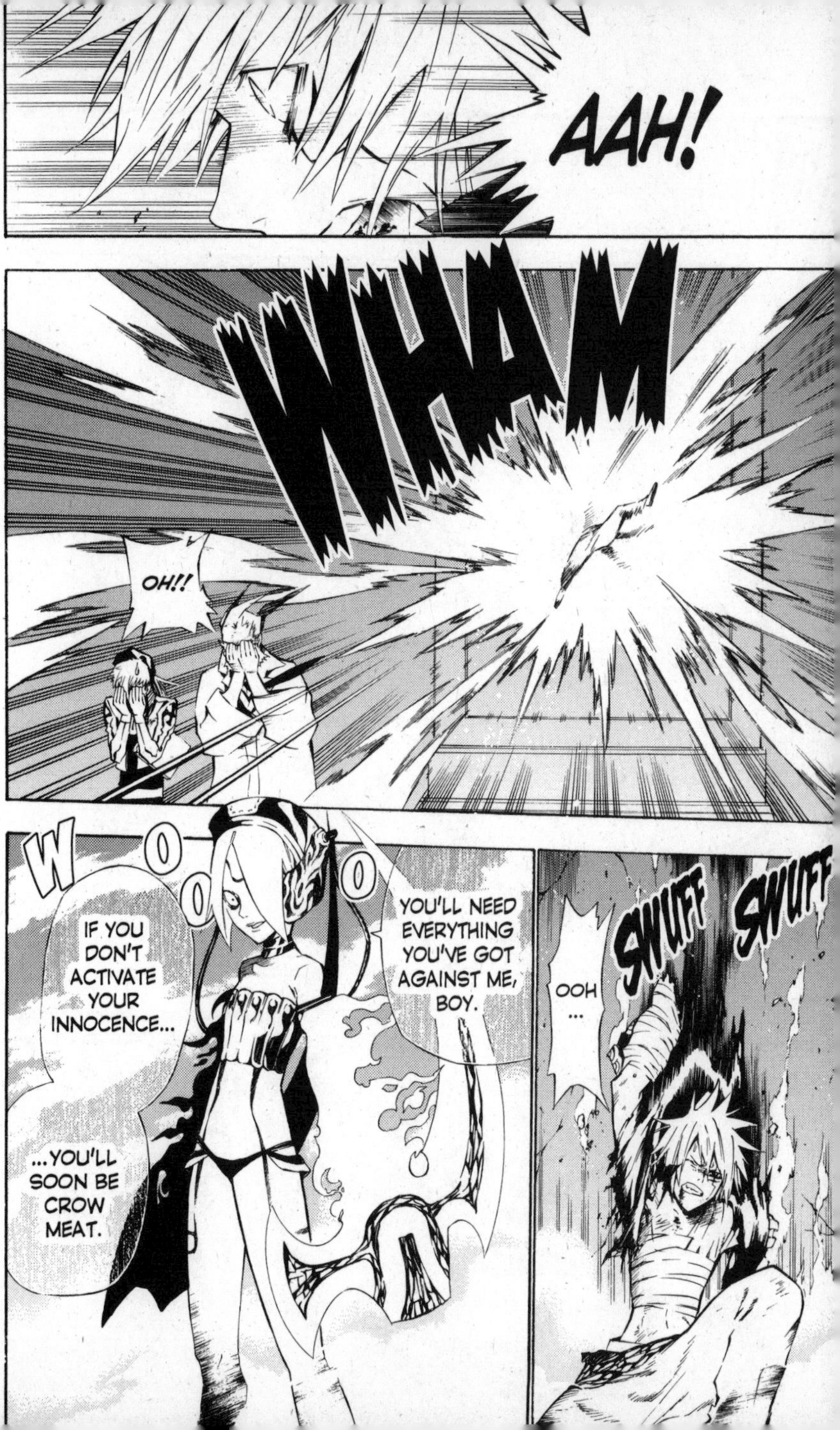
AAH!
WHAM
OH!!
SWUFF SWUFF
OOH ...
WOOO
YOU'LL NEED EVERYTHING YOU'VE GOT AGAINST ME, BOY.
IF YOU DON'T ACTIVATE YOUR INNOCENCE...
...YOU'LL SOON BE CROW MEAT.

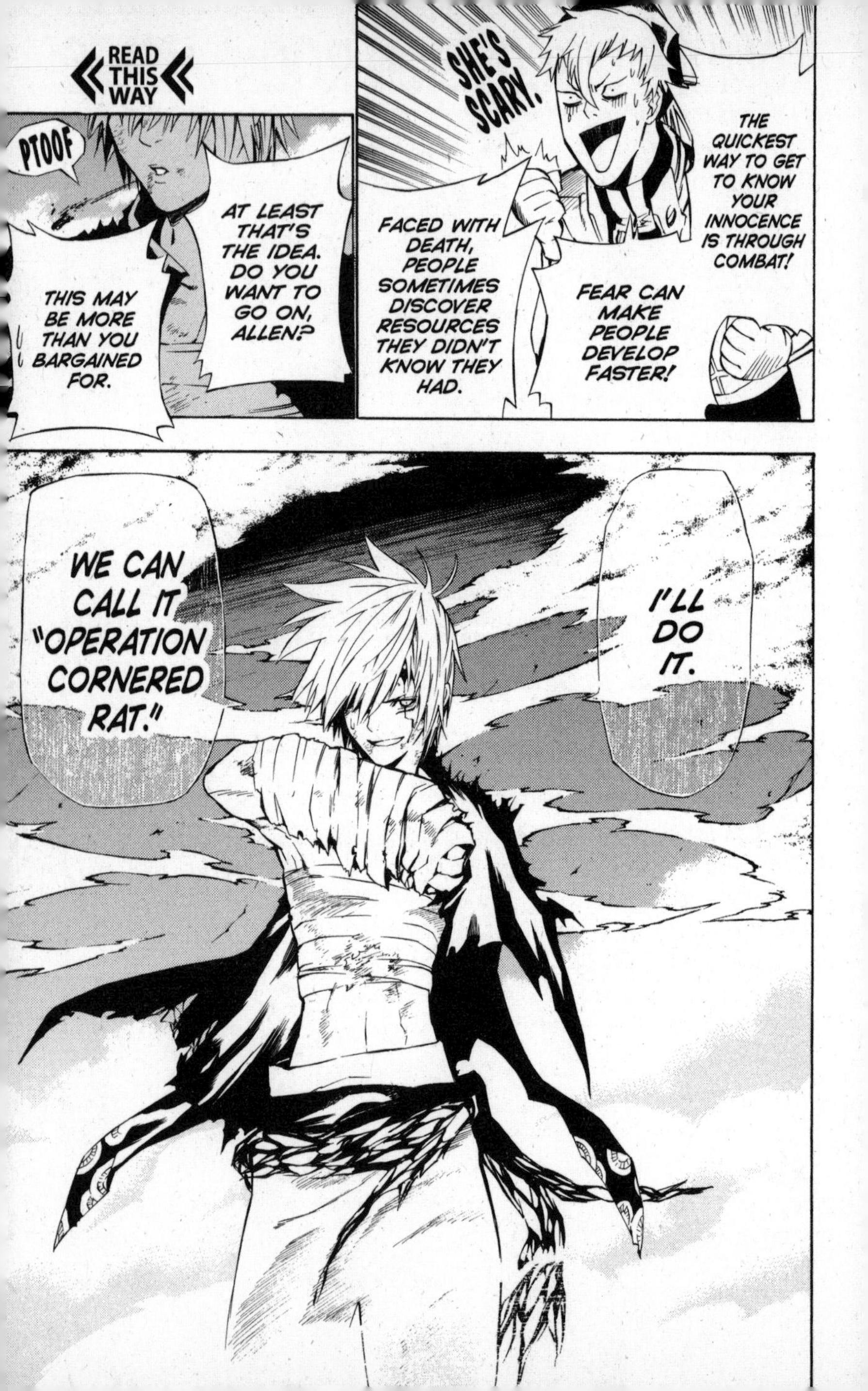
READ THIS WAY
THE QUICKEST WAY TO GET TO KNOW YOUR INNOCENCE IS THROUGH COMBAT!
SHE'S SCARY.
FEAR CAN MAKE PEOPLE DEVELOP FASTER!
FACED WITH DEATH, PEOPLE SOMETIMES DISCOVER RESOURCES THEY DIDN'T KNOW THEY HAD.
AT LEAST THAT'S THE IDEA. DO YOU WANT TO GO ON, ALLEN?
PTOOF
THIS MAY BE MORE THAN YOU BARGAINED FOR.
I'LL DO IT.
WE CAN CALL IT "OPERATION CORNERED RAT."

KOMUI'S DISCUSSION ROOM, VOL. 6

Q: WHAT TYPE OF WOMAN DOES LAVI GO FOR?
A: (LAVI) HMM...MY TYPE? I LIKE WIDOWS.
(ALLEN) I BET LAVI LIKES OLDER WOMEN. (GLARE)
(LAVI) NOT EXACTLY. AFTER ALL, I'M INTERESTED IN LENALEE. MOSTLY I GO FOR LADIES BETWEEN THE AGES OF 18 AND 40. (GLINTING EYES)
(ALLEN) ...
Q: IF LAVI AND ALLEN WERE TO HAVE A STARING CONTEST, WHO WOULD WIN?
A: (LAVI) HEY!
(ALLEN) SHALL WE?
♬LET'S HAVE A STARE OFF. HERE WE GO!♪
(ALLEN & LAVI) ... (MAKING FACES)
...10 SECONDS PASS
(ALLEN & LAVI) ... (LAVI ACTIVATES HIS SPECIAL FACIAL EXPRESSION)
...20 SECONDS PASS
(ALLEN & LAVI) ... (ALLEN ACTIVATES HIS SPECIAL FACIAL EXPRESSION)
(LAVI) WA HA HA HA HA HA HA HA HA HA HA HA HA HA HA HA HA HA HA HA!!!
(ALLEN) I WIN! (MAKING FIST)
(LAVI) W-WOW, THAT WAS SOME LOOK. (TEARS IN EYES)
(ALLEN) YOU WERE PRETTY GOOD TOO, LAVI. BUT IT LOOKS LIKE I'M OUT OF MITARASHI DANGO, SO CAN I GO NOW?
(LAVI) YEAH, I'M OUT OF SNACKS TOO.
OKAY THEN, THIS INSTALLMENT OF THE "DISCUSSION ROOM" IS OVER.
BYE-BYE!

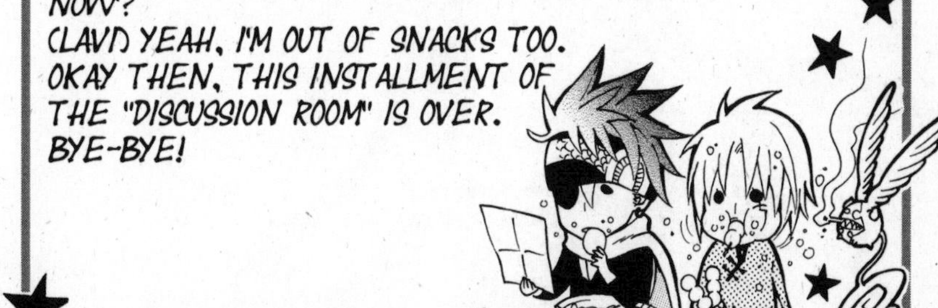

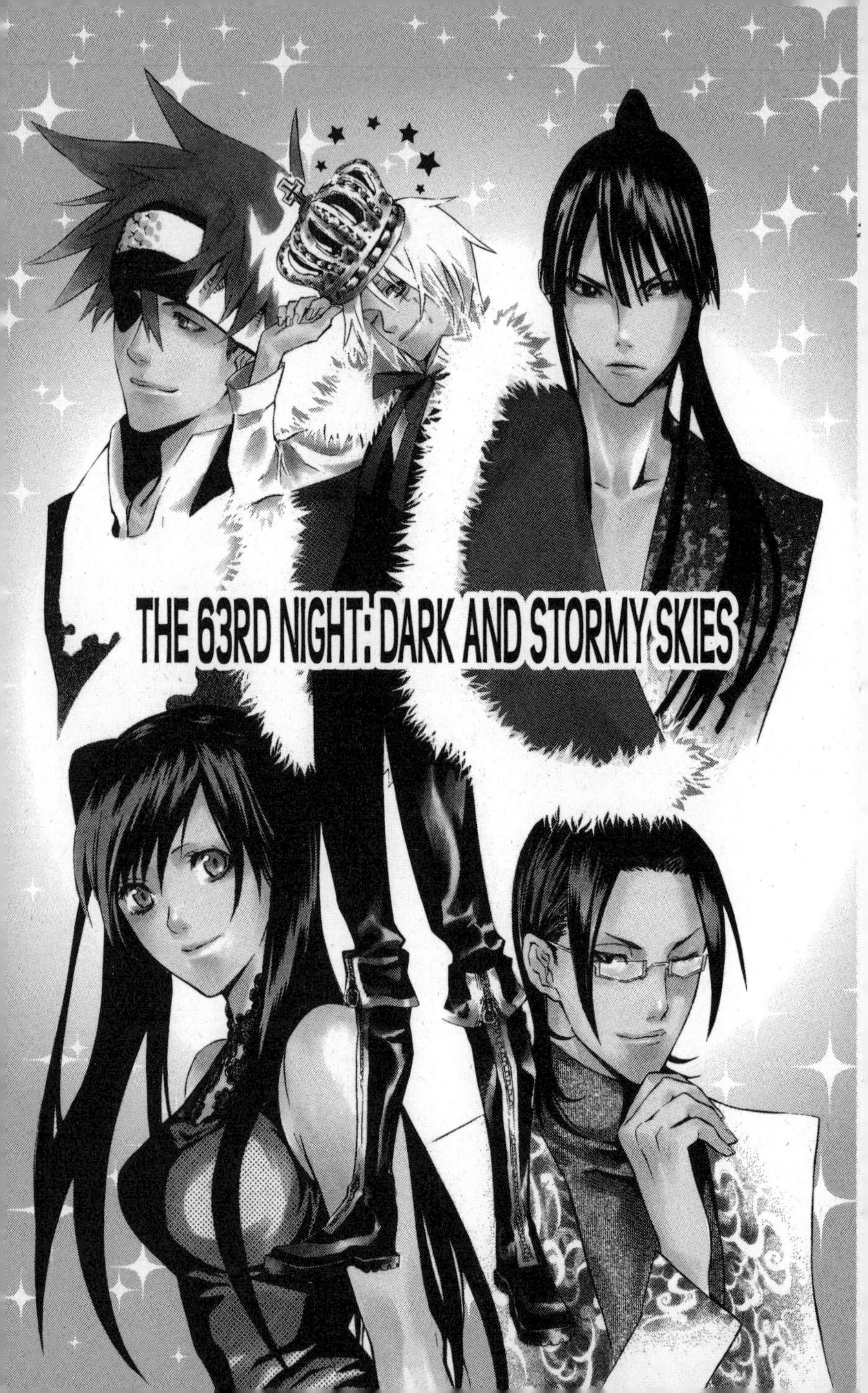
THE 63RD NIGHT: DARK AND STORMY SKIES

D.Gray-man
ANNOUNCING THE TOP TEN!
THE FIRST ANNUAL CHARACTER POPULARITY POLL!!

1ST PLACE 8,062 VOTES	2ND PLACE 6,128 VOTES	3RD PLACE 5,782 VOTES
ALLEN WALKER	YU KANDA	LAVI

| 4TH PLACE 1,552 VOTES LENALEE LEE | 5TH PLACE 673 VOTES KOMUI LEE | 6TH PLACE 609 VOTES REEVER WENHAM | 7TH PLACE 602 VOTES TYKI MIKK |

| 8TH PLACE 591 VOTES ROAD KAMELOT | 9TH PLACE 406 VOTES MIRANDA LOTTO | 10TH PLACE 383 VOTES CROSS MARIAN | SEE PAGE 132 FOR 11TH THROUGH 20TH PLACES! |

* THIS POPULARITY POLL WAS CONDUCTED TO COMMEMORATE *D.GRAY-MAN'S* FIRST ANNIVERSARY IN *WEEKLY SHONEN JUMP*.

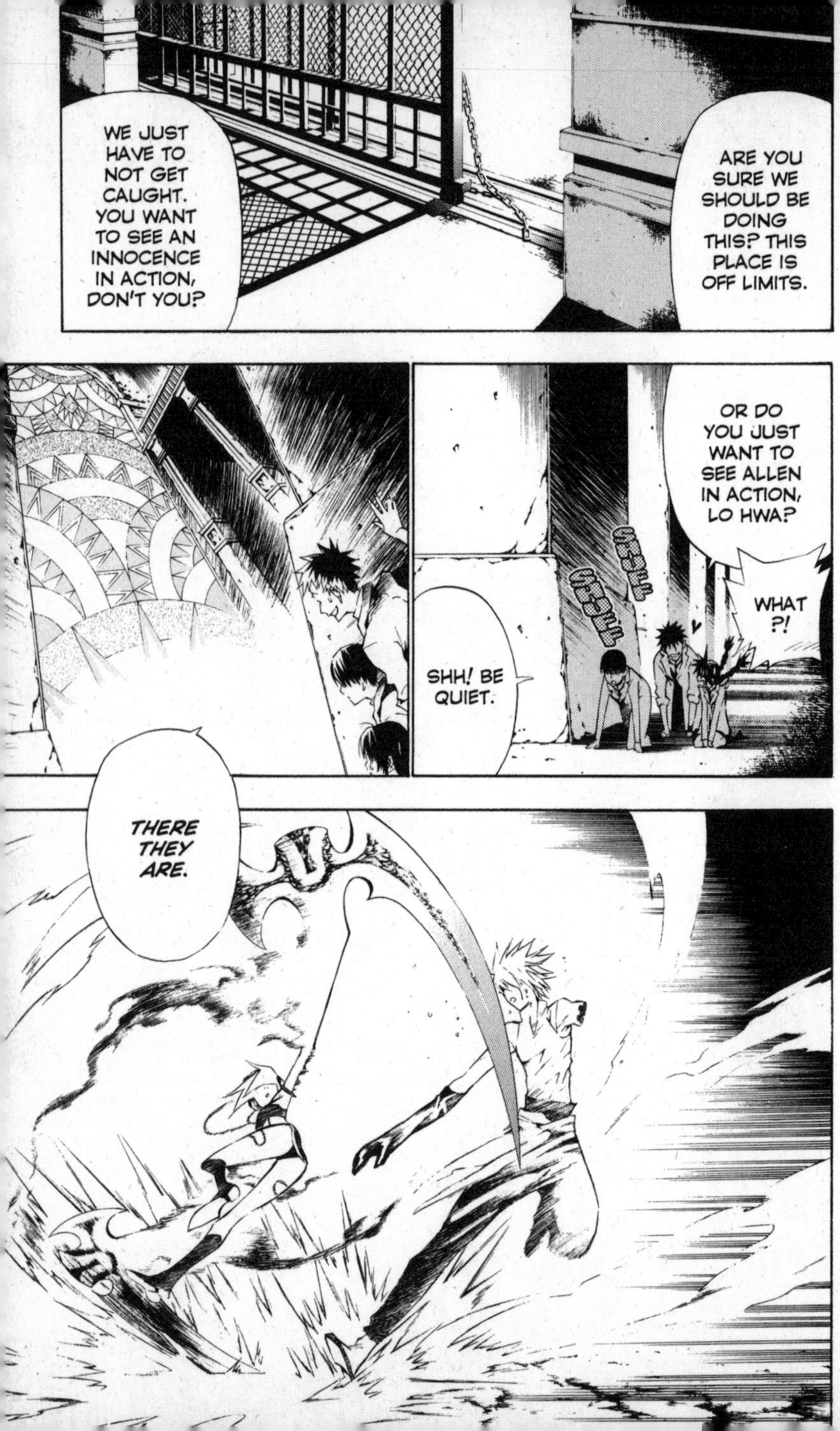
ARE YOU SURE WE SHOULD BE DOING THIS? THIS PLACE IS OFF LIMITS.
WE JUST HAVE TO NOT GET CAUGHT. YOU WANT TO SEE AN INNOCENCE IN ACTION, DON'T YOU?
OR DO YOU JUST WANT TO SEE ALLEN IN ACTION, LO HWA?
WHAT?!
SHH! BE QUIET.
THERE THEY ARE.

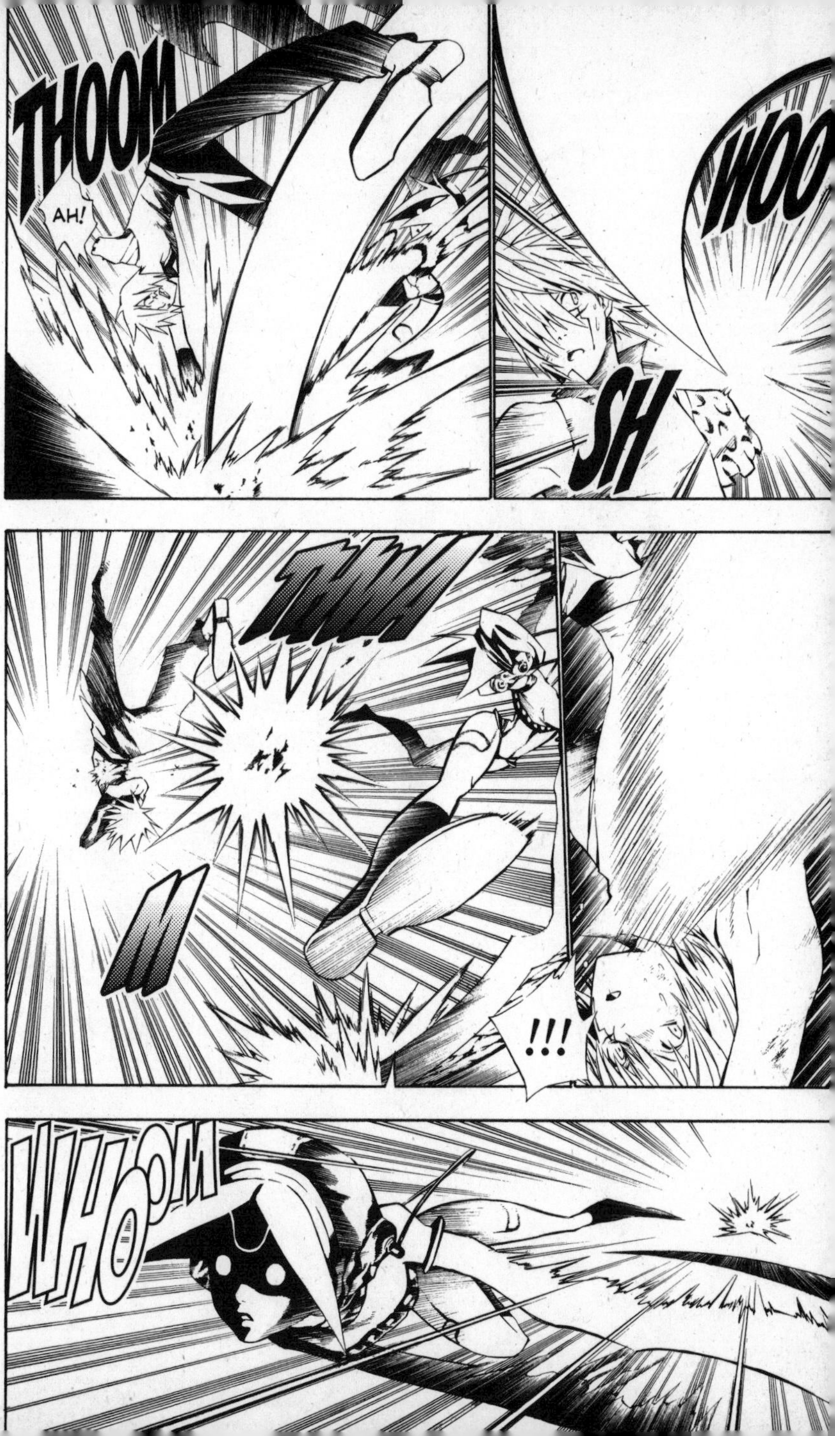
WHOO
SH
THOOM
AH!
!!!
THWAM
WHOOM

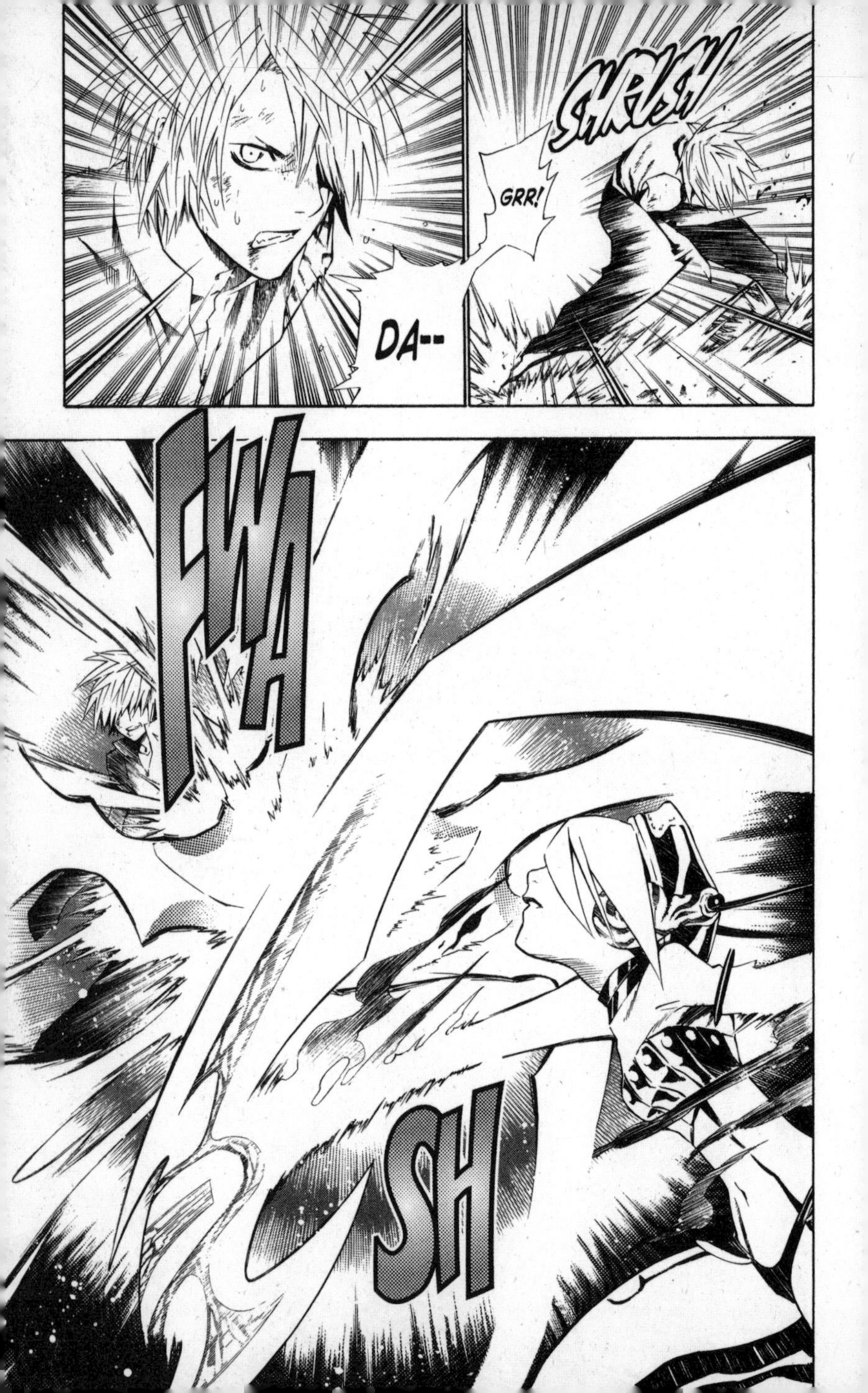
GRR!
DA--
FWA
SH

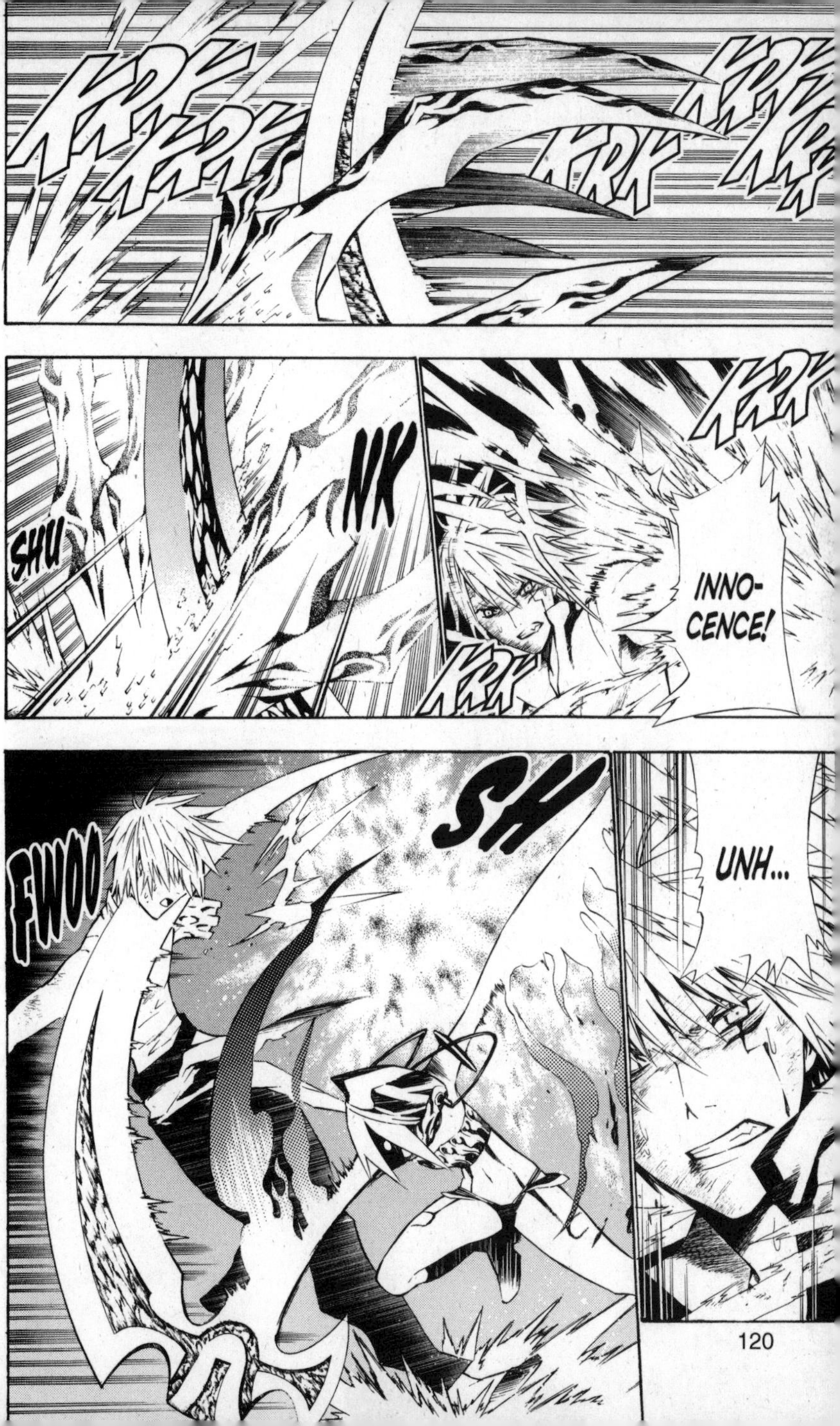
KRK
KRK
KRK
KRK
KRK
INNO-
CENCE!
KRK
NK
SHU
UNH...
SH
FWOO

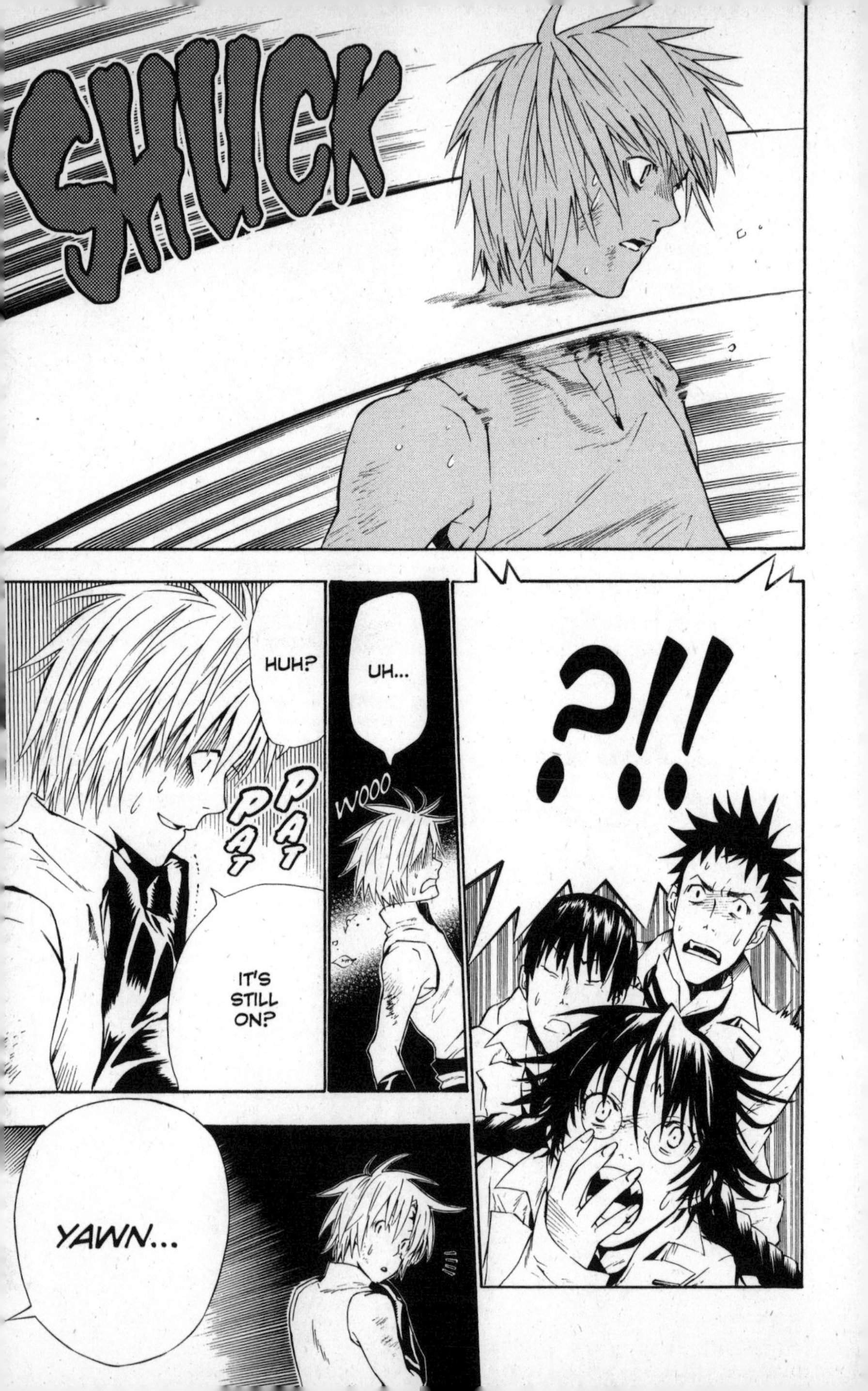
SHUCK
?!!
UH...
WOOO
HUH?
PAT PAT
IT'S STILL ON?
YAWN...

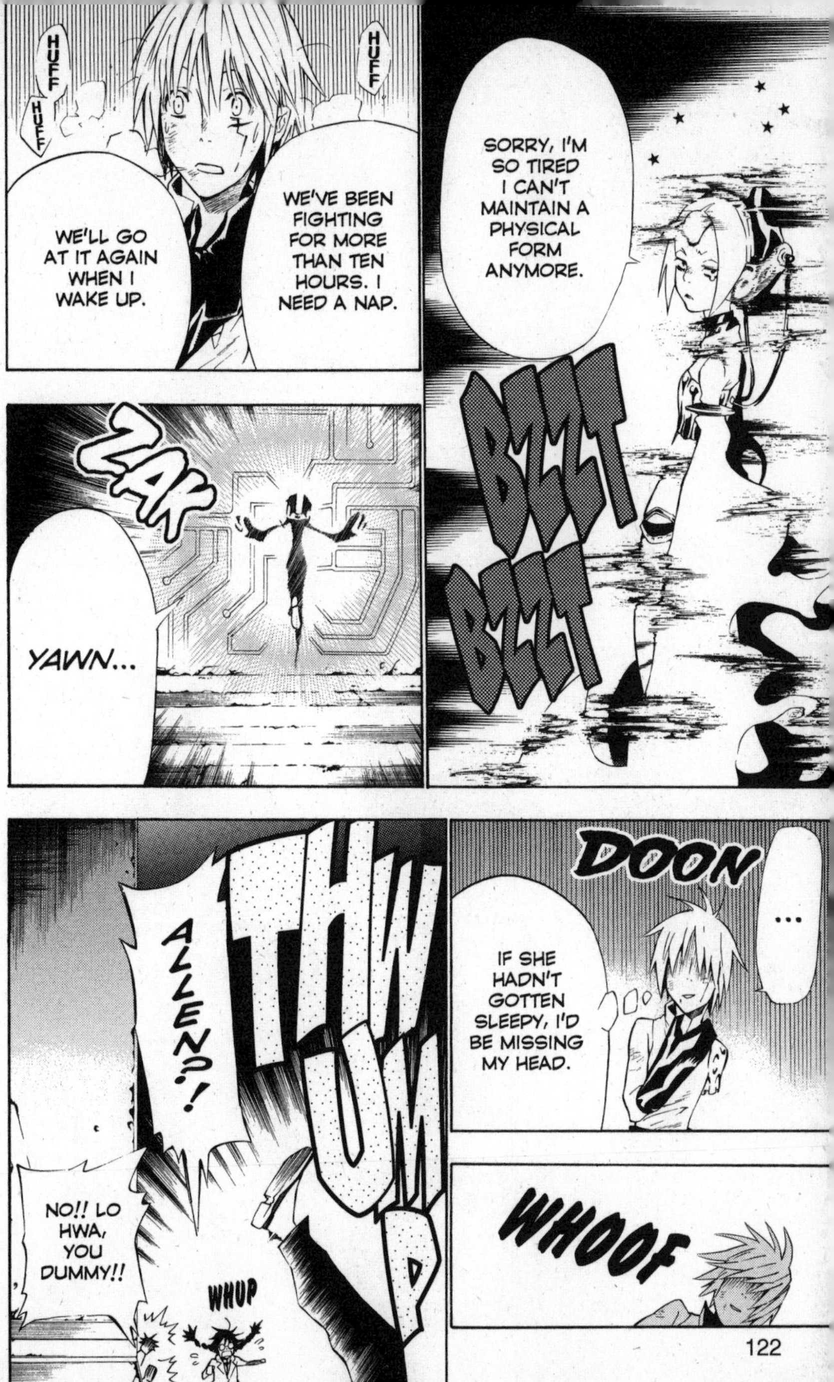
SORRY, I'M SO TIRED I CAN'T MAINTAIN A PHYSICAL FORM ANYMORE.
BZZT BZZT
HUFF
HUFF
HUFF
WE'VE BEEN FIGHTING FOR MORE THAN TEN HOURS. I NEED A NAP.
WE'LL GO AT IT AGAIN WHEN I WAKE UP.
ZAK
YAWN...
DOON
...
IF SHE HADN'T GOTTEN SLEEPY, I'D BE MISSING MY HEAD.
WHOOF
THWUMP
ALLEN?!
NO!! LO HWA, YOU DUMMY!!
WHUP

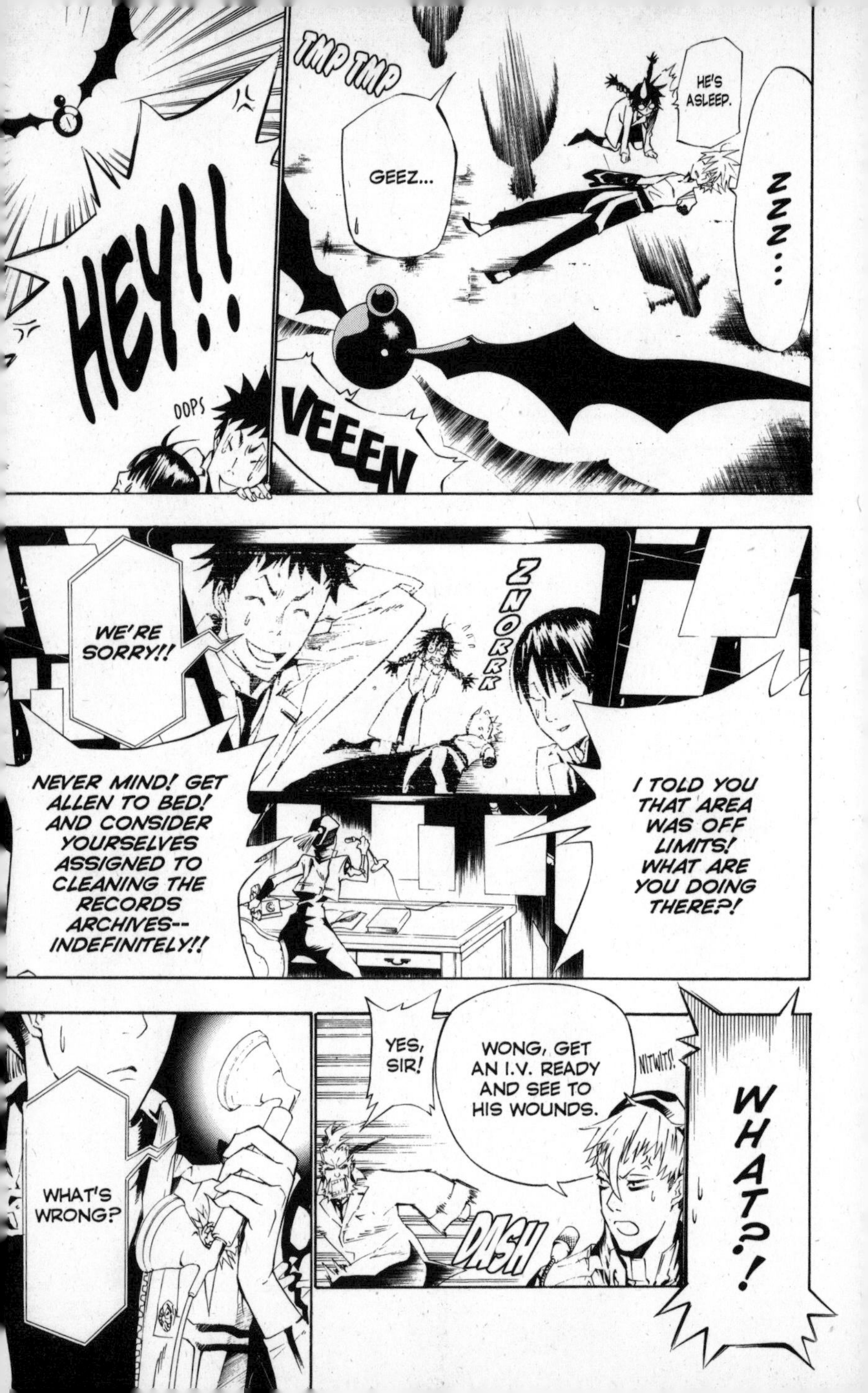
HE'S ASLEEP.
ZZZ...
TMP TMP
GEEZ...
VEEEN
HEY!!
OOPS
ZNORRK
I TOLD YOU THAT AREA WAS OFF LIMITS! WHAT ARE YOU DOING THERE?!
WE'RE SORRY!!
NEVER MIND! GET ALLEN TO BED! AND CONSIDER YOURSELVES ASSIGNED TO CLEANING THE RECORDS ARCHIVES--INDEFINITELY!!
WHAT?!
NITWITS!
WONG, GET AN I.V. READY AND SEE TO HIS WOUNDS.
YES, SIR!
DASH
WHAT'S WRONG?

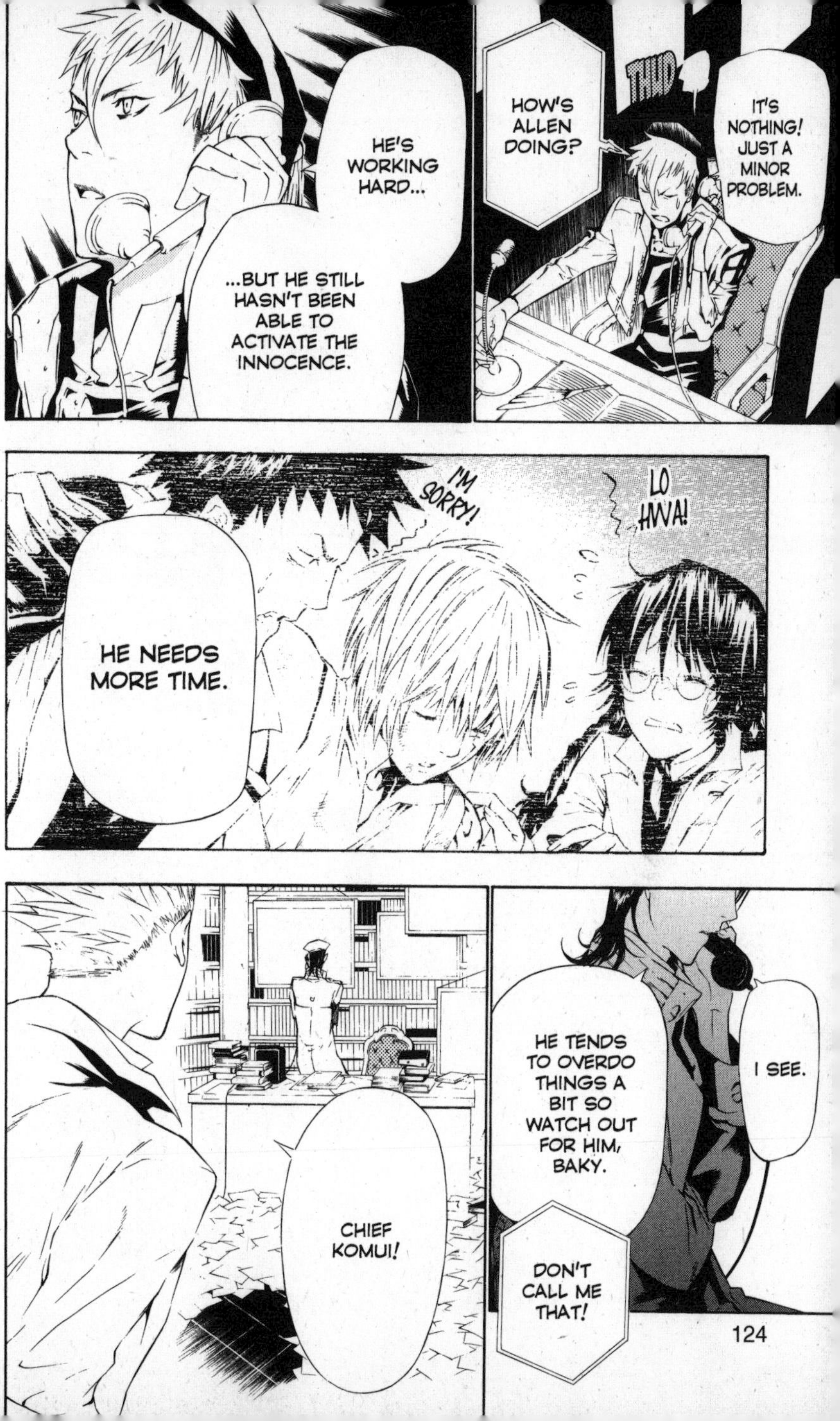
THUD
IT'S NOTHING! JUST A MINOR PROBLEM.
HOW'S ALLEN DOING?
HE'S WORKING HARD...
...BUT HE STILL HASN'T BEEN ABLE TO ACTIVATE THE INNOCENCE.
LO HWA!
I'M SORRY!
HE NEEDS MORE TIME.
I SEE.
HE TENDS TO OVERDO THINGS A BIT SO WATCH OUT FOR HIM, BAKY.
DON'T CALL ME THAT!
CHIEF KOMUI!

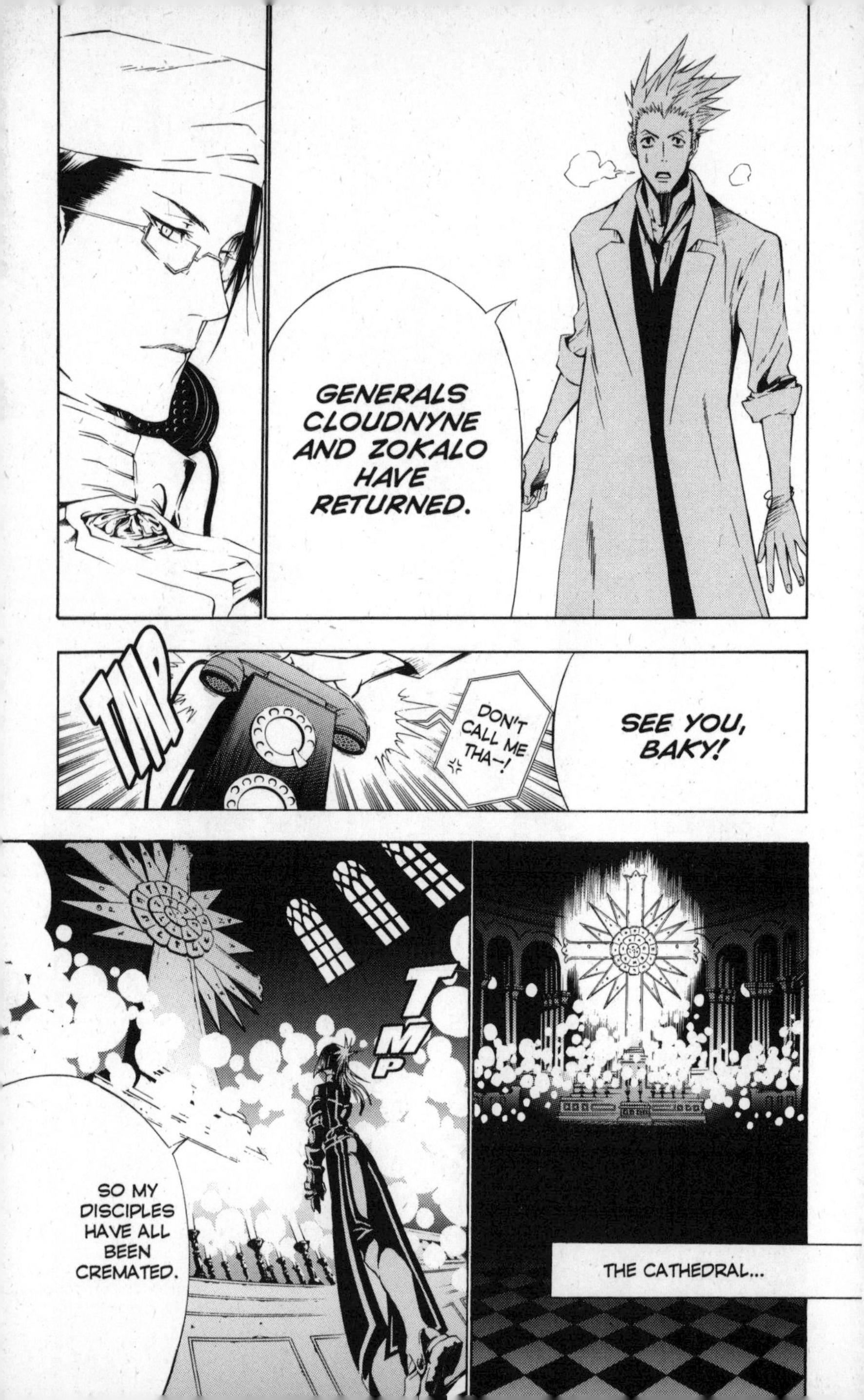
GENERALS CLOUDNYNE AND ZOKALO HAVE RETURNED.
SEE YOU, BAKY!
DON'T CALL ME THA--!
TMP
THE CATHEDRAL...
TMP
SO MY DISCIPLES HAVE ALL BEEN CREMATED.

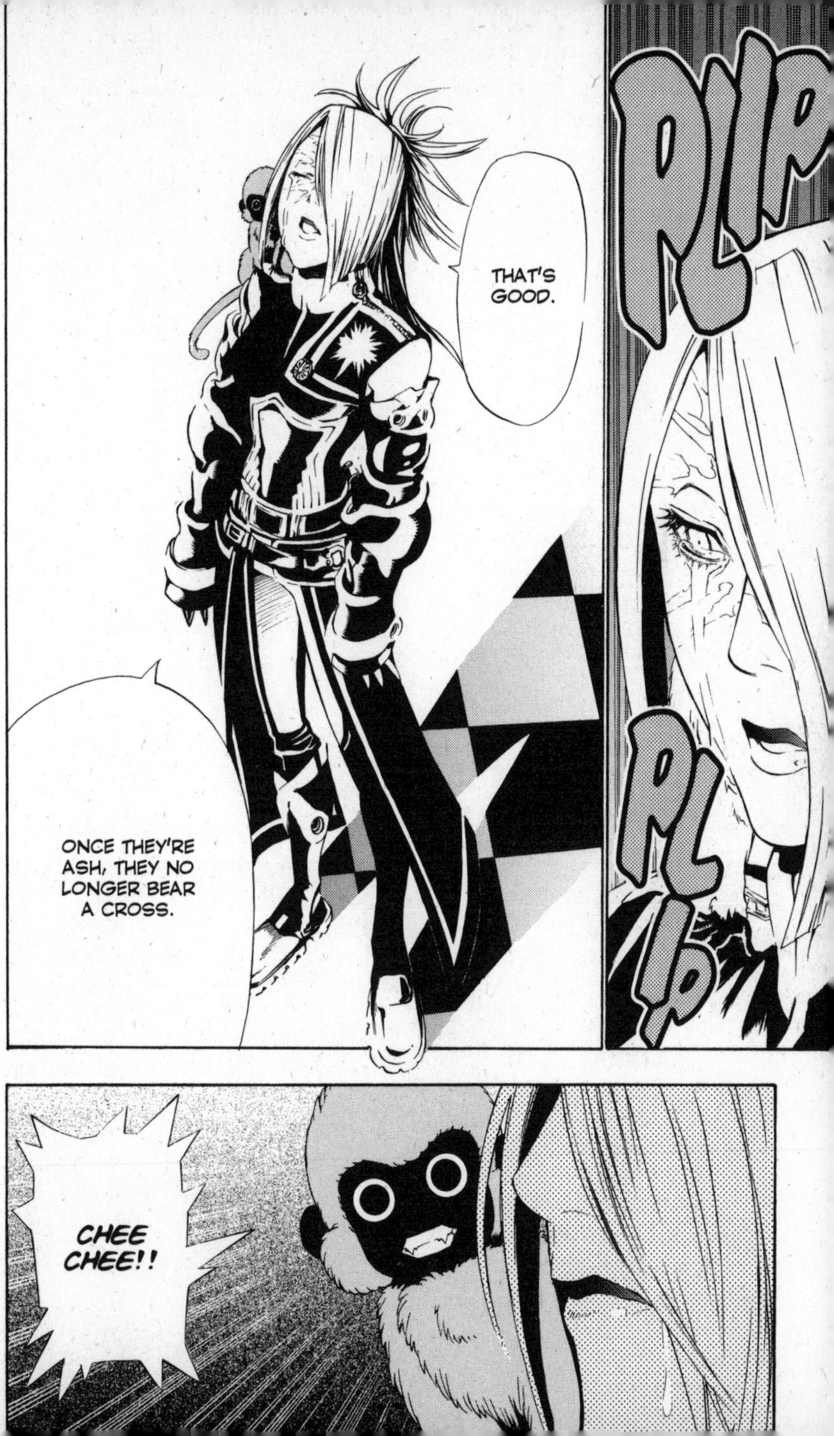
PLIP
PLIP
THAT'S GOOD.
ONCE THEY'RE ASH, THEY NO LONGER BEAR A CROSS.
CHEE CHEE!!

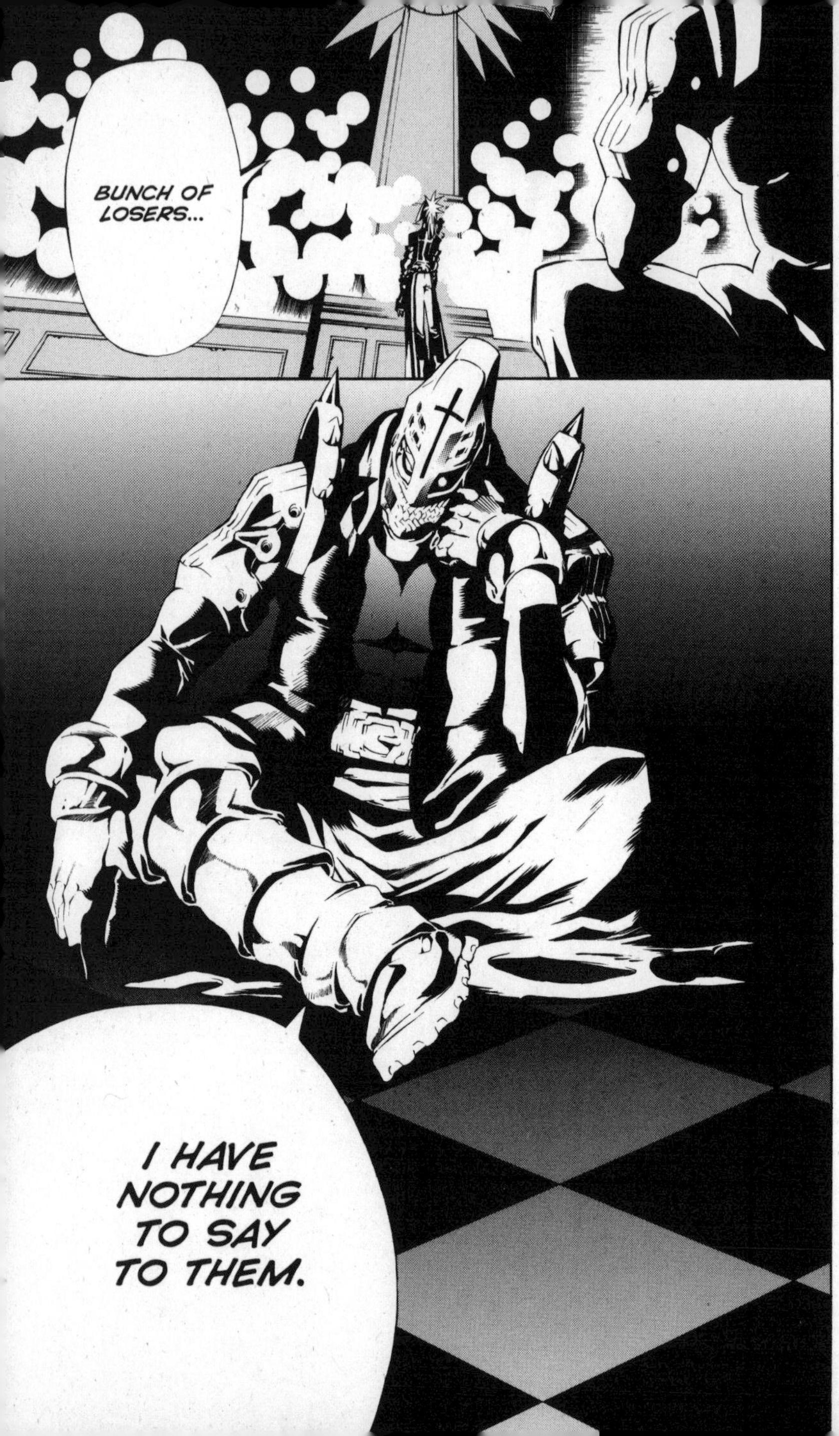
BUNCH OF LOSERS...
I HAVE NOTHING TO SAY TO THEM.

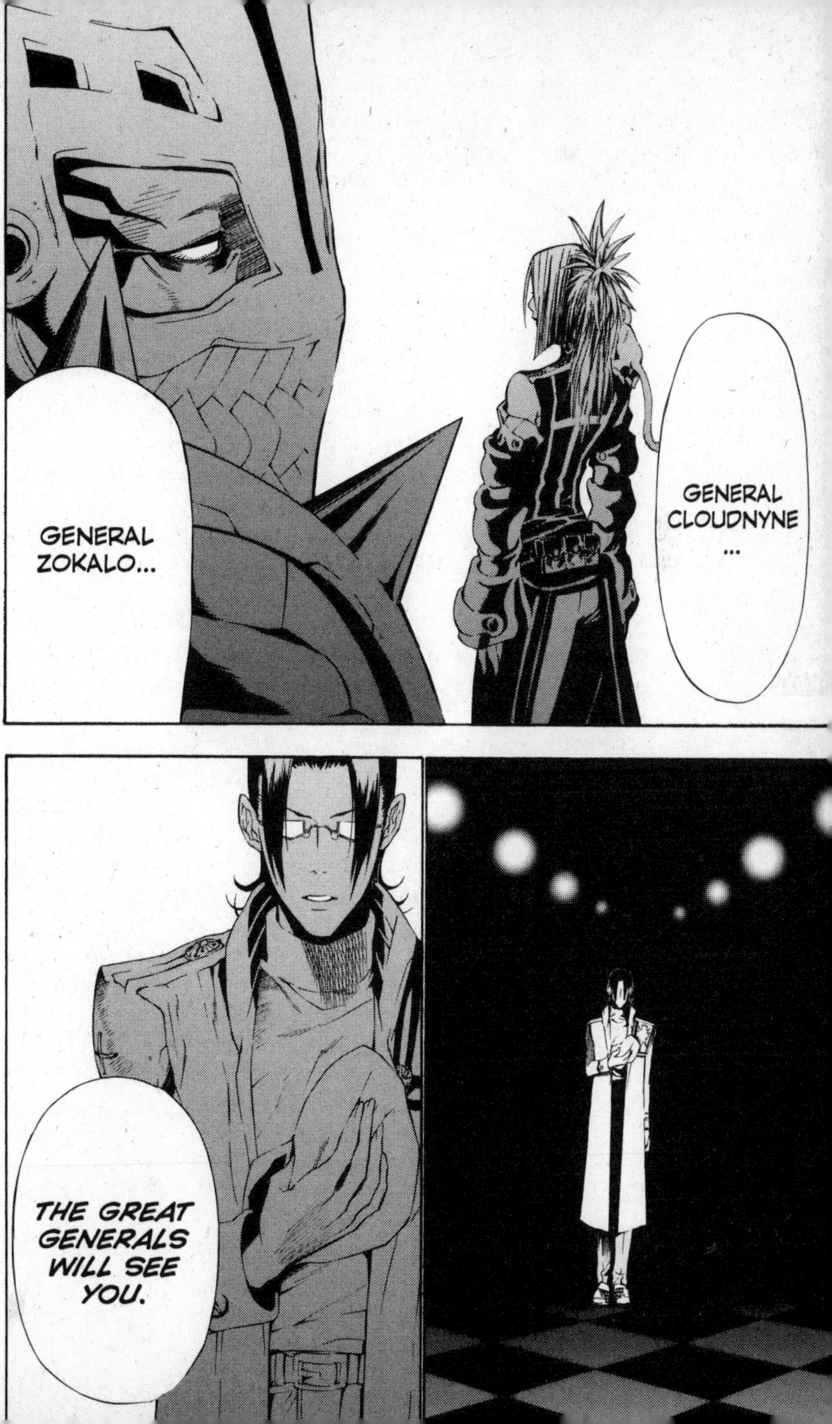
GENERAL CLOUDNYNE ...
GENERAL ZOKALO...
THE GREAT GENERALS WILL SEE YOU.

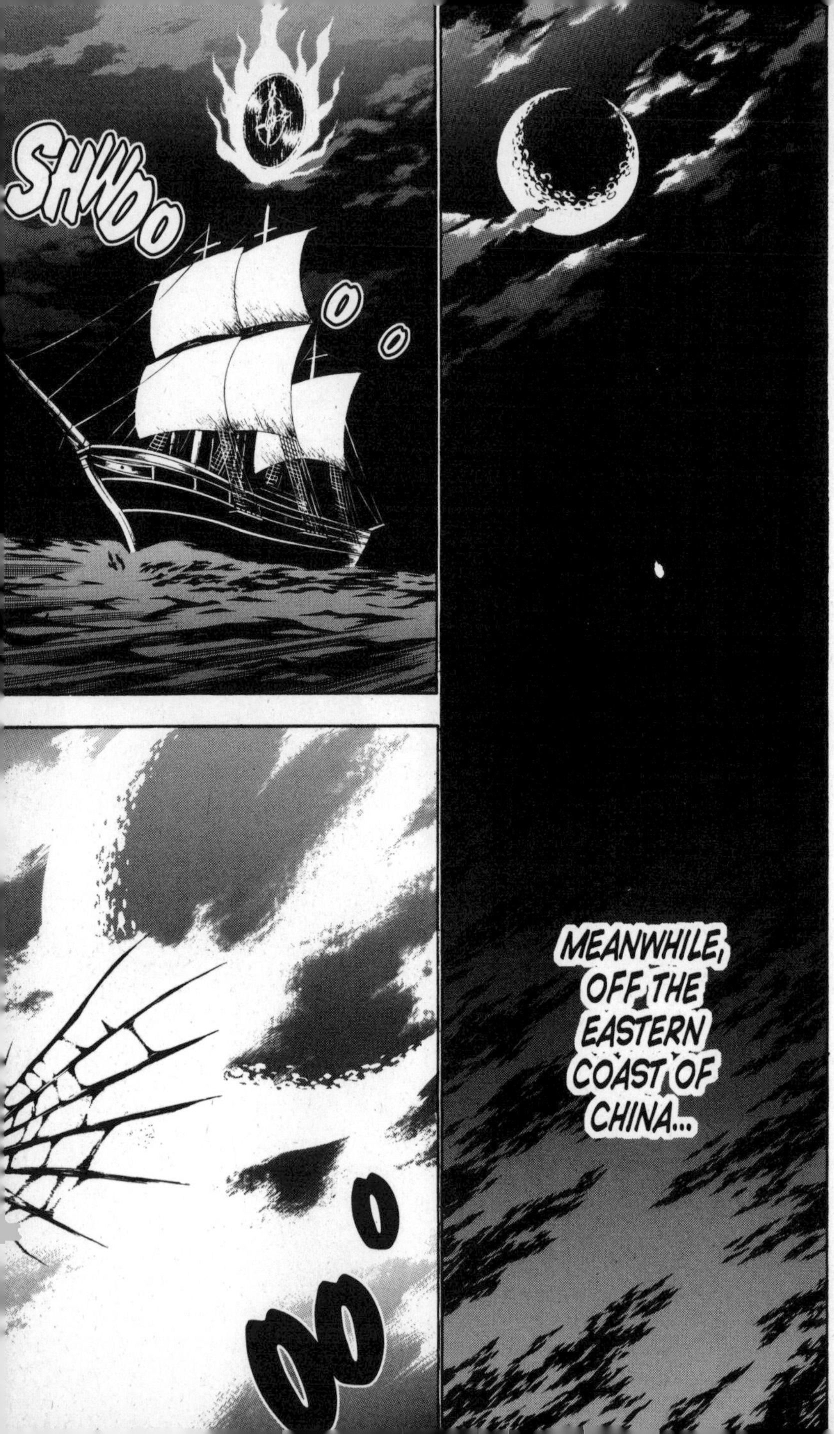
MEANWHILE, OFF THE EASTERN COAST OF CHINA...
SHWOO

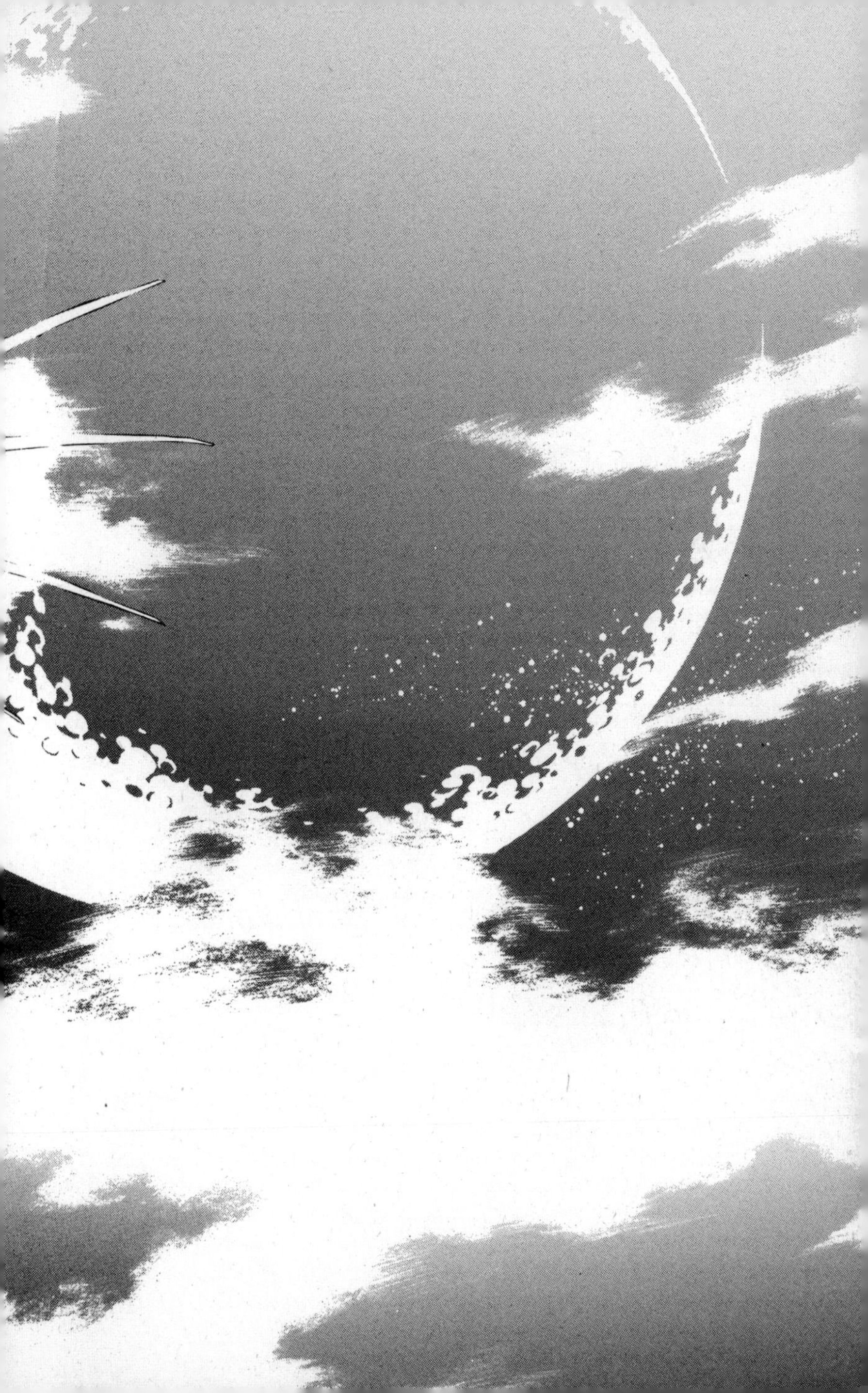

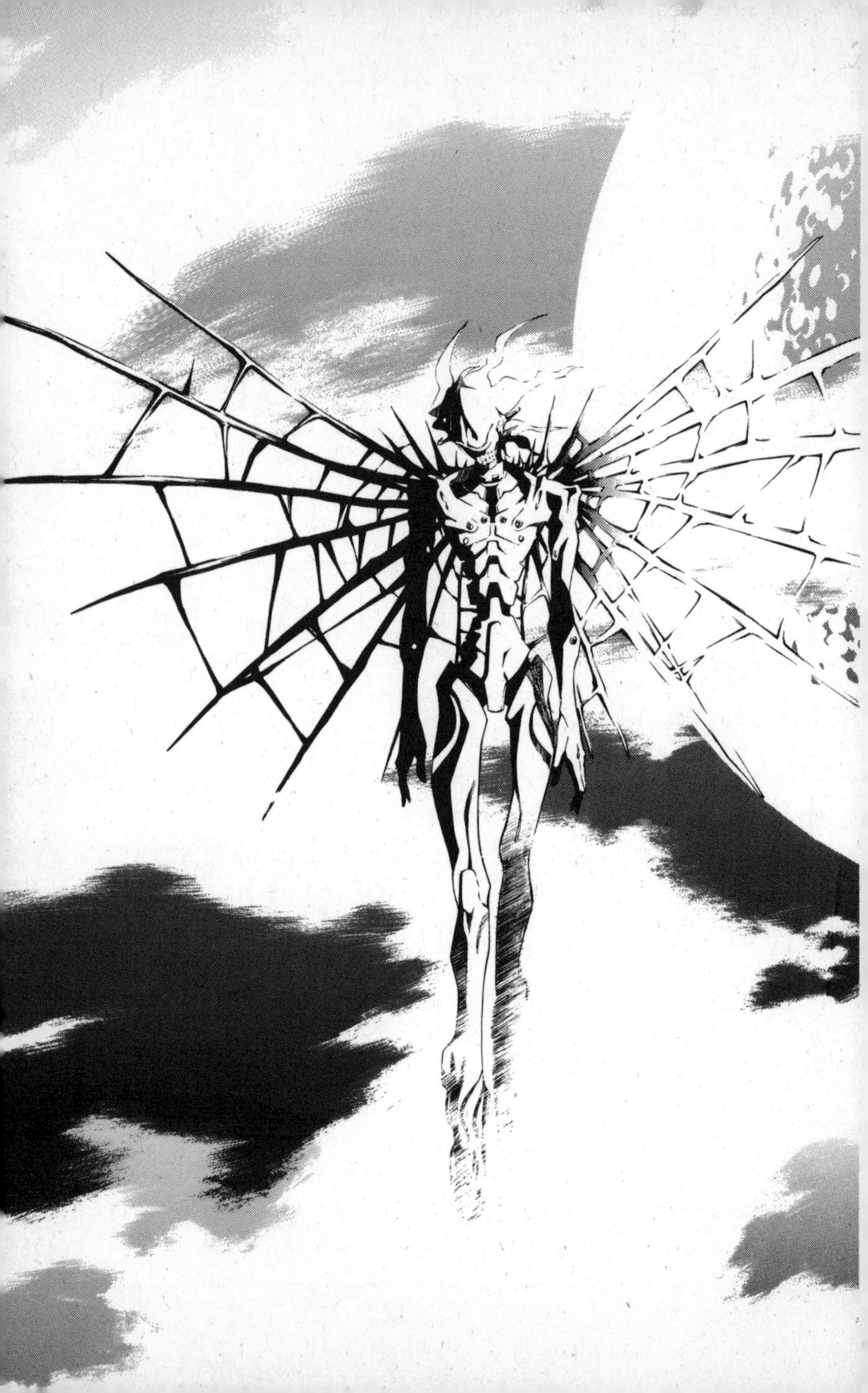

THE FIRST ANNUAL CHARACTER POPULARITY POLL!!

ANNOUNCING 11TH-20TH PLACE IN THE RANKINGS!

11TH PLACE
372 VOTES
TIMCANPY

12TH PLACE
324 VOTES
ARYSTAR KRORY

13TH PLACE
200 VOTES
DAISYA BARRY

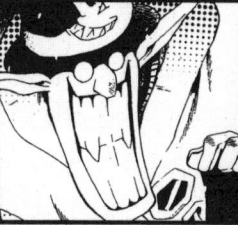

14TH PLACE
105 VOTES
ELIADE

14TH PLACE
105 VOTES
KATSURA HOSHINO

16TH PLACE
93 VOTES
THE MILLENNIUM EARL

17TH PLACE
86 VOTES
LALA

18TH PLACE
75 VOTES
MOA HESSE

19TH PLACE
65 VOTES
JOHNNY GILL

20TH PLACE
62 VOTES
YOSHI

SEE PAGE 150 FOR THE REST!!

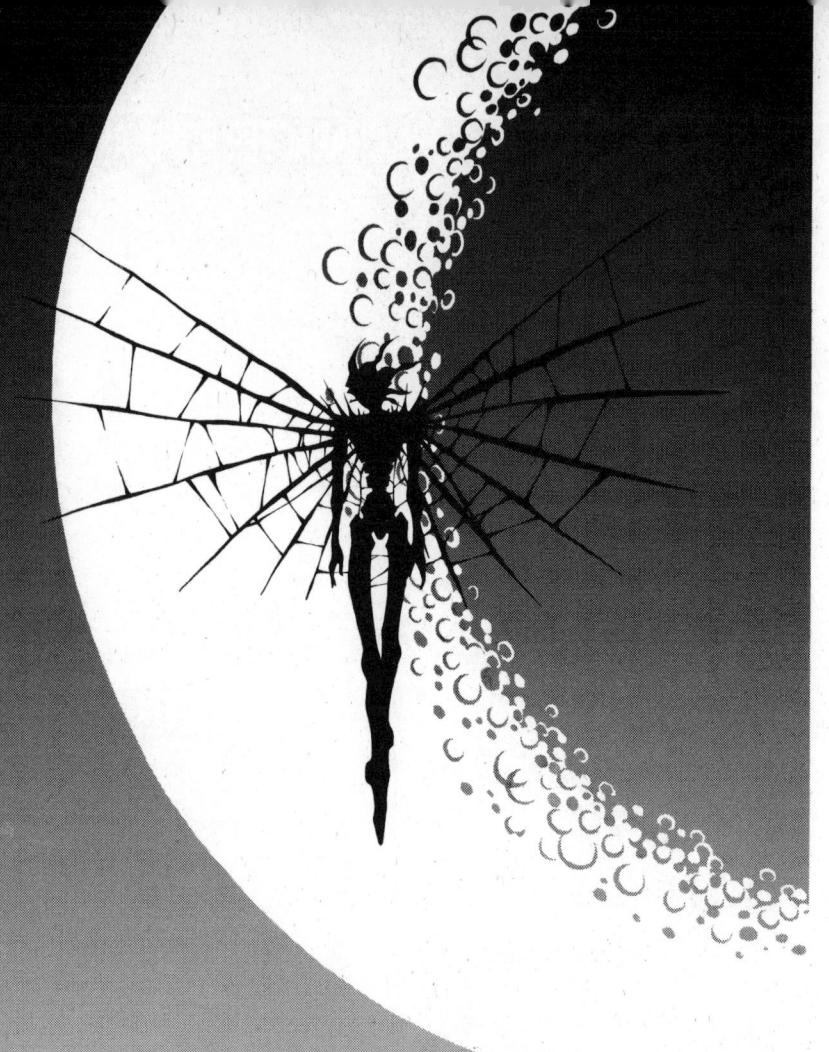

THE 64TH NIGHT: LEVEL 3

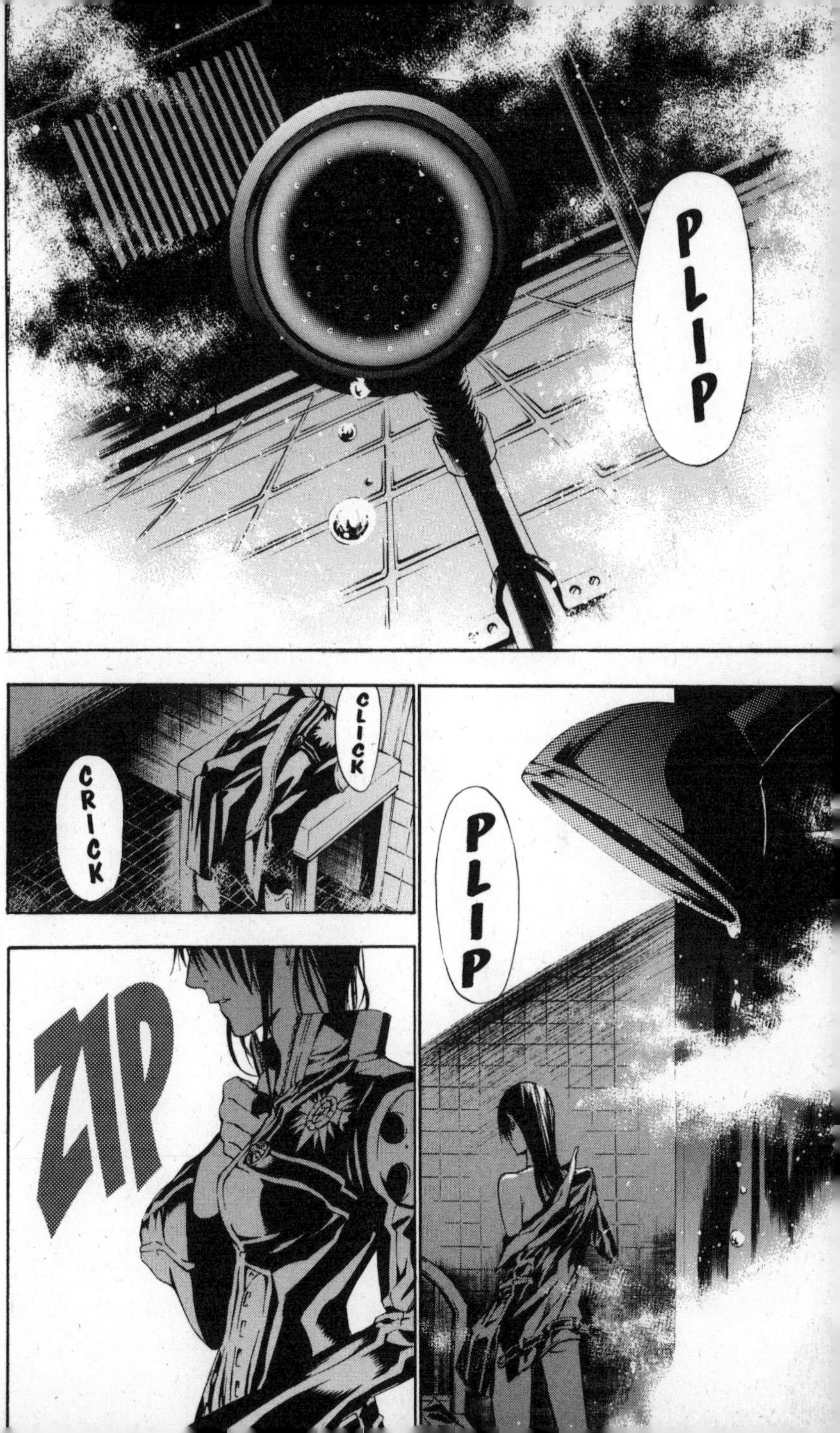
PLIP
CLICK
CRICK
PLIP
ZIP

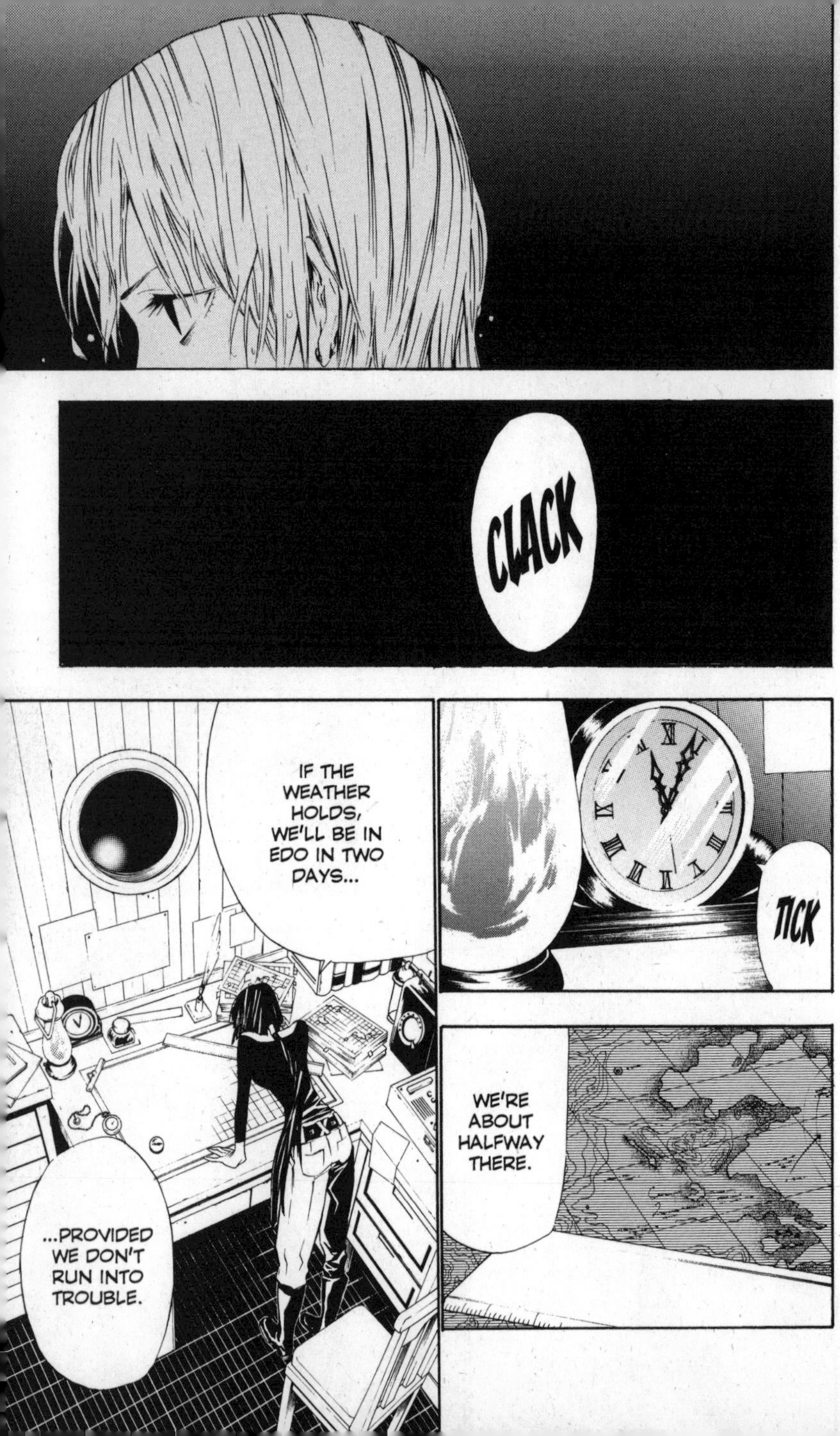
CLACK
TICK
WE'RE ABOUT HALFWAY THERE.
IF THE WEATHER HOLDS, WE'LL BE IN EDO IN TWO DAYS...
...PROVIDED WE DON'T RUN INTO TROUBLE.

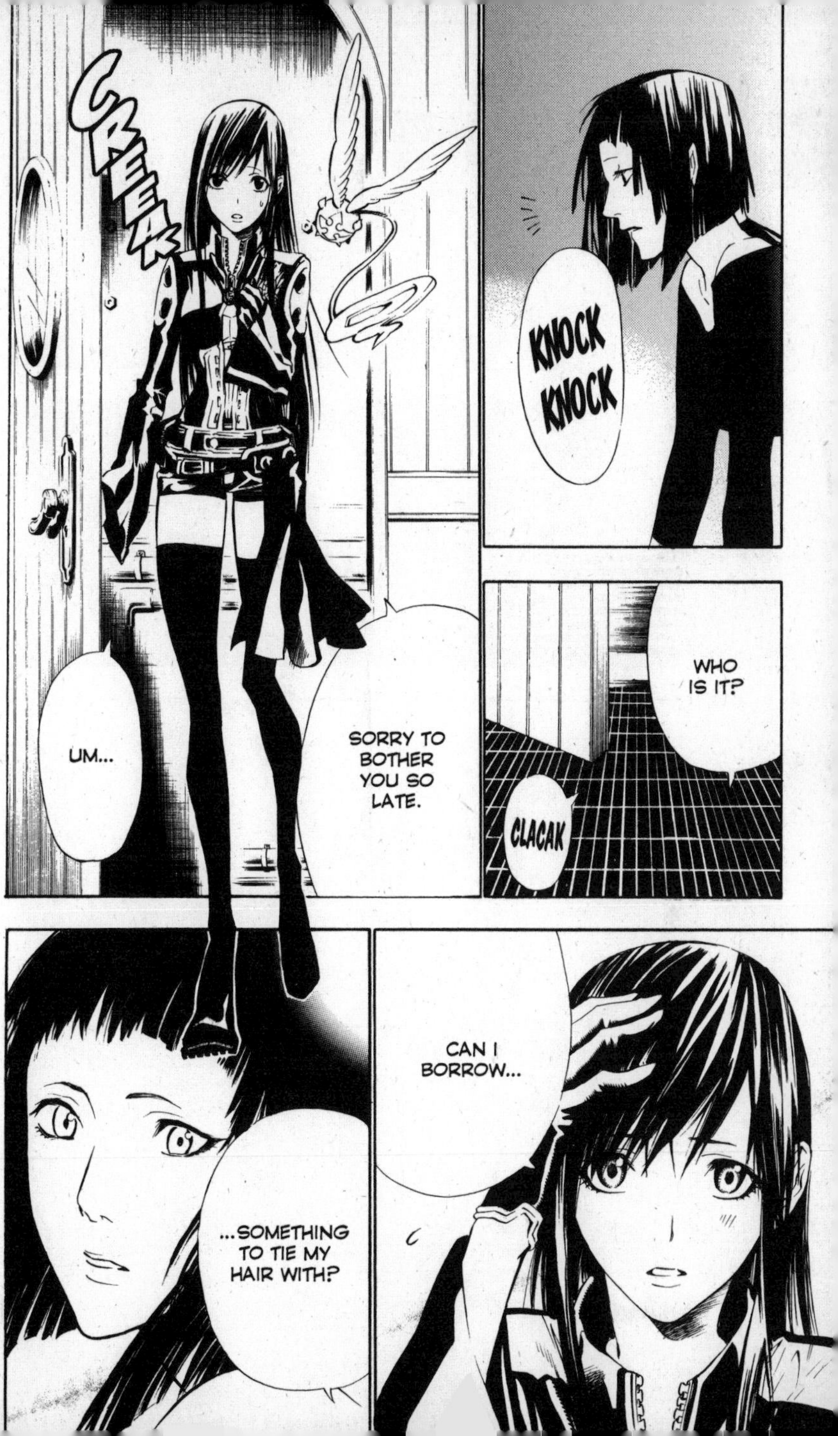
KNOCK KNOCK
WHO IS IT?
CLACAK
CREAK
SORRY TO BOTHER YOU SO LATE.
UM...
CAN I BORROW...
...SOMETHING TO TIE MY HAIR WITH?

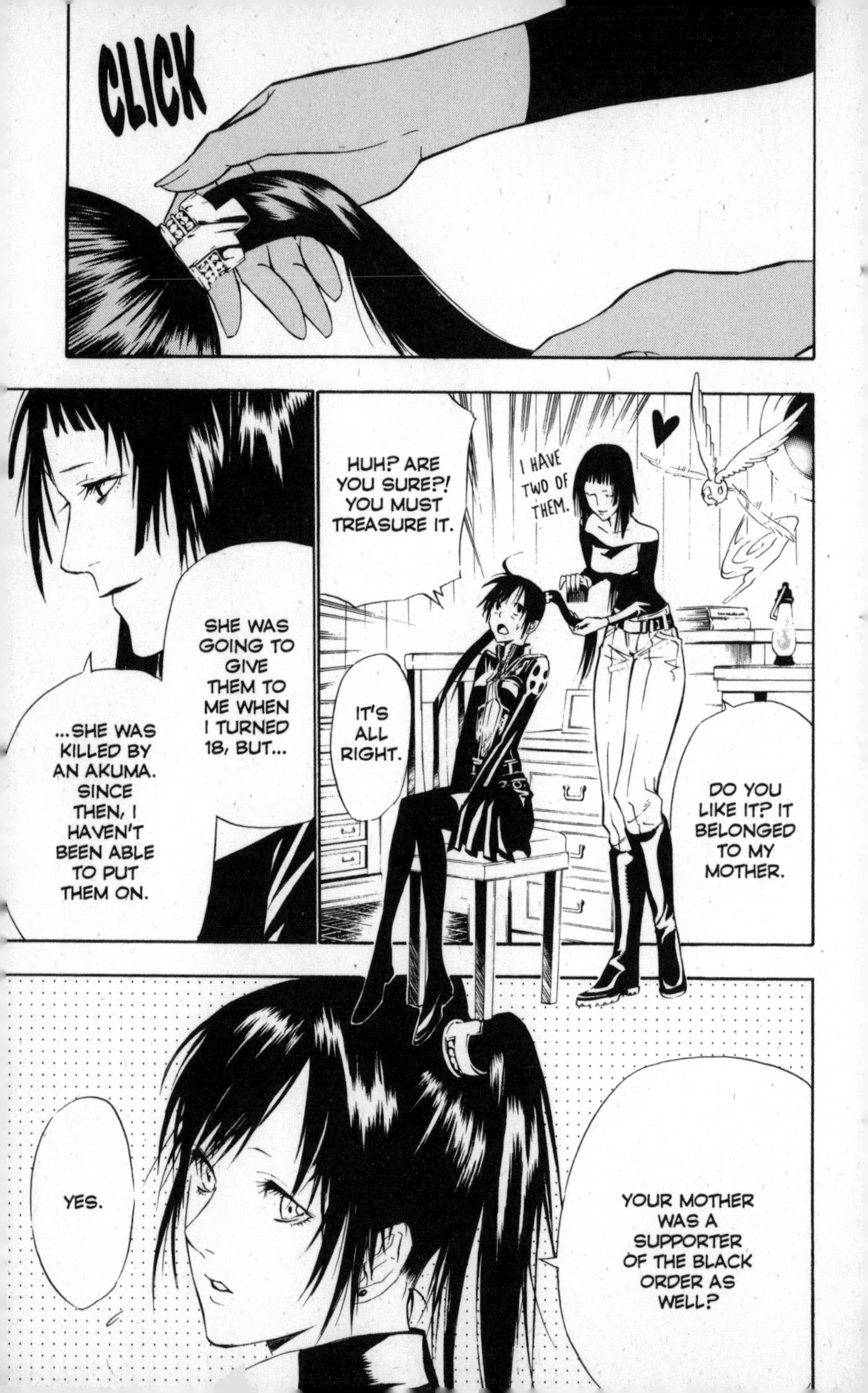
CLICK
DO YOU LIKE IT? IT BELONGED TO MY MOTHER.
IT'S ALL RIGHT.
HUH? ARE YOU SURE?! YOU MUST TREASURE IT.
I HAVE TWO OF THEM.
SHE WAS GOING TO GIVE THEM TO ME WHEN I TURNED 18, BUT...
...SHE WAS KILLED BY AN AKUMA. SINCE THEN, I HAVEN'T BEEN ABLE TO PUT THEM ON.
YOUR MOTHER WAS A SUPPORTER OF THE BLACK ORDER AS WELL?
YES.

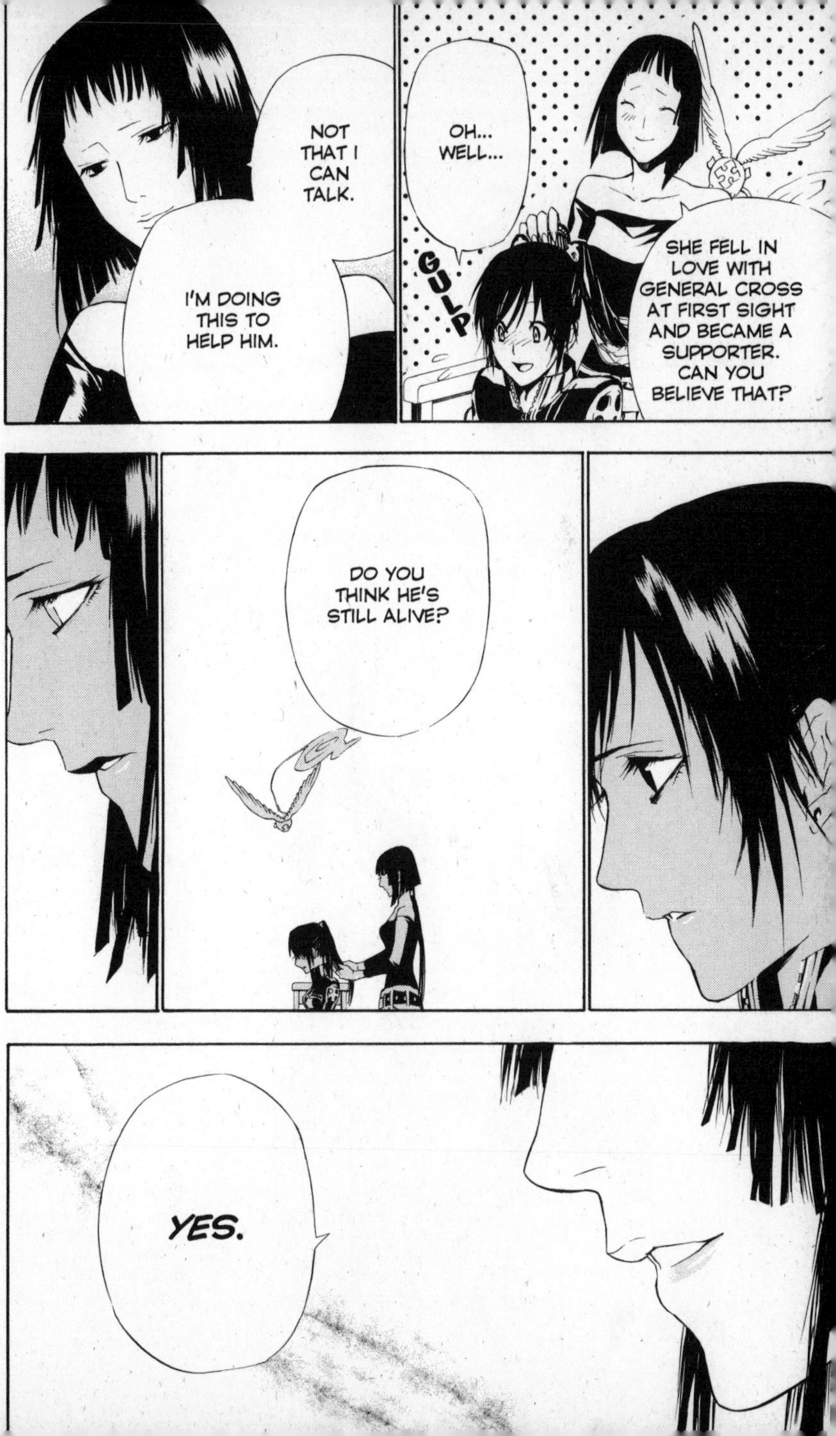
SHE FELL IN LOVE WITH GENERAL CROSS AT FIRST SIGHT AND BECAME A SUPPORTER. CAN YOU BELIEVE THAT?
OH... WELL...
GULP
NOT THAT I CAN TALK.
I'M DOING THIS TO HELP HIM.
DO YOU THINK HE'S STILL ALIVE?
YES.

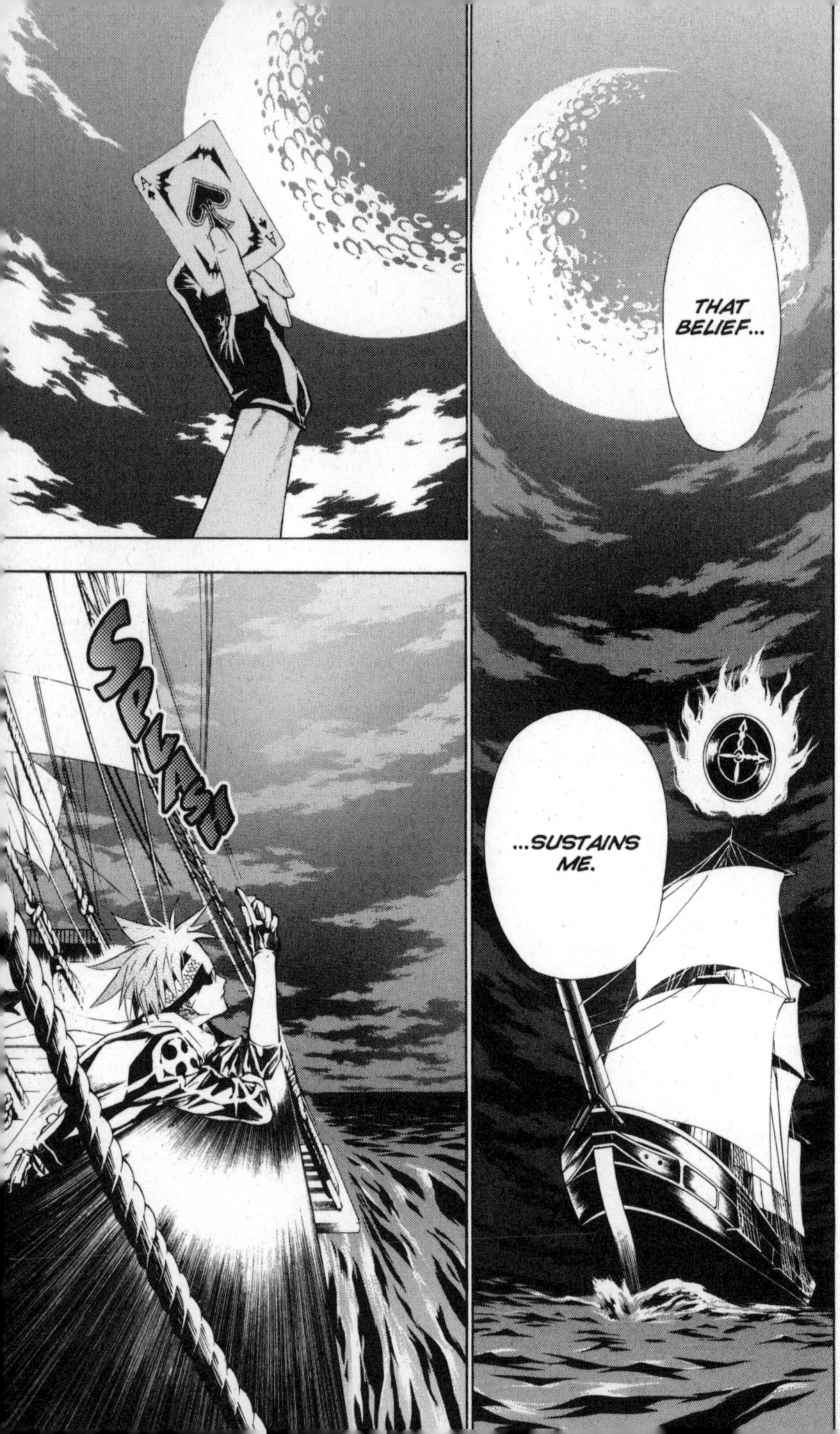
THAT BELIEF...
...SUSTAINS ME.
SPLASH!

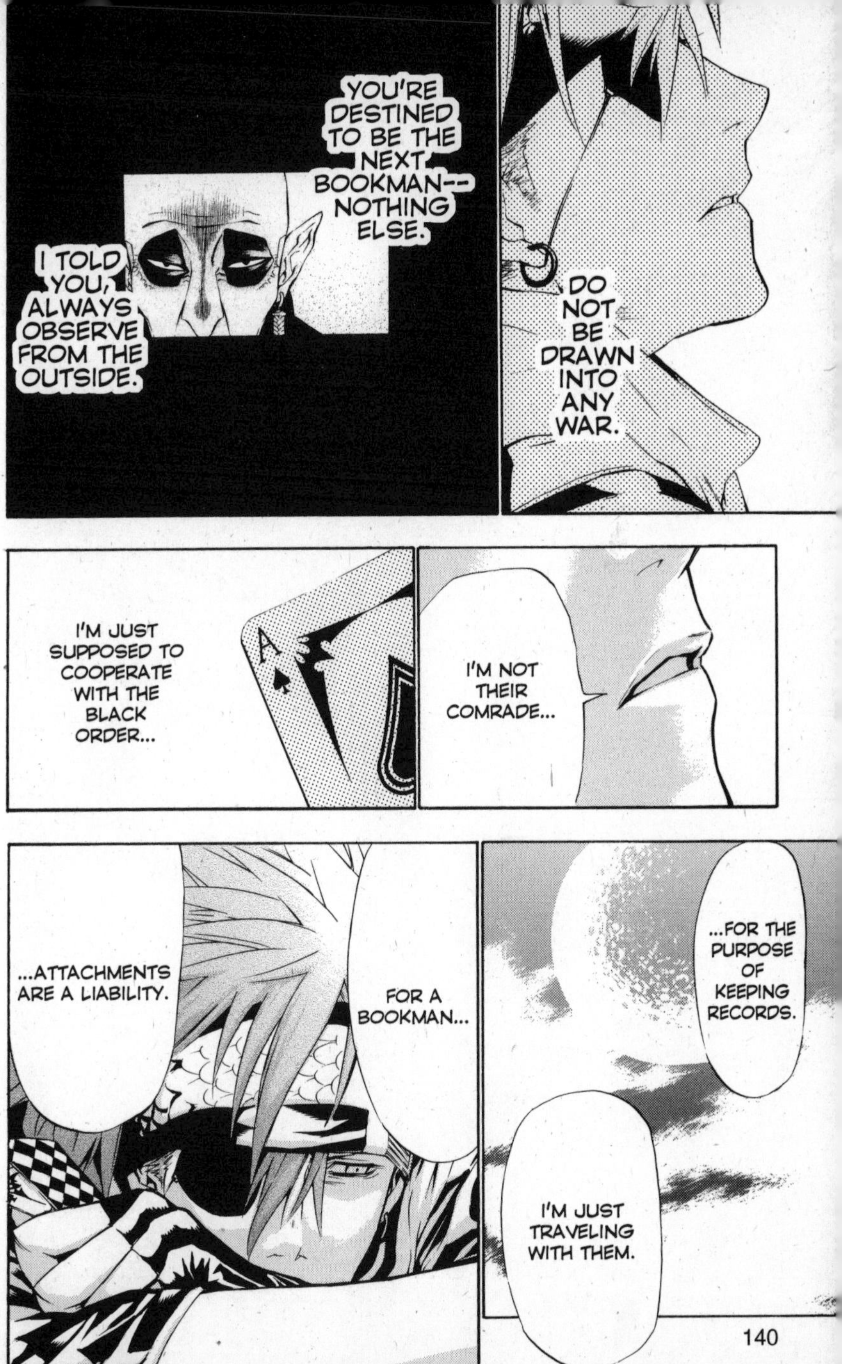
DO NOT BE DRAWN INTO ANY WAR.
YOU'RE DESTINED TO BE THE NEXT BOOKMAN-- NOTHING ELSE.
I TOLD YOU, ALWAYS OBSERVE FROM THE OUTSIDE.
I'M NOT THEIR COMRADE...
I'M JUST SUPPOSED TO COOPERATE WITH THE BLACK ORDER...
...FOR THE PURPOSE OF KEEPING RECORDS.
I'M JUST TRAVELING WITH THEM.
FOR A BOOKMAN...
...ATTACHMENTS ARE A LIABILITY.

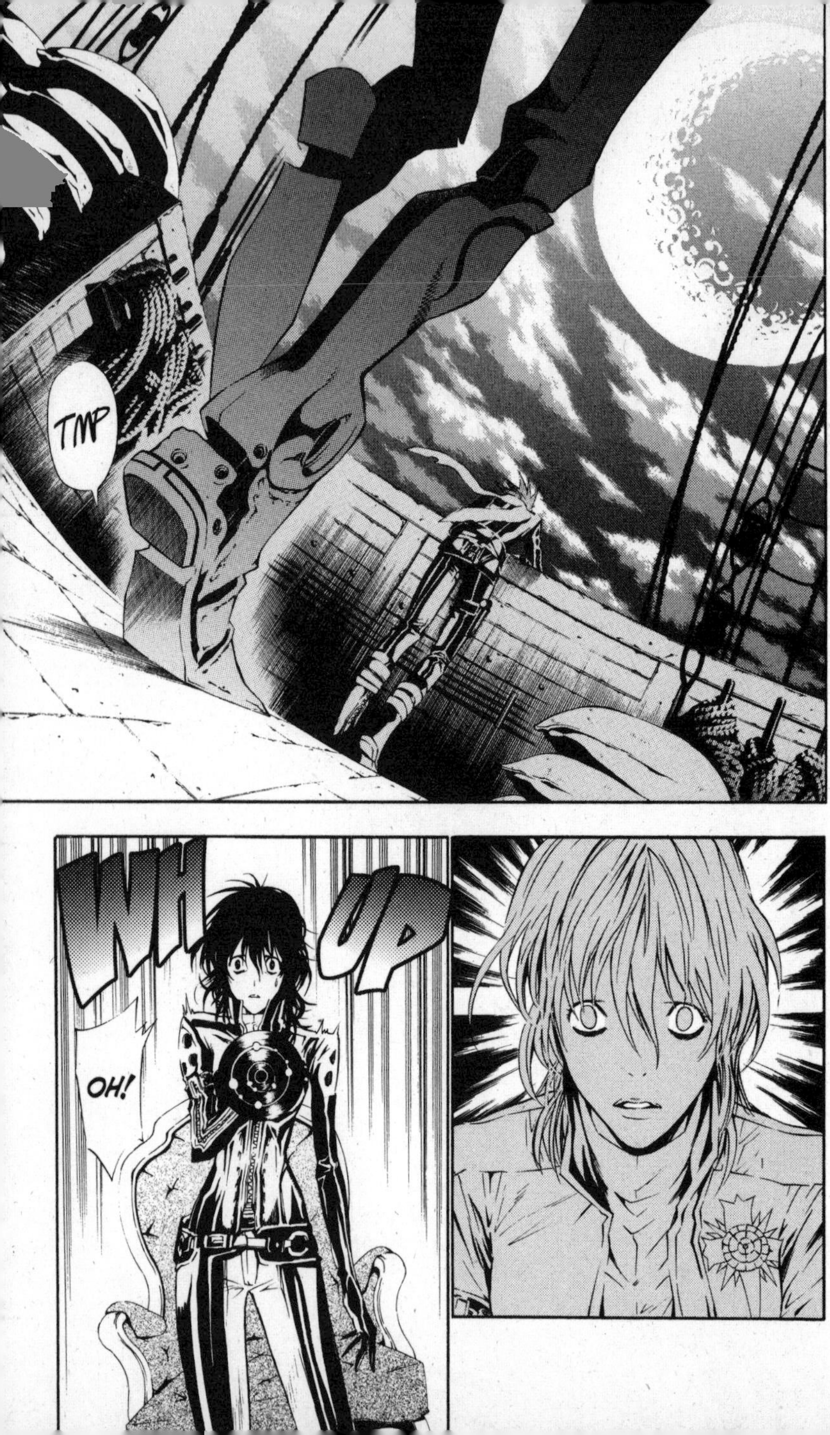
TMP
WH
UP
OH!

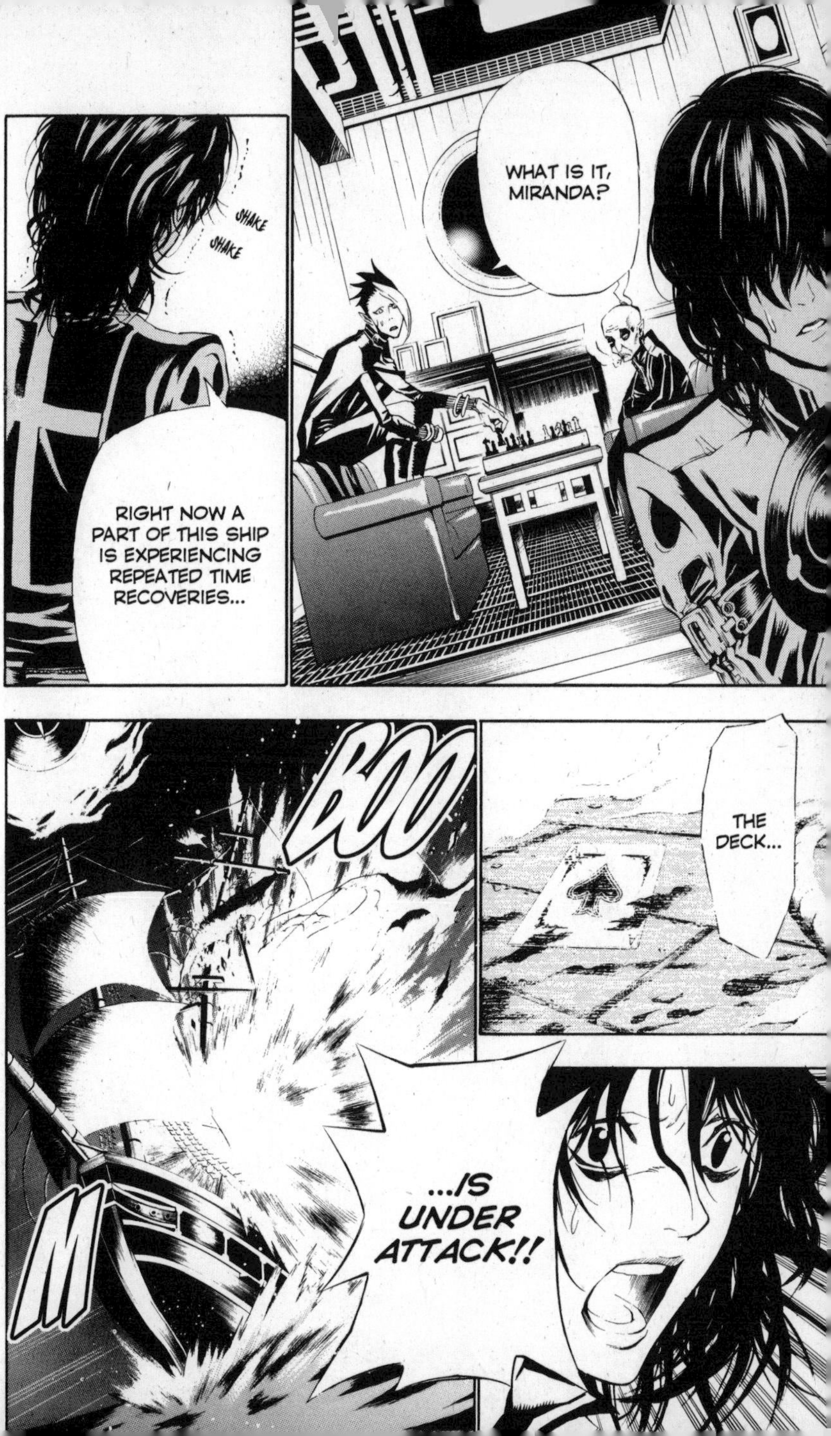
WHAT IS IT, MIRANDA?
SHAKE
SHAKE
RIGHT NOW A PART OF THIS SHIP IS EXPERIENCING REPEATED TIME RECOVERIES...
THE DECK...
...IS UNDER ATTACK!!
BOOM

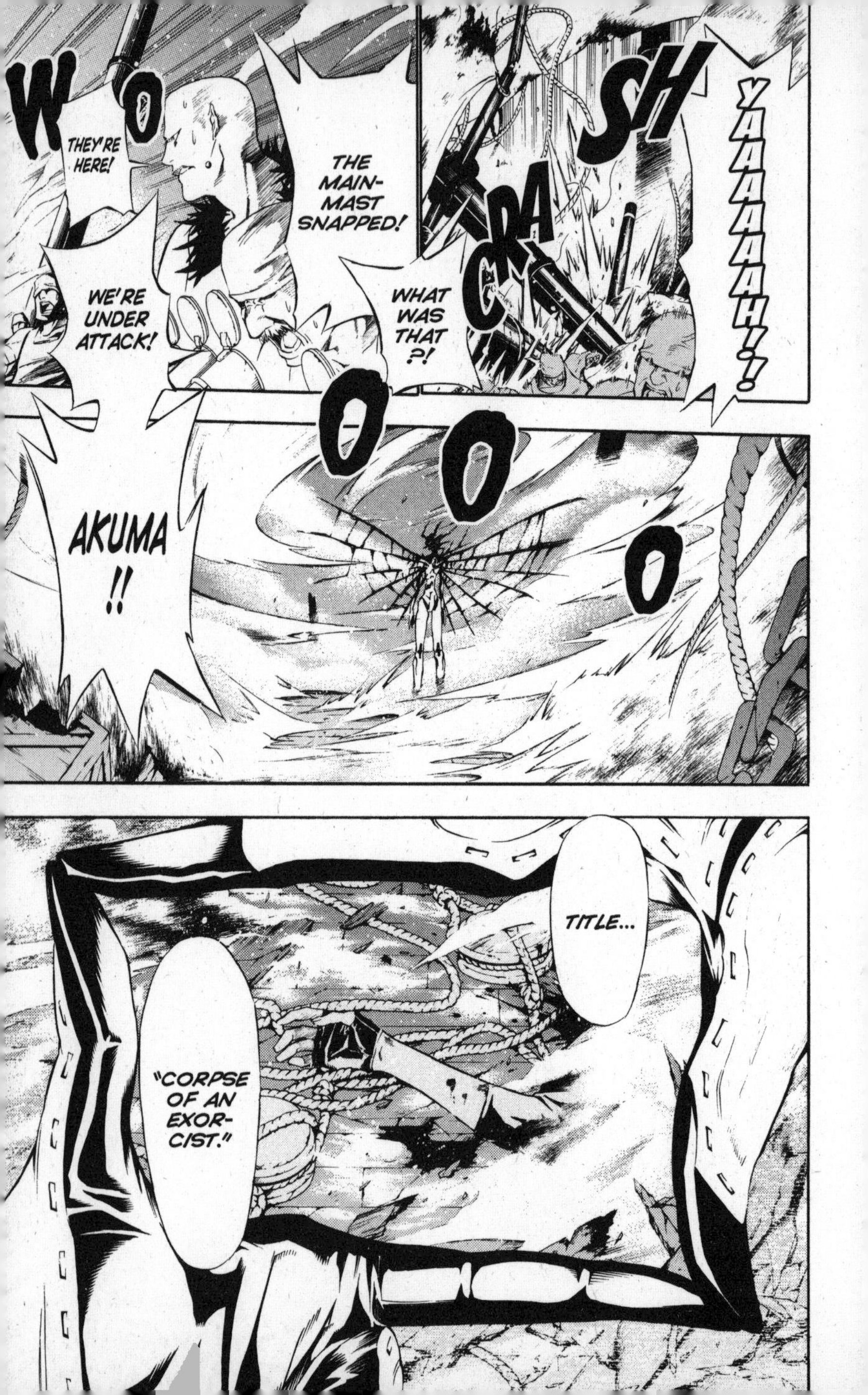
YAAAAAAAH!!
CRASH
THE MAIN-MAST SNAPPED!
WHAT WAS THAT?!
THEY'RE HERE!
WE'RE UNDER ATTACK!
WOOOOO
AKUMA!!
TITLE...
"CORPSE OF AN EXORCIST."

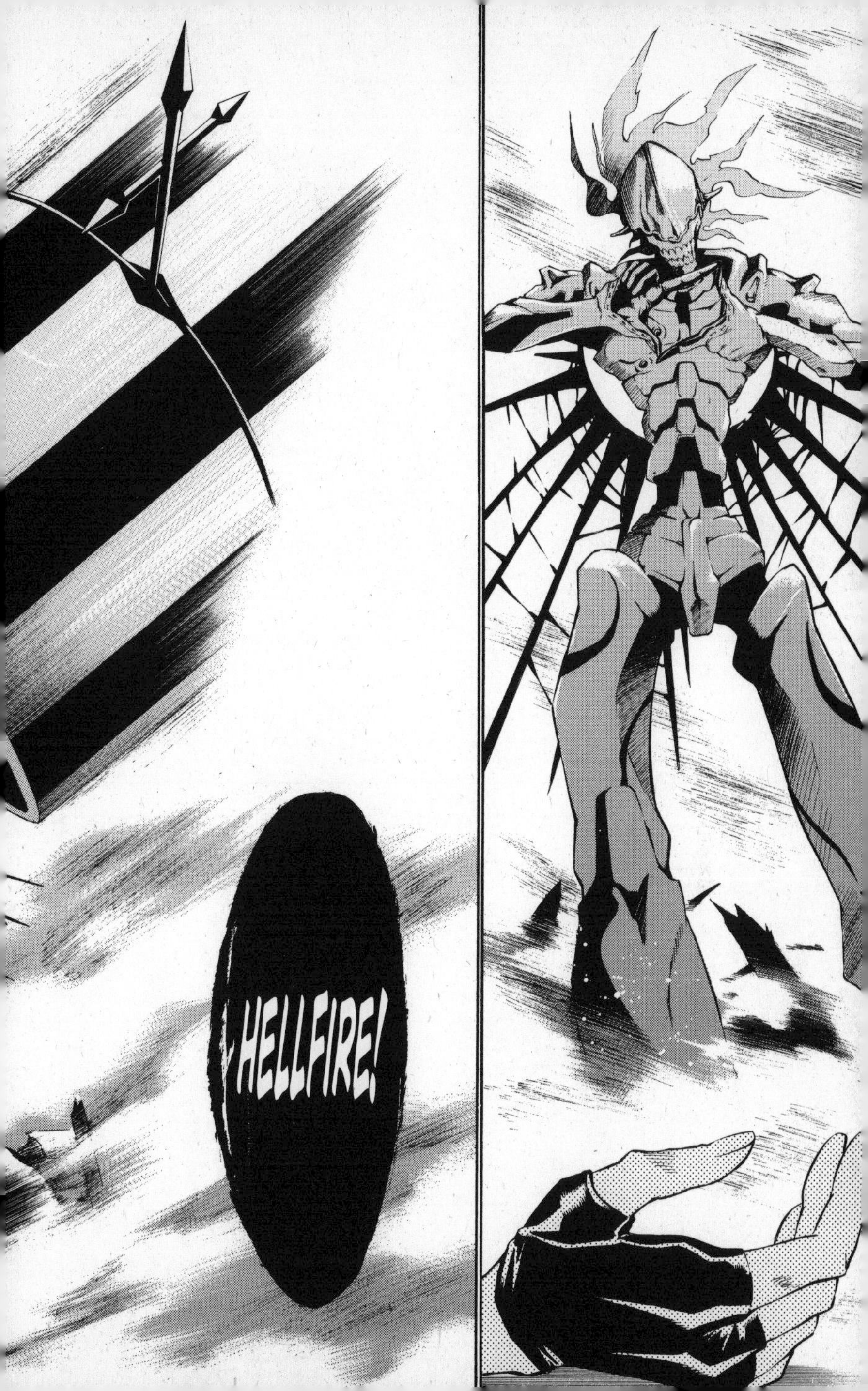
HELLFIRE!

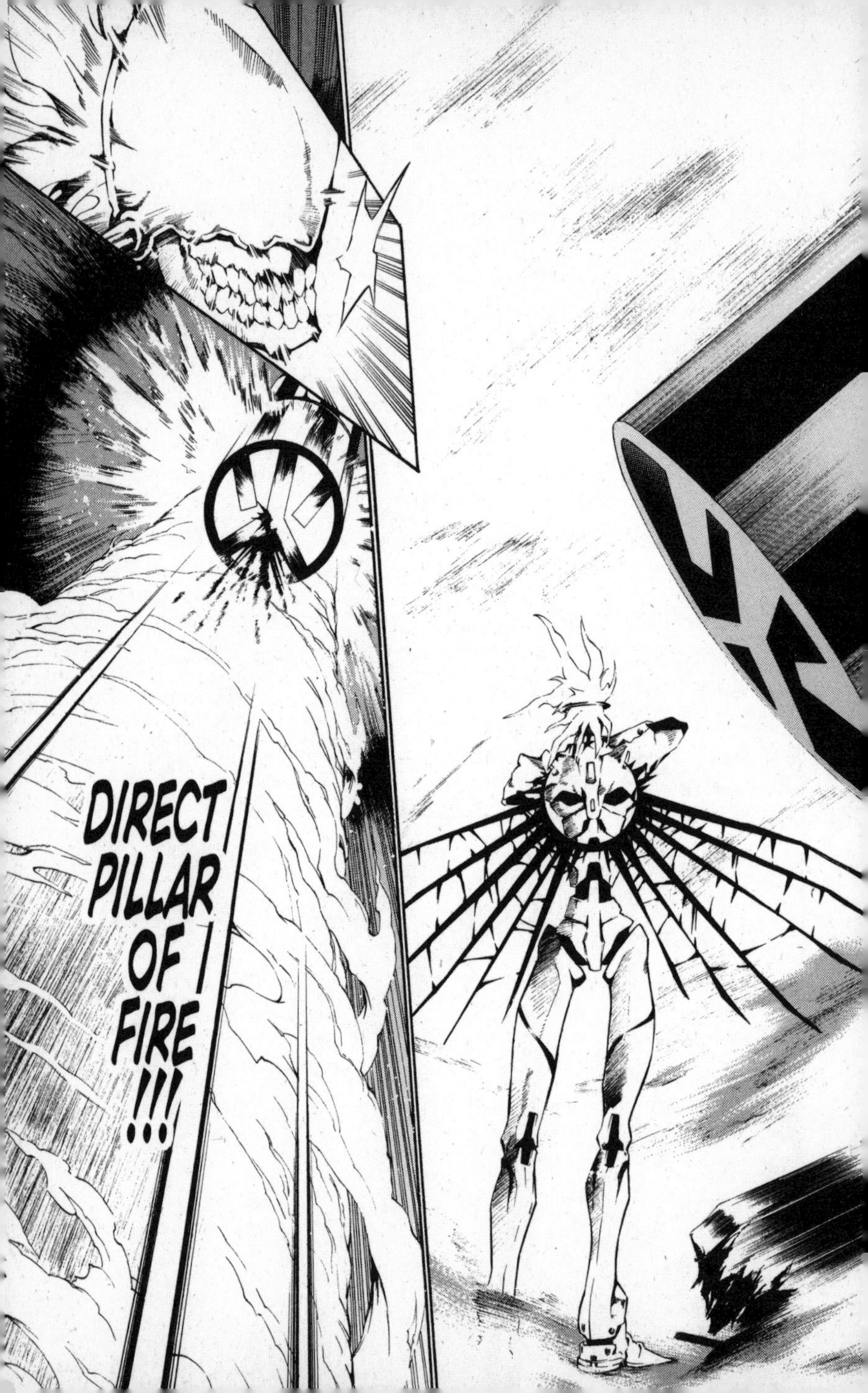
DIRECT PILLAR OF FIRE!!!

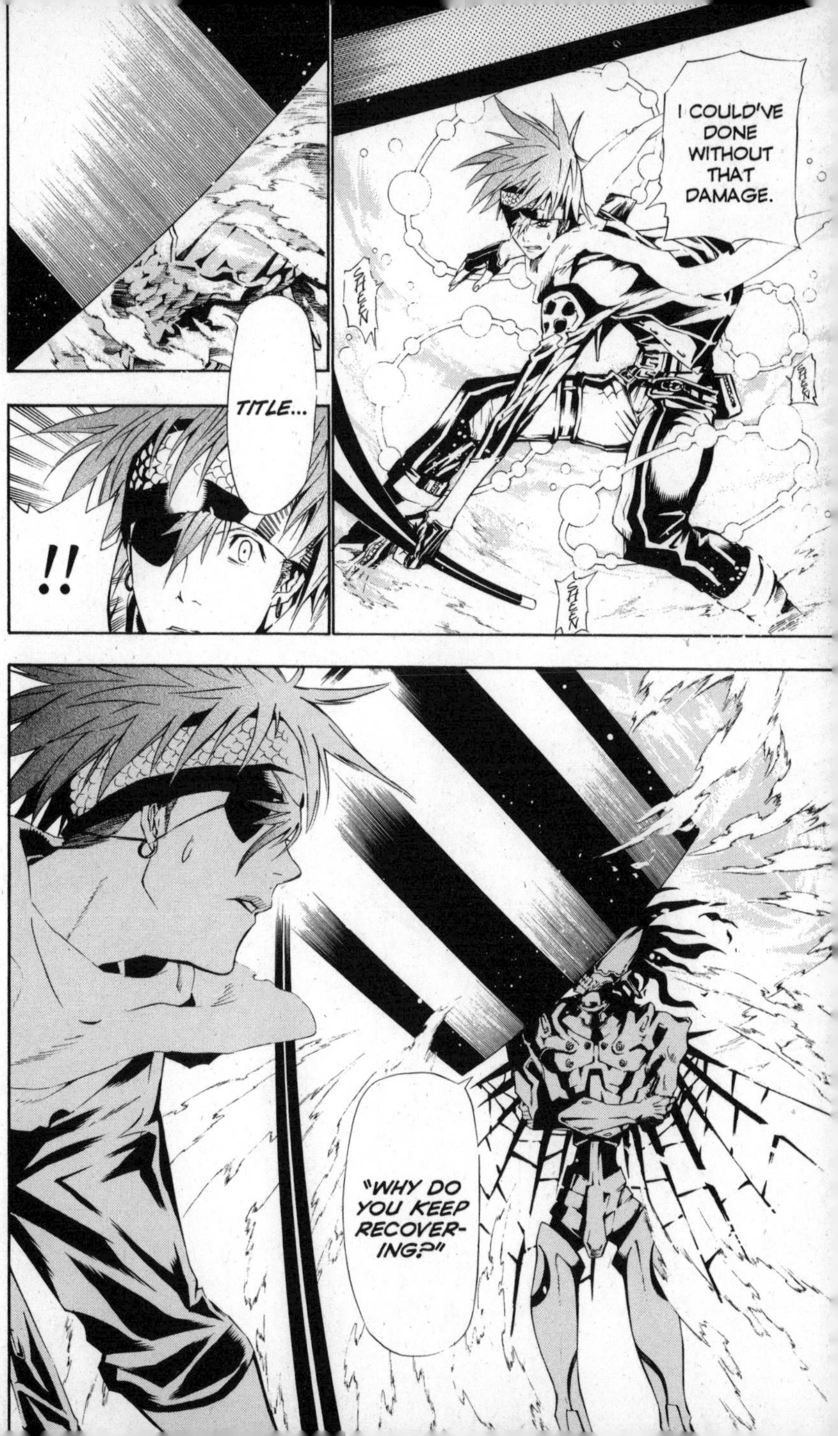
I COULD'VE DONE WITHOUT THAT DAMAGE.
SHEEN
SHEEN
SHEEN
TITLE...
!!
"WHY DO YOU KEEP RECOVER-ING?"

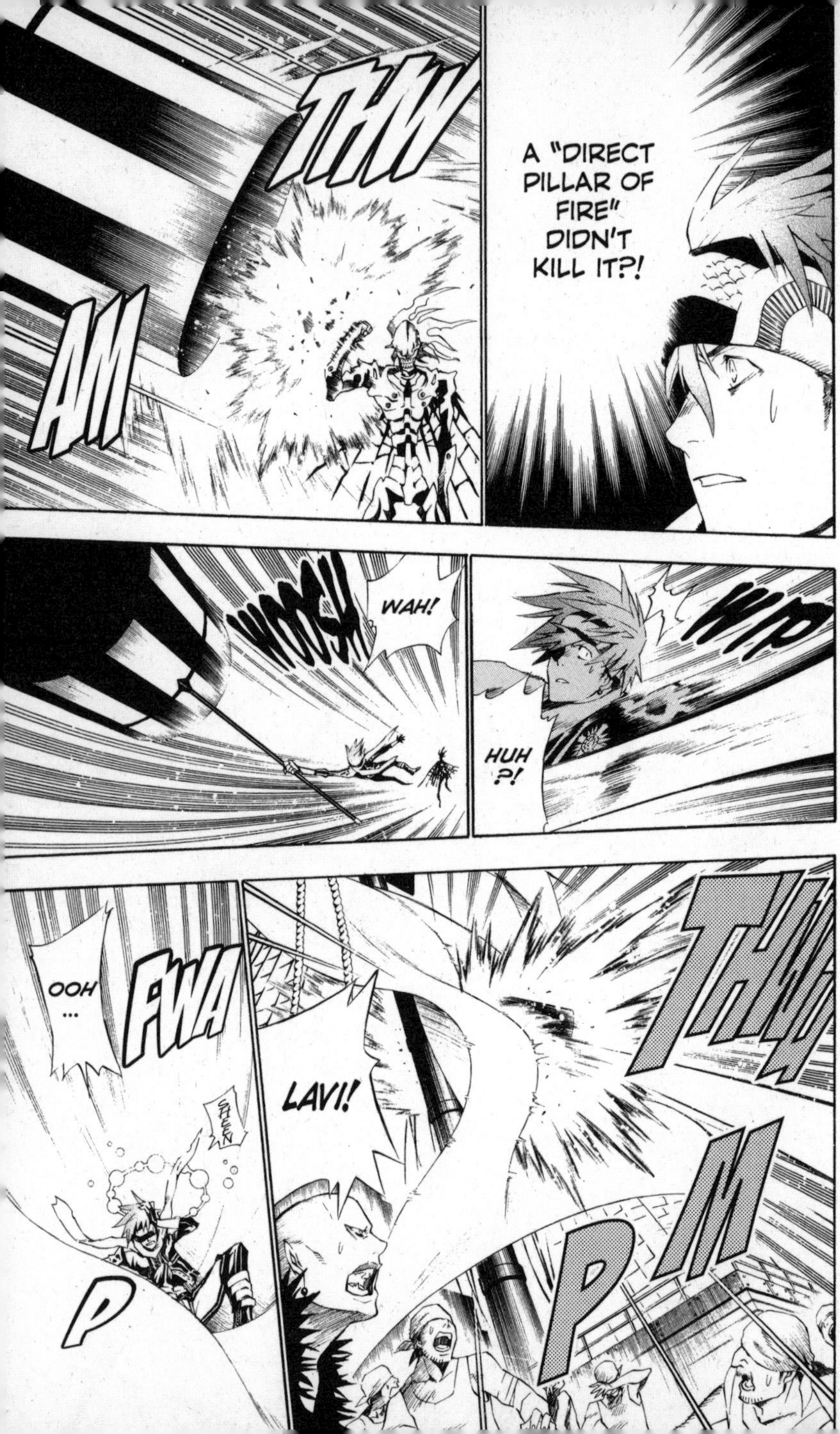
A "DIRECT PILLAR OF FIRE" DIDN'T KILL IT?!
THW
AM
WHIP
HUH?!
WOOSH
WAH!
THW
M
P
LAVI!
OOH...
FWA
SHEEN
P

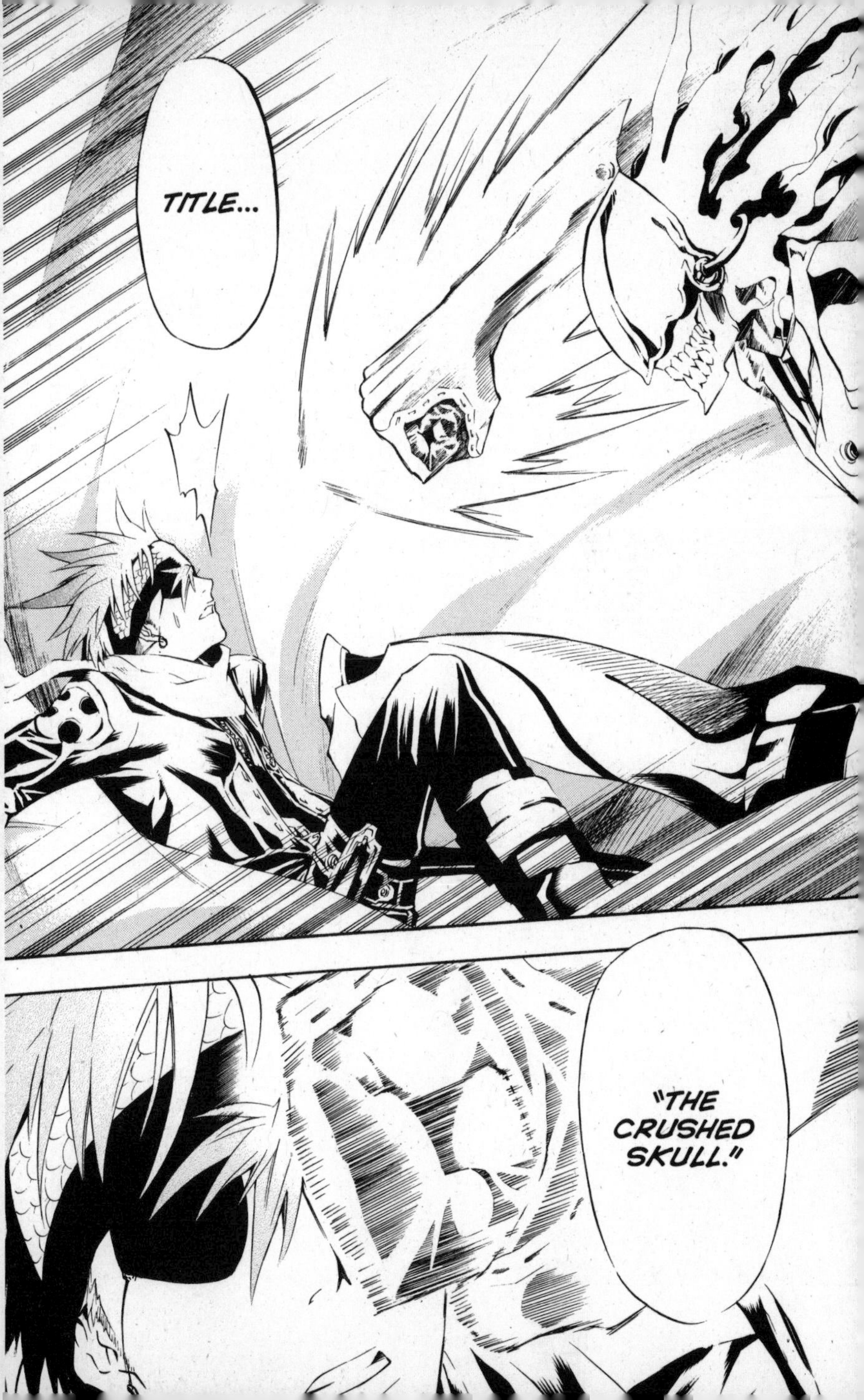
TITLE...
"THE CRUSHED SKULL."

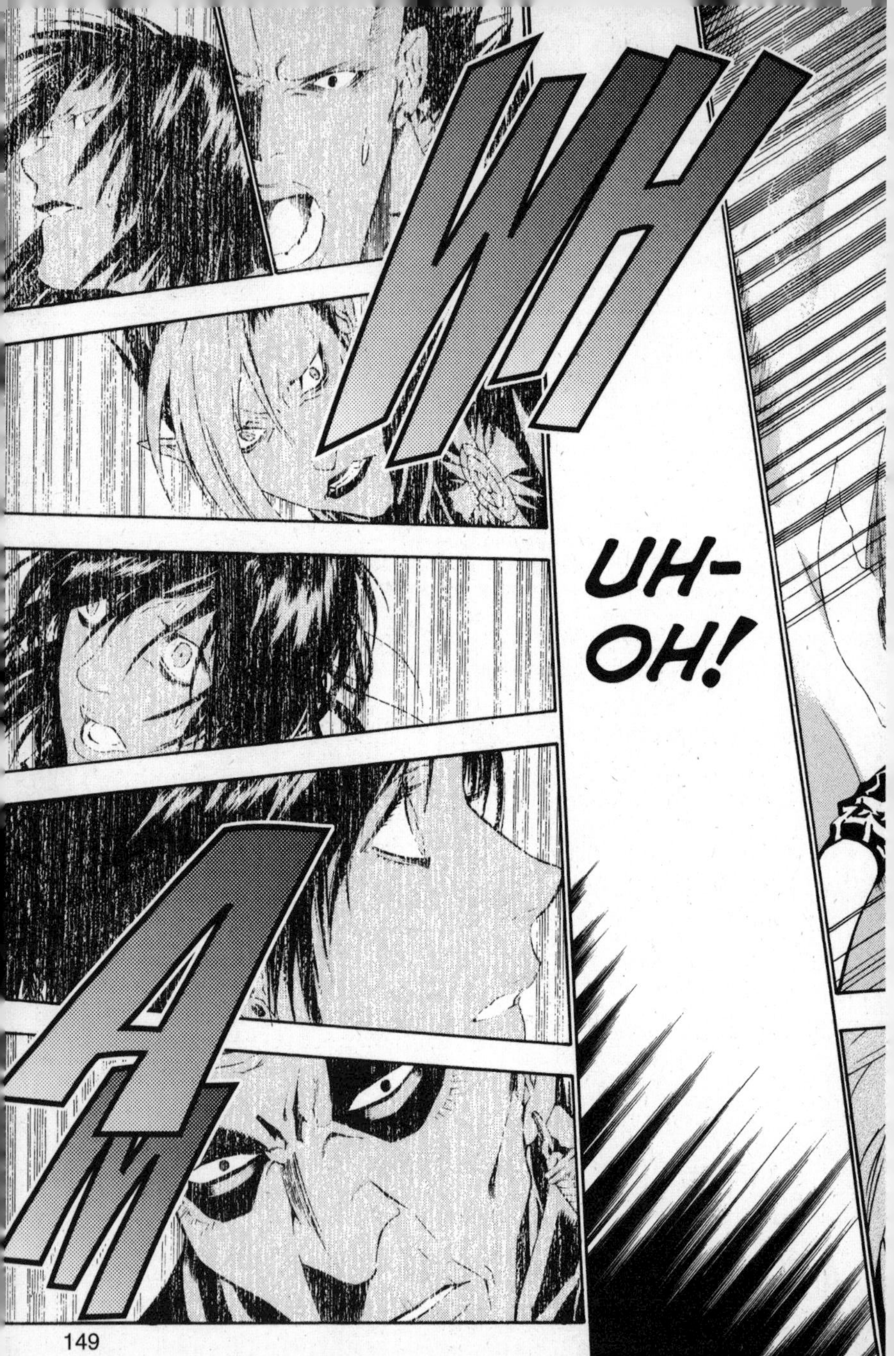
WH
UH-OH!
AH

D.Gray-man

21ST PLACE AND UP!

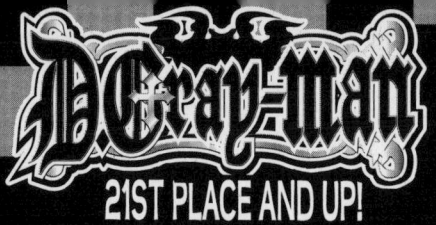

THE FIRST ANNUAL CHARACTER POPULARITY POLL!!

RANK	CHARACTER NAME	# OF VOTES	RANK	CHARACTER NAME	# OF VOTES
21	JAN	53		BEN	4
22	ARYSTAR KRORY I	51	61	KOMUSUKE KINDAICHI	3
23	MANA WALKER	47		KANDA'S GOLEM	3
24	BOOKMAN	44		CHIEF INSPECTOR	3
25	TOMA	43		GOZU	3
26	SUMAN DARK	42		DOCTOR	3
27	65	29		STOREKEEPER	3
28	JERRY	28		FRANZ	3
29	EEZE	27	68	KAZAANA LIDO	2
30	BAK CHAN	26		CLOUDNYNE	2
31	LERO	22		JAIME	2
32	ALESTINA	19		EDITOR Y	2
				FAKE ALLEN	2
33	GUZOL	16		BABA	2
	THE FALLEN ONE BOY	16		MOTHER	2
	HEVLASKA	16		CARETAKER OF MIRANDA'S HOUSE	2
36	AKUMA	14		LIZA	2
37	ANITA	13		MUGEN	2
	GENERAL TIEDOLL	13	78	ASSISTANT GUNMA	1
39	KOMLIN II	12		ASSISTANT MIYAZAKI	1
40	ROSANNE (MAN-EATING FLOWER)	11		ANGELA	1
41	VILLAGE HEADMAN GEORG 10	10		ICHIGEN	1
42	FAT CAT (THAT ATE TIMCANPY)	8		OI-CHAN	1
	PETER	8		STAFF OF THE SCIENCE SECTION	1
44	MAHOJA	7		GWEN FLAIL	1
	MARIE	7		EARL OF ST. GERMAINE	1
	COMMUNICATION GOLEM	7		GENERAL ZOKALO	1
	LAVI'S GOLEM	7		SOFIA	1
48	LEO 6	6		SOL GALEN	1
49	BELOVED CAT CORO	5		DARK BOOTS	1
	MAID AT JAN'S HOUSE	5		CHAKER RABON	1
	OFFICER CHARLES	5		TINA SPARK	1
	FAN	5		SKIN BORIC	1
	FATHER MARK	5		FAN'S MOTHER	1
	AKUMA (LEVEL 2)	5		HOMELESS GUY	1
55	INNOCENCE	4		BEAN SPROUT	1
	CLAIRE	4		TAIYO YAMAMOTO	1
	GENERAL KEVIN YEEGAR	4		69	1
	TAP DOPP	4		PLACE ROBIN	1
	PAZU	4			—

THANKS TO ALL OF YOU WHO VOTED!!

THE 65TH NIGHT: TITLE

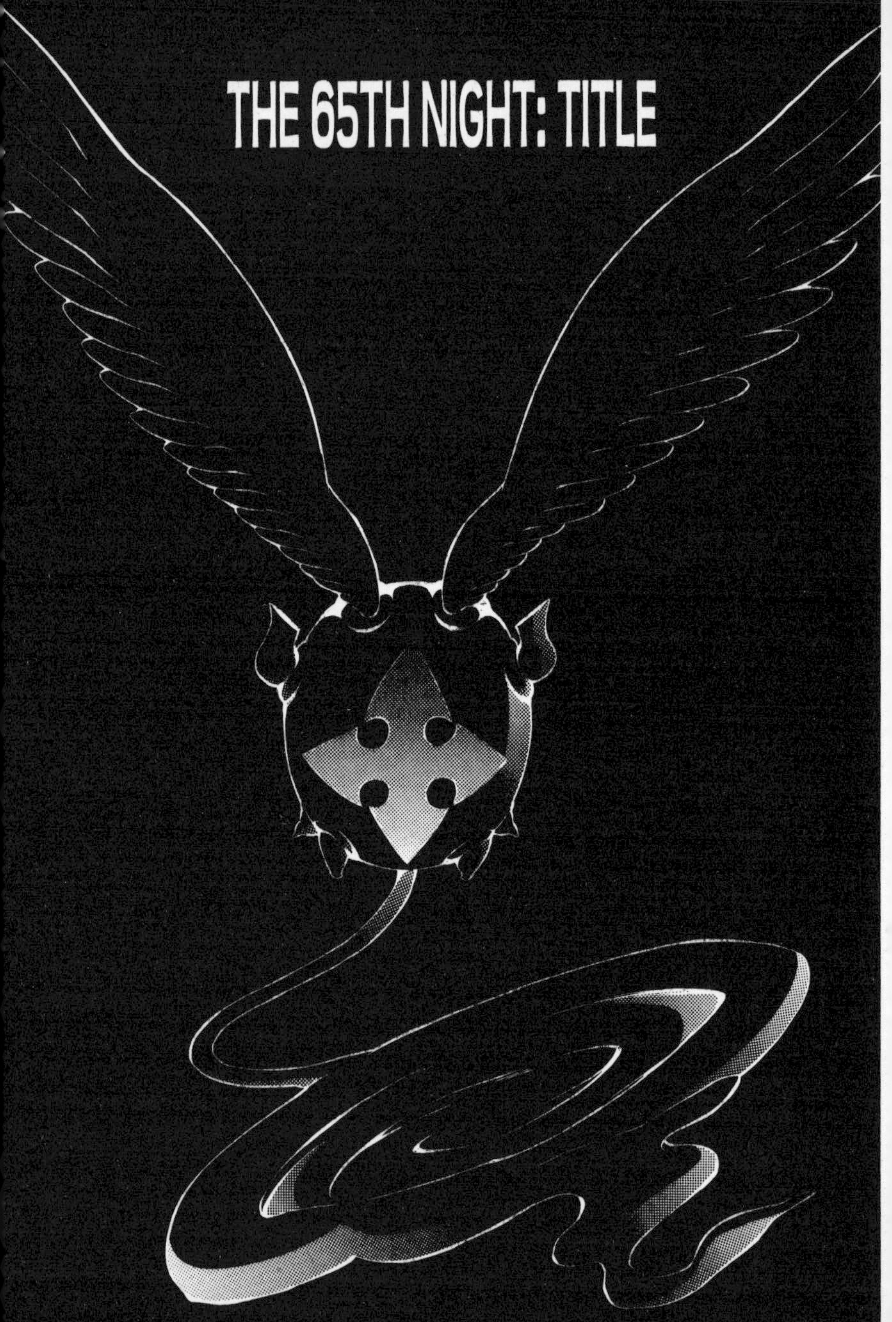

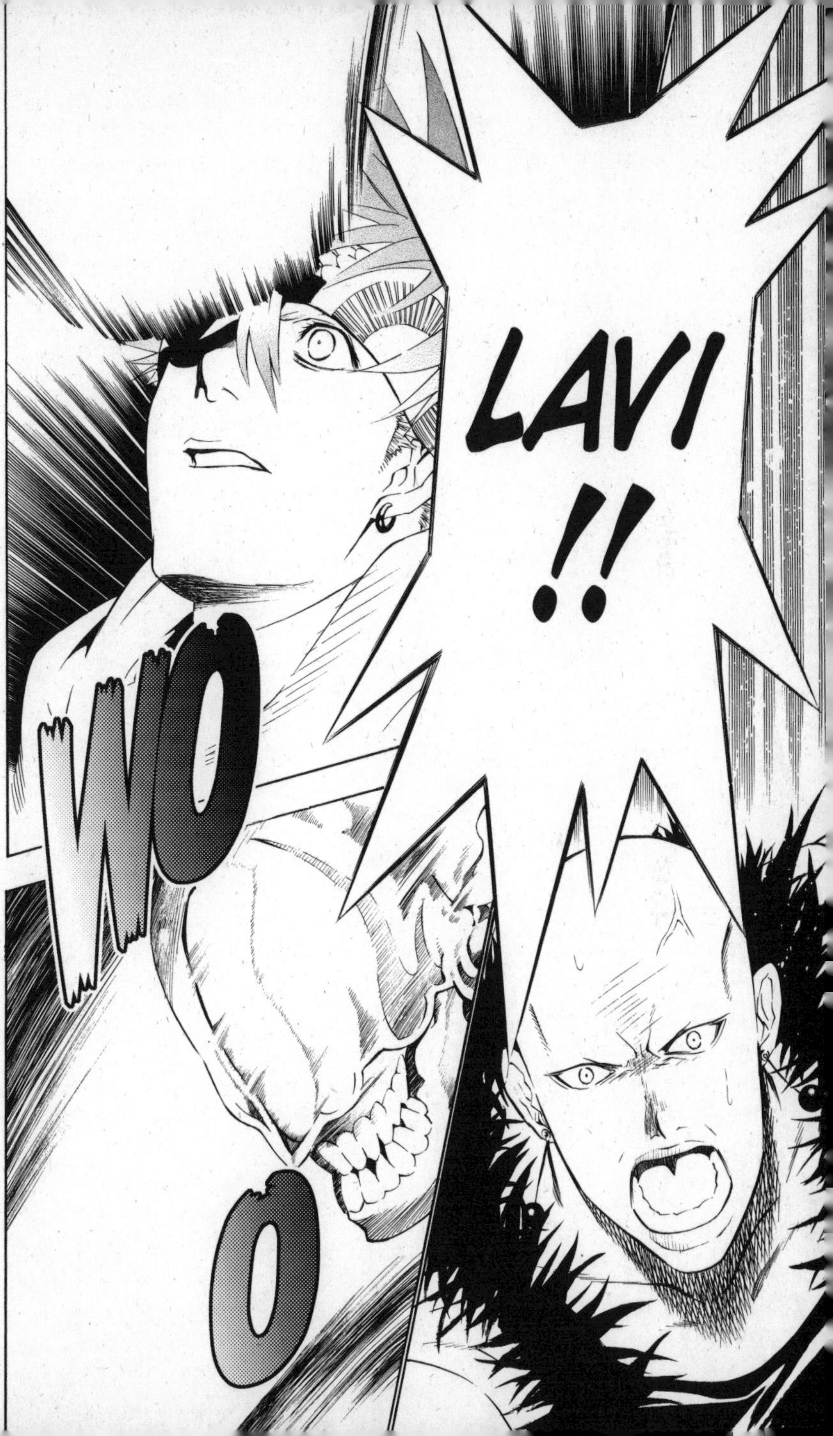
LAVI!!
WOO

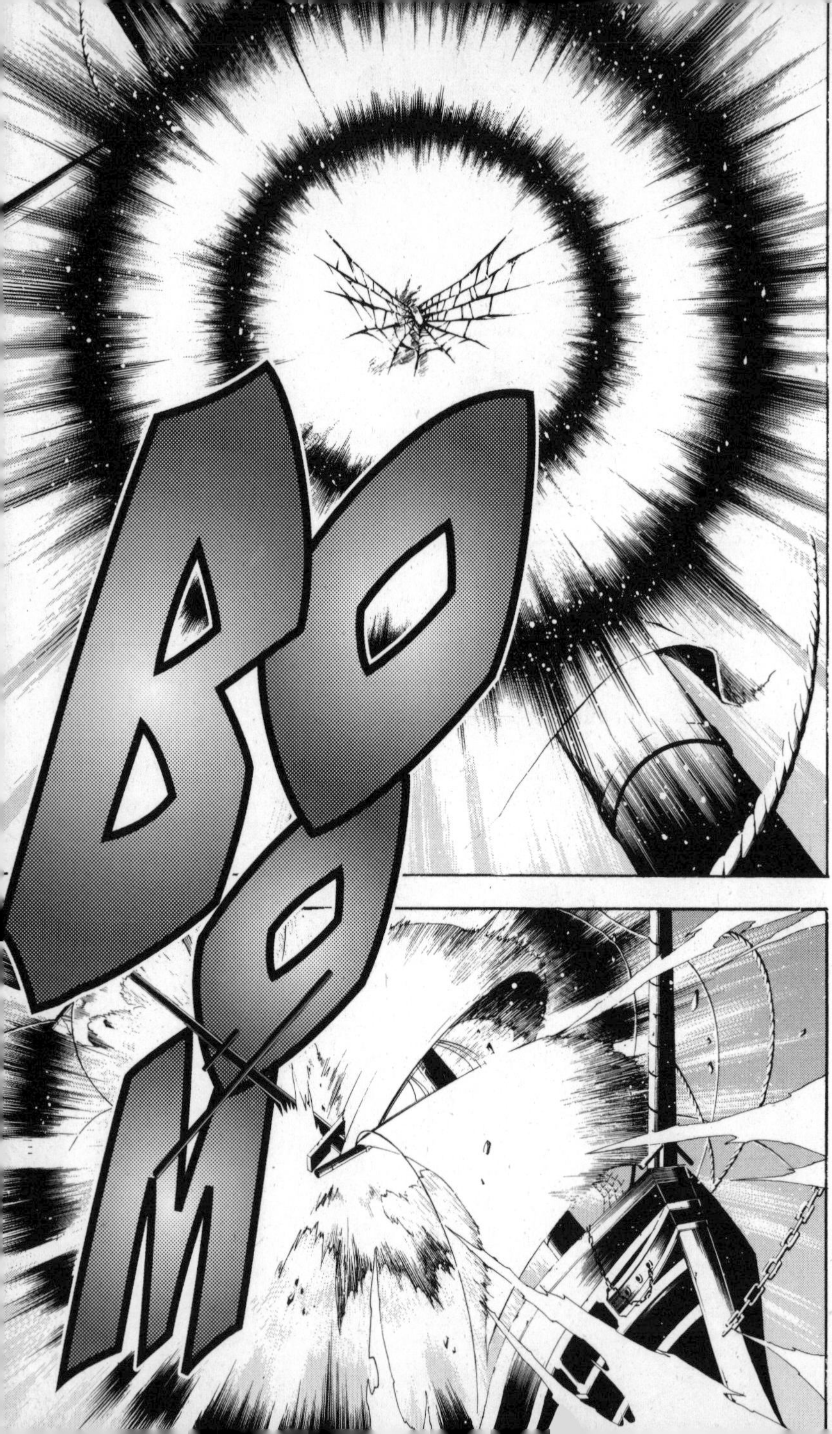
BOOM

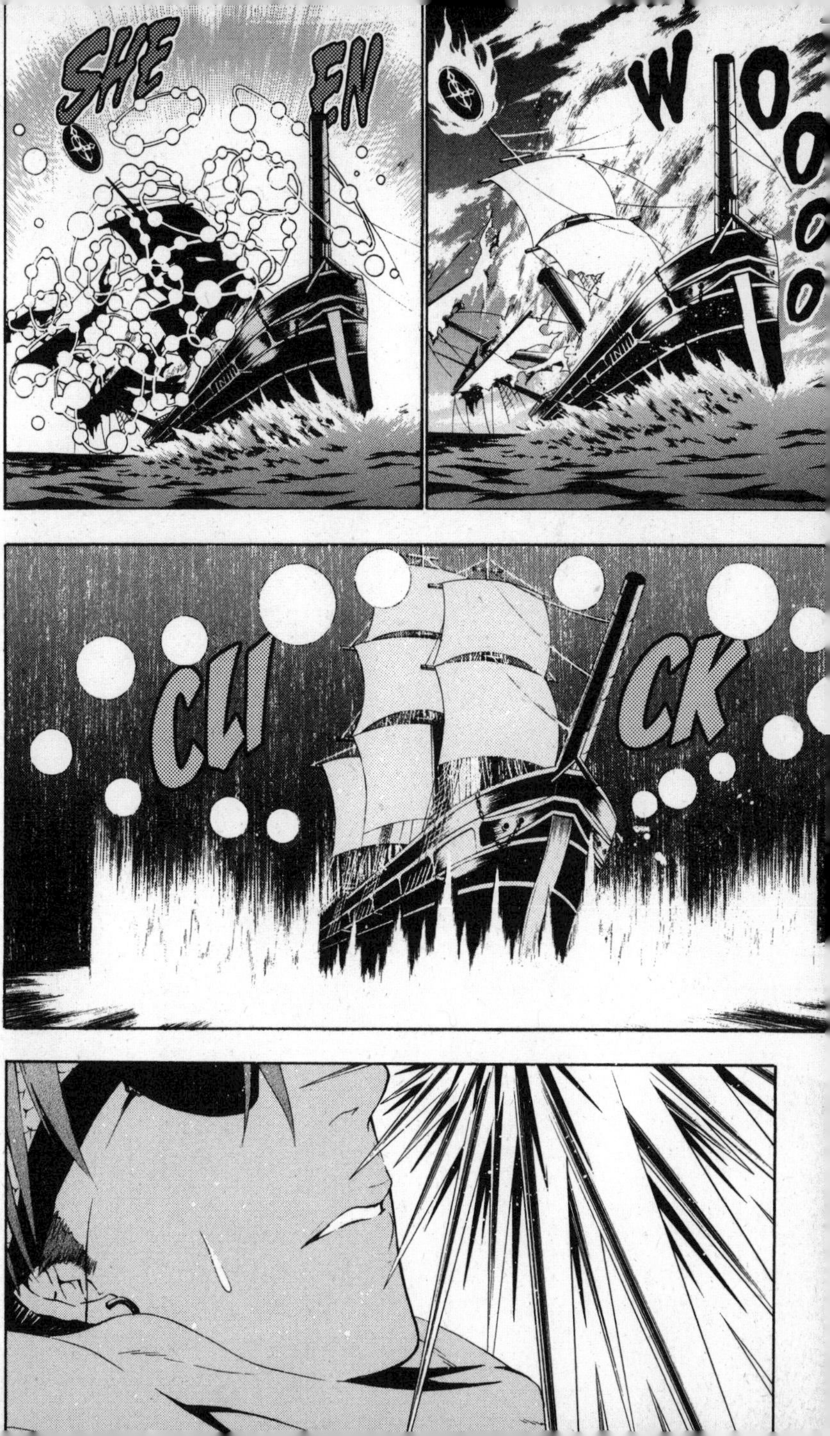
WOOOOO
SHEEN
CLICK

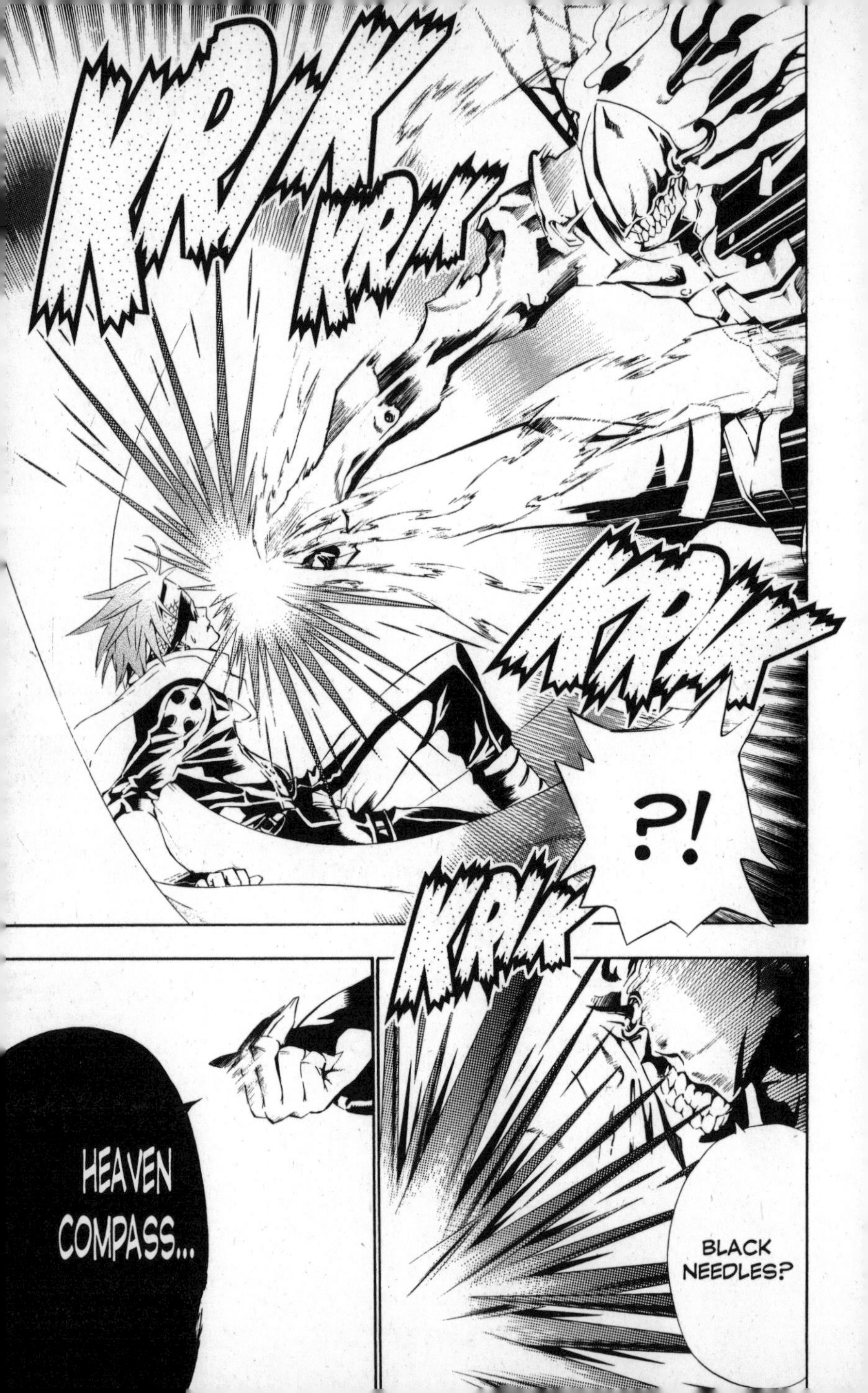
KRAK
KRAK
KRAK
?!
KRAK
BLACK NEEDLES?
HEAVEN COMPASS...

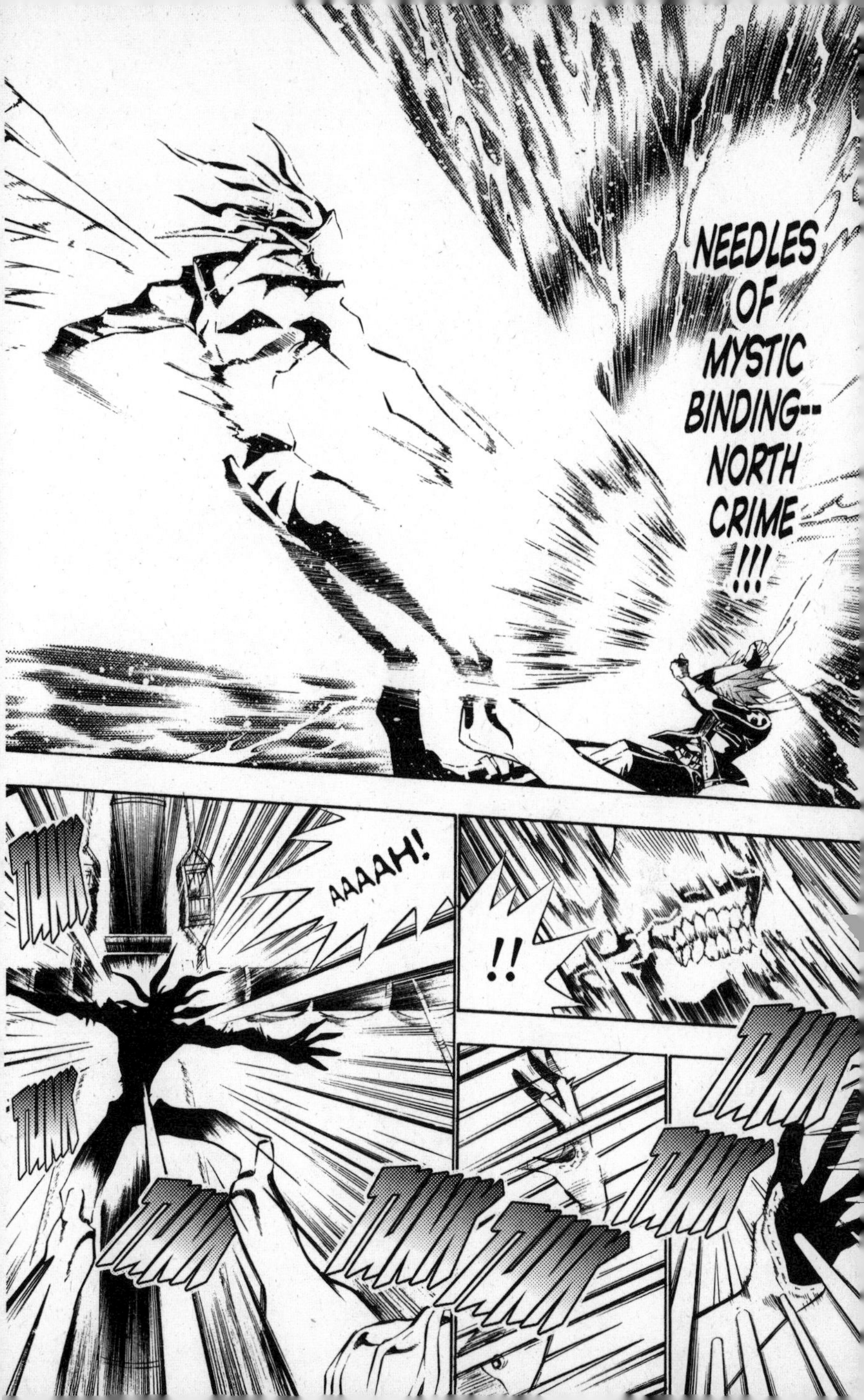
NEEDLES OF MYSTIC BINDING-- NORTH CRIME !!!
!!
AAAAH!
THNK
THNK

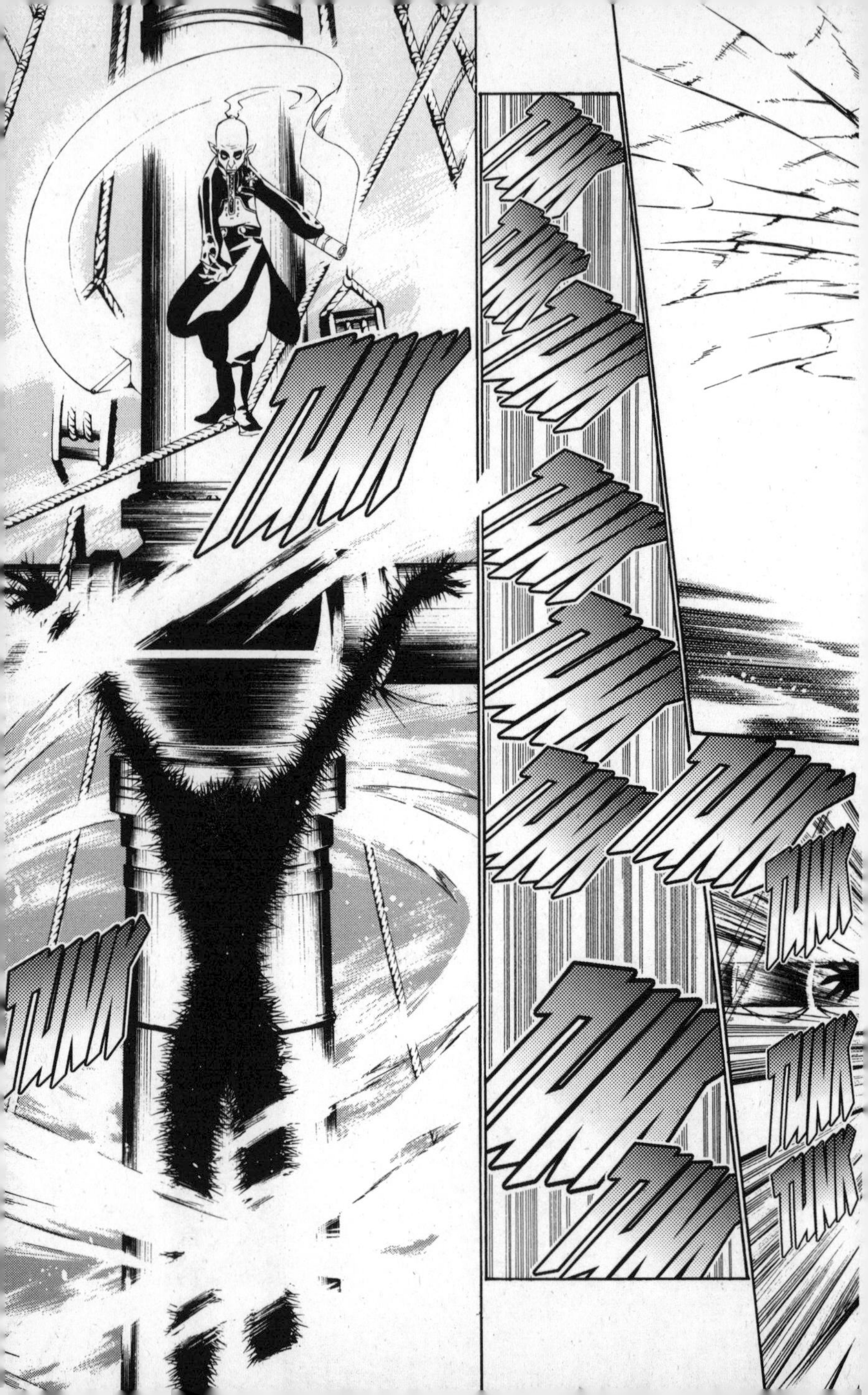
THUNK
THUNK
THUNK
THUNK
THUNK

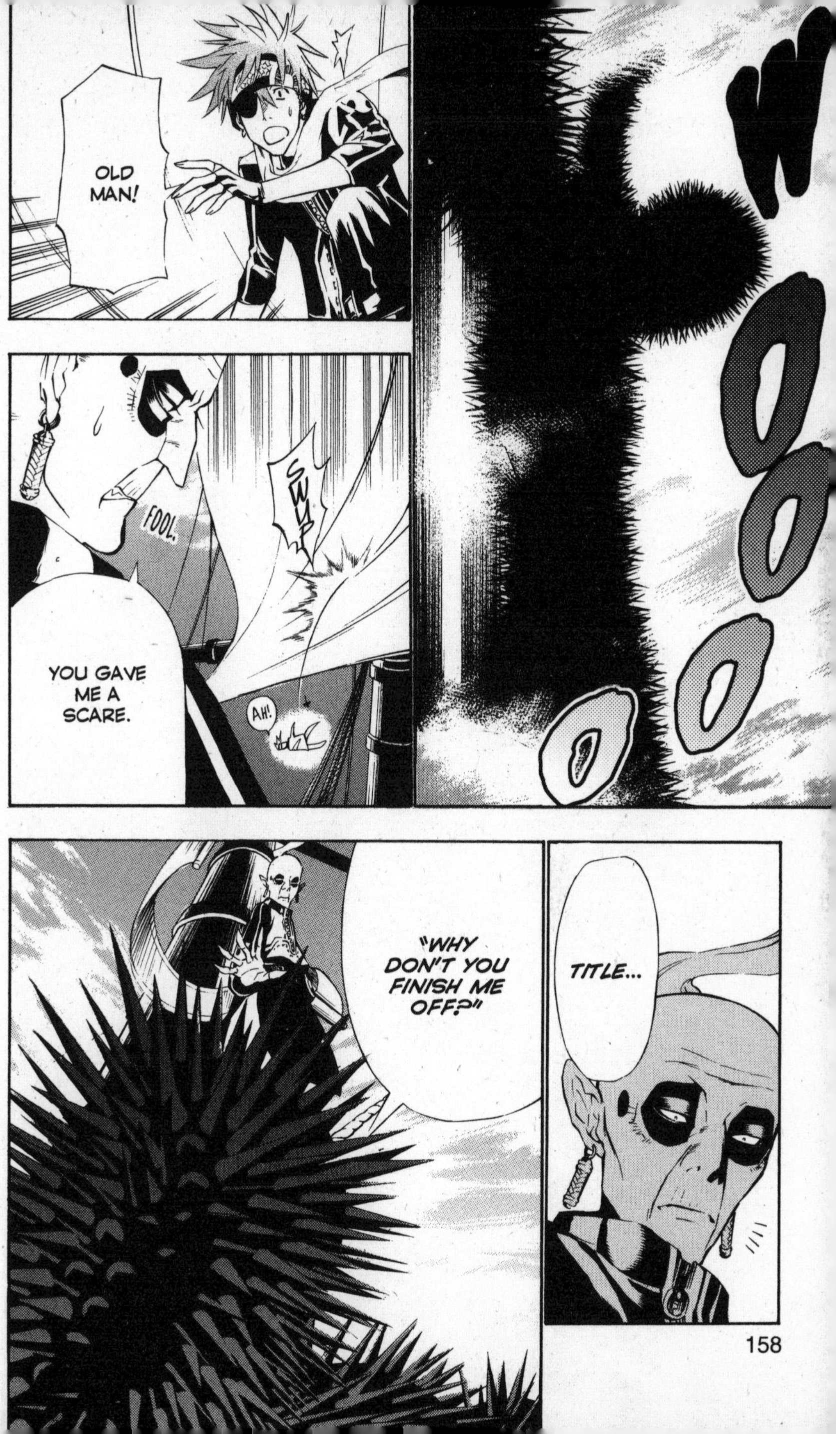
WOOOO
OLD MAN!
FOOL.
SWUP
YOU GAVE ME A SCARE.
AH!
TITLE...
"WHY DON'T YOU FINISH ME OFF?"

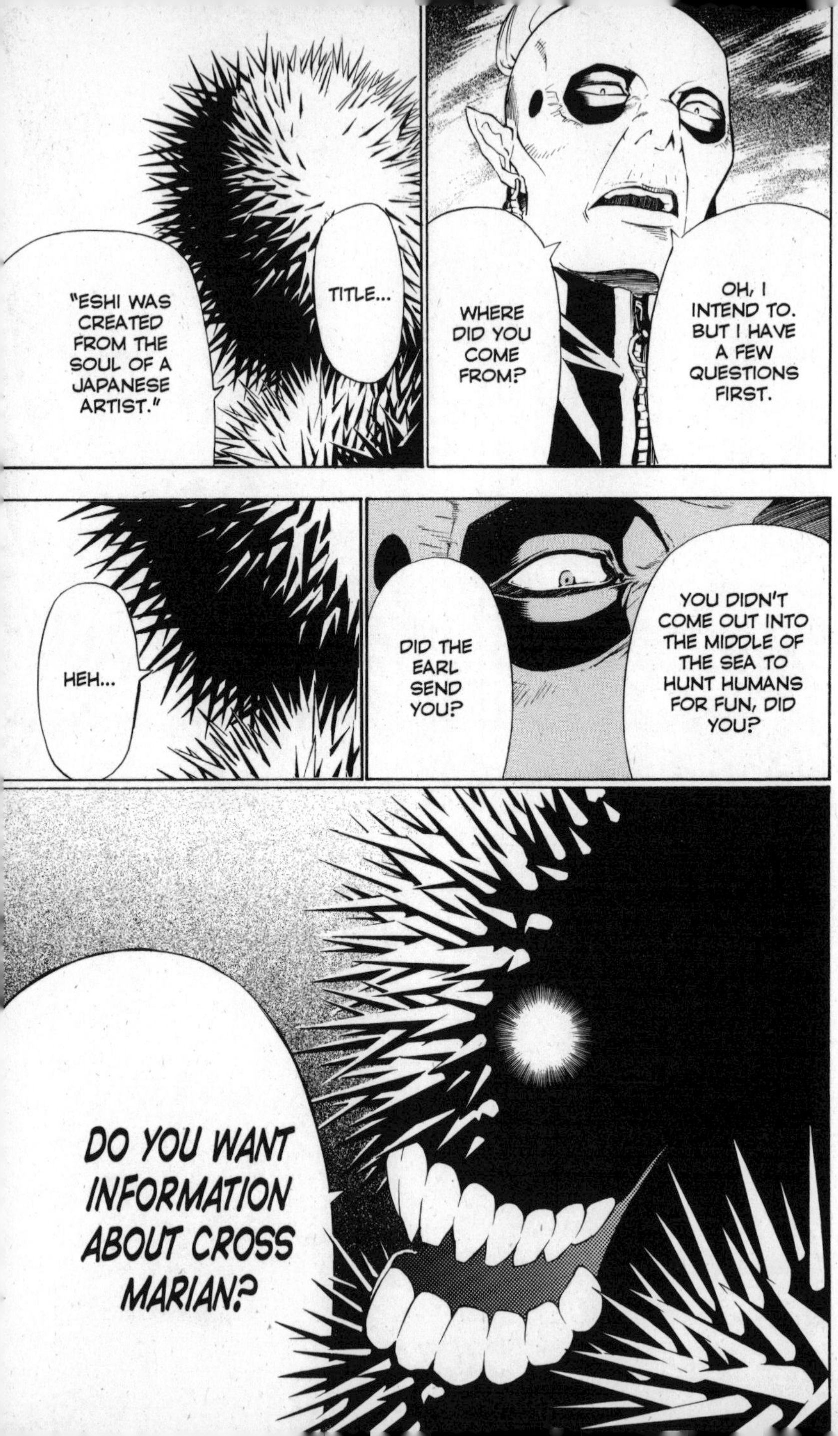
OH, I INTEND TO. BUT I HAVE A FEW QUESTIONS FIRST.
WHERE DID YOU COME FROM?
TITLE...
"ESHI WAS CREATED FROM THE SOUL OF A JAPANESE ARTIST."
YOU DIDN'T COME OUT INTO THE MIDDLE OF THE SEA TO HUNT HUMANS FOR FUN, DID YOU?
DID THE EARL SEND YOU?
HEH...
DO YOU WANT INFORMATION ABOUT CROSS MARIAN?

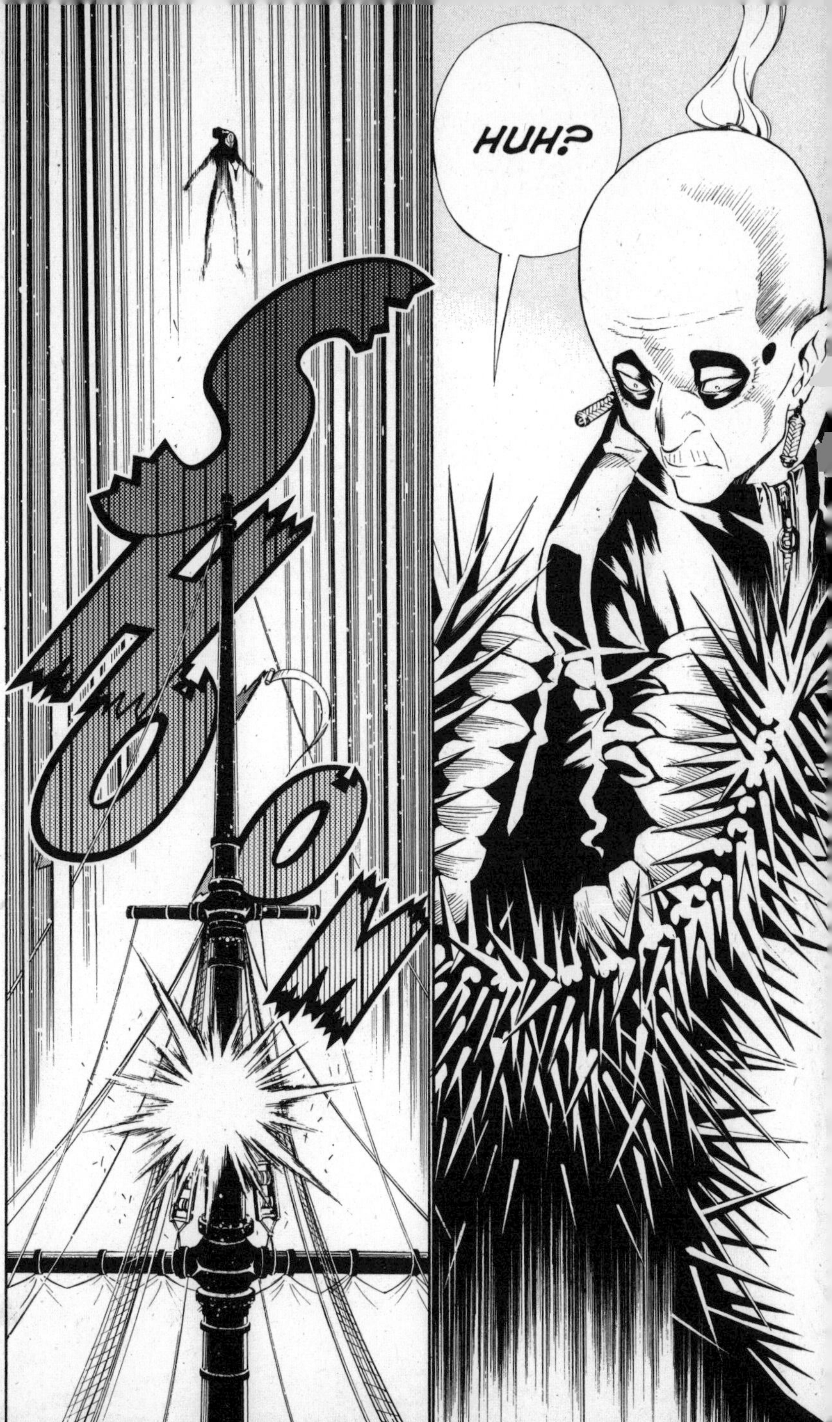
HUH?

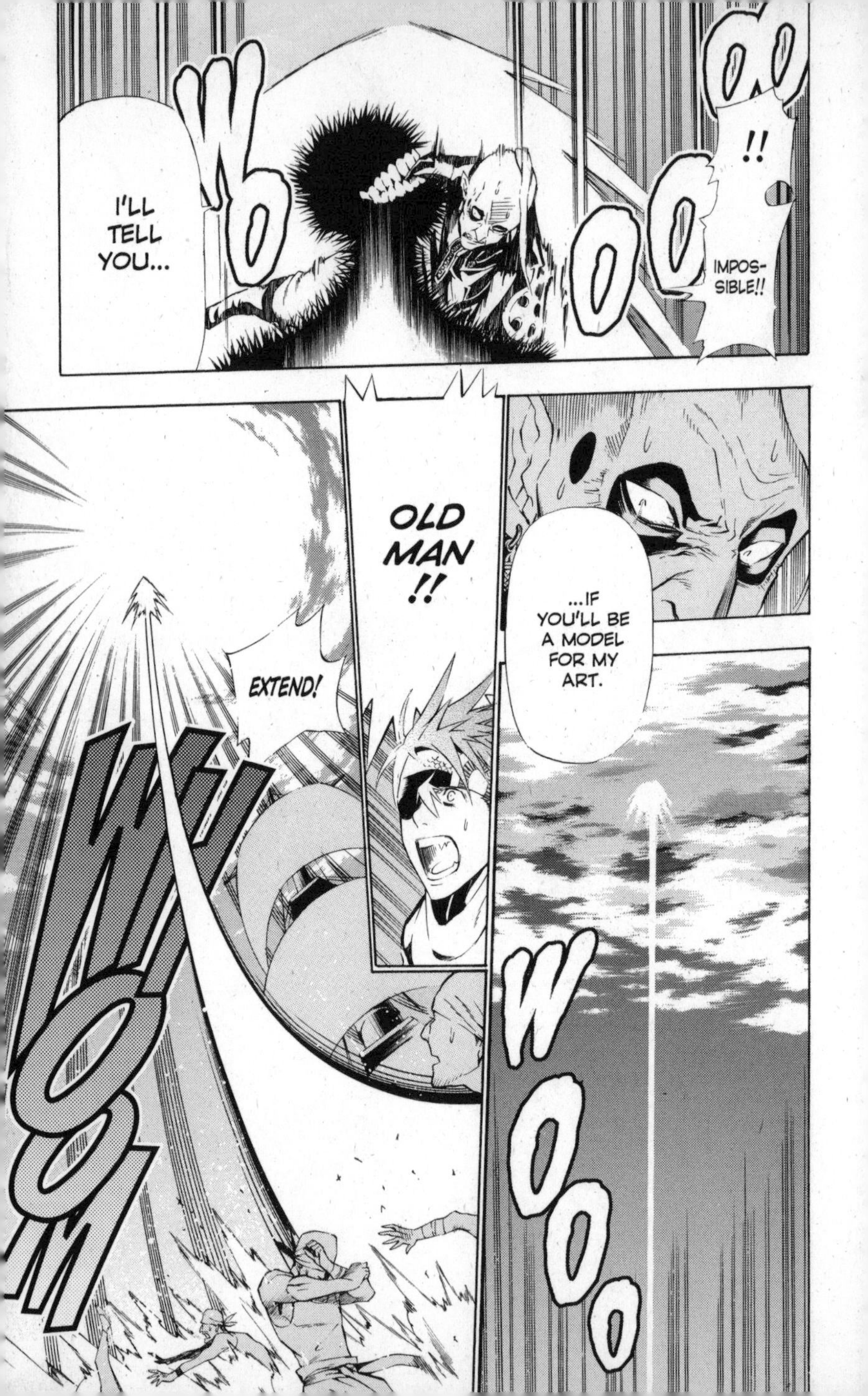
!!
IMPOS-SIBLE!!
WOOOOO
I'LL TELL YOU...
...IF YOU'LL BE A MODEL FOR MY ART.
OLD MAN!!
WOOOOO
EXTEND!
WHOOSH

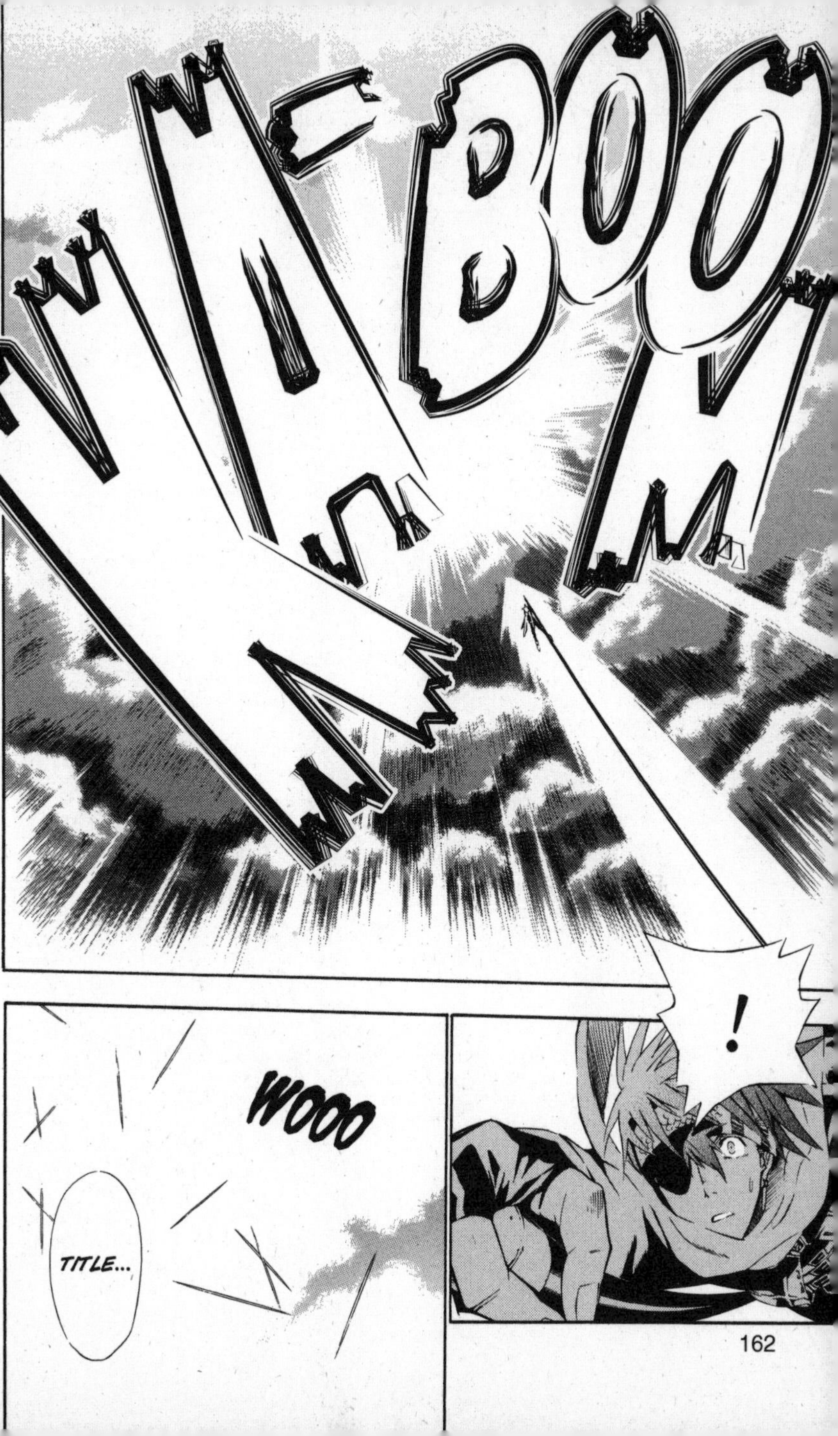
BOOM
!
WOOO
TITLE...

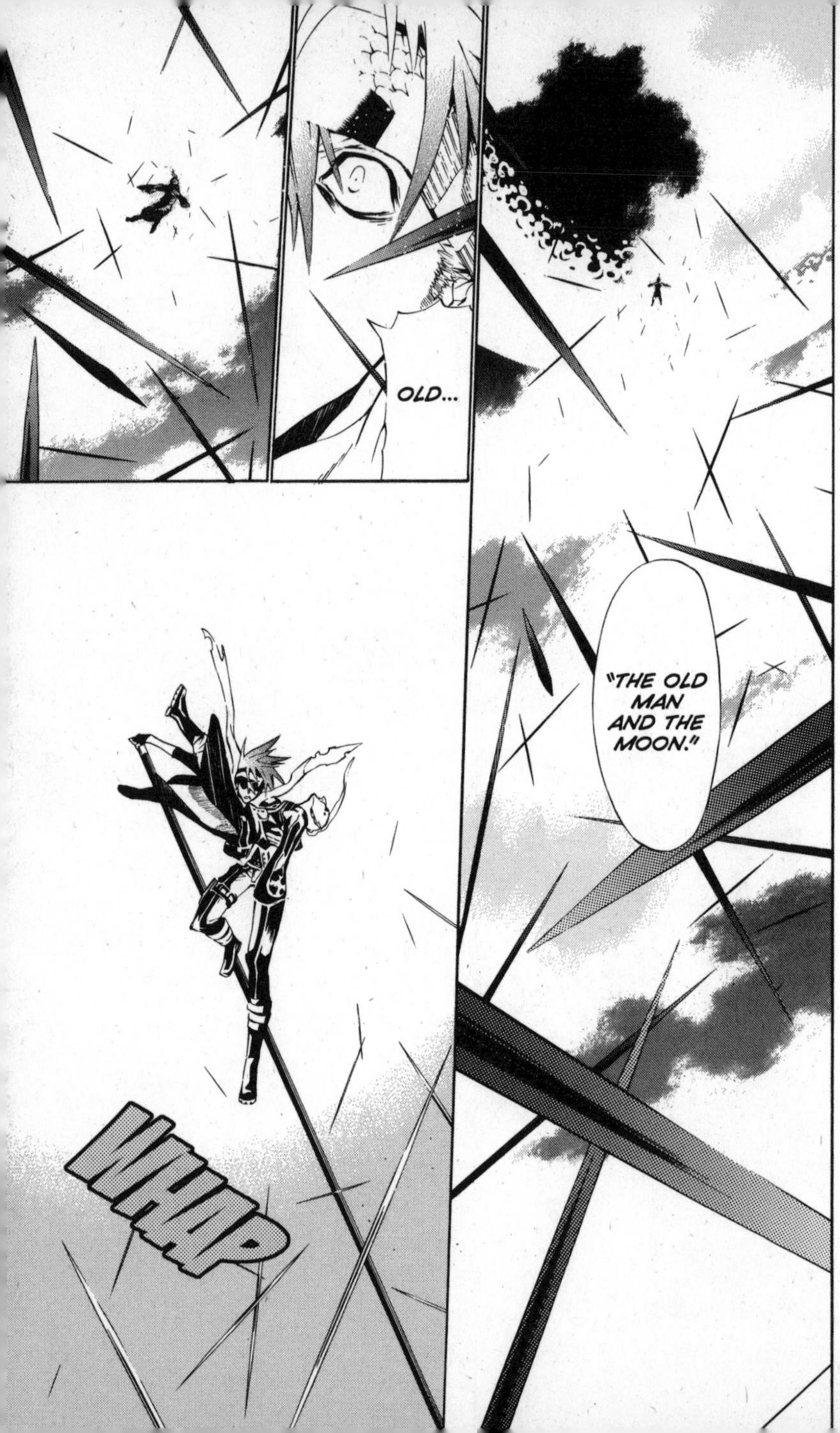
OLD...
"THE OLD MAN AND THE MOON."
WHAP

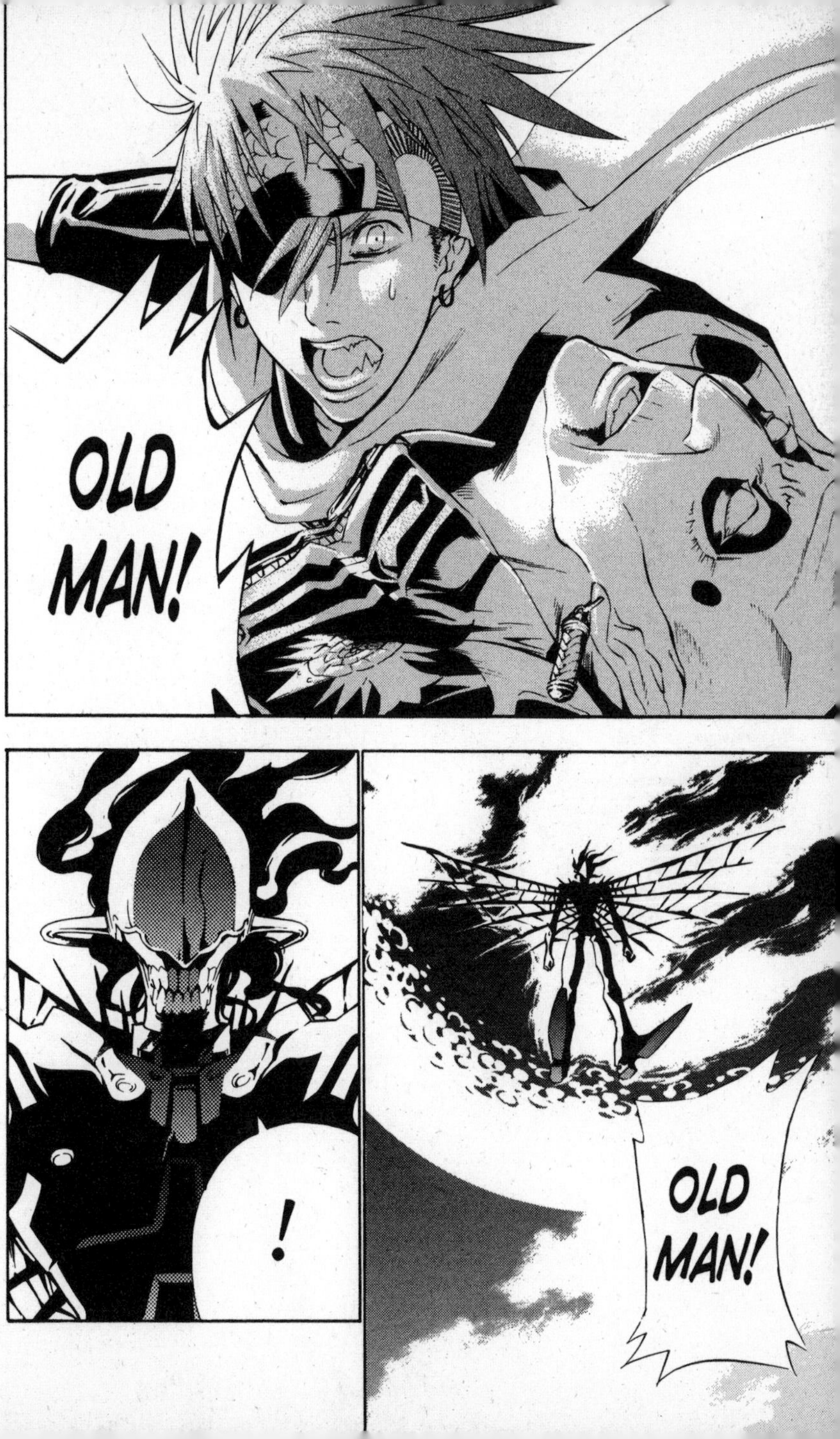
OLD MAN!
OLD MAN!
!

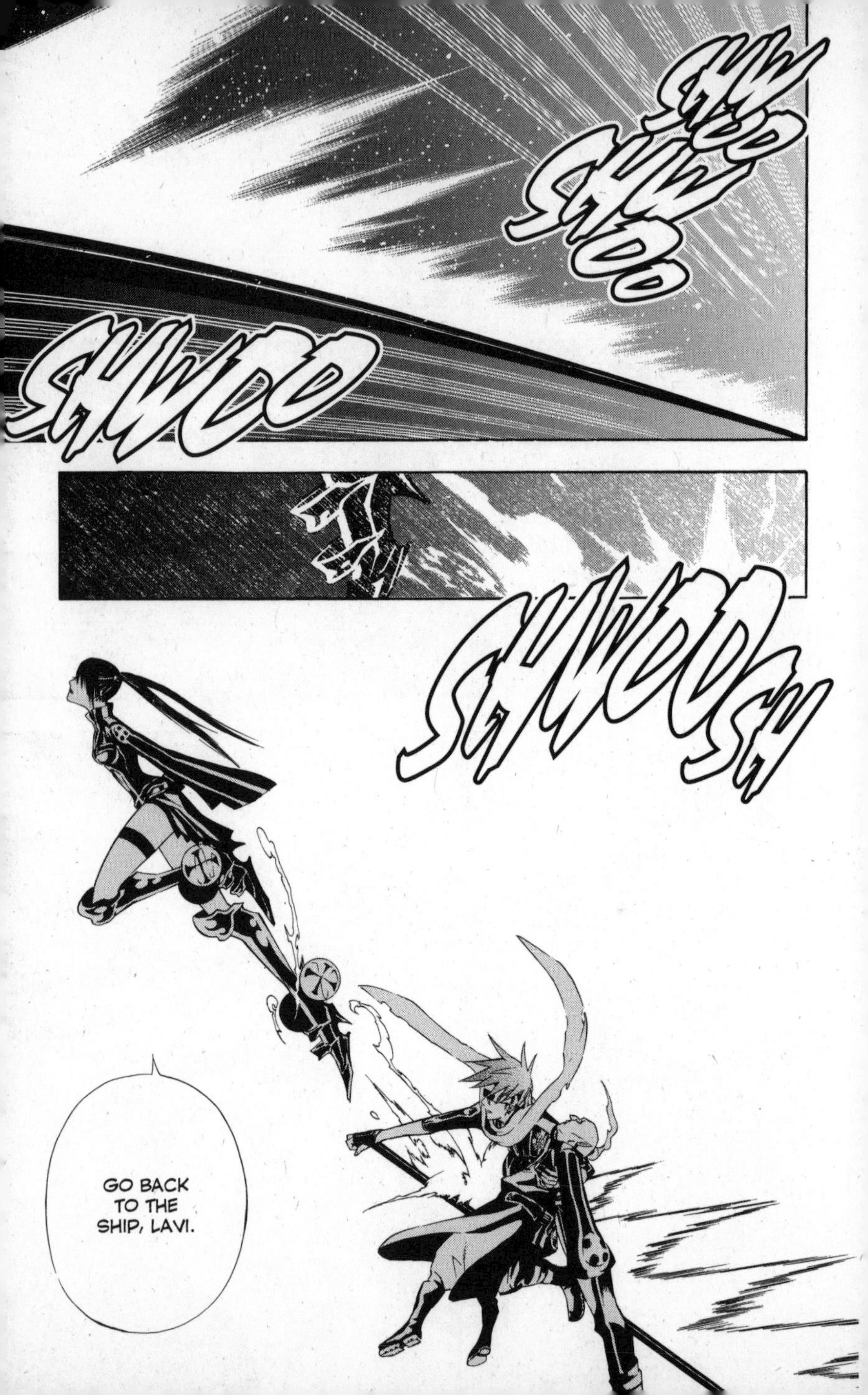
SHWOO
SHWOO
SHWOO
SHWOOSH
GO BACK TO THE SHIP, LAVI.

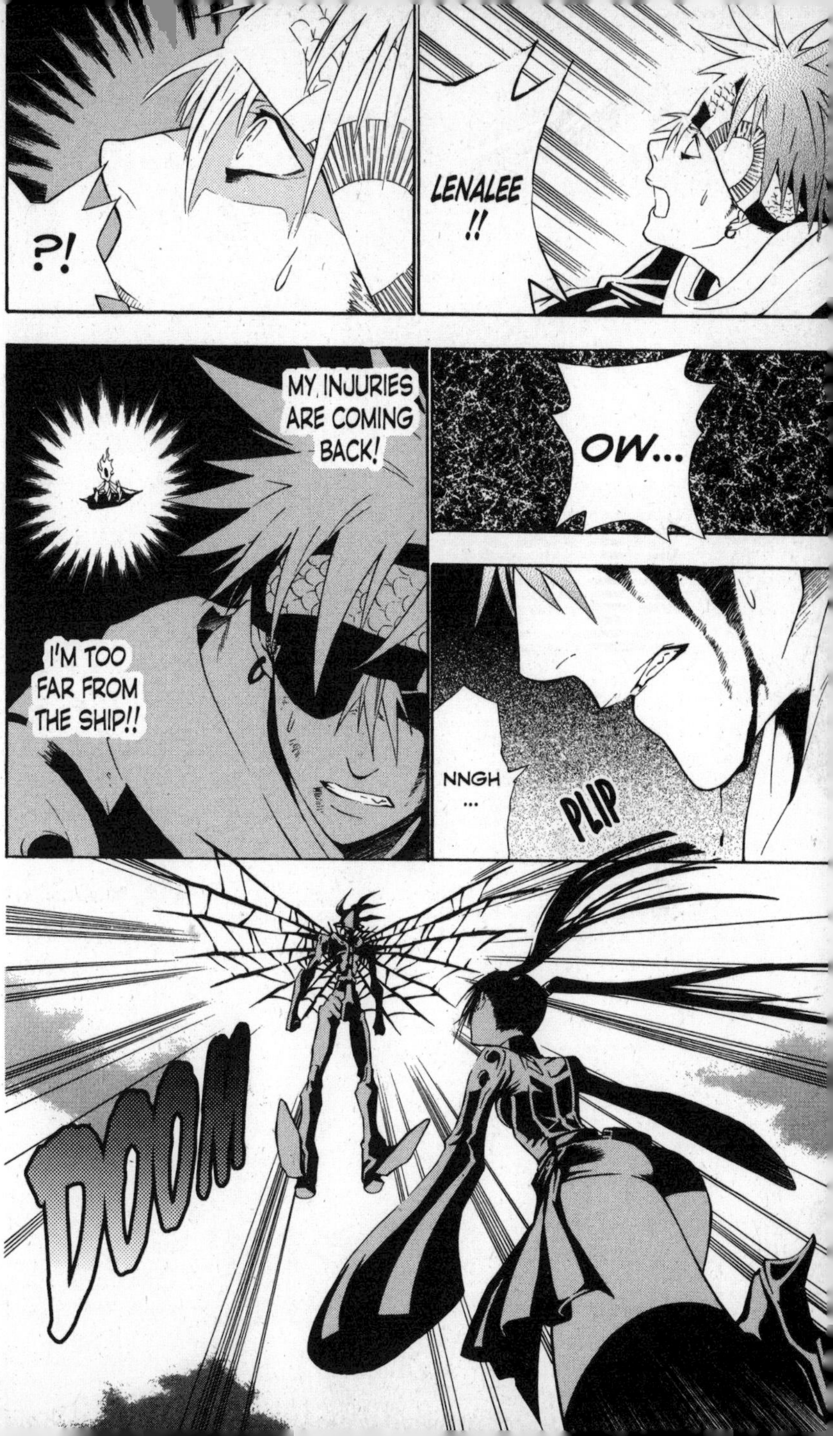
LENALEE !!
?!
OW...
NNGH ...
PLIP
MY INJURIES ARE COMING BACK!
I'M TOO FAR FROM THE SHIP!!
DOOM

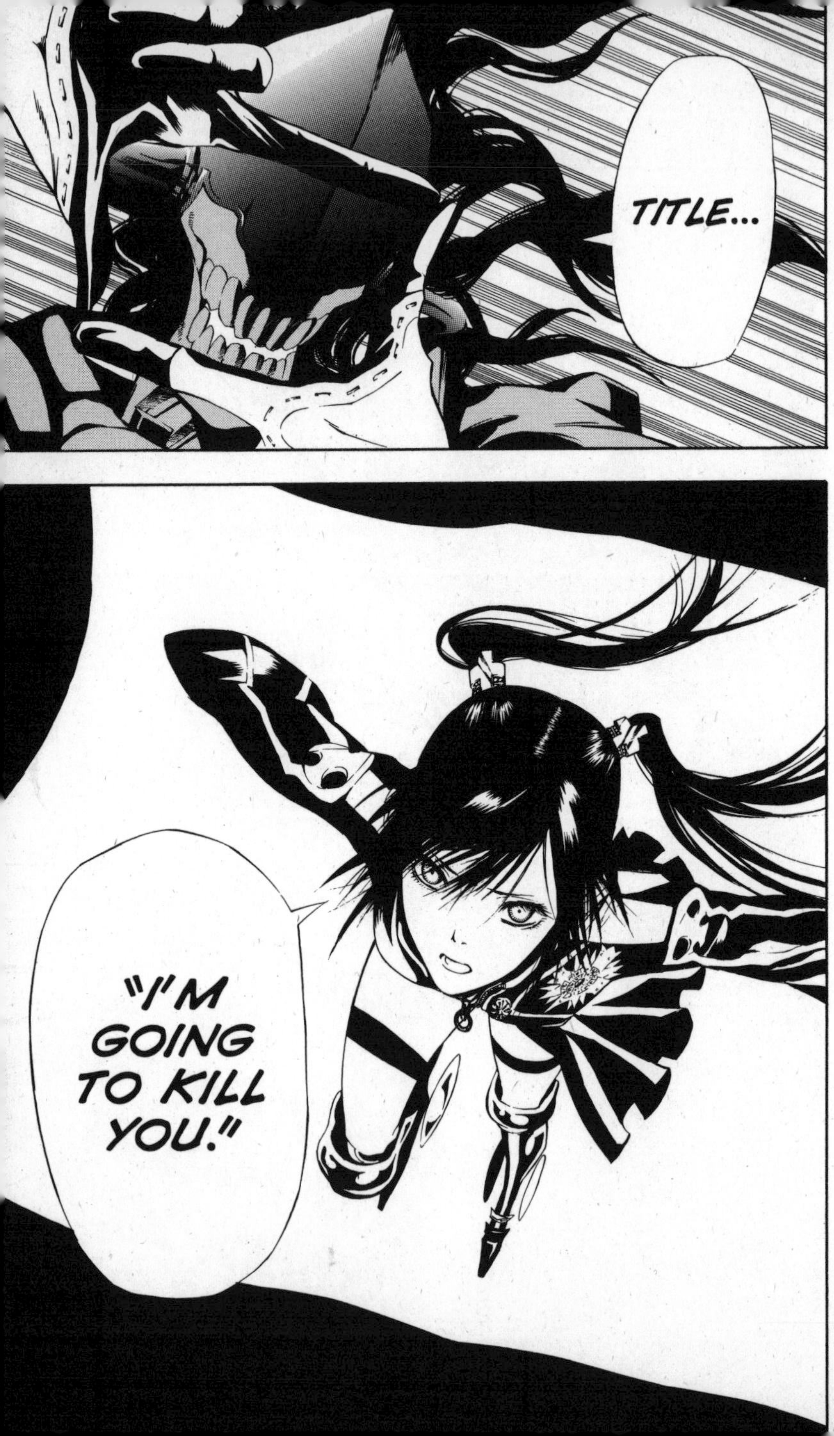
TITLE...
"I'M GOING TO KILL YOU."

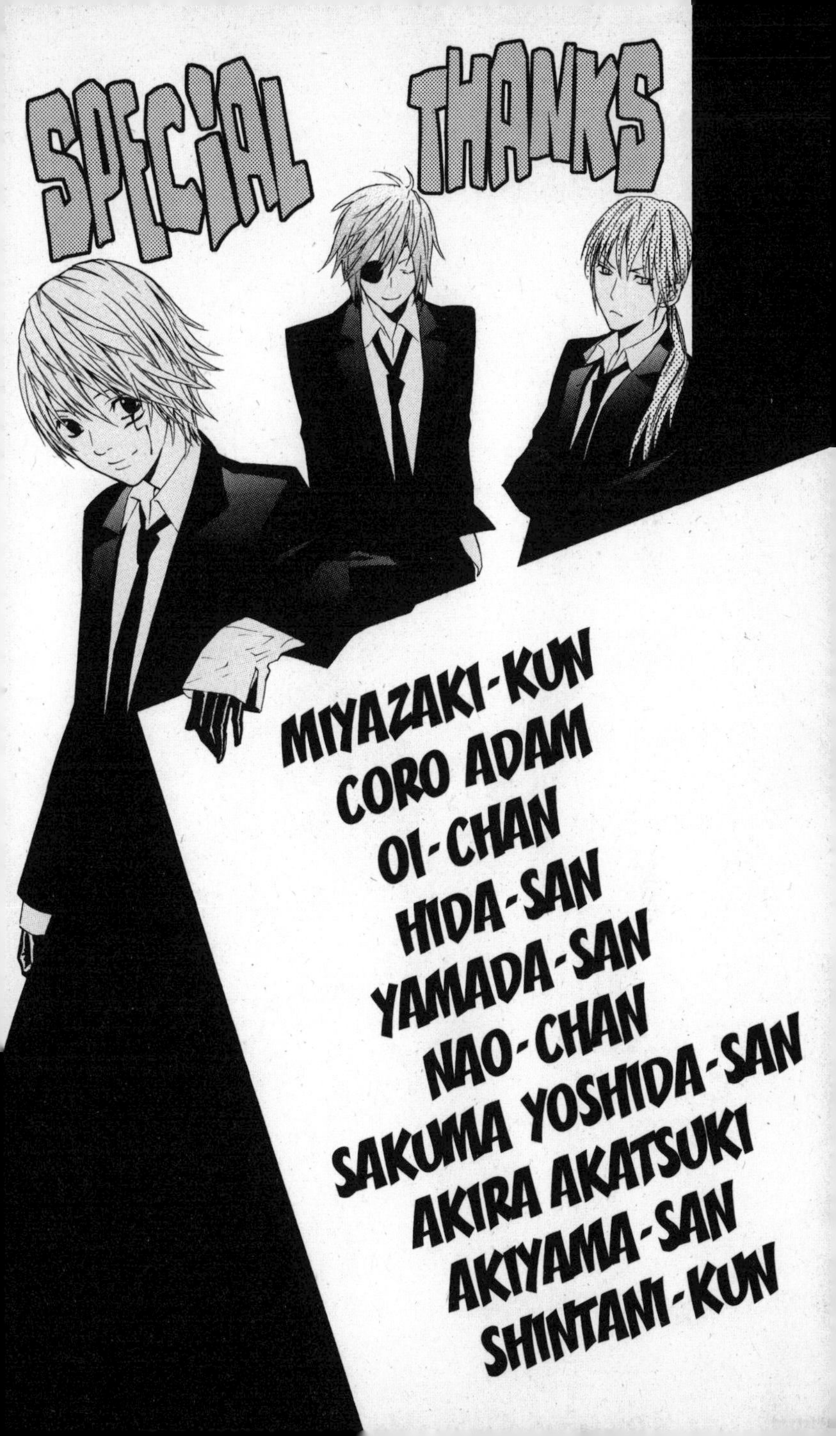
SPECIAL THANKS
MIYAZAKI-KUN
CORO ADAM
OI-CHAN
HIDA-SAN
YAMADA-SAN
NAO-CHAN
SAKUMA YOSHIDA-SAN
AKIRA AKATSUKI
AKIYAMA-SAN
SHINTANI-KUN

THE 66TH NIGHT: FROM SEA AND CLOUDS

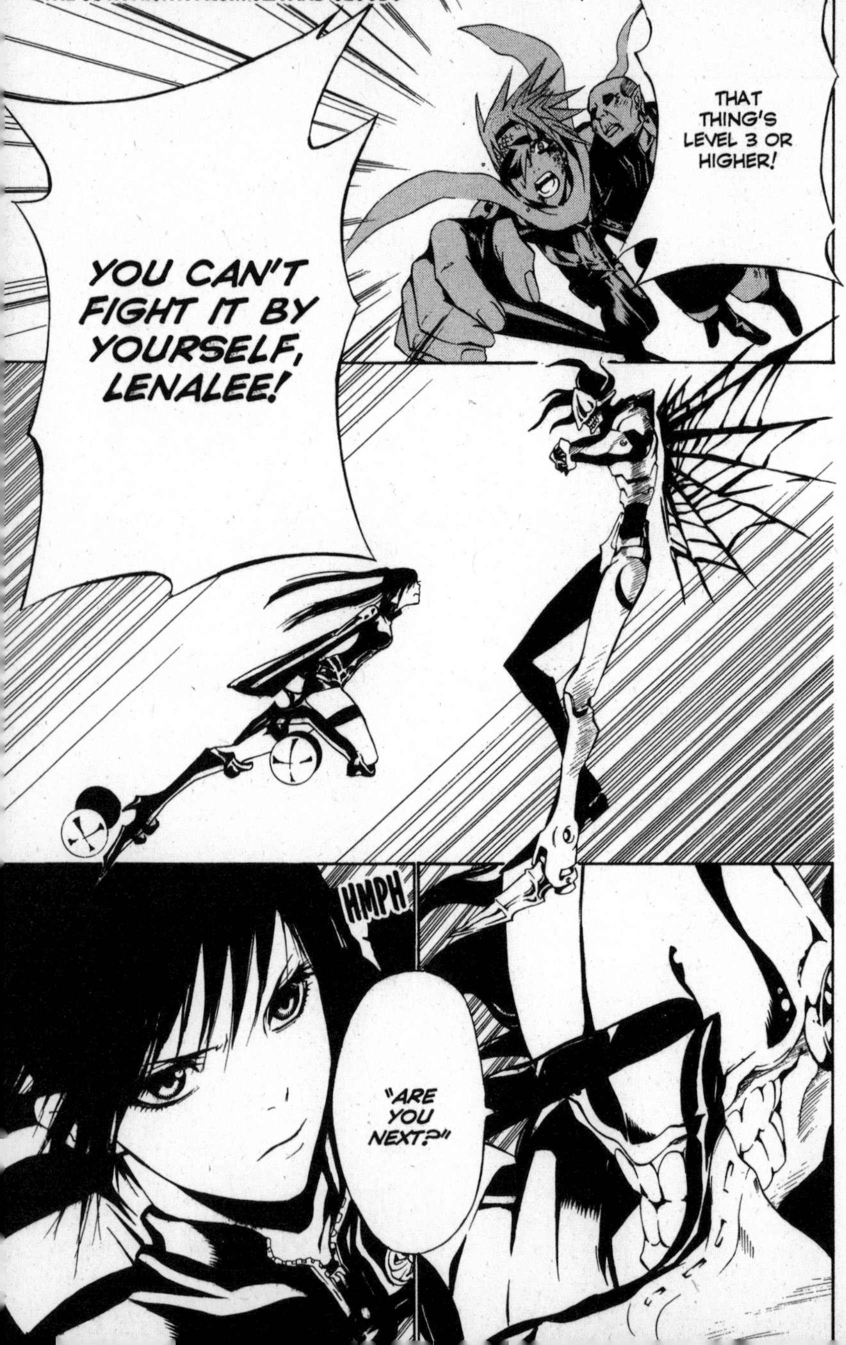
THAT THING'S LEVEL 3 OR HIGHER!
YOU CAN'T FIGHT IT BY YOURSELF, LENALEE!
HMPH
"ARE YOU NEXT?"

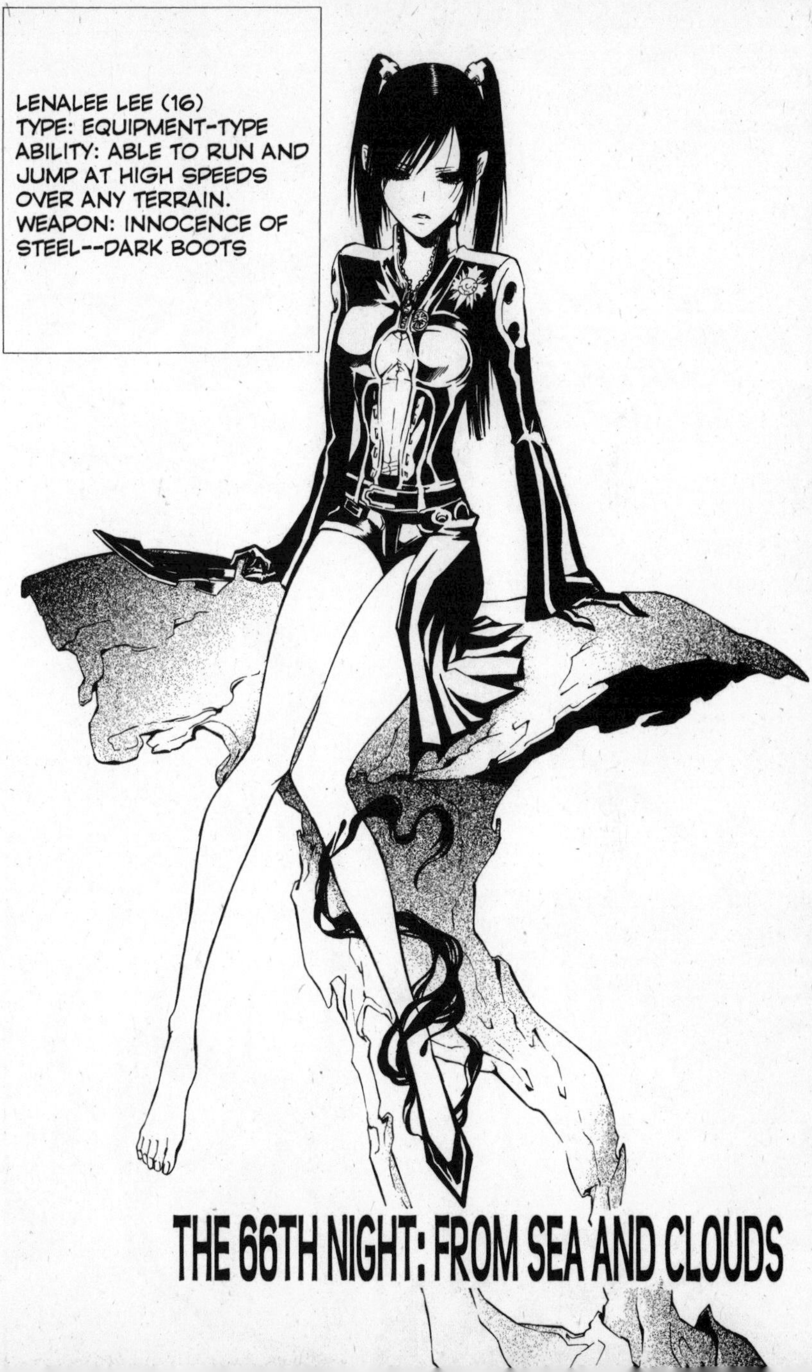
LENALEE LEE (16)
TYPE: EQUIPMENT-TYPE
ABILITY: ABLE TO RUN AND JUMP AT HIGH SPEEDS OVER ANY TERRAIN.
WEAPON: INNOCENCE OF STEEL--DARK BOOTS

THE 66TH NIGHT: FROM SEA AND CLOUDS

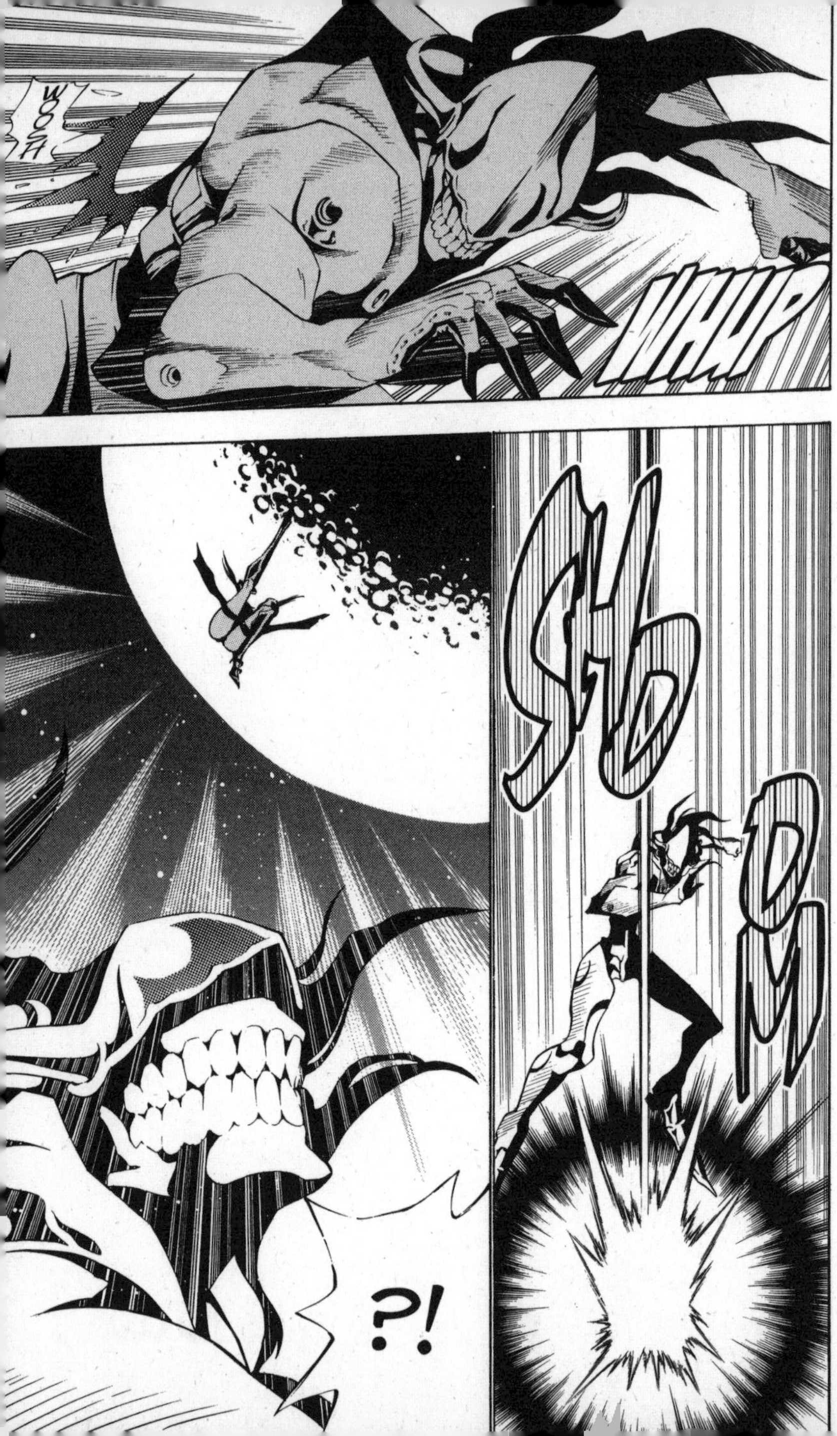
WHUP
WOOSH
SHOOM
?!

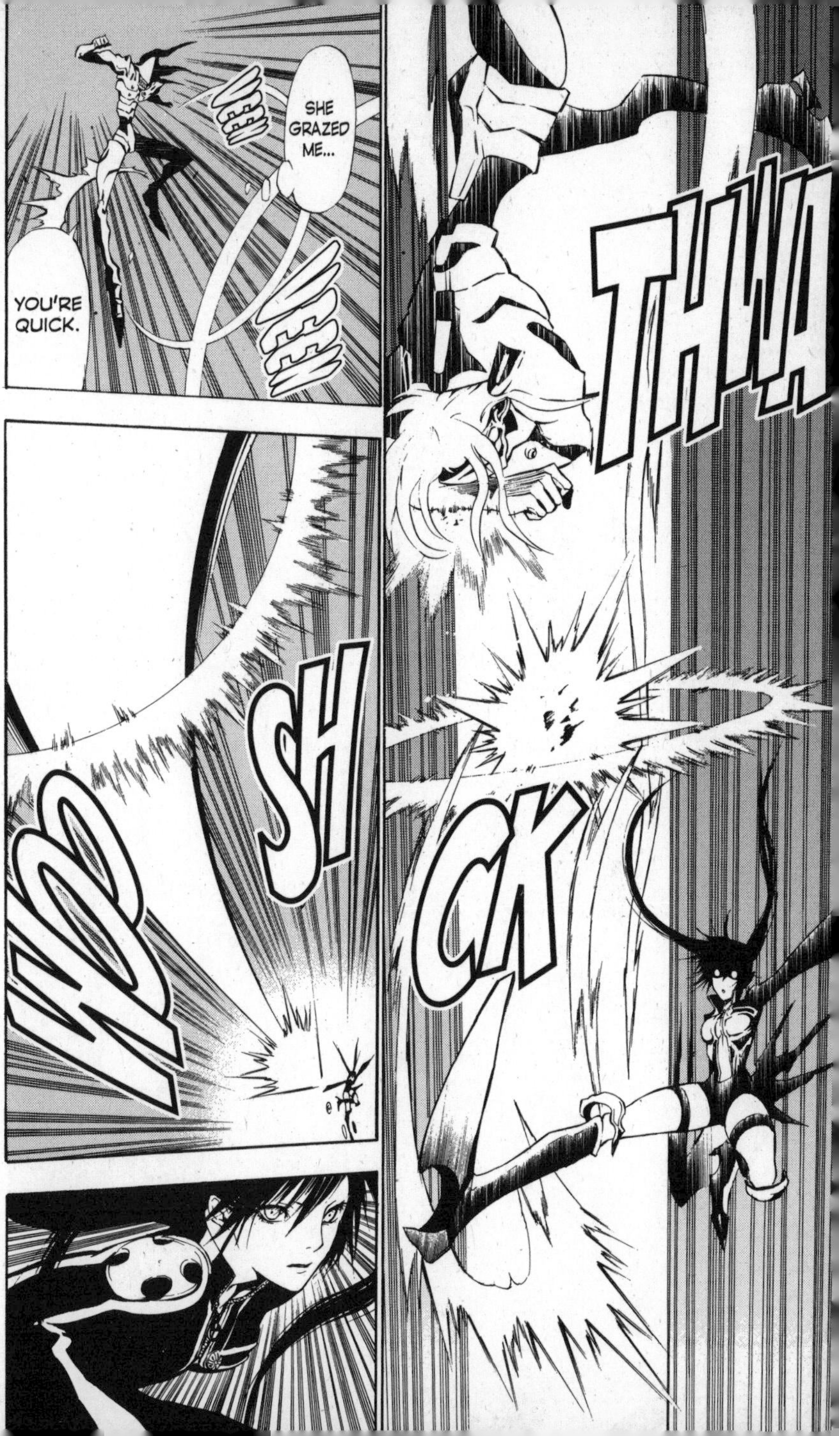
THWACK
SHE GRAZED ME...
YOU'RE QUICK.
WOOSH

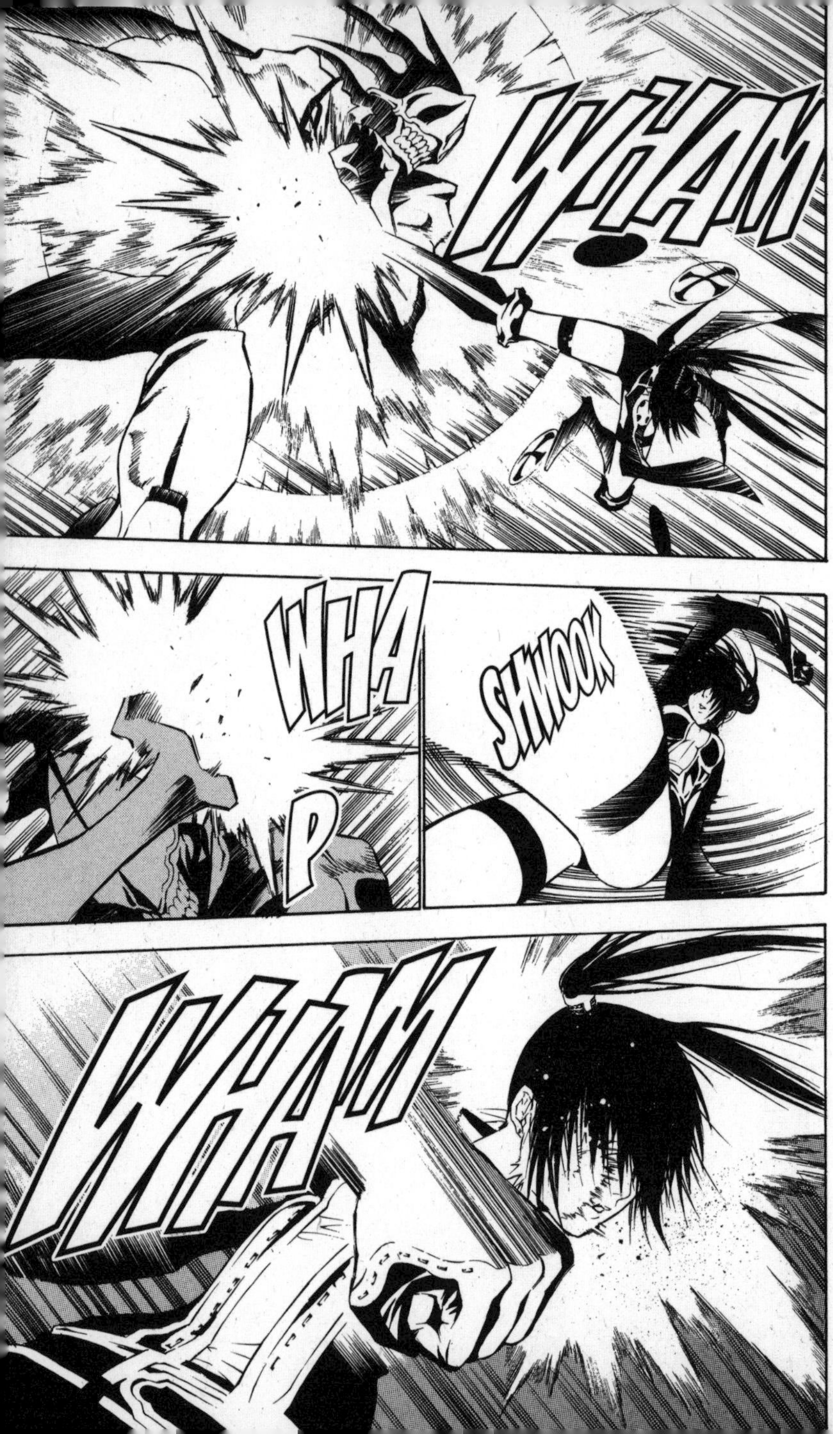
WHAM
SHWOOK
WHAP
WHAM

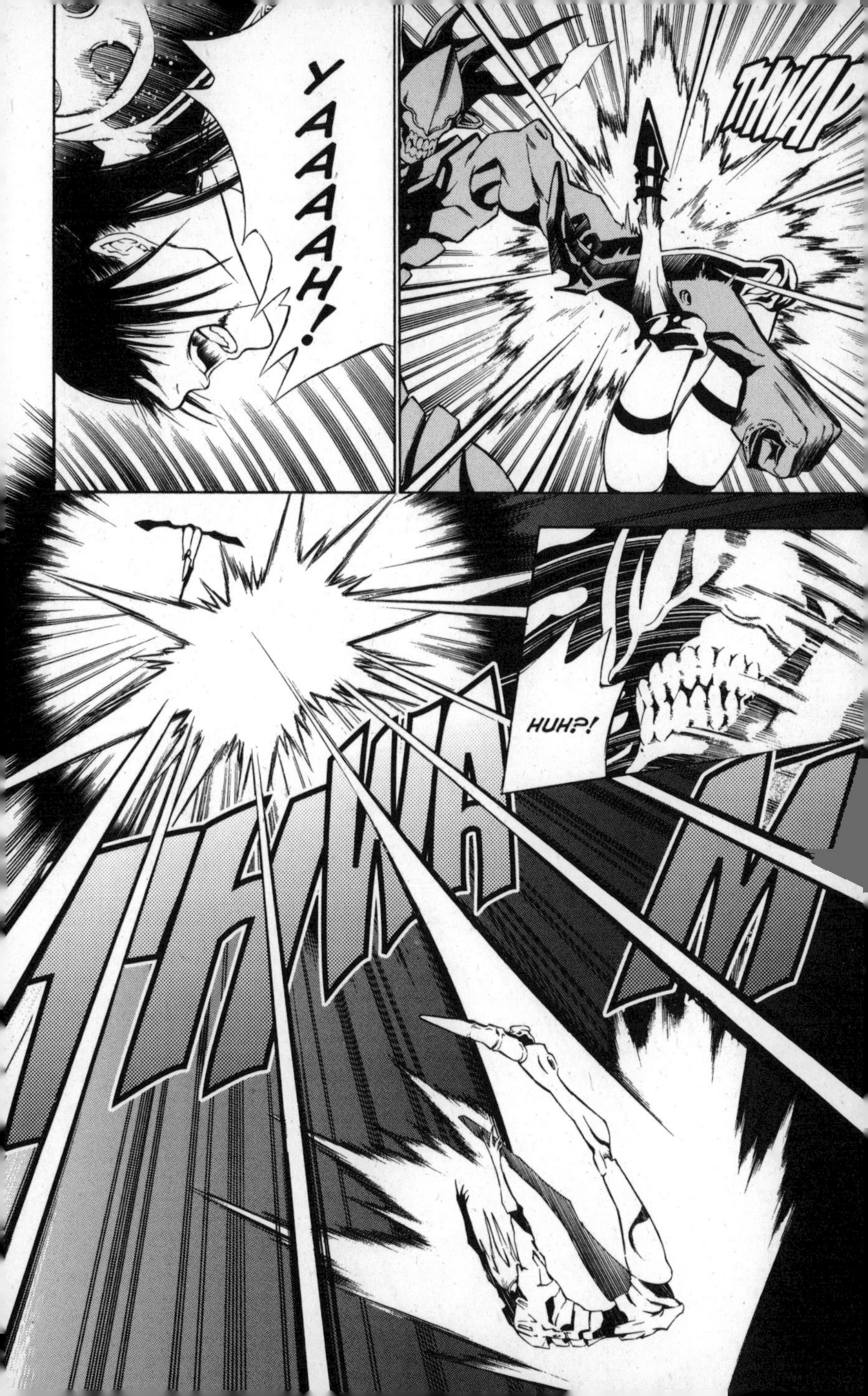
THWAP
YAAAAAH!
HUH?!
THWAM

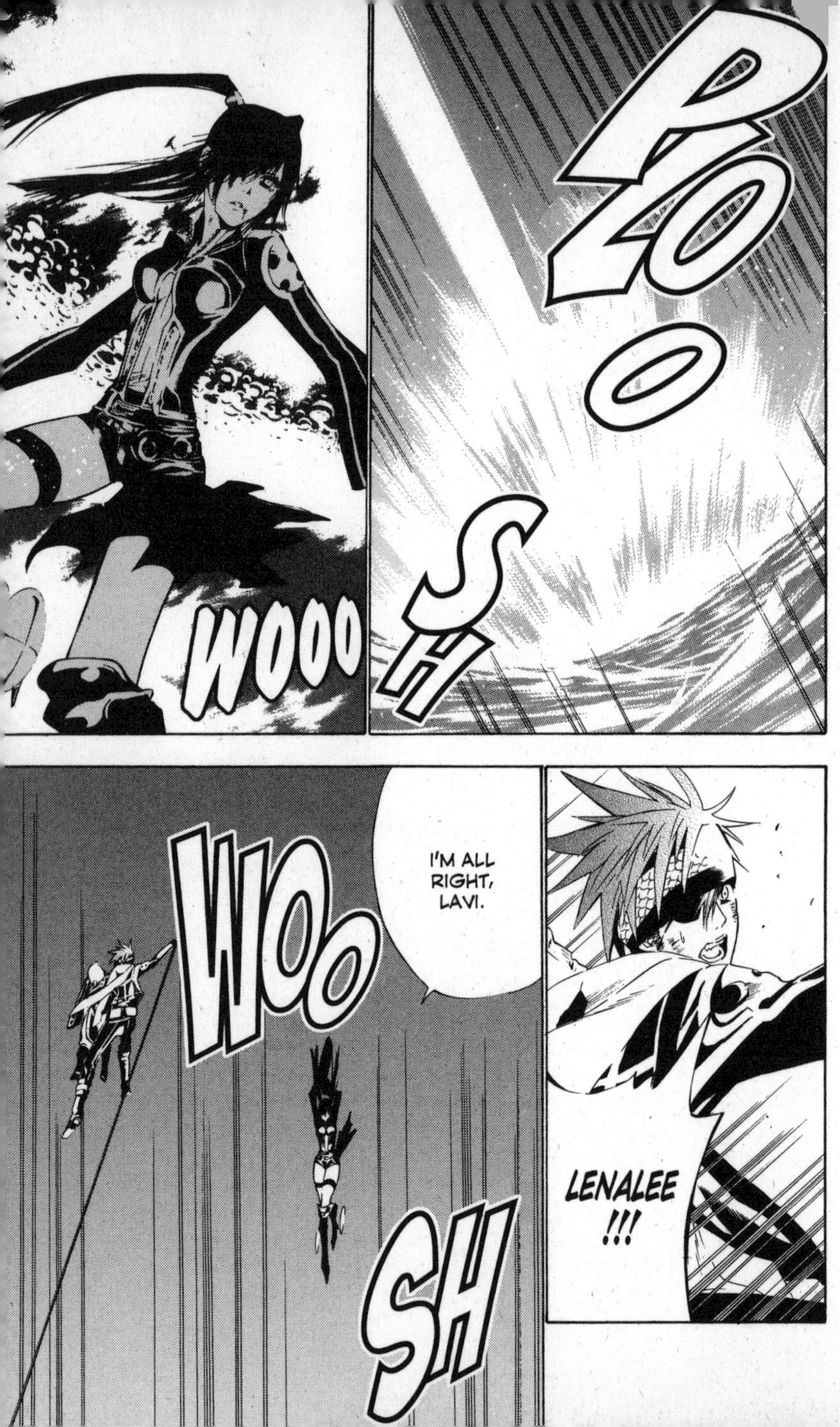
POOOSH
WOOO
LENALEE !!!
I'M ALL RIGHT, LAVI.
WOOSH

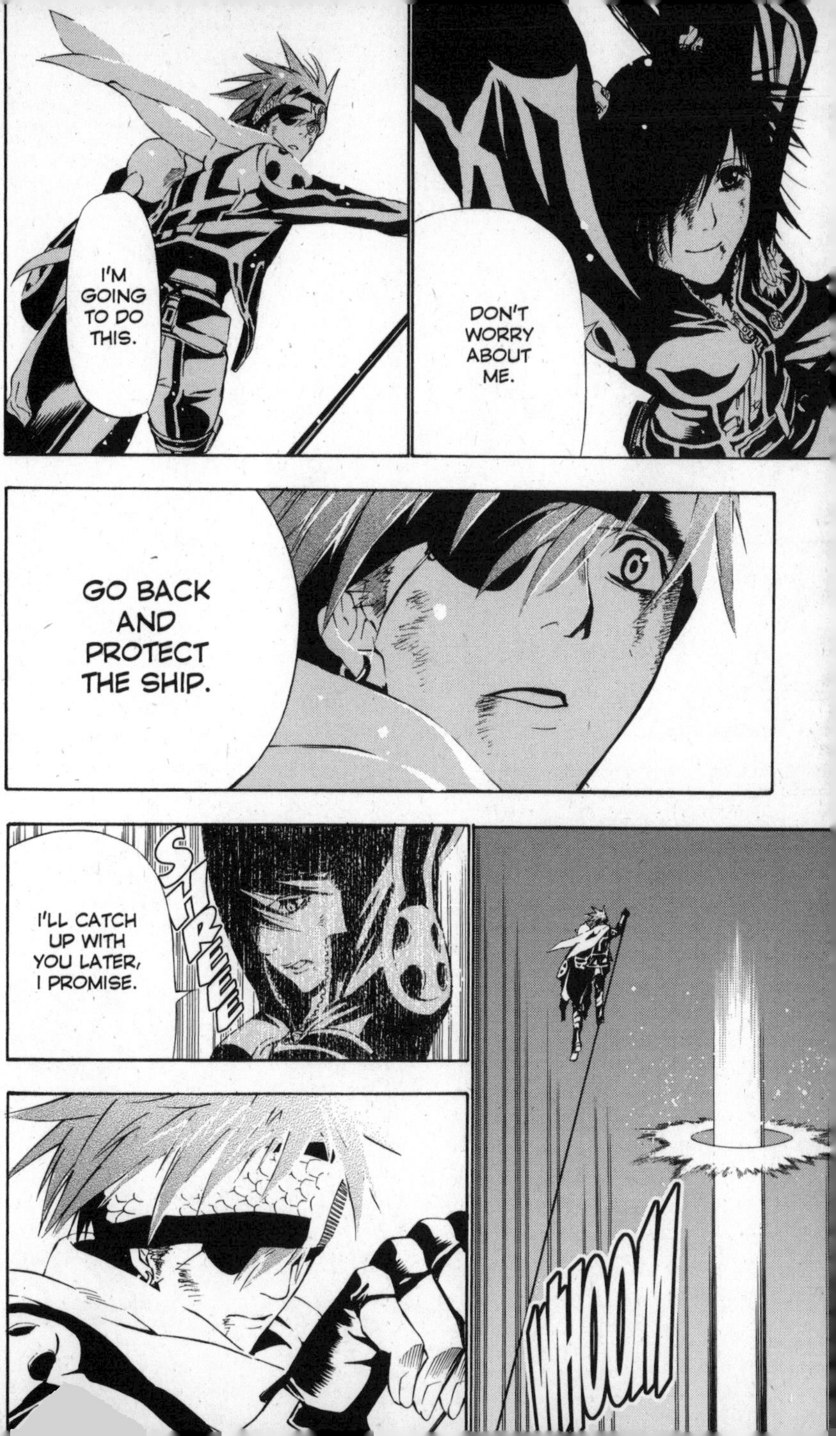
DON'T WORRY ABOUT ME.
I'M GOING TO DO THIS.
GO BACK AND PROTECT THE SHIP.
WHOOM
SHREEE
I'LL CATCH UP WITH YOU LATER, I PROMISE.

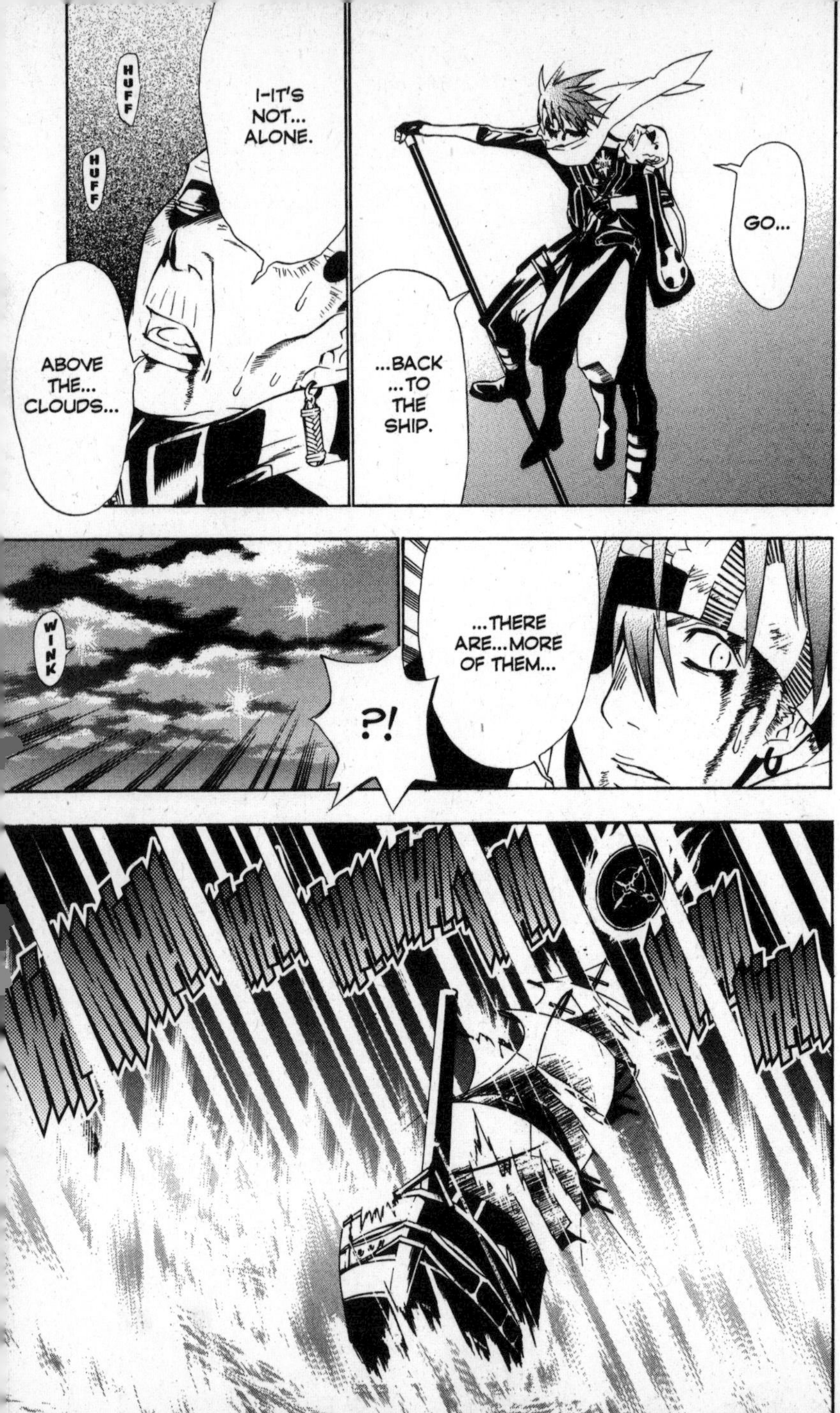
GO...
...BACK ...TO THE SHIP.
I-IT'S NOT... ALONE.
HUFF
HUFF
ABOVE THE... CLOUDS...
...THERE ARE...MORE OF THEM...
?!
WINK

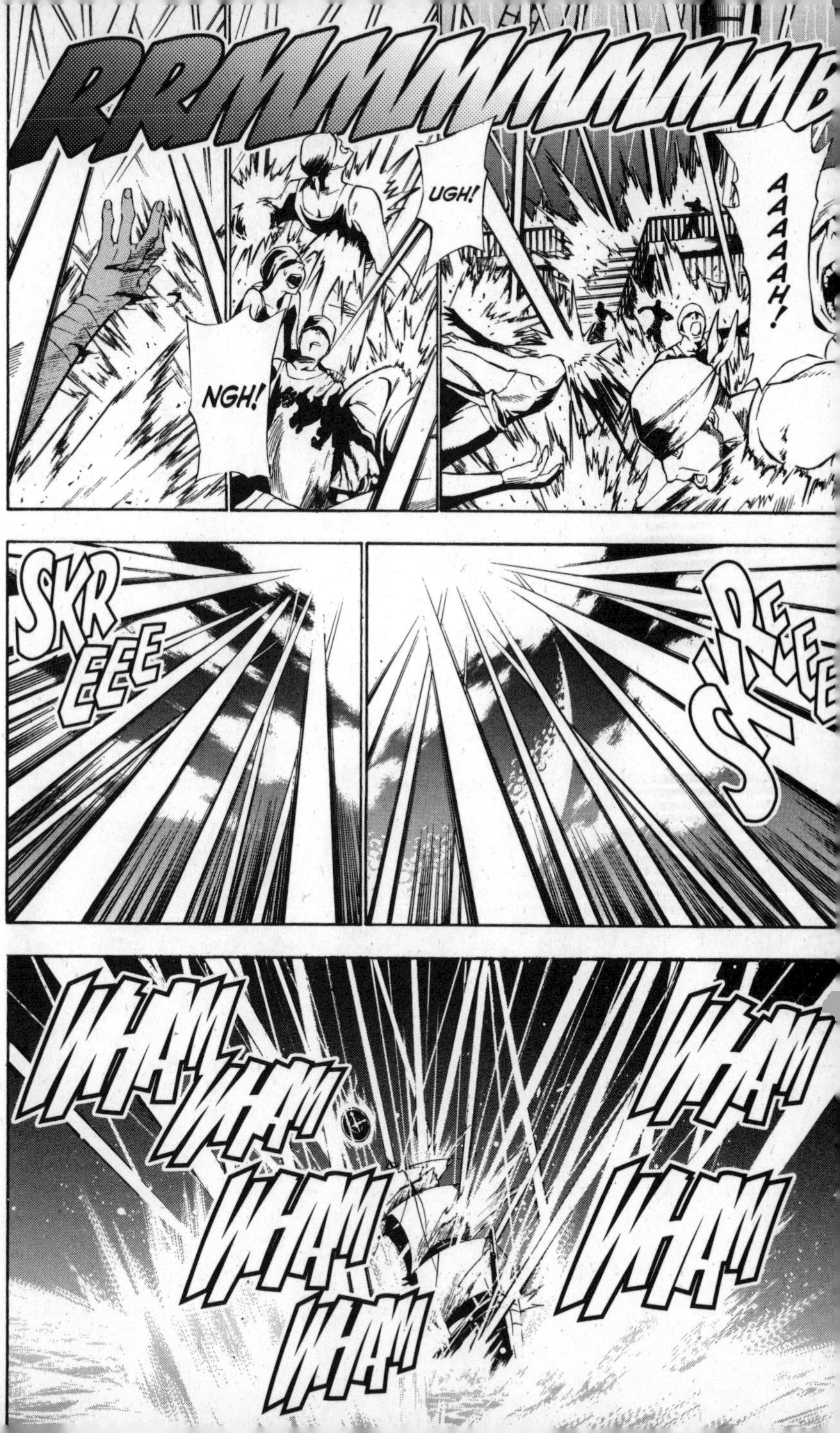

RRMMMMMMMB
AAAAAAH!
UGH!
NGH!
SKREEES
SKR EEE
WHAM
WHAM
WHAM
WHAM
WHAM
WHAM

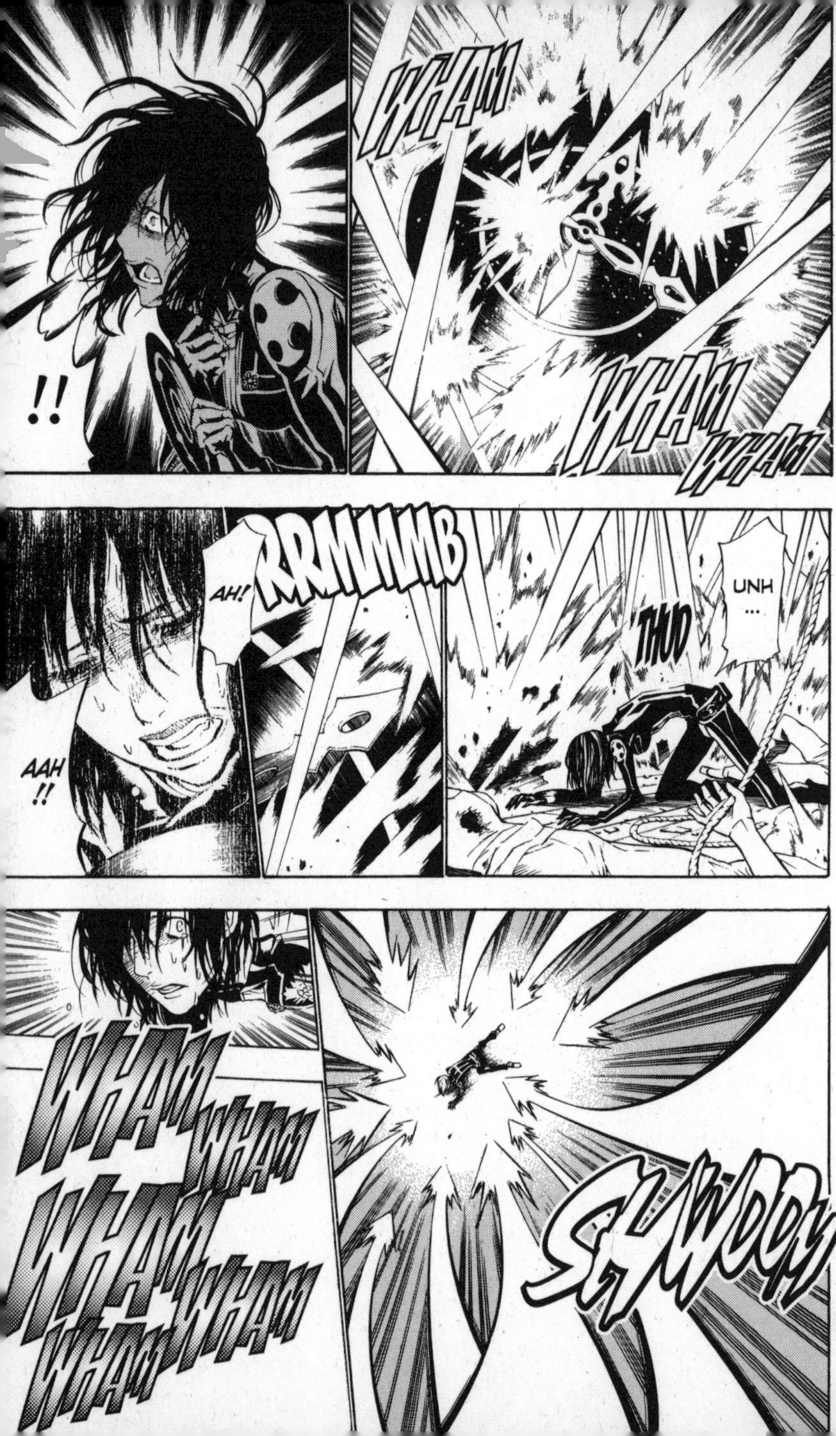
WHAM
WHAM
WHAM
!!
UNH ...
THUD
RRMMMMB
AH!
AAH !!
SHWOOM
WHAM
WHAM
WHAM
WHAM
WHAM
WHAM

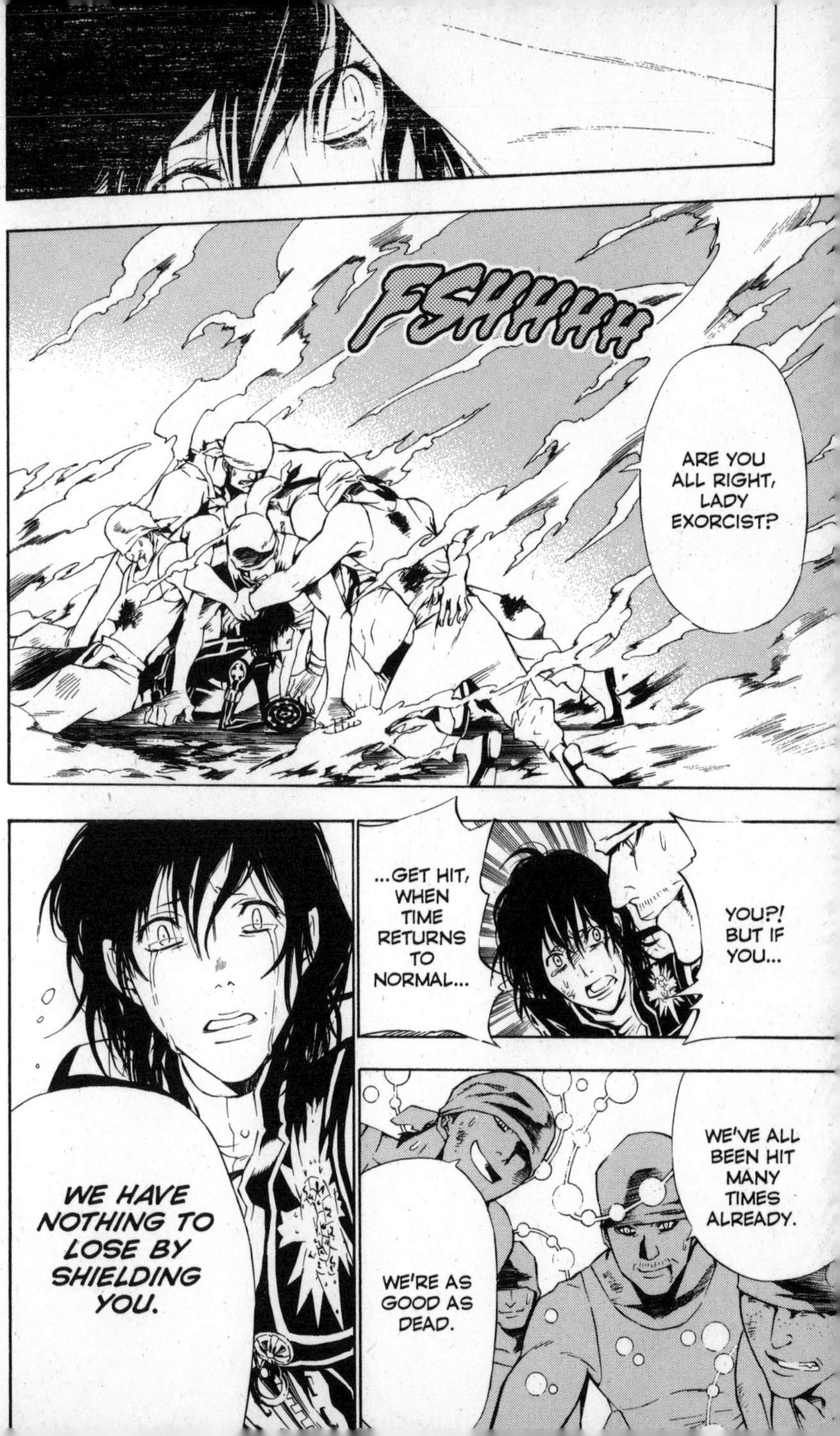
FSHHHH
ARE YOU ALL RIGHT, LADY EXORCIST?
YOU?! BUT IF YOU...
...GET HIT, WHEN TIME RETURNS TO NORMAL...
WE'VE ALL BEEN HIT MANY TIMES ALREADY.
WE'RE AS GOOD AS DEAD.
WE HAVE NOTHING TO LOSE BY SHIELDING YOU.

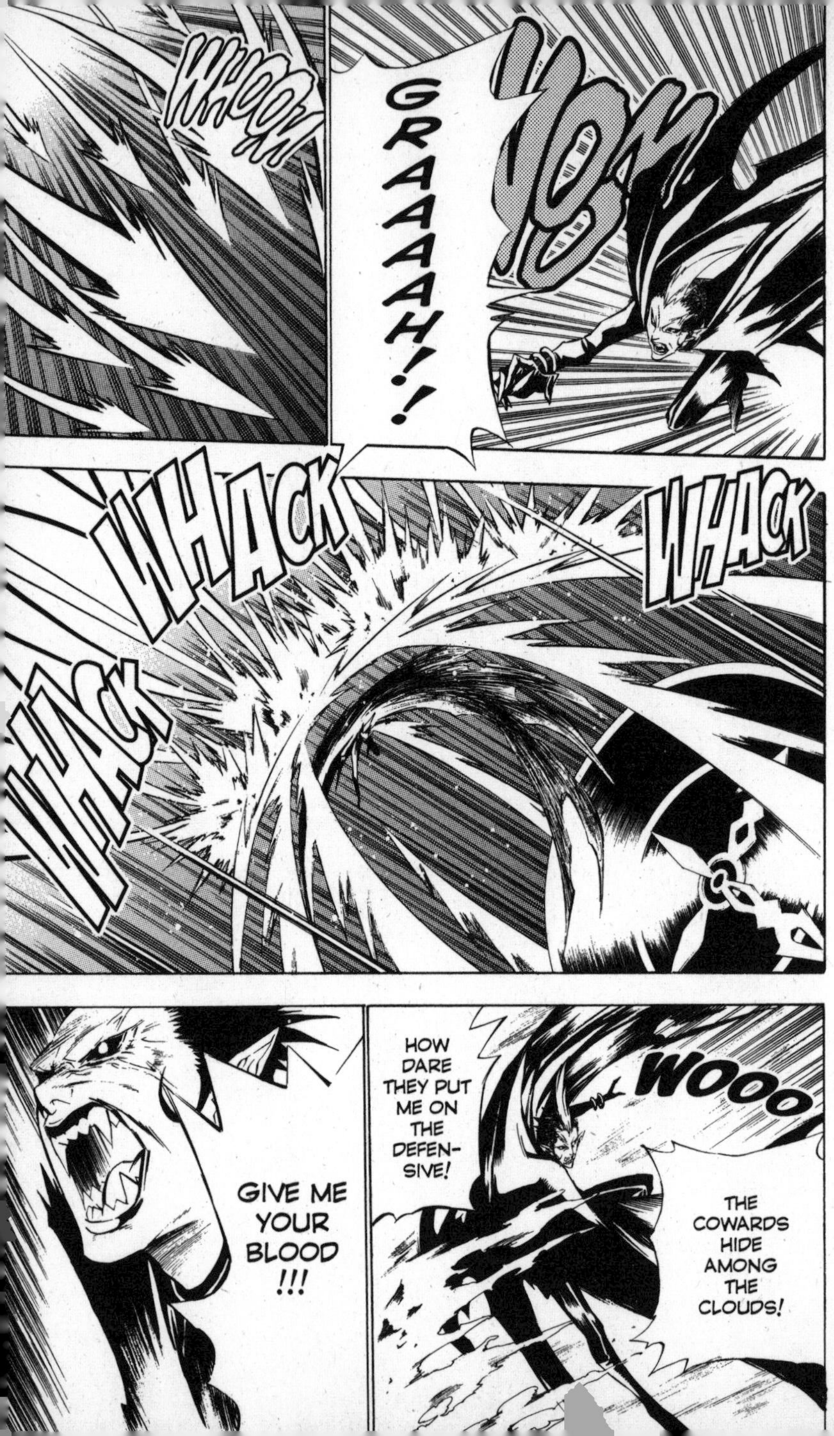
GRAAAAAH!!
WHACK
WHACK
WHACK
HOW DARE THEY PUT ME ON THE DEFEN-SIVE!
WOOO
THE COWARDS HIDE AMONG THE CLOUDS!
GIVE ME YOUR BLOOD !!!

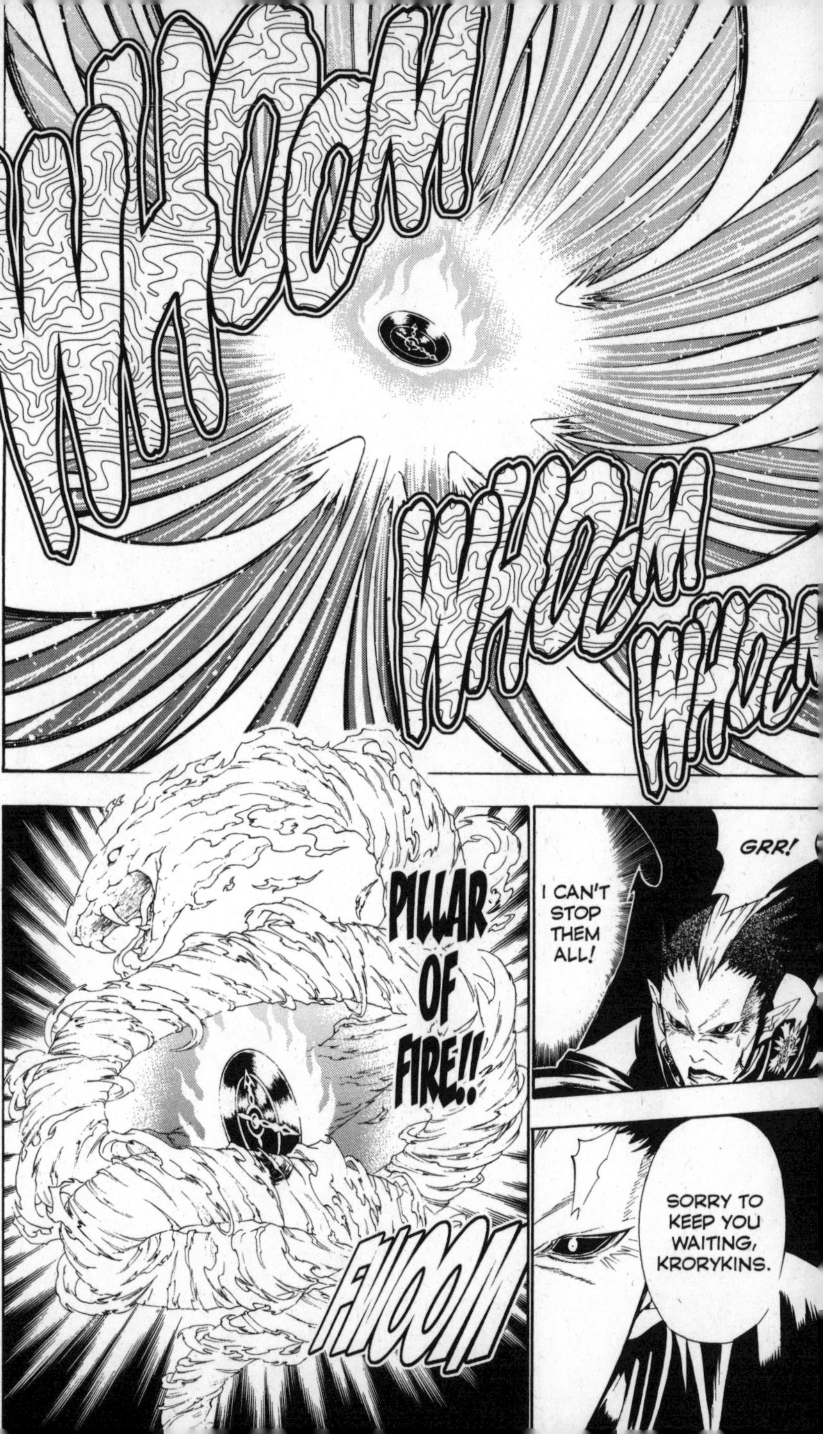
WHOOM
WHOOM
GRR!
I CAN'T STOP THEM ALL!
SORRY TO KEEP YOU WAITING, KRORYKINS.
PILLAR OF FIRE!!
FWOOM

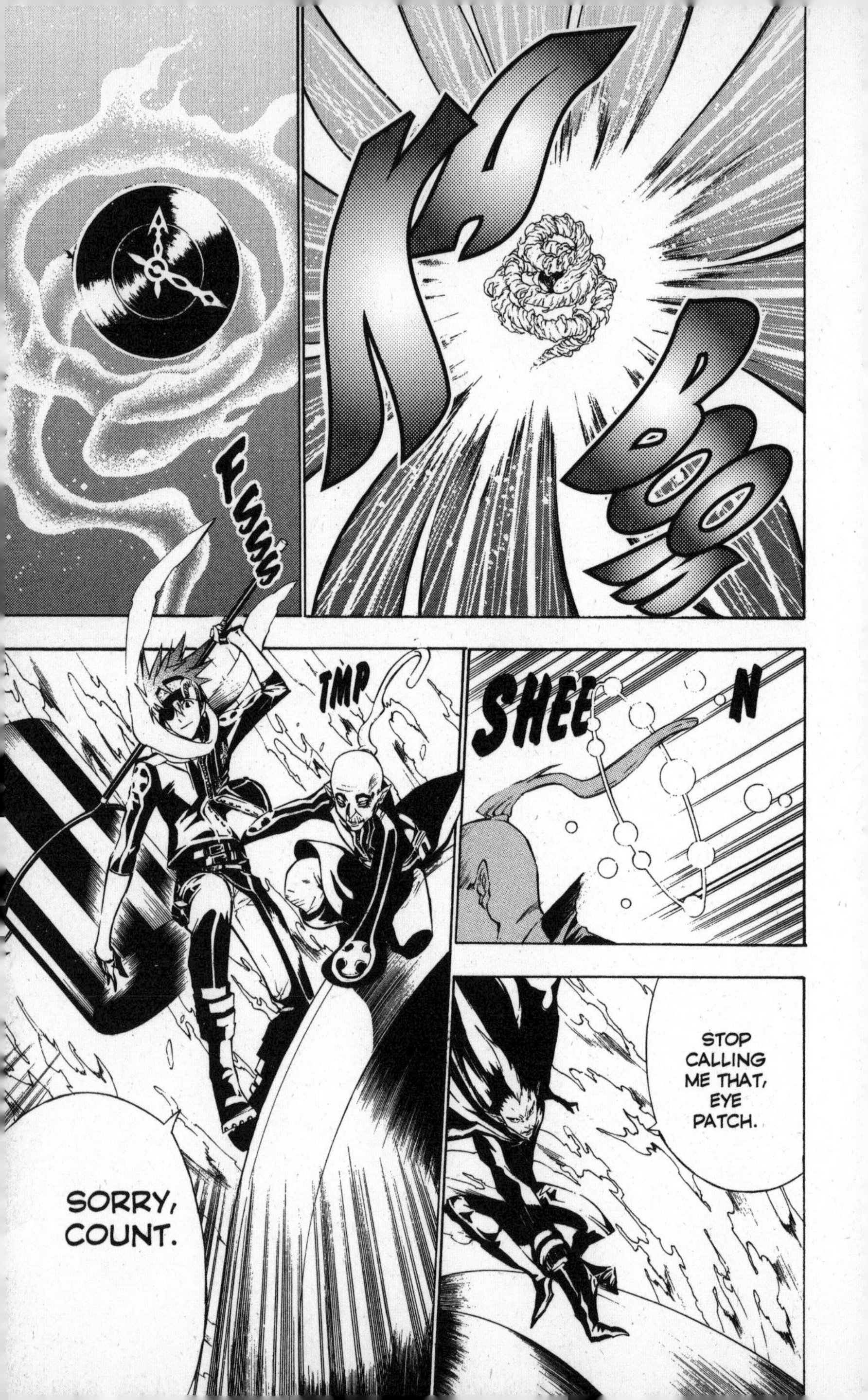
BOOM
FSSSS
SHEE N
STOP CALLING ME THAT, EYE PATCH.
TMP
SORRY, COUNT.

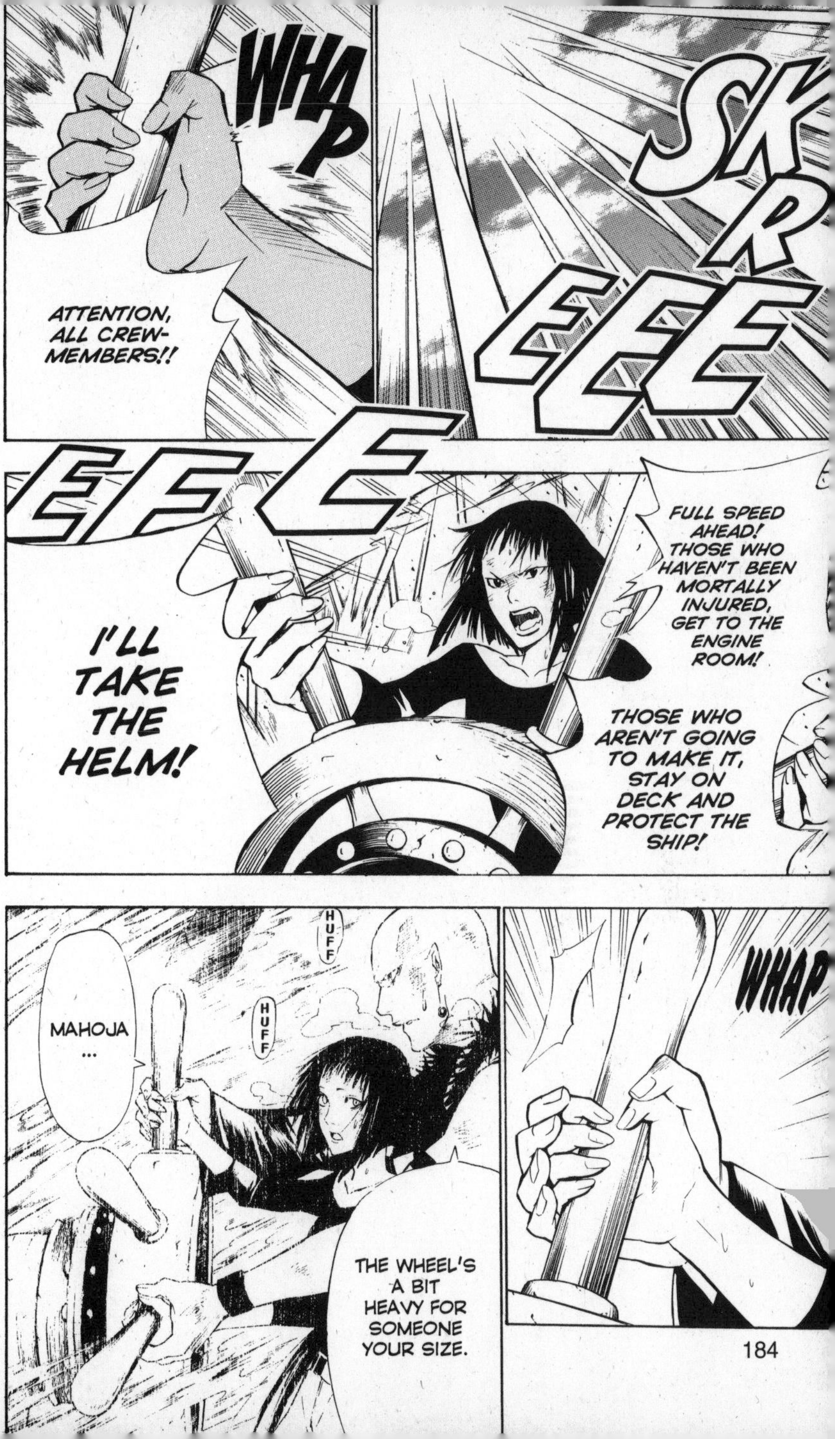
SKREEEEEE
WHAP
ATTENTION, ALL CREW-MEMBERS!!
FULL SPEED AHEAD! THOSE WHO HAVEN'T BEEN MORTALLY INJURED, GET TO THE ENGINE ROOM!
THOSE WHO AREN'T GOING TO MAKE IT, STAY ON DECK AND PROTECT THE SHIP!
I'LL TAKE THE HELM!
WHAP
HUFF
HUFF
MAHOJA ...
THE WHEEL'S A BIT HEAVY FOR SOMEONE YOUR SIZE.

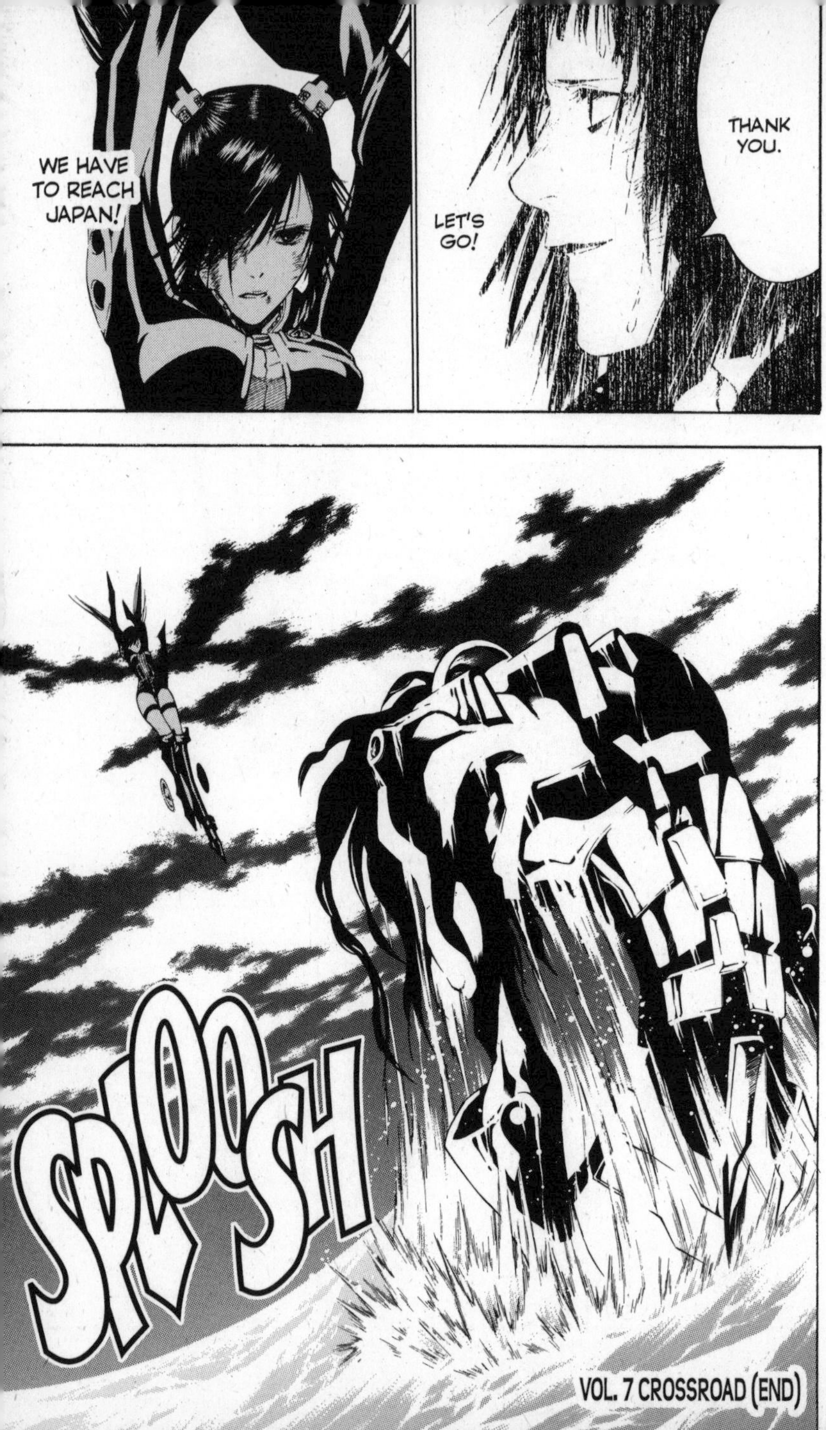
THANK YOU.
LET'S GO!
WE HAVE TO REACH JAPAN!
SPLOOSH
VOL. 7 CROSSROAD (END)

D.GRAY THEATER

CHAPTER OF EDITOR Y   ART & STORY BY SOME ASSISTANT

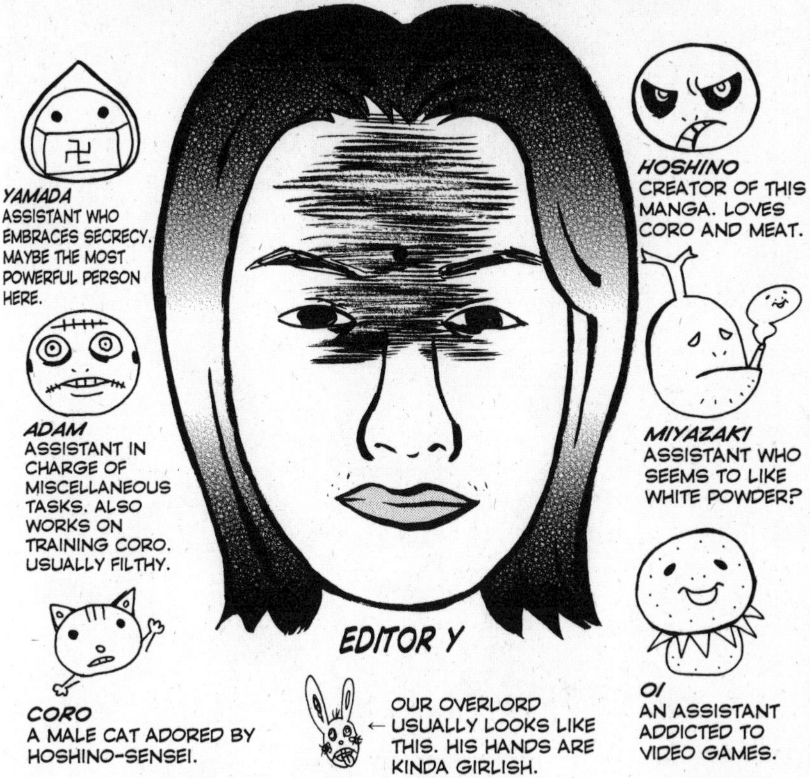
YAMADA
ASSISTANT WHO EMBRACES SECRECY. MAYBE THE MOST POWERFUL PERSON HERE.
HOSHINO
CREATOR OF THIS MANGA. LOVES CORO AND MEAT.
ADAM
ASSISTANT IN CHARGE OF MISCELLANEOUS TASKS. ALSO WORKS ON TRAINING CORO. USUALLY FILTHY.
MIYAZAKI
ASSISTANT WHO SEEMS TO LIKE WHITE POWDER?
EDITOR Y
CORO
A MALE CAT ADORED BY HOSHINO-SENSEI.
← OUR OVERLORD USUALLY LOOKS LIKE THIS. HIS HANDS ARE KINDA GIRLISH.
OI
AN ASSISTANT ADDICTED TO VIDEO GAMES.

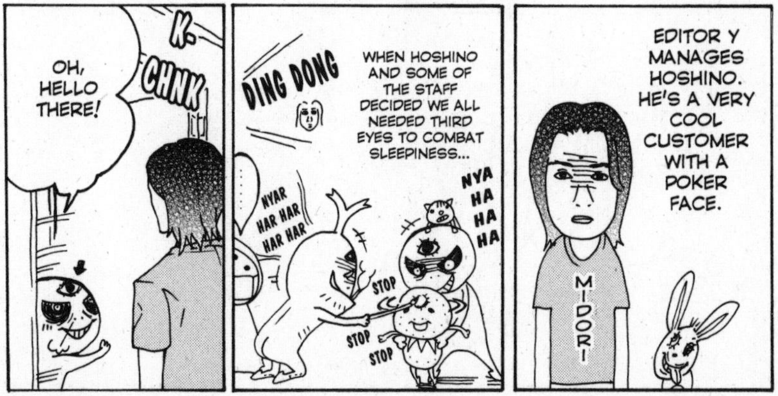
EDITOR Y MANAGES HOSHINO. HE'S A VERY COOL CUSTOMER WITH A POKER FACE.
MIDORI
WHEN HOSHINO AND SOME OF THE STAFF DECIDED WE ALL NEEDED THIRD EYES TO COMBAT SLEEPINESS...
DING DONG
NYA HA HA HA HA
NYAR HAR HAR HAR HAR
STOP
STOP
STOP
K-CHNK
OH, HELLO THERE!

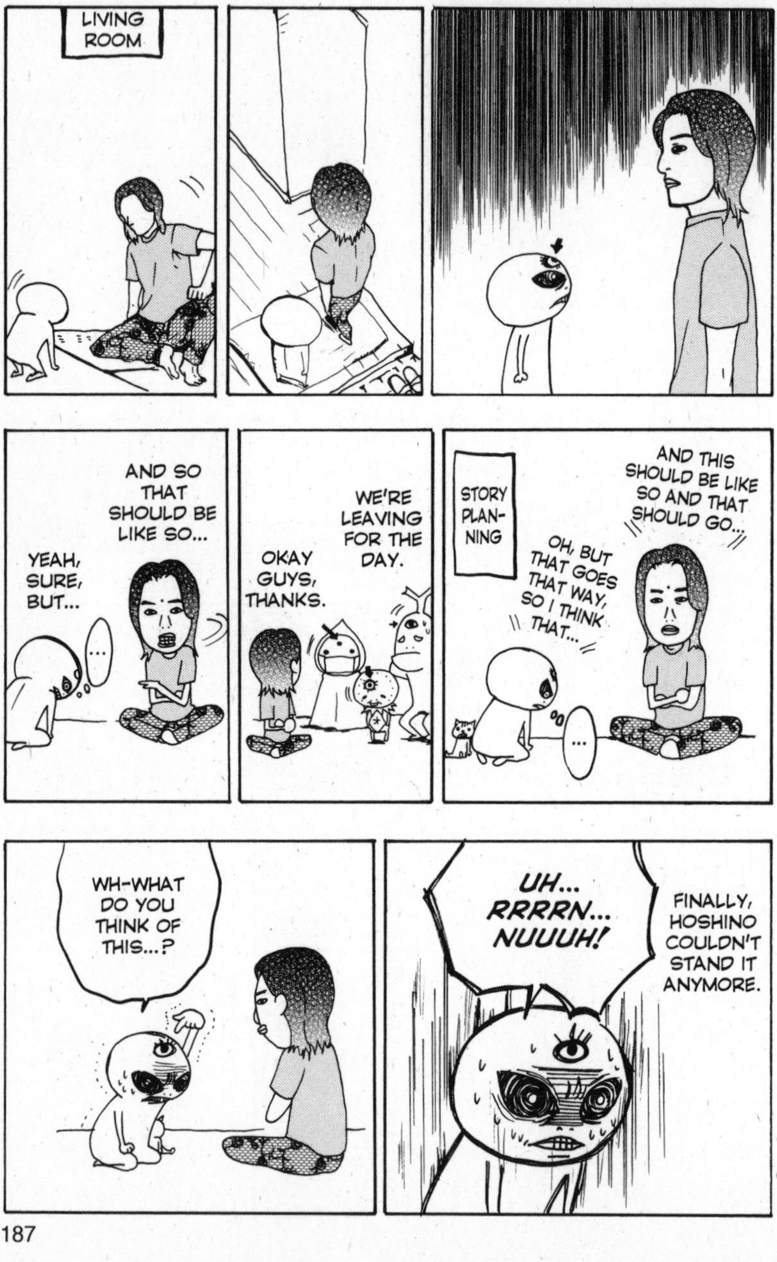
LIVING ROOM
AND THIS SHOULD BE LIKE SO AND THAT SHOULD GO...
STORY PLANNING
OH, BUT THAT GOES THAT WAY, SO I THINK THAT...
...
WE'RE LEAVING FOR THE DAY.
OKAY GUYS, THANKS.
AND SO THAT SHOULD BE LIKE SO...
YEAH, SURE, BUT...
...
FINALLY, HOSHINO COULDN'T STAND IT ANYMORE.
UH... RRRRN... NUUUH!
WH-WHAT DO YOU THINK OF THIS...?

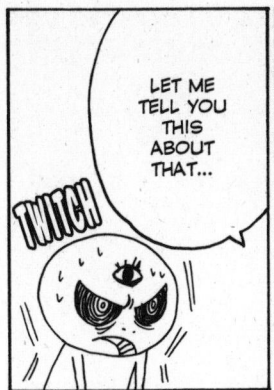

FLICK
PUUUFF
LET ME TELL YOU THIS ABOUT THAT...
TWITCH
THE MOMENT YOU ASKED THAT QUESTION, YOU LOST.
!!
YOU SHOULD SHAVE YOUR HEAD AND PUT ON A MARTIAL ARTS GI.
THE TERRIBLE EDITOR Y IS UNMOVED BY ANYTHING. HE IS A MAN WITH A STONE HEART. HARD TO BELIEVE EDITOR Y IS MARRIED.
HOW-EVER, ONE DAY...
HELLO THERE.
UM...I'M ALMOST DONE. WILL YOU WAIT IN THE LIVING ROOM?
SHOOMP
...
LIVING ROOM

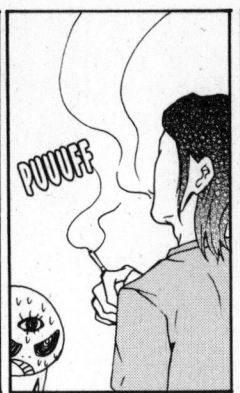

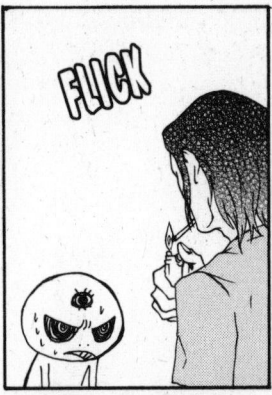

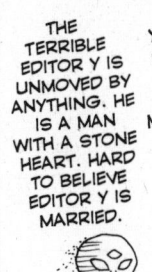

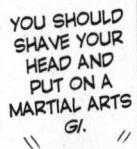

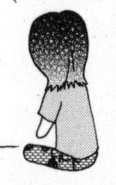

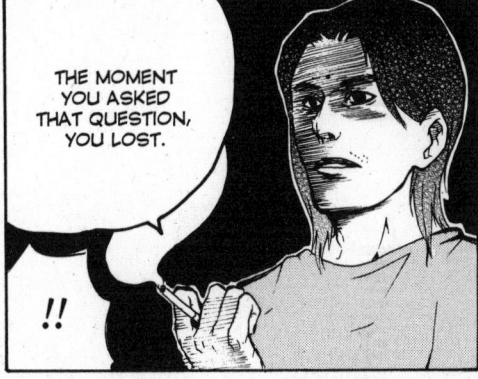

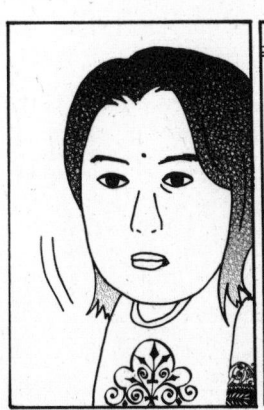

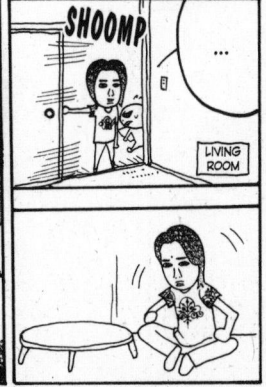

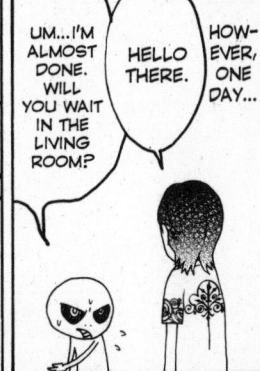

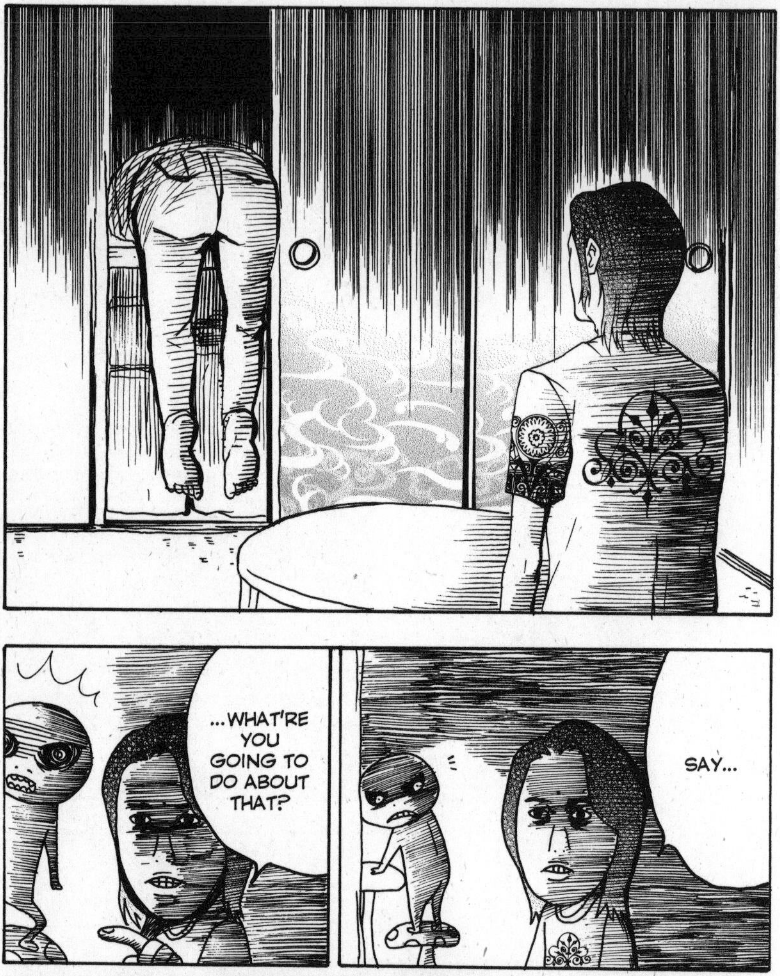
SAY...
...WHAT'RE YOU GOING TO DO ABOUT THAT?
ADAM !!!
APARTMENT
PERVERTED ASSISTANT ADAM'S ANTICS EVEN GOT THE ATTENTION OF EDITOR Y. GO FIGURE.
ADAM
SPECIAL ABILITIES: SLEEPS ANYWHERE. ESCAPES TO A FANTASY WORLD.

D.GRAY THEATER (END)

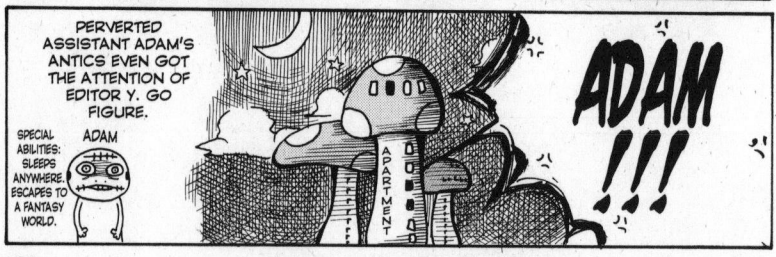

IN THE NEXT VOLUME...

The battle on the sea between the Exorcists and the akuma rages on. Lenalee speeds off to face Eshi, a Level 3 akuma, but it seems she may have bitten off more than she can chew. Her one chance is to unleash the maximum power of her Innocence, as Allen did to save Suman Dark, putting her own life on the line!

Available Now!

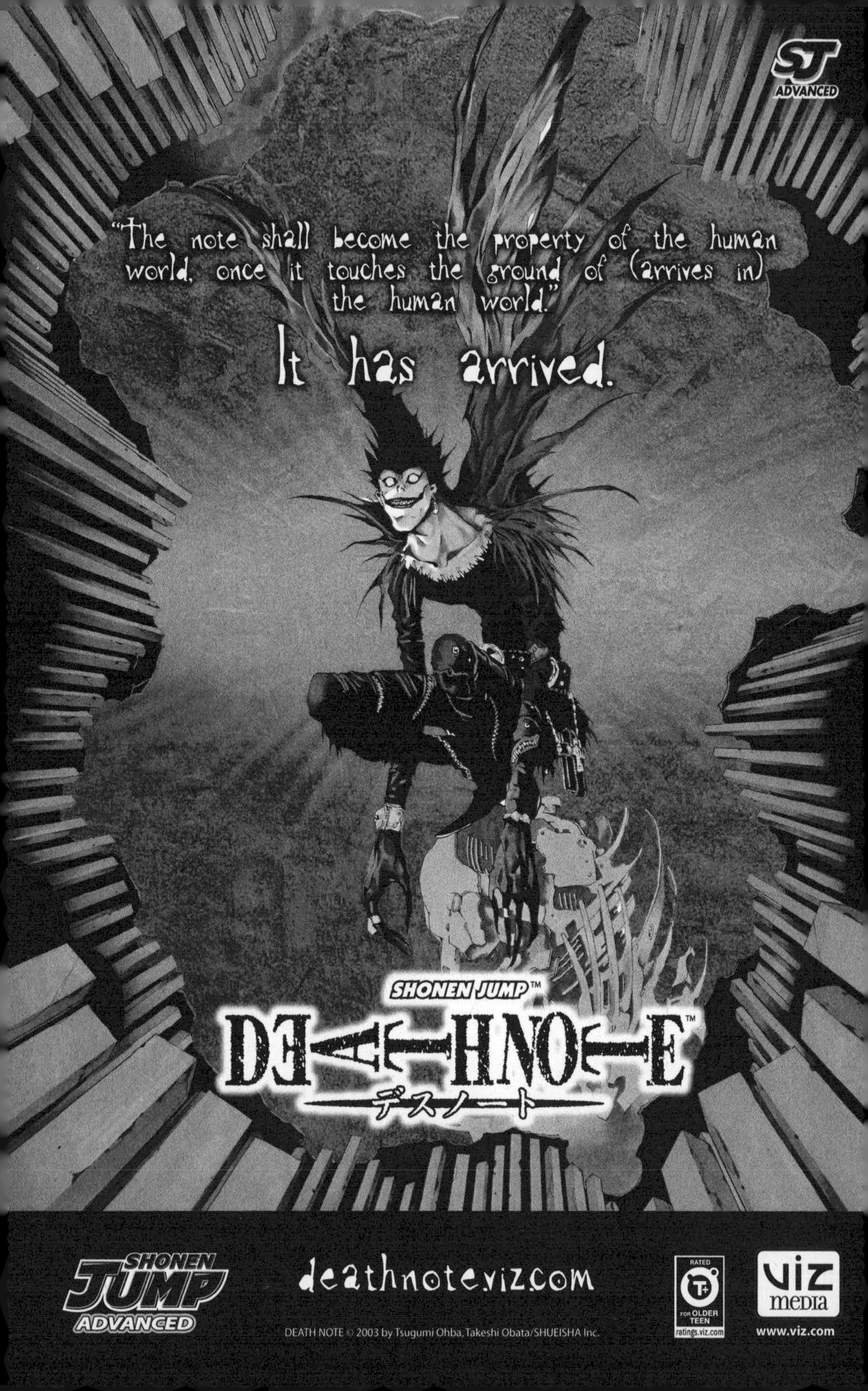
SJ ADVANCED
"The note shall become the property of the human world, once it touches the ground of (arrives in) the human world."
It has arrived.
SHONEN JUMP™
DEATH NOTE™
デスノート
SHONEN JUMP ADVANCED
deathnote.viz.com
DEATH NOTE © 2003 by Tsugumi Ohba, Takeshi Obata/SHUEISHA Inc.
RATED T+ FOR OLDER TEEN ratings.viz.com
viz media
www.viz.com

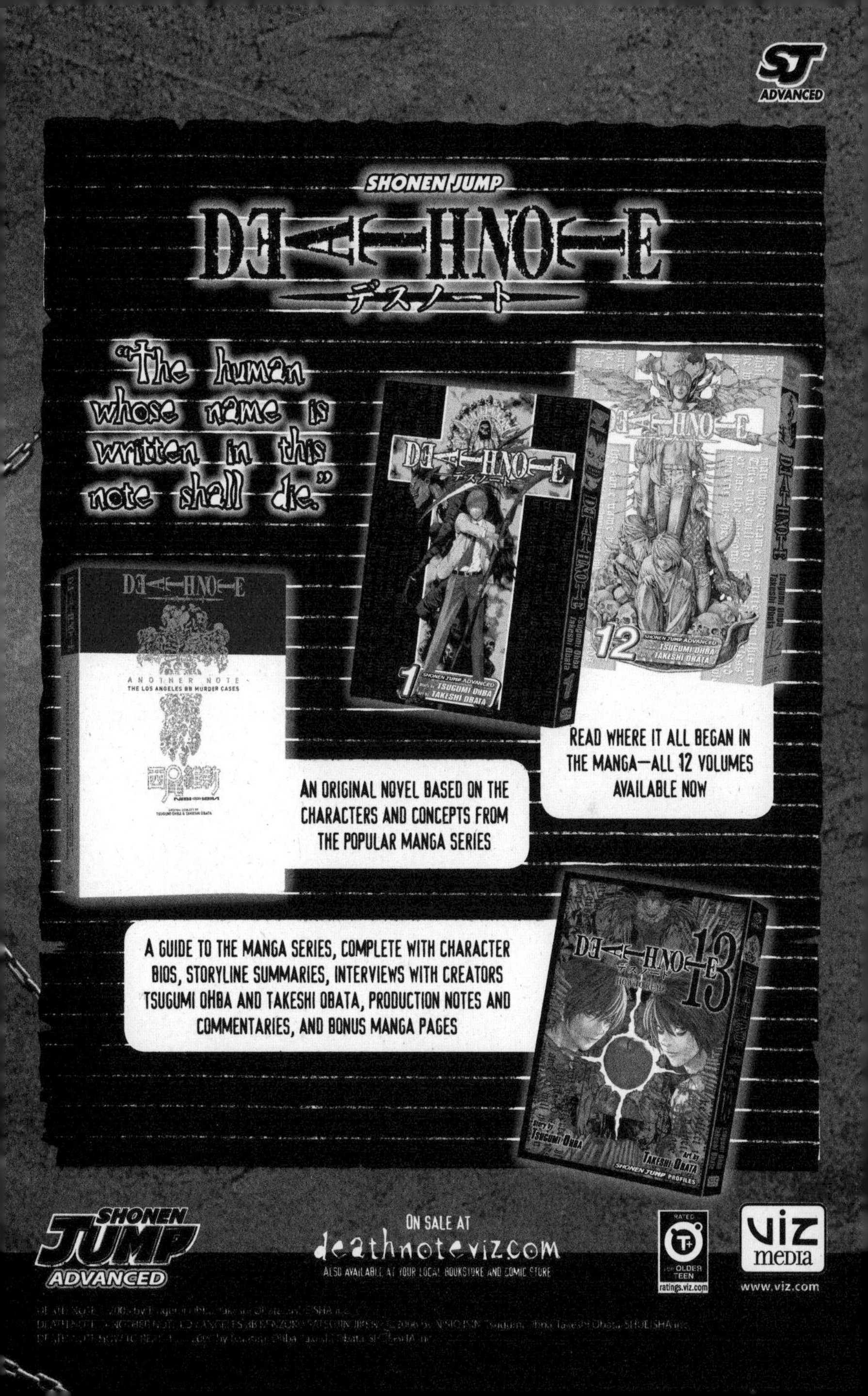

SJ ADVANCED
SHONEN JUMP
DEATH NOTE
デスノート
"The human whose name is written in this note shall die."
ANOTHER NOTE
THE LOS ANGELES BB MURDER CASES
AN ORIGINAL NOVEL BASED ON THE CHARACTERS AND CONCEPTS FROM THE POPULAR MANGA SERIES
SHONEN JUMP ADVANCED
TSUGUMI OHBA
TAKESHI OBATA
READ WHERE IT ALL BEGAN IN THE MANGA—ALL 12 VOLUMES AVAILABLE NOW
A GUIDE TO THE MANGA SERIES, COMPLETE WITH CHARACTER BIOS, STORYLINE SUMMARIES, INTERVIEWS WITH CREATORS TSUGUMI OHBA AND TAKESHI OBATA, PRODUCTION NOTES AND COMMENTARIES, AND BONUS MANGA PAGES
HOW TO READ
13
Story by TSUGUMI OHBA
Art by TAKESHI OBATA
SHONEN JUMP PROFILES
SHONEN JUMP ADVANCED
ON SALE AT
deathnote.viz.com
ALSO AVAILABLE AT YOUR LOCAL BOOKSTORE AND COMIC STORE
RATED T+ FOR OLDER TEEN
ratings.viz.com
viz media
www.viz.com

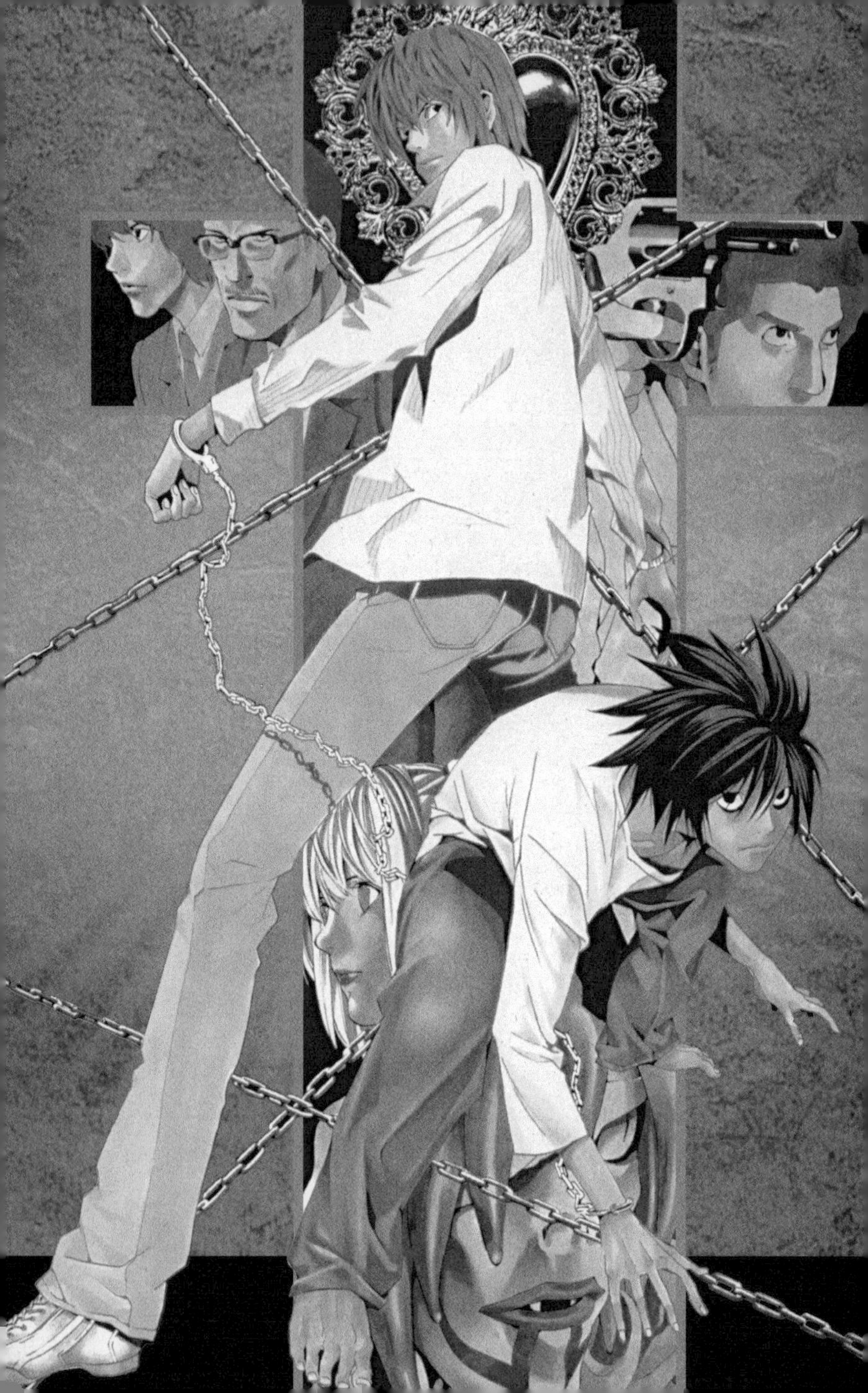

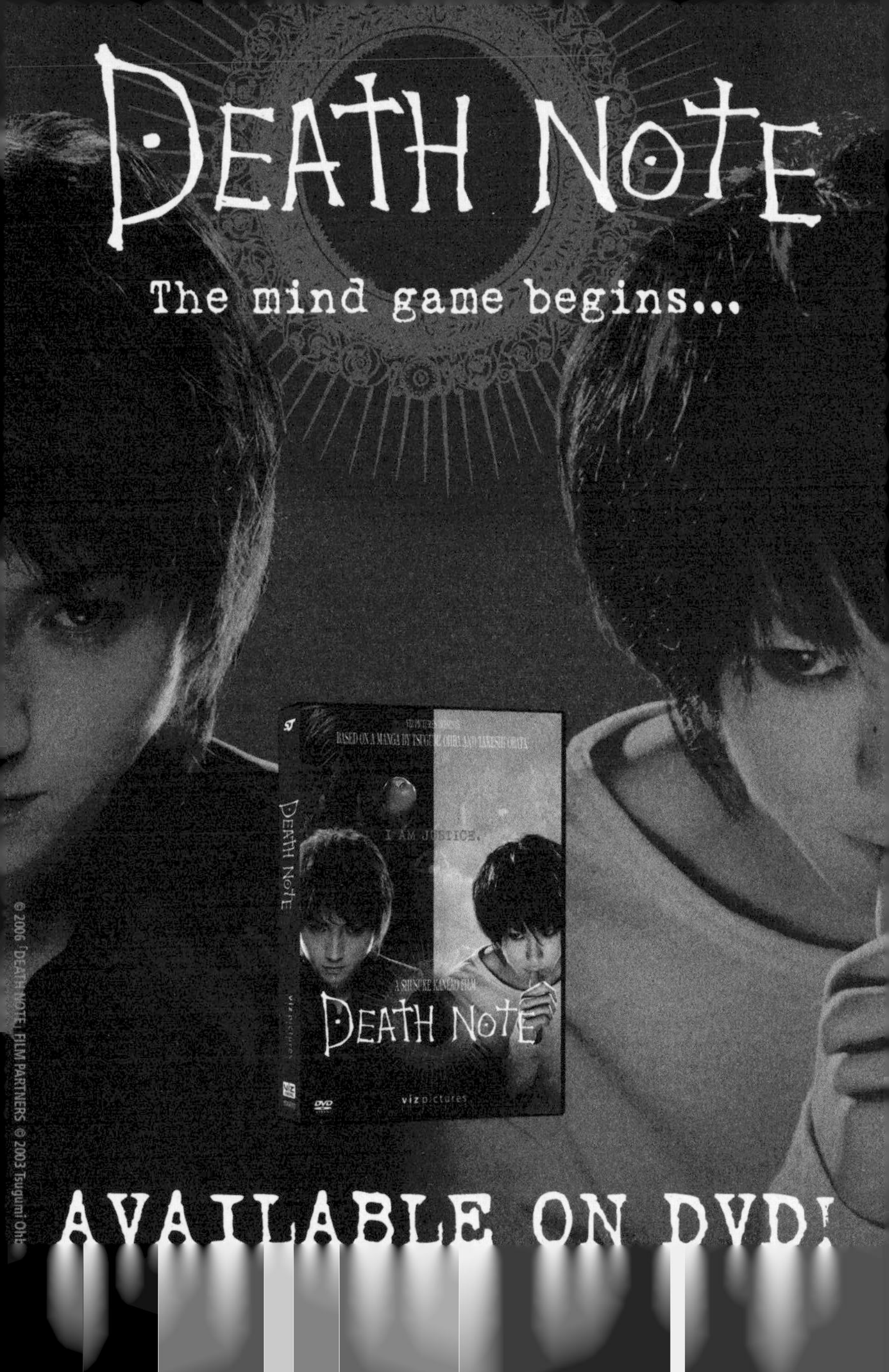
DEATH NOTE
The mind game begins...
I AM JUSTICE.
DEATH NOTE
viz pictures
AVAILABLE ON DVD!
© 2006 'DEATH NOTE' FILM PARTNERS © 2003 Tsugumi Ohb

SHONEN JUMP

THE WORLD'S MOST POPULAR MANGA

**STORY AND ART BY
TITE KUBO**

**STORY AND ART BY
EIICHIRO ODA**

**STORY AND ART BY
HIROYUKI ASADA**

JUMP INTO THE ACTION BY TELLING US WHAT YOU LOVE (AND WHAT YOU DON'T)

LET YOUR VOICE BE HEARD!

SHONENJUMP.VIZ.COM/MANGASURVEY

HELP US MAKE MORE OF THE WORLD'S MOST POPULAR MANGA!

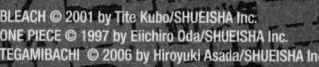 

SAVE 50% OFF
THE COVER PRICE!

IT'S LIKE GETTING 6 ISSUES
FREE!

OVER 350+ PAGES PER ISSUE

This monthly magazine contains 7 of the coolest manga available in the U.S., PLUS anime news, and info about video & card games, toys AND more!

❑ **I want 12 HUGE issues of SHONEN JUMP for only $29.95*!**

NAME

ADDRESS

CITY/STATE/ZIP

EMAIL ADDRESS   **DATE OF BIRTH**

❑ **YES**, send me via email information, advertising, offers, and promotions related to VIZ Media, SHONEN JUMP, and/or their business partners.

❑ **CHECK ENCLOSED** (payable to SHONEN JUMP) ❑ **BILL ME LATER**

CREDIT CARD: ❑ **Visa** ❑ **Mastercard**

ACCOUNT NUMBER   **EXP. DATE**

SIGNATURE

CLIP&MAIL TO:
SHONEN JUMP Subscriptions Service Dept.
P.O. Box 515
Mount Morris, IL 61054-0515

P9GNC1

  www.viz.com